AMERICAN INDIAN TRIBAL GOVERNMENTS

THE CIVILIZATION OF THE AMERICAN INDIAN SERIES

AMERICAN INDIAN TRIBAL GOVERNMENTS

By SHARON O'BRIEN

UNIVERSITY OF OKLAHOMA PRESS : NORMAN AND LONDON

Dedicated to the Indian people who have taught me with such patience and generosity and to my parents, Dale and Maurine O'Brien, who have always encouraged me to seek knowledge for the understanding and joy that it brings.

Library of Congress Cataloging-in-Publication Data

O'Brien, Sharon.
    American Indian tribal governments / by Sharon O'Brien. — 1st ed.
      p.   cm. — (The Civilization of the American Indian series : v. 192)
    Bibliography: p. 321
    Includes index.
    1. Indians of North America — Tribal government.   2. Indians of North America — Government relations. I. Title. II. Series.
  E98.T77027   1989
  323.1'197 — dc19   89–4791
  ISBN: 0–8061–2199–8 (cloth)
  ISBN: 0–8061–2564–0 (paper)

American Indian Tribal Governments is Volume 192 in The Civilization of the American Indian Series.

The paper in this book meets the guidelines for permanence and durability of the Committee on Production Guidelines for Book Longevity of the Council on Library Resources, Inc. ∞

3 4 5 6 7 8 9 10 11

CONTENTS

ILLUSTRATIONS

MAPS

FIGURES

TABLE

PREFACE

During the summer of 1982, Linda Howard, chairwoman of the Yerington Paiutes, asked me to review a meager selection of books for possible adoption in a course on tribal government that the tribe was planning to introduce in the schools. Few, if any, of the books dealt directly with the subject of tribal government, and certainly none treated it from an Indian perspective. Finding none of the books acceptable, we decided to find a means by which to develop a book on tribal governments. Shortly thereafter, the National Congress of American Indians (NCAI) renewed its interest in producing a book on tribal governments that could be used by senior high schools, colleges, tribal officials, and the general public. Later that same year the NCAI received a grant from the Rockefeller Foundation to underwrite the cost of research, and I was formally asked to write the book—to work, in effect, as a translator of information for the tribes that had agreed to participate in the project.

Basing their decisions on geographic location and political differences in governmental structures, the NCAI selected five tribes to be used as examples: the Seneca Nation of New York, the Muscogees (Creeks) of Oklahoma, the Cheyenne River Sioux of South Dakota, the Isleta Pueblo of New Mexico, and the Yakimas of Washington. My library and archival research was supplemented by weeks of travel to the tribes' homes, which yielded me with insightful information to combine with my research for a better representation of the various tribal governments. I also visited other tribes or groups that had agreed to have specific programs included in the text. To ensure accuracy, all five tribal councils, as well as specific program directors, reviewed and approved the pertinent sections of the text.

Part 1 of this book introduces the material to be discussed more fully throughout the remainder of the text and explores the central structures of traditional tribal governments. Chapter 1 presents a "case study." It details the history of the Mississippi Band of Choctaws and their current efforts to reestablish their government after a period of near dissolution throughout the years of removal, assimilation, and paternalism. Personal reasons led me to choose the Mississippi Band of Choctaws for this introductory role. I spent my early childhood in Mississippi, and my education there, not unlike that of most children everywhere, left me with the impression that all Indians there had died in the 1700s, or had been moved westward during the 1830s. Not until I be-

came interested in Indians in graduate school did I begin to
read of the Mississippi Band of Choctaws located at Philadelphia, Mississippi, and of their great strides in recovering
their government and economy. Therefore, chapter 1 is offered both as an apology to them for my ignorance and as a
means of congratulating them on their success.

Chapter 2 presents the traditional tribal governments of
the five groups mentioned above and serves to inform readers
on the structures, complexities, and responsiveness of traditional tribal governments. At a time when Europeans labored
under authoritarian, hierarchical governments, most tribes
possessed democratic and responsive governments. Many
tribes practiced universal suffrage and incorporated provisions for recall, referendums, and other political processes,
thought later to have been developed by American and European political theorists. Today, for example, arbitration is
heralded by the legal establishment as a new and important
procedure for administering justice, but the process was long
used by traditional tribal governments.

Since it is impossible to understand the current status of
tribal governments without understanding their historical
and political development, part 2 (chapters 3, 4, and 5) provides a background of tribal-white relations from the time
non-Indians and Indians first came in contact with each
other.

In chapters 6–10 the history and current governmental
structure of the five groups discussed in chapter 2 are exam-
ined in detail. These five chapters, along with chapter 11,
which examines the general powers of tribal governments,
form part 3, the heart of the book. These six chapters are
meant to provide readers with a detailed understanding of
the development and current rights of tribal governments.

By their nature and source tribal governments lie partly
outside the federal framework and also legally possess a
status higher than that of the states. Nonetheless, tribal governments are highly constrained by the laws and legal decisions that circumscribe their relationships with the federal
and state governments. Part 4 examines the parameters of
tribes' relationships with the federal and state governments
and briefly considers the future of tribal governments.

This book was written to fill a large gap in the literature.
Very little published information of either a general or
a scholarly nature exists on tribal governments. The area
has been overlooked by historians, political scientists, legal
theorists, and anthropologists. One reason for this is that the
subject is one of considerable complexity, requiring understanding and intellectual maturity in a number of disciplines.
It is my hope that this book will provide other scholars with
a basis from which to write improved and more far-reaching
treatises.

At the same time, I am aware that this book may not please

some members of the scholarly community, accustomed to rigidly applied scholarly theories and painstaking footnotes. It has, however, always been the intention of those involved in the development of this project that it be a book easily understood by and accessible to a wide audience. I undertook this project at the request of tribal members looking for a means to educate their people and their white neighbors. Despite its foreseen shortcomings, including the exclusion or underemphasis of some material in the interest of providing a practical and affordable book, I believe that this book will begin to produce an appreciation for the operation of traditional tribal governments, the role of history in destroying those governments, and the tenacity of the Indian people's desire to continue providing for their welfare against incredible odds.

Many people have contributed to the final form of this book. This entire project would not have been possible without the original inspiration of Linda Howard, of the Yerington Paiutes, and Ron Andrade, formerly of the National Congress of American Indians, and without the support of the Rockefeller Foundation. I received information, support, and encouragement from numerous tribal members and representatives, including Mississippi Choctaw Chief Philip Martin and Skip Bridges, tribal planner for the Mississippi Choctaws; Elmer John and George Abrahm of the Seneca Nation; Robert Trepp of the Muscogee Nation; former Governor Frank A. Jojola of the Isleta Pueblos; Iyonne Garreau and Manson Garreau of the Cheyenne River Sioux; and Russell Jim of the Yakima Nation.

Several other people have assisted me in the technical process of making this book. Steve Hayes of the Hesburgh Library, University of Notre Dame, answered innumerable requests for information on federal-Indian relations. Lin Vacca and Patricia Dornbusch have helped make the manuscript readable and logical. Bruce Bittle has given freely of his graphic arts talents to produce the maps and charts that illustrate the text. Fernando Dreaming Bear of the Pine Ridge Reservation provided some of the illustrations. Photographs have been gleaned from a number of sources, including the Smithsonian Institution, the Museum of the American Indian, several state historical societies, generous individuals such as Donald L. Fixico and Helen Clausen, of the *Eagle Butte News*, and from the tribes themselves. The Institute for Scholarship in the Liberal Arts, University of Notre Dame, gave me a grant to purchase some of these photographs. I thank Donald L. Fixico, of the University of Wisconsin–Milwaukee, and John Sugden and other colleagues from the Newberry Library, Chicago, Illinois, for their assistance in the final reading of the manuscript and Jennifer Thomas for her help in compiling the photograph collection. Finally, I would like to give special thanks to my parents, family, friends, especially Donald L. Fixico, colleagues, and student assistants, who have provided substantial assistance and continual support throughout the long period during which this book was taking shape. Despite this help, some errors are likely to remain. They are, of course, my responsibility.

SHARON O'BRIEN

South Bend, Indiana

AMERICAN INDIAN TRIBAL GOVERNMENTS

In future your business dealings with the whites are going to be very hard, and it behooves you to learn well what you are taught here. But that is not all. We older people need you. In our dealings with the white men, we are just the same as blind men, because we do not understand them. We need you to help us understand what the white men are up to. My Grandchildren, be good. Try and make a mark for yourselves. Learn all you can.

CHIEF JOSEPH, NEZ PERCÉ, 1879

PART 1

INTRODUCTION

This book is about the struggle of Indian tribes and their governments to achieve their goals of freedom and self-determination. Chapter 1 introduces the experiences of the Mississippi Choctaws—a tribe whose past and present are both unique and similar to the experience of the more than six hundred tribes native to the United States. The story of the Mississippi Choctaws reflects the issues and events that will be discussed throughout this book.

Chapter 2 introduces the structure, function, and values of the traditional governments of five Indian nations: the Haudenosaunee (the Iroquois League), the Muscogees, the Lakotas, the Isleta Pueblo, and the Yakimas. These five groups were chosen for their geographic and cultural diversity. Yet despite their differences, it will be apparent that all five groups shared, with each other and with most other tribes, a high degree of democracy and emphasis on personal responsibility to the community. Each tribe, exercising its inherent sovereignty, structured its government according to its special needs, made and enforced its own laws, and conducted relations and trade with other tribes.

CHAPTER 1

THE MISSISSIPPI CHOCTAW TRIBAL COUNCIL: INDIAN SELF-GOVERNMENT IN ACTION

The 16 members of the Mississippi Choctaw Tribal Council sat attentively one autumn day in 1962, earnestly discussing the problems facing their tribe. These council members had been elected to represent the 3,500 members of their tribe, who lived in seven communities scattered across the hot, pine-covered, rolling hills of east-central Mississippi. The hills were part of the region where the Choctaws—or Chatas, as they called themselves—had lived for more than seven thousand years. Oral tradition told how their ancestors, and those of the Muscogees, Chickasaws, and Cherokees, sprang from Nanih Waiya, the "Mother Mound," near the present town of Preston, Mississippi. The other tribes had spread throughout the Southeast, but the Choctaws had stayed, heeding their "Great Mother," who warned that they would die if they ever left her side.

The tribal council members who met that day in 1962 were descendants of Choctaws who had remained in Mississippi against appalling odds. Their ancestors had endured wars, "removal" policies designed to relocate them to Indian Territory (present-day Oklahoma), poverty, epidemics, and health conditions so devastating that at one point the formerly populous nation dwindled to just over a thousand survivors.

In 1519, when whites first made contact with the Choctaws, the large and powerful tribe controlled more than 26 million acres in what is now the southeastern United States. The Spanish explorers who came first were followed by French and English explorers. By the 1700s all three nations had permanent, competing settlements in the region.

The Choctaw Nation became caught in power plays among Spain, France, Great Britain, and, eventually, the United States. In 1786 the tribe signed its first treaty with the United States: the Treaty of Hopewell. In it the United States acknowledged the Choctaws as an independent nation and established trading relations with the tribe.

The Choctaws remained loyal to this treaty. During the War of 1812 they fought with Gen. Andrew Jackson and his forces against the Muscogees in the decisive Battle of Horseshoe Bend. They also supplied 750 warriors under Chief

The hatchet shall be forever buried and the peace given by the United States of America, and the friendship reestablished between the said states on the one part, and all the Choctaw nation on the other part, shall be universal; and the contracting parties shall use their utmost endeavors to maintain the peace given as aforesaid, and friendship reestablished.

Article XI,
Treaty of Hopewell, 1786

Nanih Waiya, the Choctaws' sacred "Mother Mound," in central Mississippi. (Courtesy Mississippi Band of Choctaw Indians.)

Pushmataha in the Battle of New Orleans against the British. In response to federal insistence that they "become civilized," the Choctaws adopted many of their white neighbors' practices: they opened schools, adopted a tribal constitution, and improved their farms so much that their white neighbors became envious.

The Choctaws' assistance, loyalty, and willingness to change got them nowhere, however. Instead of appreciating the Choctaws' efforts, the federal government made repeated demands for further land cessions and implemented a proposal to move all eastern tribes west across the Mississippi River. By 1820 the Choctaws had ceded almost 13 million acres of land to the United States, and pressure continued to remove the Choctaws from Mississippi entirely. In 1829 the state of Mississippi, with federal approval, passed laws turning Choctaw lands into Mississippi counties, dissolving tribal government, and levying large fines and prison sentences against any Choctaw who assumed a tribal office.

One year later, in 1830, Congress passed the Indian Removal Act, which authorized the federal government to negotiate treaties with tribes for their removal westward. Congress passed this act at the urging of President Andrew Jackson, under whom the Choctaws had fought so valiantly in the battles of Horseshoe Bend and New Orleans. Late in 1830 the Choctaws, stripped of tribal leaders, divided, and fearing the armed reprisal of the federal army, signed away their remaining lands in Mississippi and agreed to move to Indian Territory. The journey west was filled with suffering, heartbreak, disease, and death. The farms the tribe left behind were among the richest and most productive in Mississippi, and their tribal school system was the best in the entire state. Some tribal members opted to remain behind under the terms of their treaty; their lives too were filled with hardship and despair.

The treaty had promised land allotments of 640 acres to any Choctaw head of a family remaining in Mississippi. More than 8,000 of the 19,200 tribal members stayed, but only a few actually received their allotments. To survive, some Choctaws worked as sharecroppers for fifty cents a day on land that was once theirs. By 1910 the population had dwindled to 1,253. A flu epidemic in 1917 killed 20 percent of the remaining population. A year later the federal government finally acknowledged its long-ignored responsibility to the tribe and established the Choctaw Agency to help the tribe improve economic, health, and educational levels. In 1921 the federal government began the purchase of 17,000 acres of scattered lands that today comprise the Choctaw Reservation.

In 1945 the Choctaws reestablished a formal tribal government. They adopted a new constitution and elected a tribal council. For the next fifteen years this council met four times a year and functioned as an advisory body to the non-Indian representatives of the federal government who ran the Choctaw Agency, administered the few federal programs, and allocated the meager funds.

Realizing that its limited voice rendered it ineffective, the tribal council eventually began taking a greater and more aggressive role in tribal matters. In the 1960s the tribal council began expanding its governing powers and developing programs to improve the lives of its people. The Choctaws' economic resources were limited, but their human and cultural resources were great. Despite pressures to relocate and assimilate, the Choctaws and their culture had survived. The Choctaw language flourished as the primary language of more than 90 percent of the population. Tribal dances and songs endured, a testament to the strength of Choctaw values and traditions. The tribal council resolved to build on these strengths to overcome the tribe's problems.

Meeting at first in the kitchen of the Choctaw Agency headquarters, the council discussed the employment, housing, educational, and health needs of its people. Most Choctaws were impoverished and had few decent employment opportunities; many were unemployed. The widely scattered tribal lands were in parcels too small and infertile for productive farming. Housing was substandard, often with no running water. The educational level among tribal members was extremely low. Many had attended schools for only a few years. The federal government had not established schools in the area until 1926, and those went only to the eighth grade. Until 1963, to gain even a high-school education, tribal

Each Choctaw head of a family being desirous to remain and become a citizen of the States, shall be permitted to do so, by signifying his intention to the Agent within six months from the ratification of this Treaty, and he or she shall thereupon be entitled to a reservation of one section of six hundred and forty acres of land. . . . Persons who claim under this article shall not lose the privilege of a Choctaw citizen. . . .

Article XIV,
Treaty with the
Choctaws, 1830

We, the Choctaw Indians, members of the Mississippi Band of Choctaw Indians, desiring to promote the achievements of self-government for the Choctaw people do, for our welfare and benefit, hereby adopt and proclaim the following constitution and bylaws.

Preamble, Constitution
and Bylaws of the Mississippi
Band of Choctaw Indians, 1945

Stickball was, and still is, one of the most popular games among the Choctaws and other tribes of eastern North America. Games were once played to settle intertribal and intratribal disputes. As a diplomatic measure somewhere between peace and war, stickball became a means of expressing and managing tribal political relationships. The Muscogees even called the game "the little brother of war" and held matches between competing chiefdoms after weeks of negotiation and preparation. As part of an elaborate body of ceremonial ritual, stickball drew groups together and reinforced solidarity in clan and tribe. The George Catlin painting above, depicts a stickball game among southeastern Indians in the 1800s. The lower photos show the game as it is played today. Sticks are about three feet long and have a shallow, webbed leather scoop at one end. The ball, of leather woven around a hard core, is about the size of a golf ball. Players may not touch the ball with their hands but may bat or throw it with their sticks or run with it cradled in the scoop. Stickball is played on a field the size of a football field; points are scored when the ball strikes the opponents' goalpost. (Illustrations courtesy Mississippi Band of Choctaw Indians.)

members had to leave family and community and attend a boarding school for Indians in Oklahoma.

These conditions took an appalling toll on the Mississippi Choctaw community. In 1960 the average life expectancy for all Indian men was only forty-four years compared to the national average of sixty-six. The Indian infant mortality rate across the nation for the same year was 49 per 1,000 live births compared to 28 per 1,000 live births among the general population. Deaths from heart attacks, suicide, accidents, and alcoholism were many times higher for Indians than for any other group. Tuberculosis, almost nonexistent elsewhere, was a constant deadly presence on reservations. Living conditions for the Mississippi Choctaws were so poor that only in the 1960s did the birth rate begin to inch above the death rate. The only health-care facility open to the tribe was a thirty-five-bed hospital established in 1926 in Philadelphia, Mississippi. It was inadequately supplied, understaffed, and miles from the homes of most tribal members.

Conditions have changed drastically for the Choctaws since 1962. Economic development, education, and health-care programs administered by the tribal council have improved living conditions on the reservation, and the council is still involved in issues that will affect the tribe's future. But today, twenty years and countless meetings after that autumn meeting in 1962, the tribal council no longer meets at the Choctaw Agency but in its own council hall, built in 1978. A tribal office building, completed in 1975 by a tribal construction company, houses the more than sixty programs that have been shifted from federal to tribal control. The Choctaw Agency, headed by a Choctaw since 1973 at the tribe's insistence, no longer directs tribal affairs but serves the tribe in an advisory capacity.

In 1974 tribal members approved a revised constitution and bylaws. The new constitution provides for the election of a chief by the entire tribe instead of a chairperson appointed by the tribal council. The chief presides over council meetings, carries out policies established by the council, and directs the operation of tribal programs. With the council's approval, the chief negotiates contracts and agreements on behalf of the tribe. The council members, whose seats are apportioned by population among the seven communities, are responsible for regulating tribal property, managing tribal funds, employing legal counsel, establishing and enforcing tribal ordinances, levying taxes, developing economic policies, establishing an executive department, and promoting and protecting the "health, peace, morale, education and general welfare of the tribe." Each council member reports regularly to his or her local community organization.

Some of the council's recent activities and accomplishments are summarized below.

Chata Enterprises, one of the largest businesses established by the Choctaws in central Mississippi, has become a successful manufacturer of automobile parts. (Courtesy Mississippi Band of Choctaw Indians.)

ECONOMIC DEVELOPMENT

The Choctaws began an aggressive economic development plan in 1963 when they used proceeds from the sale of tribal timber to hire a Choctaw tribal member as tribal business manager. In 1969 the tribe created the Chata Development Company. This tribally owned construction firm has since renovated over two hundred houses and built more than four hundred new ones in addition to schools, offices, an adult correction center, community meeting halls, community baseball stadiums, and a health center.

In 1966 the tribe constructed the eighty-acre Choctaw Industrial Park. By the late 1980s the park had 300,000 square feet of industrial manufacturing space housing six separate plants and employing more than one thousand people. One of these businesses, established in 1979, is Chata Enterprises, a company that supplies the General Motors Corporation with wire harnesses for automobile instrument panels. Today this company operates three plants, employs over six hundred people, and has a higher acceptance rate of its product than all other manufacturers of the harnesses. Chata Greeting Enterprises, the third largest greeting-card production company in the world in terms of volume, began operation in 1982.

In 1985 the tribe established the Choctaw Federal Credit Union to provide banking services to its members. Three years later the tribe completed the Choctaw Shopping Center, a tribally owned shopping center that houses, among other enterprises, a grocery store, bank, restaurant, gas station, and a barber and beauty shop. In the mid 1980s, the tribe, working with the state of Mississippi, began examining the feasibility of constructing an on-reservation dam and reservoir to develop recreation and tourist facilities on the reservation.

Since its inception, the Choctaw economic development program has won numerous minority business awards and has been one of the most successful among all tribes' programs.

EDUCATION

Educational development has been a high priority among the Choctaws for the last twenty years. In 1963 the long-awaited high school was completed. Currently the Choctaw school system serves more than eleven hundred students in grades kindergarten through twelve. In addition to a basic primary and secondary school curriculum the tribe has designed programs to meet the educational needs of all its members. For instance, a preschool program helps prepare youngsters from age three through five for primary school.

Improving education is a primary objective of the Choctaw tribe. Both younger and older members of the tribe are shown here developing their educational skills in the tribal school and library. (Courtesy Mississippi Band of Choctaw Indians.)

An adult education program offers day and evening classes
to prepare adults for eighth-grade and high-school diplomas.
Adults may also take courses in health, nutrition, consumer
economics, driver education, Choctaw history, and Choctaw
arts and crafts. A training center teaches vocational and technical skills. A grant program operated by the tribe has helped
more than sixty Choctaw students earn college degrees.

Education issues facing the tribal council include decisions about funding for educational programs. For instance, when President Ronald Reagan vetoed appropriations
for tribally controlled colleges, the council had to decide
whether to delay that aspect of its educational program until
federal or tribal funds became available or to seek private
outside funding.

HEALTH

A fully accredited 40-bed hospital and three satellite clinics have served the reservation since 1975. In 1987 the
tribe opened a newly constructed 120-bed nursing home.
The Choctaw Health Center provides general medical and
dental care to all reservation residents. The Choctaw Health
Department also oversees a community nursing and training program, an ambulance service, and mental-health and
alcohol-abuse programs. The department also monitors water and sanitation conditions on the reservation. Health-
related issues currently facing the council include questions
of where in the seven communities, if anywhere, it is feasible
and desirable to open new clinics.

Although most tribes have not suffered the pain and loss of
being separated into two distinct groups, many were removed from their homelands to lands unwanted by whites,
and numerous tribes repeatedly have had their treaties broken by the United States. Most important, all Indian tribes
across the nation, like the Choctaws, are fighting today for
self-determination, struggling to regain freedom from federal
control, respect for their culture, and the economic prosperity that once was theirs.

Federal-tribal relations over the past two hundred years
are the main reason why the path toward tribal freedom
has been—and still is—difficult. History reveals that non-
Indians have frequently failed to understand or respect Indian ways. The federal government has periodically sought
to take away Indian lands, to destroy tribal culture, and to
dismantle tribal governments. As late as the 1960s, Congress
implemented legislation to end or terminate tribal status
and lands. Tribes have fought these and other pressures for
more than four centuries, since whites first came to North
America. Indian tribes and their governments are now facing
crucial decisions. In one direction is the end of tribal rights
and freedom. In the other direction is self-determination and
the chance to survive as a unique and unified people.

Members of younger and older generations participating in the annual Choctaw Fair held in Philadelphia, Mississippi. (Courtesy Mississippi Band of Choctaw Indians.)

Chapter 2 will introduce the traditional tribal governments of five tribes whose governments represent some of the different structures and degrees of complexity with which Indian governments traditionally met the needs of their people. Examining these traditional tribal governments will also reveal the major differences in values and basic philosophy between tribal governments and the governments of the countries that colonized the Americas.

CHAPTER 2

TRADITIONAL TRIBAL GOVERNMENTS

When Europeans "discovered" the New World, between 75 and 100 million people were already living in the Western Hemisphere. As many as 12 million, in more than 600 tribes, inhabited what is now North America. Each tribe possessed its own language or dialect, its own set of beliefs and traditions, and its own form of government.

Although tribes and their governments varied widely, to be a member of a tribe meant sharing a common bond of ancestry, kinship, language, culture, and political authority with other members. This feeling of oneness and distinctness from other groups is illustrated by the widespread custom of Indian tribes naming themselves with a word or words meaning "the People." The names by which tribes are known today are often the names they were given by early explorers or trappers. Nez Percé, for example, is a French phrase meaning "Those with Pierced Noses." The Nez Percés call themselves "Nimipu," meaning "the People." The word *Sioux* comes from the Chippewa word for snake, an insulting term the Chippewas used for their traditional enemies. The Teton Sioux refer to themselves as "Lakota" (the Allies). The Cherokees call themselves "Ani Yun Wiya," or "Real People."

Each tribe considered itself separate, distinct, and sovereign, or independent. *Sovereignty* is the force that binds a community together and represents the will of a people to act together as a single entity. A sovereign community possesses certain rights, including the rights to structure its government as it desires, to conduct foreign relations and trade with other nations, to define its own membership, to make and enforce its own laws, and to regulate its resources and property. The manner in which each tribe traditionally exercised these rights varied according to its distinct cultural practices and the needs imposed by its environment. Despite differences in structure, however, traditional tribal governments shared certain values, ideas of leadership, and styles of decision making.

Traditional Indian cultures made little distinction between the political and the religious worlds. Political wisdom was synonymous with religious power. All political actions were undertaken with spiritual guidance and oriented toward spiritual as well as political fulfillment. Indian reli-

TRIBAL DISTRIBUTION, 1500

Graphic by Bittle Productions

This map shows the estimated locations of a portion of the hundreds of Indian nations, tribes, and bands that inhabited in the 1500s what is today the United States.

gious and political values were based on the belief that a spiritual force lived within every natural being. The primary goal of religion and politics was to achieve harmony between all elements—the land, plant and animal life, and the human community. Human beings were not considered superior to and above nature but rather were thought to be connected to and part of nature. People did not *own* the land and resources; instead, individuals had a responsibility toward all aspects of life.

Traditional tribal governments reflected these religious values of responsibility and harmony. The community and an individual's responsibility to the community were more important than the individual and his or her rights within society. A person's rights and privileges never exceeded that person's duties and responsibilities. Power came from the community and flowed upward to the leaders. A large number of Indian societies were egalitarian and classless. A person's status and position were based on individual performance and ability.

These systems were unlike the highly structured and hierarchical European governmental systems in which a monarch held total power and the people had only those rights

MAJOR CULTURE AREAS, 1500

Graphic by Bittle Productions

On the basis of the organization of daily and seasonal life, family and kinship systems, economic structure, and other factors, Indian cultures have been classified into the eleven major culture areas shown above.

granted to them by the monarch. Indian governments in general were highly decentralized and democratic, based on rule by the people. Leaders lacked the power to dictate or to enforce their decisions. Their rule depended on their performance, their powers of persuasion, and the respect they were accorded. To remain in power, they needed the support and approval of their people. The ideas of majority rule and minority rights, however, were political concepts not used in their governing systems. Tribes made decisions based on consensus because their cultures stressed harmony of the whole. Since unanimity was necessary, dissension and disharmony were avoided. Many tribal governments contained provisions for initiatives, referendums, and recall. The right of male and female suffrage was the norm among many tribes.

The particular structures that embodied these values were as varied as the methods of coping with diverse environments. Some small bands and tribes, the Yakimas of the Columbia River area, for instance, operated with simple govern-

The authority of these rulers is gained by, and consists wholly in the opinion that the rest of the Nations have of their wisdom and integrity. They never execute their resolutions by force upon any of their people. Honor and esteem are their principal rewards; as shame, and being deposed, their punishment.

Cadwallader Colden,
Lieutenant Governor
of New York, 1727

ing bodies. All members of the tribe, meeting in a daily general council, discussed and decided on matters of general importance. Such a system is an example of the purest form of democracy. Leadership in such tribes fell naturally to the elders, who were respected for their wisdom, and to individuals who exhibited fairness, generosity, bravery, or particular hunting or fishing skills, depending on a community's needs. Such leaders had no inherent right to their positions. They governed only with the ongoing support of others. When that support was withheld, the old leader lost the position and new leaders emerged as needs arose.

At the other extreme from direct democracies were the complex, highly structured governments of such tribes as the Iroquois (who lived in what is now the northeastern United States), the Muscogees (who lived in what is now the southeastern United States), the Pueblos (of the Southwest), and the Lakotas (of the Plains).

The structure and operation of the traditional governments of these five groups are discussed below. Although the circumstances of life have changed drastically from what they were before white people came, it is important to realize that tribal governments continue today. As part 3 will illustrate, tribal governments are not a thing of the past.

THE HAUDENOSAUNEE (IROQUOIS LEAGUE)

Competition, bloodshed, and warfare marked the early relations between the Iroquois tribes of the northeastern woodlands. Although closely related linguistically and culturally, these tribes (the Onondagas, Mohawks, Oneidas, Senecas, and Cayugas) lived constantly at loggerheads with each other, frequently involved in skirmishes or out-and-out fighting. Then, sometime between A.D. 1000 and 1500, a great, visionary leader, Deganwidah, proposed that the warring tribes form a confederacy. Deganwidah, a Mohawk, had

> Their great Men, both Sachems and Captains, are generally poorer than the common People for they affect to give away and distribute all the Presents or Plunder they get in their Treaties or in War, so as to leave nothing for themselves. There is not a Man in the Ministry of the Five Nations, who has gain'd his Office, otherwise than by Merit; there is not the least Salary, or any Sort of Profit, annexed to any Office, to tempt the Covetous or Sordid; but, on the contrary, every unworthy Action is unavoidably attended with the Forfeiture of their Commission; for their Authority is only the Esteem of the People, and ceases the Moment that Esteem is lost.
>
> Cadwallader Colden
> Lieutenant Governor
> of New York, 1727

The final council at the formation of the Iroquois League is depicted in this life-size diorama in the Public Museum, Milwaukee, Wisconsin. (Courtesy Museum of the American Indian, Heye Foundation.)

a commanding presence and a deep spirituality. He was assisted by an Onondaga orator named Hiawatha. The two men eloquently persuaded the various Iroquois tribes to put down their weapons and form a political confederacy, the Great Peace.

This Great Peace (known by whites as the Iroquois League, or Iroquois Confederacy) remains in existence. It was founded on the principles Deganwidah and his kinspeople cherished and nurtured: freedom, respect, tolerance, consensus, and brotherhood. These values contrasted sharply with the principles that underlay European governments of the same time. In the 1500s, European governments were based on notions such as authoritarian rule by monarchs and the use of force and coercion to bring about unquestioning obedience.

Five nations—the Mohawk, Oneida, Onondaga, Cayuga, and Seneca (the five largest tribes in the area)—formed the original Great Peace Confederacy. A sixth nation, the Tuscarora, forced out of the Carolinas by European settlement, was admitted as a "junior" member around 1722. Of lower status, the Tuscarora Nation held no official position.

The confederacy was organized around three units: the Mohawks and Senecas were known as the Older Brothers; the Cayugas and Oneidas as the Younger Brothers; and the Onondagas as the Keepers of the Council Fire. As firekeepers (*adodarhonk*), the Onondagas were the council's moderators; their task was to promote agreement among the other four members. As a group these five nations came to be called the Haudenosaunee, or "People of the Longhouse."

Under the terms and spirit of the Ne Gayaneshagowa, or "Great Binding Law," to which all parties pledged themselves, the confederacy's constitution provided for a governing council of fifty civil chiefs, the Council of Fifty. Each of the fifty seats was named, ranked, and associated with a particular duty or responsibility. Since the Onondagas, in their role as moderators, held the most critical position in the confederacy, the head of the council was, by constitutional law, an Onondaga. Two more Onondagas served as his councillors, and yet another was designated as Keeper of the Council Wampum (the wampum was a woven belt beaded with shells used to record politically important agreements). Of the fifty seats on the council, the Onondagas held fourteen, the Cayugas ten, the Mohawks and Senecas nine each, and the Oneidas eight.

Each year the Onondagas called together the Council of Fifty to discuss matters of mutual concern and resolve differences peacefully. Matters of interest strictly to one tribe or another were handled by that tribe individually, but anything involving two or more tribes was discussed by the Council of Fifty.

When an issue was brought before the council, the Mohawks and Senecas discussed it first, then informed the

I, Deganawidea, and the Confederated Chiefs, now uproot the tallest pine tree, and into the cavity thereby made we cast all weapons of war. Into the depths of the earth, deep down into the under-earth currents of water flowing to unknown regions, we cast all weapons of strife. We bury them from sight and we plant again the tree Thus shall the Great Peace be established. . . .

We bind ourselves together, for many purposes, members of one family, by taking hold of each other's hands so firmly and forming a circle so strong that if a tree should fall upon it, it would not shake nor break it, so that our people and grandchildren shall remain in the circle of security, peace and happiness. Our strength shall be in union and our way the way of reason, righteousness and peace.

Deganwidah

An Iroquois longhouse. The Iroquois tribes called themselves Ongwanonhsioni, "We Longhouse Builders," and the Iroquois League came to be called Haudenosaunee, "People of the Longhouse." Today the term has structural, political, social, and religious significance. Traditional longhouses were rectangular, barrel- or pointed-roofed structures covered by elm-bark shingles. Each one served as home to an extended matriarchal family. Each nuclear family within a longhouse had its own room with sleeping platforms and storage areas along the walls. Fire and cooking areas were shared. The women of the house shared farming plots and the men hunted, fished, and fought together. When a man married, he joined his wife's longhouse. The term *longhouse* symbolized the Iroquois League, because all tribes within the league dwelt together and worked out their mutual problems. Each member tribe had a name referring to its place within the longhouse. Thus the Mohawks were known as "Guardians of the Eastern Door"; the Senecas as "Guardians of the Western Door"; and the Onondagas as "Keepers of the Council Fires." The longhouse today also has a religious meaning in Iroquois life. Members of the Handsome Lake religion, often referred to as the Longhouse Religion, hold their ceremonies in a longhouse. (Drawing by Fernando Dreaming Bear.)

Younger Brothers, the Cayugas and Oneidas, of the conclusions they, as Older Brothers, had reached. If the Older and Younger Brothers disagreed, the Onondagas task was to search for paths of compromise and renewed discussion. The Onondagas would then return the issue to the Older and Younger Brothers for further consideration.

When both brotherhoods finally reached agreement, the Onondagas were responsible for confirming the decision or subjecting it to further discussion. Ideally, final decisions were unanimous. All council members were to be of "one heart, one mind, one law." This system gave all five nations equal power, although they had different numbers of representatives on the council. When the council could not reach agreement despite its best efforts, the Onondagas extinguished the confederacy council fire, thereby giving each member nation the right to pursue an independent policy.

Women were not eligible for seats on the Council of Fifty, but they did hold considerable power within the Iroquois tribes. In certain clans, the clan mother (the oldest woman

> In all cases the procedure must be as follows: when the Mohawk and Seneca Lords have unanimously agreed upon a question, they shall report their decision to the Cayuga and Oneida Lords who shall deliberate upon the question and report a unanimous decision to the Mohawk Lords. The Mohawk Lords will then report the standing of the case to the Firekeepers, who shall render a decision . . . as they see fit in case of a disagreement by the two bodies, or confirm the decisions of the two bodies if they are identical. The Fire Keepers shall then report their decision to the Mohawk Lords who shall announce it to the open council.
>
> Ne Gayaneshagowa, "The Great Binding Law" (Constitution of the Iroquois League)

in the clan) was responsible for nominating the chiefs, or *sachems*, of the group. She would normally do this after consulting other women in the clan and identifying the clansmen most suited for leadership by virtue of their generosity, truthfulness, reliability, courage, and religious spirit. After the clan mother made her nomination, the entire tribe and the Council of Fifty met to confirm it. Sometimes the clan mother nominated an exceptionally promising but young boy for a position; in that case she herself served as his surrogate, or substitute, until he reached an age to assume full responsibility for the job. Clan mothers also possessed the authority to dismiss leaders guilty of misconduct.

Although the Council of Fifty was the primary governing body of the Great Peace Confederacy, another group of men, known as the Solitary Pine Trees, was also important. The men in this group were not eligible to vote in council discussions—only the fifty civil chiefs could do that—but they had the right to speak at council meetings. They earned this right through merit and bravery in warfare. The Solitary Pine Trees acted as ombudsmen for their communities, conveying their people's wishes, complaints, and questions to the Council of Fifty.

The Iroquois governmental system was sophisticated, spreading political power over a wide base and also providing the society with a system of checks and balances. Power was delegated by the people to the Council of Fifty, the clan mothers, and the Solitary Pine Trees. Iroquois law further decreed that civil chiefs should not also serve as war leaders. If a chief felt obliged to lead a war expedition, he was required to relinquish his civil position. All leaders, whether civil or war chiefs, exerted their influence not by coercion or physical force but through diplomacy and persuasion and by personally earning their people's respect. The requirement that tribal and confederacy decisions be unanimous meant that leaders had to consider and balance all viewpoints. In the Iroquois League, rule by council consensus did not mean rule by a few or even by a majority, but rule by all.

THE MUSCOGEE (CREEK) NATION

The Muscogees, or Creeks, as the whites called them, originally lived in a large area extending throughout present-day eastern Alabama, Georgia, and neighboring areas. By 1500 the Muscogee Nation, composed of many independent tribes, had formed a strong political confederacy of more than twenty thousand people. The primary governing body of the confederacy was the Great Council, which met every summer. This council was composed of the leaders of each town, or *talwa*, in the confederation. At its meetings the council debated and decided matters of national importance, such as treaties, wars, and the admission of new groups to the confederacy. The council meetings had political, religious, and social significance and were times of great cele-

When a Lordship title becomes vacant through death or other cause, The Royaneh women of the clan in which the title is hereditary shall hold a council and shall choose one from among their sons to fill the office made vacant. Such a candidate shall not be the father of any Confederate Lord. If the choice is unanimous the name is referred to the men relatives of the clan. If they should disapprove it shall be their duty to select a candidate from among their number. If then the men and women are unable to decide which of the two candidates shall be named, then the matter shall be referred to the Confederate Lords in the Clan. They shall decide which candidate shall be named. If the men and the women agree to a candidate his name shall be referred to the sister clans for confirmation. If the sister clans confirm the choice, they shall then refer their action to their Confederate Lords who shall ratify the choice and present it to their cousin Lords, and if the cousin Lords confirm the name then the candidate shall be installed by the proper ceremony for the conferring of Lordship titles.

Ne Gayaneshagowa, "The Great Binding Law" (Constitution of the Iroquois League)

bration. The council, however, did not discuss matters of local concern, respecting the right of each *talwa* to organize its own affairs.

The *talwa* was the basic unit of confederation in the Muscogee Confederacy, and each *talwa* had its own governing council, mediated its own disputes, and punished its own offenders. The clan system in Muscogee culture also played a role in maintaining social harmony. The structure and governmental functions of the Muscogee *talwa* and clan systems are discussed below.

Each *talwa* was built around a central, ceremonial square, and adjacent to the town were its hunting grounds and the agricultural fields where the community grew its corn, grain, beans, squash, pumpkins, and sunflowers. There were approximately one hundred *talwas* in the Muscogee Confederacy, ranging in population from under one hundred to over one thousand inhabitants. Four *talwas*—Tukabahchee, Koweta, Knsita (or Cussetah), and Abihka—held the title of "mother *talwa*." These four towns were centers of commerce and communication and often took the lead in political affairs.

Like many other southeastern tribes, the tribes in the Muscogee Confederacy had a dual system of political and social organization. Towns and clans were divided into two groups: one symbolized by the color white and the other by the color red. White Towns and White Clans were generally associated with the activities and responsibilities of peace, while Red Towns and Red Clans were associated with war-related matters.

The clan system of the Muscogees, like those of other eastern tribes, including the Iroquois, was matriarchal and exogamous. In a *matriarchal* system newborn children become members of their mother's clan and *talwa*. The Muscogees were also *matrilocal*, meaning that a new bridegroom lived with his wife's family. As an *exogamous* society, the Muscogees required individuals to marry outside their clan. Because of these practices, a family with several children would typically become related through marriage to several other clans, often those in neighboring *talwas*. This meant that several or possibly all the clans might be represented in a single *talwa*. Since clan members were regarded as "family," this system promoted close ties and interrelationships throughout the nation.

The clan system provided the basic political and social structure of each *talwa*. Each clan within a *talwa* had specific duties and farming areas and often provided leaders for specific offices. Clans were responsible for the social behavior of their own members and, except in unusual cases, for punishing crimes and settling civil grievances. The eldest male member of a clan served as its teacher and counselor. It was his job to talk with clan members who behaved improperly and to determine punishments in the case of a serious of-

fense. Unresolvable disputes between two clans were referred to the council of the *talwa*, which represented all the
clans.

An offense against one member of a clan was considered
an offense against all members, and it was the responsibility
of all members to seek redress against the offender. A clan's
honor depended upon determining the truth in a dispute and
making proper settlements for the wrongs committed by any
of its members. Punishments were determined by the crime
and by the character of the defendant. Stolen goods were
repaid twofold. If a thief had poor standing in the community, clan members might deliver him or her to the victim for
whipping. In the case of killing (no distinction was made
between an accidental killing and a murder), one of several
alternatives existed. The killer, if well respected, might be
adopted by the wronged clan to take the victim's place, or he
or she might be ordered to perform certain services or deeds,
such as providing food, for the victim's family. If the killer
was a person of ill repute, the members of his or her clan
might consent to the death penalty, with the victim's clan
carrying out the execution. Punishments were undertaken
with two goals in mind: to mend the law that had been broken and, as a cleansing process, to wash away the crime.
Once the sentence had been carried out, the culprit was considered innocent of the crime.

Further reflecting the duality of the town and clan system,
each *talwa* had two leaders: a civil chief and a war chief. The
civil chief, or *micco*, received ambassadors, negotiated treaties, dispensed food from the public granaries, and established feast days to celebrate successful hunts. *Miccos* were
generally chosen by the opposing group. That is, in White
Towns the Red Clan members chose the *micco* from among
the White Clans' membership. In Red Towns, White Clan
members chose the *micco* from among the Red Clans.

The *micco*, a person who had achieved great honor and
trust, ruled by persuasion, not command or coercion. A
micco who failed to achieve harmony and consensus among
members and who brought divisiveness to *talwa* affairs was
relieved of the position.

A three-tiered system of advisers appointed by the *micco*
assisted in the administration of public duties. The war chief,
or *tvstvnvke*, was chosen by the *micco* from among members
of the Red Clans. He advised the *micco* on matters of war,
organized warriors for battle, maintained public order, and
arranged the important stickball games played between Red
and White Towns. The "second men," *henneha*, or public-
works advisers, were responsible for constructing new dwellings, organizing work in the communal fields, and preparing
the "black drink," an important, tealike beverage consumed
at weekly *talwa* council meetings. One of the *henneha* served
as the *micco*'s Speaker, or chief spokesman. Well versed in
law, the Speaker was responsible for conveying the *micco*'s

. . . there is no coercive
power. . . . Their Kings can do
no more than persuade. All the
power they have is no more than
to call their old men and captains
and to propound to them the
measures they think proper. After
they have done speaking, all the
others have liberty to give their
opinions also; and they reason
together with great temper and
modesty, till they have brought
each other into some unanimous
resolution. Then they call in the
young men and recommend the
putting in execution the resolution with their strongest and most
lively eloquence. In speaking to
their young men they generally
address to the passions; in speaking to their old men they apply to
reason only.

James Oglethorpe, governor of
Georgia, speaking
of the Muscogees, 1764

decisions to the people. The "beloved old men," or *este vcakvlke*, were the third group of advisers. These elders had distinguished themselves throughout their lives and were highly valued for their wisdom and good advice.

The *micco* and his three groups of advisers formed the *talwa*'s governing council. Besides overseeing the administration of each advisory group's specific duties, the council levied fines for infractions against the community, such as failing to participate in the Green Corn Ceremony or not doing one's share in the public planting and harvesting. Working together, the three advisory groups and the *micco* formed a participatory and thoroughly democratic body in which all people had the right to express their own views. Through discussion and compromise, the *talwa* leaders sought harmony and the reconciliation of differences among all members.

Harmony was so highly valued among the Muscogees that a special system was devised to maintain it even when a major issue could not be settled to everyone's satisfaction. If a member or several members of a *talwa* continued to disagree with the majority on a policy, they were free to move and establish their own community, with the support—not the enmity—of those whose *talwa* they were leaving. When a dissident group established a new town (and also when a neighboring tribe joined the Muscogee Confederacy), an ember from one of the mother *talwas* was used to start the fire of the new settlement as a symbol of continuity and unity. When the Muscogees were removed to Indian Territory in the 1800s, they carefully took the embers and other symbols of their *talwas* with them.

THE LAKOTA (TETON SIOUX) NATION

The three divisions of the Sioux people are the Santee (Dakota), the Yankton (Nakota), and the Teton Sioux (Lakota). The Lakota Nation was a confederation of seven bands: the Oglala (Scatter One's Own), the Sicangu (Burnt Thighs), the Minneconjou (Those who Plant by the Stream), the Hunkpapa (Those who Camp at the Entrance), the Itazipco (Without Bows), the Sihasapa (Blackfeet), and the Oohinunpa (Two Kettles).

At its greatest extent, in the mid-1800s, the Lakota Nation reached from the Platte River north to the Heart River and from the Missouri River west to the Bighorn Mountains. Unlike the Iroquois and the Muscogees, who had established large, permanent settlements, the Lakotas were nomadic hunters who traveled over vast territories in search of buffalo, which provided food, hides for shelter and clothing, and bones for weapons and utensils. The *tiyošpaye*, a small group of related families, was the basic unit of Lakota society. Highly mobile, a *tiyošpaye* could move almost daily if necessary to stay in contact with the buffalo and other game on which it depended.

Everything the Power of the World does is done in a circle. The sky is round, and I have heard that the earth is round like a ball, and so are all the stars. The wind, in its greatest power, whirls. Birds make their nests in circles, for theirs is the same religion as ours. The sun comes forth and goes down again in a circle. The moon does the same, and both are round. Even the seasons form a great circle in their changing, and always come back again to where they were. The life of man is a circle from childhood to childhood, and so it is in everything where power moves. Our tepees were round like the nests of birds, and these were always set in a circle, the nations hoop, a nest of many nests, where the Great Spirit meant for us to hatch our children.

Black Elk, Oglala Sioux

Sam Kills Two working on his winter count. Along with warriors
and medicine men, the tribal historian, keeper of the Winter Count,
was held in high esteem among the Lakota and Kiowa nations. Each
winter the tribal elders met to discuss the events of the past year
and decide which should be recorded on that year's Winter Count,
a pictorial record of the tribe's history. The tribal historian depicted
the event on a large, stretched buffalo hide. The pictographs served
as reminders to the historian, who would relate the tribe's history
to its members on long winter nights. (Courtesy John A. Anderson
Collection, Nebraska State Historical Society.)

Each *tiyošpaye*, led by a headman, or leader, included
thirty or more tipis, or individual households. A headman
achieved his position by possessing family status and demonstrating bravery, fortitude, generosity, wisdom, and spiritual powers gained through dreams and visions. Headmen
were also expected to sponsor ceremonies and attain membership in the tribe's important fraternal societies.

Fraternal societies played a significant role in maintaining
the well-being of Lakota society. Each of the seven Lakota
bands formed its own societies, but there were two main
kinds: *akicitas* and *nacas*. Membership in the *akicitas*, or police societies, was by invitation only and limited to the band's
most promising young men. Each season one of the *akicitas*
was given the task of maintaining order during camp move-

ments and communal buffalo hunts. Membership in the *aki-citas* helped develop the leadership skills of young men.

The *nacas*, or civil societies, on the other hand, capitalized on the wisdom of maturity. Of all the *nacas* societies, the group called Naca Ominicia was the most important. Composed of former headmen, hunters, warriors, and shamans, the Naca Ominicia functioned as the tribal council. The council could act only by consensus. Its responsibilities were broad, ranging from determining the time and place of tribal hunts and relocations to appointing tribal administrators and executives to declaring war and peace.

Seven to ten members of the Naca Ominicia were appointed *wicaša itancans*. This group acted as an executive committee and was responsible for interpreting and enforcing the broad decisions of the council. Two to four *wicaša*, or "shirt wearers," headed this smaller council. Their duties ranged from negotiating with foreign nations to reconciling quarrels between individuals and families. The Naca Omini-

This scene, photographed in 1915, is reminiscent of life before the coming of non-Indians. Eleven members of the Blackfeet Tribe are shown in Glacier National Park, Montana. (Courtesy Smithsonian Institution, National Anthropological Archives.)

This steatite pipe is said to have belonged to Crazy Horse, one of the most renowned of all Lakota warriors. Pipes played an important religious and political role in the societies of the eastern, midwestern, and plains tribes. A special pipe was smoked at the beginning of all important councils and ceremonies to symbolize the harmony and unity of the universe. The pipe's bowl served as the altar for the burning tobacco, which many tribes considered to have mystical properties. The shaft was the pathway for the smoker's breath. The breath, or spirit, joined with the sacred smoke and traveled heavenward in thanks to the Great Spirit. (Courtesy Museum of the American Indian, Heye Foundation.)

cia also appointed two to four *wakincuzas*, or "pipe owners." Serving under the shirt wearers, the pipe owners were responsible for the Pipe Ceremony (a religious ceremony involving prayer and use of the sacred pipe) and for organizing camp moves, assigning camping locations, and guarding against attacks. Another important figure in Lakota society was the *wicaša wakan*, or "medicine man." Medicine men were highly respected for their curative powers and wisdom and were consulted by the *wicaša itancan* about important tribal decisions.

The government of the Lakota Nation had a structure similar to that of each of the seven bands. Every summer the bands assembled to decide matters of national importance, to participate in the Sun Dance, and to renew acquaintances. The *nacas* of each band formed the national council. The national council appointed four *wicaša yatapikas*, or "supreme owners of the nation." Occupying positions of esteem, honor, and trust, the supreme owners were responsible for formulating national policy, approving or disapproving actions taken by the leadership of the separate bands during the previous year, and sitting in judgment on offenses against national unity and security.

. . . peace . . . comes within the souls of men when they realize their relationship, their oneness, with the universe and all its powers . . .

Black Elk, Oglala Sioux

THE PUEBLOS

The Pueblo Indians have lived in the beautiful canyons, plateaus, and mesas of the Southwest for more than ten thousand years. The Pueblos are descendants of the Mogollan and Anasazi people who settled in the area that is now the states of Arizona, New Mexico, Colorado, and Utah. Agriculturalists who farmed the arid lands using a sophisticated irrigation system, these ancient peoples lived in large villages built from local materials, such as adobe and sandstone, and practiced the arts of basket weaving and pottery making. Toward the end of the fourteenth century many of the largest settlements were abandoned, perhaps because of drought and a decreasing food supply. By the time of Francisco Coronado's expedition in 1540, the Pueblo Indians were living in numerous communities scattered across what is now New Mexico.

The Spanish called these Indians "Pueblos" because their houses were fashioned around closely clustered communities similar to the *pueblos* (villages) of Spain. The Pueblos were not one people or tribe; rather, they were a diverse collection of tribes who shared the same geographic area, used similar architecture, and organized their societies in similar ways. Each Pueblo was autonomous, having its own social organization, leadership, and language. All were highly religious and possessed complex systems of ceremonies and dances, and each produced its own crops of chile, corn, beans, and squash.

To an even greater extent than most other Indian cultures, the Pueblos did not establish divisions between religious and nonreligious (or *secular*) life. Religious beliefs and practices were an integral part of all political and social behavior. In fact, Pueblo spiritual life was not just a part of life but was life itself. Religion was not categorized or institutionalized but represented a whole system of beliefs that found expression throughout all of nature.

Pueblo beliefs were, and still are, based on the idea that there is a spiritual force within all of nature. Nature and God are one. Humankind's task is to maintain a harmonious relationship with nature. An intricate system of dances and celebrations reinforces the Pueblos' quest for this oneness with God and Nature. The Pueblos give thanks and prayer for all aspects of their lives: the rains that fall, the crops that grow, the game they hunt, their good health, and their fellow human beings. Commitment to this pervasive spiritual relationship, combined with community duties, created a tightly knit and highly integrated society. Emphasis was on cooperation and the subordination of personal interest to the interests of the group.

Most Pueblo communities were divided into two moieties. Every individual was a member of one of the two moieties. Every individual was also a member of a clan. The clans formed the basis of Pueblo spiritual and religious life. Coordination of the numerous Pueblo dances and celebrations was the responsibility of the moieties and the various clans, or societies, which included curing (or medicine) societies, hunting societies, kachina societies, clown societies, and warrior societies. Individuals could change their moiety affiliation and rarely their clan membership, which was based on lineage and inherited from one's mother. Clan members maintained strong attachments to each other throughout their lives. Clan leaders were responsible for regulating the behavior of their members. In some pueblos, the leaders of curing societies had to belong to certain clans.

In many pueblos, parents chose a kiva or kachina society into which their children would be initiated. Kiva societies, generally only for males, were housed in a kiva, a special ceremonial chamber. Kiva societies taught children the ceremonies and rituals associated with the community. Throughout his or her lifetime, a person often became associated with other societies as well. Various societies were responsible for specific community functions and ceremonial practices. A clown society, for instance, performed at special solstice dances, providing comic relief as well as maintaining ceremonial order. Hunt societies made preparations for suc-

Interior view of a facsimile model of a kiva. (Courtesy Museum of Northern Arizona.)

cessful hunts, while war societies prepared for success in war. Curing societies were responsible for the physical and spiritual health of the village. Men and women each had specific roles in these societies.

Traditionally, each pueblo was governed by one or more priests (if two, then each ruled for half the year). Since there was no distinction between religious and political life, traditional Pueblo government is often described as a theocracy—a government by religious leaders. Among the Hopi Pueblos the leader was called the *kikmongwi*; at Jemez, the *whivela*; and at Isleta, the *taikabede*. The Spanish referred to Pueblo leaders as the "cacique." (Taken from a Caribbean Indian word meaning "leader," *cacique* is the term used by outsiders today when speaking of a Pueblo religious leader.) In some pueblos the leader of a specific clan became the cacique. In other pueblos a council of the elders chose the cacique, who then held the position for life.

The cacique was the titular head of all societies. He counseled but did not command. He gave formal endorsement after a consensus had been reached by the community. As overseer of the community's values and beliefs, he remained removed from many common village chores. The community provided the cacique and his family with food and firewood, thereby allowing him to direct his attention to spiritual matters.

The cacique's staff traditionally consisted of an Outside Chief and two assistants, the war captains. These officials looked after the practical needs of the pueblo, leaving the cacique free to attend to important community matters. Together they oversaw irrigation, planting, livestock care, and building repair. They also settled disputes, provided for the pueblo's defense, and represented the tribe in its outside relations.

A council of leaders also assisted the cacique. They aided in lawmaking and judicial enforcement. A decision was usually debated until all were in agreement. This council was responsible for introducing new policies and procedures, sponsoring changes in customs and traditions, and recommending punishment for such crimes as disloyalty, witchcraft, or the betrayal of community secrets.

THE YAKIMAS

The ancestors of the modern Yakima Nation came to the plains, valleys, and mountains of what is now the state of Washington at least fourteen thousand years ago. Their homeland stretched from the forested Cascade Mountains on the west to the sagebrush desert and rocky canyons of the Columbia River basin on the east. Dependent on food gathering, hunting, and fishing, they lived in harmony with the physical world. Their life followed the rhythms of nature as they moved with the changing seasons from one location to another.

The Seasons kept our people on the move.
With an eye to winter's needs:
Spring saw us in the river valley for celery
Summer took us to the foothills for roots
Fall brought us to the high mountains for the huckleberry
Winter in the shelter of the lowlands
Was made possible by those gatherings.

Yakima Nation Cultural Center

These early people wintered in the Yakima Valley, several families sharing single dwellings. During the winter they lived on the food they had gathered during the spring and summer and used the long, cold season to mend their fishing nets, make weapons and utensils, and fashion buckskin clothing. With the first signs of spring, the villages disbanded, and family groups traveled to favorite root-digging locations on the alpine slopes of the Cascades. Here, in the foothills, they harvested camas root, wild onions, wild potatoes, and wild carrots and prepared them for storage.

By late May and early June, the Yakimas, Palouses, Klickatats, Se-ap-cats, and other tribes had begun congregating at their traditional fishing sites on the Columbia River and its tributaries. Every family member kept busy throughout July catching, drying, and packing salmon—king, sockeye, chinook, and steelhead—the mainstay of their winter diet. In late August the bands returned to their wild and beautiful mountains to harvest berries. As autumn settled in, the women gathered fruits and nuts and the men hunted deer, antelope, elk, bear, and smaller game.

Depending on their needs, families might stay in the mountains during late autumn for further gathering and hunting or return to the Columbia River for the fall salmon run. After horses were introduced to the area in the 1700s, the tribes of the Columbia Plateau became skilled horsemen. They often took journeys lasting several months to the plains east of the Rockies to hunt for buffalo.

The Yakimas recognized the beauty and sanctity of all nature and felt a deep spirituality for and emotional attachment to the land. Gratitude for nature's bounty and the desire to give thanks and protect it formed the basis of their life. They returned nature's bounty with thanksgiving and celebration and, like other Indian tribes, differentiated scarcely at all between the sacred and the secular.

The Yakima Indians, and other Plateau tribes, lived in small, politically autonomous groups linked by culture, shared resources, and similar languages. The basic unit of social organization was the village, made up of several extended families. Villages varied from one to fifty dwellings and housed a total of 50 to 1,500 people, with the average village population being 100 to 150. Dwelling size varied too, with the largest huts being sixty feet long and housing 50 or 60 individuals.

Closely interconnected villages joined together to form bands. In times of crisis, several villages or bands might unite temporarily, but no regular structure existed for formal joint action. There were no clans among these tribal groups. Intermarriage, trade, cooperation, and frequent contact at fishing sites created whatever close ties existed among the villages and bands in a region.

The Yakimas, Umatillas, Nez Percés, Cayuses, and other tribes of the area enjoyed an egalitarian society based on co-

> Plants ask that we leave some for
>   other creatures,
> That we remember seasons to
>   come,
> And the people to come.
> Plants are not ours to own.
> But to use and protect.
>
> **Yakima Nation Cultural Center**

> My Mother is the earth, my
> Father the light, when I die, my
> body returns to my Mother and
> my spirit to my Father.
>
> **Yakima Nation Cultural Center**

Yakima Indian fishing in the traditional manner. The tribes of the Northwest made salmon their primary food and worshipped the fish, believing that they were not fish but godlike people who lived beneath the sea. When a salmon was killed, its spirit was believed to change to a humanlike form and return to its sea village. But the transformation could be ruined by human failure to give thanks and respect to the salmon for its gift. To give thanks, the village gathered each year to celebrate the First Salmon Ceremony. The first salmon caught was specially prepared in an elaborate ceremony, then roasted and eaten before sundown. Its heart was burned in the fire and its bones carefully placed at the water's edge, to be reclaimed by the fish's spirit. (Courtesy Eastern Washington State Historical Society.)

operation, sharing, hospitality, and responsibility for common welfare. "Giveaways" (similar to the potlatches of the northwestern coastal tribes) formed an important part of ceremonial and social life. It was an honor both to give and to receive, but the greater honor was to give.

Yakima Indians on horseback, reminiscent of life before non-Indian settlement. (Courtesy Washington State Historical Society.)

Village leadership rested in the hands of a male elder respected for his generosity, wisdom, powers of persuasion, and abilities as a warrior and hunter. The leader held authority through the consent of the people, and he could lose his position if his actions ceased to command confidence and respect. After contact with whites, positions of leadership came more and more to remain within certain families, although leadership never became strictly hereditary. The headman was assisted in his decision making by an informal council of village elders, both men and women. Any disagreements were resolved by arbitration and mediation. Each day the headman's spokesperson (similar to a town crier) reported the leader's and the council's decisions and announced plans for the following day. Other persons of leadership and esteem in the village included recognized warriors, shamans or medicine men, heads of hunting and fishing parties, religious leaders, leaders of root-digging expeditions, and athletes.

The extended family regulated social behavior and handled misbehavior. Individualism and the autonomy of the individual, family, and band were highly valued, but overall there was a clear sense of responsibility both for one's own actions and for the welfare of others. Children were taught early to be self-sufficient. Older family members usually settled family disagreements, although the headman and council were sometimes asked to resolve particularly difficult disputes. At times, fines or floggings were levied for serious crimes.

Years of contact with European governments and the U.S. government have changed the structure of tribal governments as well as the kinds of power they exercise and the manner in which they meet the needs of their people. Part 3 will outline the history of Indian-white relations, demonstrating how this relationship has affected the structure and powers of tribal governments.

PART 2

THE EFFECTS OF INDIAN-WHITE RELATIONS
ON TRIBAL GOVERNMENTS:
A HISTORY

To understand the tribal governments of today, it is necessary to understand not only their traditional governmental systems but how and why those systems have changed over the years. To enhance that understanding, part 2 reviews the history of the relations between Indians and non-Indians from the time Christopher Columbus "discovered" America, in 1492, to the present.

Chapter 3 reviews the Indian nations' relationships with the European powers that invaded and settled their lands. The first colonizers, the Spanish, originally sought to conquer and enslave the Indians of Latin America in the name of Christianity. In later years, following the example of other European powers, Spain concluded treaties of equality with the Indian nations. The French, who came primarily to trade, treated Indians with respect, eager to learn their ways of the woods. The Dutch, whose stay was brief, nonetheless established an important political relationship that was later inherited by the English. The English, who came to farm, concluded over five hundred treaties with various tribes in an effort to obtain their lands and gain their alliance against competing European powers.

After the formation of the United States, that nation gradually became the dominant force in Indian-white relations. Chapter 4 examines the relationship of the Indian nations with the United States in the period from the 1780s through the 1890s. Originally, the U.S. Congress respected Indian nations as independent sovereigns and regulated their relations with them through treaties. By the 1830s the eastern United States had filled with settlers, and Congress embarked on a policy of forced removal of eastern tribes to lands west of the Mississippi River. As western lands grew scarce, the government established reservations, frequently fighting battles of attrition and starvation to force tribes to relinquish their lands.

After finally subduing the tribes, Congress passed a series of laws designed to assimilate Indians into white society. Legislation passed included bills aimed at destroying tribal government, culture, language, and communal landholdings. In the 1930s, Congress reversed the worst aspects of these laws with the passage of the Indian Reorganization Act (IRA), a bill designed to strengthen tribal governments. Twenty years later Congress reversed itself again with policies designed to terminate the government's relationship with and responsibilities to the tribes. In 1975, recognizing its historical and moral commitment to tribes, Congress initiated the present era of self-determination. Today tribes are striving to strengthen their governments, establish social services, and obtain economic self-sufficiency. Chapter 5 surveys the various and contradictory U.S. government policies in force since the end of the Indian wars and analyzes their effects on tribal governments.

CHAPTER 3

THE NEWCOMERS

In 1492 the Taino Indians of the Bahamas discovered Christopher Columbus on their shores. Others, Scandinavians and perhaps even the Irish, may have preceded him, but they failed to establish permanent settlements. Those who followed Columbus—"discoverers," adventurers, missionaries, and, later, settlers—did stay. Columbus came to the New World seeking a direct route to India and its luxury goods: jewels, silk, porcelain, and spices. Instead he found vast new lands of astonishing size and variety, populated by "men of great deference and kindness."

Following Columbus's expedition, reports and rumors of a land rich in gold, furs, and rich soil quickly spurred new expeditions. John Cabot, Giovanni da Verrazano, Jacques Cartier, Hernando de Soto, Francisco Coronado, and Martin Frobisher led the scramble for claims in North America, while Vasco da Gama, Amerigo Vespucci, Vasco Balboa, Juan Ponce de León, Hernando Cortes, Francisco Pizarro, and Sir Francis Drake led expeditions to Central and South America.

The European discovery of the Americas had a tremendous impact on the Old World. The new, vast, and rich continents were sources of national wealth for European powers and provided an outlet for individuals seeking wealth and fleeing religious persecution. The gold taken by Spain from Latin America supported the Spanish national treasury for decades. French fur-trade profits added considerably to the wealth and prestige of the French Crown. The English colonies provided raw materials and markets for Great Britain's rapidly expanding manufacturing trade. The introduction of Indian crops, such as white potatoes, corn, and tomatoes, improved European diets and aided a population explosion and an improved standard of living, especially in Great Britain. European medicine welcomed more than 170 new drugs, such as quinine, used to treat malaria, and novocaine, an anesthetic. Transportation and entertainment changed as Europeans began using snowshoes, canoes, rubber, and hammocks. Tobacco and chocolate added to personal enjoyment. Warfare also changed as Europeans adopted Indian styles of guerrilla military strategy.

Despite their debts to Indian culture, Europeans' treatment of Indians was generally hostile and always self-serving. The pattern varied from virtual extermination by the Spanish to hostile dismissal by the English to grudging respect by the French. European civilization was based on individualism, hierarchy, and materialism, and Europeans considered their

They are loving people, without covetousness. . . . They love their neighbors as themselves, and their speech is the sweetest and gentlest in the world.

Christopher Columbus

way vastly superior to Indian cultures. Reared in societies
that emphasized acquisition through competition and control, Europeans were simply unable to appreciate or even understand cultures that deemphasized those values.

SPANISH CLAIMS AND INDIAN RIGHTS

Spain and Portugal, the first nations to establish permanent
settlements in the New World, quickly laid claim to the entire Western Hemisphere on the basis of discovery. The
Western Hemisphere, however, was not unpopulated. It had
already been "discovered" by its approximately 90 million
inhabitants. To support their claims, Spain and Portugal
sought the support of Pope Alexander VI, "the appointed servant of God." The whole earth belonged to God, and the
pope, as God's representative, had the authority, the Spanish
and the Portuguese argued, to dispose of it as he saw fit. In
1493, Pope Alexander VI issued the encyclical "Inter Caetera." This papal proclamation, which was reaffirmed in the
1494 Treaty of Tordessillas, drew a north-south line through
the Western Hemisphere. All of the New World to the west
of the line was under Spain's control; everything to the east,
under Portugal's. What the line actually meant—whether it
granted land ownership or merely divided the hemisphere
into areas where the Spanish and the Portuguese could convert the native populations to Christianity—was disputed for
decades.

Spain's presence in the New World lasted for almost three
hundred years. During that time the Spanish occupied colonies in all areas of Latin America, Florida, the Gulf of Mexico
coast, the entire Southwest, and, for a time, the area that
eventually became the Louisiana Purchase. In the early years
of its colonial administration, Spain's treatment of the native
populations was rivaled in cruelty only by that of the Russians, who established colonies in Alaska and northern California between 1741 and 1867.

Spain's overriding interest in the New World was gold.
Wealth and power in Europe at this time were determined
by the amount of gold bullion a nation held in its treasury.
To extract gold and other metals from the New World, Spain
conquered and enslaved the native populations. The near extermination of numerous Indian villages through forced labor was so appalling that, in 1537, Pope Paul III issued a
proclamation directed at preventing the use of Indians as
beasts of burden: "Indians are truly men. . . . They may and
should freely and legitimately enjoy their liberty and the
possessions of their property; nor should they be in any way
enslaved; should the contrary happen, it shall be null and
void and of no effect."

The pope's proclamation had little effect, however. Spain
argued that conquest and enslavement were necessary to
convert the natives to Christianity. To legitimize this argument, Spanish court advisers drew up a document called the

> We trust that, as long as you
> are on earth, you will compel and
> with all zeal cause the barbarian
> nations to come to the knowledge
> of God, the maker and founder of
> all things, not only by edicts of
> admonitions, but also by force
> and arms, if needful, in order that
> their souls may partake of the
> heavenly kingdom.
>
> Pope Clement VI
> to Charles V, King of Spain
> May 8, 1529

"Requerimiento." This document was to be read to the native populations by priests who accompanied each conquistador. The document urged the Indians to convert to Catholicism and warned that if they did not, the Spanish Army would "legally and morally" wage war against them. The Indians, who did not understand Spanish, were generally nowhere in sight when the Spanish arrived. More often than not, the document was read in a loud voice to the surrounding trees.

Enslavement of Indians was part of the *encomienda* system, which was established in 1512 to organize the governing of the New World. Under the encomienda system, large grants of land were given to conquistadors and settlers. Indians were allocated as property along with the land and required to work for the *encomendero* (the landowner). In return, the colonists were to Christianize and "civilize" the Indians.

By the 1550s more than one-third of the Indian population under Spanish control had perished, and many tribes had become extinct. As reports filtered out of the New World, Spain's treatment of the natives became a subject of national and international debate. In 1550 the Spanish king convened a council of respected thinkers and theologians to decide the issue as presented by two well-known Spanish thinkers, Bartolomé de las Casas and Juan Ginés de Sepulveda. Las Casas, the defender of the Indians, argued that the tribes could not be enslaved nor their lands taken by conquest. To support his arguments, he cited the works of the influential Spanish thinkers Francisco de Vitoria and Francisco Suárez. The Indians, Vitoria had written in his important work *De Indis*, were the true owners of their lands. If Spain wished to secure these lands, it should do so by making treaties with the natives. These views were echoed by Suárez, who argued that the pope's demarcation line did not grant title but only divided the world for the purpose of conversion to the Catholic faith. Conversion, Las Casas emphasized, was not a moral and legal argument for conquest. Sepulveda argued that Indians were inferior and that their labor was necessary to Spain's national interest.

The Spanish Court never officially decided the debate. Gradually, however, Las Casas's view became more accepted. By the time Spain withdrew from the New World in the 1800s, the Spanish Crown had adopted a policy of recognizing Indian land rights and sovereignty, especially in Florida and the Gulf Coast area.

In the 1590s, when Spain began colonizing the Southwest, however, the encomienda system still held sway. For eighty years the Pueblo Indians were subjected to the harsh directives of the system. Under threat of death, they were forced to labor in the fields, manufacture goods, tend livestock, perform domestic work, and submit to religious conversion and the destruction of their religious and cultural life.

In 1680 a Pueblo medicine man named Popé organized the Pueblo villages in a concerted effort to overthrow the Span-

. . . we ask and require [that] you . . . acknowledge the Church as the Ruler and Superior of the whole world and the high priest called Pope and in his name the King and Queen Dona Juana our lords and kings of these islands. . . . But if you do not do so, I certify to you that, with the help of God, we shall forcibly enter your country and shall make war against you in all ways and manners that we can, and shall subject you to the yoke and obedience of the Church, and of their Highnesses. . . .

Requerimiento

We command that the sale, grant, and composition of lands be executed with such attention, that the Indians shall be left in possession of the full amount of lands belonging to them, either singly or in communities, together with their rivers and waters; and the lands which they shall have drained or otherwise improved, whereby they may, by their own industry, have rendered them fertile, are reserved in the first place, and can in no case be sold or alienated. And the Judges who shall have been sent thither, shall specify what Indians they may have found on the land, and what lands they shall have left in possession of each of the elders of tribes, caciques, governors, or communities.

It being our wish that the Indians be protected and well treated, and that they be not molested nor injured in their person or property.

Law of the Indies

ish and wipe out all traces of European presence, including Catholicism and all imported plant and animal life. The first Pueblo attack resulted in the deaths of more than four hundred Spanish soldiers, friars, and colonists. A subsequent attack on Santa Fe in cooperation with Apache allies led to the expulsion of more than seventeen hundred Spaniards from New Mexico. For the next thirteen years the area remained free of Spanish intrusion and dominance. When Spain regained dominance in the area, it took care to honor tribal rights and sovereignty. Gradually the Laws of the Indies (the Spanish laws that governed Spanish actions in the New World) came to reflect the theories of Vitoria, Suárez, and Las Casas, dictating respect for tribal land rights and independence.

FRENCH-INDIAN RELATIONS

France, Holland, and England had little use for and were not deterred by Spanish claims to the Western Hemisphere. By the 1530s, French fur trappers were present along the Saint Lawrence River. In 1608, Samuel de Champlain established the first permanent French settlement at Quebec. That same year Champlain concluded the first known treaty in the New World, with the Hurons and Montagnais. By 1682, René-Robert Cavelier de La Salle had navigated down the Mississippi River and claimed the vast Mississippi Valley region for France.

The interests of the French and their relationship to the tribes differed considerably from those of Spain and England. France's preoccupation lay in profits from the lucrative fur trade. With the exception of the Foxes, the Chickasaws, and the Natchez (whom the French decimated through repeated battles), the French established successful alliances with many of the Indian nations of the region. The secret to France's success lay in its personal and political dealings with the tribes. The Frenchmen who traveled to the New World were trappers, and the Indians, already experienced trappers, were necessary to the expansion of the fur trade. Furthermore, the trappers had little interest in Christianizing or "civilizing" the natives. They needed to learn from the Indians the skills to trap and survive in the forests. Many French trappers married Indian women, learned Indian languages, and encouraged the tribes to settle near their trading posts. The French even established "exchange programs" in which a young French trapper would live with a tribe for a year or two while a young brave traveled to France so that each might learn the language and skills of the other.

French dependence on the tribes for furs and their regard for Indian cultures produced a respectful and open political relationship between the two groups. France recognized tribal sovereignty and land rights and treated tribal leaders well. Each May, the tribes and French leaders met in a large, diplomatic conference to negotiate treaties, discuss prob-

When the Frenchmen arrived at these falls, they came and kissed us. They called us children and we called them father. We lived like brothers in the same lodge, and we always had wherewithal to clothe us. They never mocked at our ceremonies, and they never molested the places of our dead. Seven generations of men have passed away, and we have not forgotten it.

Chippewa Chief speaking of the arrival of the French

There must be in their [the Indians'] social band something singularly captivating, and far superior to anything to be boasted of among us; for thousands of Europeans are Indians, and we have no example of even one of those Aborigines having from choice become Europeans.

Hector St. John Crevecoeur, 1782, *Letters from an American Farmer*

lems, and settle disputes. For three months of the year, the governors of Canada and Louisiana visited the various tribes, paying their respects.

Despite cordial relations, the ultimate effect of the French fur trade on the tribes was disastrous. Epidemics of diseases introduced to North America by the trappers killed an estimated one-fourth to one-half of many tribes' members. Access to trade goods, firearms, steel knives, metal utensils, and cloth made tribal members aware of material acquisitiveness. Indian men increasingly left their families and tribal obligations to go trapping in the forests for long periods. Competitiveness and individualism slowly began to compete with the traditional values of sharing and cooperation. Most important was the impact of the fur trade on intertribal relations. As hunters depleted animals in one region, tribes moved into lands held by their neighbors. Wars were frequent as Indian nations sought control of the richest lands. Competition between the Iroquois, who traded their furs to the Dutch along the Atlantic Coast, and the Hurons and Wyandots, who were allied with the French, was particularly bloody.

THE DUTCH-IROQUOIS ALLIANCE

Holland's stay in the New World was brief (1608–64) but important. The Dutch established a trade alliance with the Iroquois that halted French expansion in the early 1600s and gave Holland's successor, England, an important political ally. Dutch colonial relations, like those of France, Sweden, and, occasionally, England, were governed by royal companies. European monarchs chartered these companies to reap profits for their national treasuries and the companies' stockholders. The companies were authorized to regulate affairs with the tribes, including negotiation of treaties, purchase of land, and declaration of war.

In 1624 the Dutch West Indies Company purchased Manhattan Island from the Wappingers, making that region the center of the New Netherlands. The Dutch's primary interest was in furs, which placed them in direct competition with France. Unlike the French, who lived and trapped with the tribes, the Dutch relied on a system of trading stations. They increased their trading edge by bartering highly prized wampum beads—made in their own small factories in New Amsterdam—with the tribes.

The first thirty years of Dutch presence were peaceful. The company recognized and respected tribal sovereignty and land rights and negotiated fair and equitable treaties. By the 1630s, however, the once easily obtainable furs on the eastern seaboard had become scarce. To supplement their supply, the Dutch concluded their alliance with the Mohawks, to the west, who were members of the Iroquois League.

The Iroquois-Dutch alliance was beneficial to the Iroquois League. The Iroquois had long been concerned about France's alliance with their traditional enemies to the west, the Hurons. Commercial relations with the Dutch gave the league access to trade goods and much-needed firearms. During the seventeenth and eighteenth centuries, the Iroquois had two political aims: conquering surrounding tribes and maintaining their independence in the face of growing French dominance. The league succeeded in both areas. In 1649, Mohawks and Senecas invaded the territory of their traditional enemies, the Hurons. Caught unaware, the Hurons fought for two days before scattering in disarray. As was the custom, many of the conquered Hurons were adopted by the Iroquois tribes, while others joined neighboring tribes. (The remainder regrouped, becoming known as the Wendats, or Wyandots.) Over the next six years the Iroquois League successfully conquered other tribes in the region: the Tobacco People in 1649, the Neutral Confederacy in 1651, and the Eries in 1655.

By 1655 the French were seriously worried about the Iroquois's successes, since each new victory for the league meant the loss of an Indian ally for France. In 1666 the French launched a full-scale war against the league, burning villages and destroying crops. Exhausted by earlier tribal fighting, the Iroquois League suffered a major defeat. Within ten years, however, the league had regained its former strength, as evidenced by its conquest of the neighboring Delaware and Susquehanna tribes in the mid-1670s.

Mindful of the diminishing availability of furs, the Dutch West Indies Company decided to supplement its activities with colonies. As the number of Dutch colonists increased, so did the need for land. In 1639, William Kieft became governor of New Amsterdam. Under his leadership the colony's policies toward the tribes changed from diplomacy to extermination. The small eastern tribes of the area were no longer useful to the Dutch and had become an obstacle to Dutch settlement. For the next thirty years the tribes in the region were scattered and killed. To encourage their demise, Kieft instituted bounty payments for Indian scalps, a practice later adopted by most of the colonies.

THE RISE OF THE ENGLISH

The Dutch presence ended in 1664, when English troops, intent on expanding British-Indian trade relations and the British land base, marched on New Amsterdam and forced Dutch West Indies Company officials to surrender. The British originally had colonized land to the south of the Dutch. Their first settlement was founded in 1585, at Roanoke, Virginia. Although that colony was short-lived (it mysteriously disappeared a few years later without a trace), other English settlements, such as Jamestown (1607) and Plymouth (1620), were more successful.

Unlike the French and the Dutch, the English colonists were farmers who came for land and who came to stay. Their initial relations with the tribes were cordial. The English

They are extraordinarily charitable one to another, one having nothing to spare, but he freely imparts it to his friends, and whatever they get by gaming or any other way, they share one to another, leaving themselves commonly the least share.

English pamphlet
encouraging immigration,
1670

A meeting between English colonists and an eastern tribe is depicted here in this engraving by an unknown artist. (Courtesy Library of Congress.)

settlements at Jamestown and Plymouth had survived only with the aid of the local Powhatan Confederacy, under the leadership of Powhatan, Pocahontas's father, and of the Wampanoag tribe, under the leadership of Massasoit. These tribes taught the settlers to plant crops, build shelters, and hunt game. Some of the early English colonists followed the Dutch practice of purchasing tribal lands and respecting tribal rights. As warfare and disease decimated the tribes of the area, some colonies set aside small reservations for the tribes' benefit. The colony of Connecticut established a number of reservations to protect the small, Christianized tribes that had been decimated by epidemics. Its first reservation was established in 1638 and consisted of twelve hundred acres set aside for the remaining forty-seven members of the Quinnipiac tribe. By 1670, Connecticut had established fourteen reservations.

After this initial friendliness, however, the conflict inherent between European and Indian interests and values quickly became apparent. Outright hostility followed and soon turned into bloodshed. The hospitable sharing of tribal lands and resources began to threaten tribal existence as game and tribal agricultural lands became scarce. In 1622, Opechancanough, Pocahontas's uncle, responded to the prob-

Why will you take by force what you may obtain by love? Why will you destroy us who supply you with food? What can you get by war? . . . We are unarmed, and willing to give you what you ask, if you come in a friendly manner . . .

Powhatan's speech at Werowocomico (Gloucester County, Virginia), 1609

lem by uniting thirty tribes in a confederacy to evict the intruders. In a series of battles, Opechancanough's warriors
wiped out nearly half of the existing English settlements in
the eastern part of what is now the state of Virginia.

Despite Opechancanough's victory, European settlements
continued to spread and to deplete Indian lands and game.
As settlements increased and the English vied with the Dutch
and Swedish for lands and trade, the tribes became pawns,
drawn increasingly into fierce competition. In 1636 the English, concerned about the Pequots' alliance and exclusive
trading pact with the Dutch, invaded Pequot territory, in
present-day Connecticut. In battles over the next two years
the English exterminated most of the tribe and sold the survivors as slaves in the West Indies. Eight years later, after
twenty years of fighting, the English finally defeated Opechancanough in the colony of Virginia. Over ninety years old
when captured, he died soon afterward, and his death put an
end to the powerful Powhatan Confederacy.

By 1664, England had defeated both the Powhatan Confederacy and the Pequot tribe and had evicted the Dutch
(and the Swedish) from the New World. England's rising
power deeply concerned Metacom, son of Massasoit, the
Wampanoag leader who had befriended the Pilgrims. Metacom (known to the English as King Philip) told an English
friend: "But little remains of my ancestor's domain. I am resolved not to see the day when I have no country." Metacom
formed an alliance of local tribes in the area of present-day
Rhode Island, Vermont, and New Hampshire, and for over a
year his warriors (representing almost twenty thousand Indians) fought against fifty thousand colonists. King Philip's
War, as it was called, is one of the most costly wars in American history in terms of percentage of total population killed.
The war ended in 1676, with Metacom's death. Once again
the English sold the defeated tribal members—including
Metacom's widow and son and hundreds of others who had
surrendered under a promise of protection—into slavery.

King Philip's War changed English attitudes toward Indians. No longer looked upon as "children of nature" worthy
of conversion, Indians were considered savages who should
be exterminated. In the Carolina colonies the tribes were
thrust brutally aside to make way for plantations. Although
considered inferior to blacks as slaves, they were nonetheless
used to harvest tobacco. In 1715 the colonists nearly wiped
out the Yamasees and the Catawbas. A few years later the
Tuscaroras left the area and migrated to the Northeast, where
they joined the Iroquois League.

The relationship between the English colonies and the Iroquois was an exception to the general British mistreatment
of Indians. The reason for this exception became obvious.
The Iroquois were powerful militarily, and the English des-
perately needed their friendship against the French. Num-

Whereas the Indians . . . in-
habiting in the Eastern and
Northern Parts of His Majesty's
Territories of New England . . .
have . . . been guilty of the most
perfidious, barbarous and inhu-
man murders of divers of his Majesty's English Subjects; and have
abstained from all Commerce
and Correspondence with His Majesty's said Subjects for many
Months past; . . . I have therefore
thought fit to issue this Proclamation and to Declare the Indians
. . . to be Enemies, Rebels and
Traitors To His Most Sacred Majesty: And I do hereby require His
Majesty's subjects of this Prov-
ince to embrace all Opportunities
of pursuing, captivating, killing
and destroying all and any of the
aforesaid Indians. . . .

For every Male Indian Prisoner
above the Age of Twelve Years,
that shall be taken and brought to
Boston, Fifty Pounds.

For every Male Indian Scalp,
brought in as evidence of their
being killed, Forty Pounds.

For every Female Indian Prisoner, taken and brought in as
aforesaid, and for every Male Indian Prisoner under the Age of
Twelve Years, taken and brought
in as aforesaid, Twenty-five
Pounds.

Proclamation by His Excellency
William Shirley, Esq., Captain
General and Governor in Chief
of Massachusetts Bay,
June 12, 1755

This engraving by J. C. McRae depicts Indians in council. (Courtesy Library of Congress.)

bering about 25,000, the Iroquois controlled an area six hundred miles wide that stretched from Maine to Lake Michigan and from the Ottawa River, in Canada, to Tennessee. During this period the league strengthened its internal unity and established a policy of independent neutrality. This policy helped maintain a balance of power between the French and the English for one hundred years. Had the French been able to gain the league's alliance during this period, the United States may well have become Les États Unis.

THE FRENCH AND INDIAN WAR AND THE LOSS OF A VALUABLE INDIAN ALLY

In a series of wars beginning in the late seventeenth century, France and England, who had been enemies for centuries, fought for supremacy in Europe and the New World. In 1754 the fourth war between the two powers in sixty years erupted. The conflict started between Britain's Virginia

Colony and France over control of the upper Ohio River Valley. The French and Indian War, as it became known, lasted for seven years.

From the beginning of the war both the English and the French realized that gaining and maintaining Indian allies would be vital. To plan their strategy, representatives of seven colonies met at Albany in 1754. They also met with delegates from various Indian nations. The colonies realized that without the support, or at least the neutrality, of the Iroquois League, the war would be lost. As the secretary of the Pennsylvania Colony wrote to William Penn, "If we lose the Iroquois, we are gone."

The tribes made no specific promises in response to British appeals. Instead they repeated their complaints about fraudulent land deals and unfair trading practices. Echoing Benjamin Franklin, who had tried but failed to convince the colonies that they needed to unite, the tribes also pointed out how difficult it was to negotiate with so many colonial governments, each one quite different in its relations with the Indians.

The British authorities took the Indian nations' observations seriously. In 1755, Britain transferred responsibility for Indian affairs from the individual colonies to two regional representatives, one for the northern colonies and one for the southern colonies. The head of the Northern Department, William Johnson, was a fur trapper and longtime friend of the Iroquois. His marriage to Molly Brant, sister of Mohawk chief Joseph Brant, consolidated his friendship with the Iroquois. Edmund Atkins headed the Southern Department. These two men functioned as ambassadors and were responsible for negotiating boundaries and alliances and handling commercial relations between the British Crown and the various Indian sovereigns.

Despite these English efforts, the French were more successful in gaining Indian allies—with the important exception of the Iroquois. The French formed alliances with tribes ranging from the Caughnawagas in Canada to the Muscogees and Cherokees in the South. With all their Indian allies, the French clearly held the advantage at the beginning of the war. In 1754 and 1755 they defeated English attempts to capture the strategically situated Fort Duquesne. But as the war dragged on, the greater numbers of British soldiers and the dwindling French supplies began to take a toll.

In a last-ditch attempt to contain the British, the great Ottawa leader Pontiac inspired eighteen tribes from western Pennsylvania and northern Ohio into a powerful alliance. In well-planned, spontaneous attacks in 1763, Pontiac and his warriors captured eight of the ten British forts east of Fort Niagara. Two thousand British troops and settlers were killed in the attack. Sir Jeffrey Amherst, commander in chief of the British forces in North America, in perhaps the first example

Our wise forefathers established union and amity between the Five Nations, this has made us formidable; this has given us great weight and authority with our neighboring nations. We are a powerful Confederation; and by your observing the same methods our wise forefathers have taken, you will acquire strength and power; therefore whatever befalls you, never fall out with one another.

Canasteo, Chief of the
Onondagas,
advising the English to follow
the Iroquois example

It would be a very strange thing if Six Nations of ignorant savages should be capable of forming a scheme for such a union, and be able to execute it in such a manner as that it has subsisted for ages, and appears indissoluble; and yet that a like union should be impracticable for ten or a dozen English colonies, to whom it is more necessary and must be more advantageous, and whom cannot be supposed to want an equal understanding of their interests.

Benjamin Franklin,
letter to a friend, 1751

No people in the World understand and pursue their true National Interest better than the Indians . . . in their publick Treaties no People on earth are more open, explicit and Direct. Nor are they excelled by any in the observation of them.

Edmund Atkins,
Superintendent
of Indian affairs, Southern
Department, 1750s

Pontiac, Ottawa leader of the uprising against the British in 1763, is depicted in this portrait by Jerry Farnsworth. (Courtesy Museum of the American Indian, Heye Foundation.)

of biological warfare, retaliated by sending "gifts" of small-pox-infected blankets to the tribes allied with the French.

Despite Pontiac's brilliant achievements, the French were eventually defeated. In the Peace of Paris of 1763, which ended the war, France ceded Canada and all French-claimed lands east of the Mississippi River to England. In the same treaty, France gave the city of New Orleans and all its claims west of the Mississippi River to Spain, while Spain ceded Florida to England. Upon hearing that his French allies had capitulated, Pontiac reluctantly ended his five-month siege of

Out of our regard to them [the Indians] we gave them two Blankets and an Handkerchief out of the Small Pox Hospital. I hope it will have the desired effect.

William Trent's description of a "gift" to the Delawares, 1763

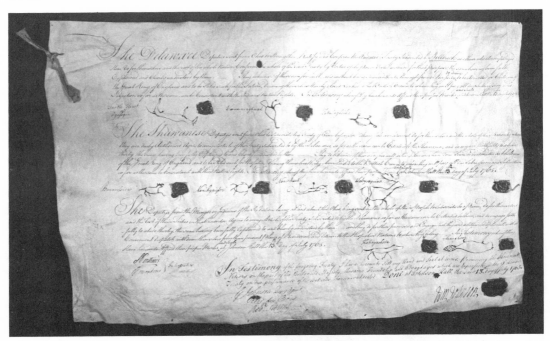

The July 13, 1765, treaty between the Delaware, Shawnee, and Mingo nations and the British. (Courtesy Museum of the American Indian, Heye Foundation.)

Detroit. In 1765 he signed a peace treaty at Detroit with Great Britain.

The defeat of the French meant the loss of the Indian nations' most sympathetic ally and protector. Even the Iroquois, who had officially maintained a neutral position during the war and had unofficially lent aid to England, were harmed by the French defeat. With the French gone, the Iroquois could no longer pit the French against the English, and they found themselves in a dangerous political position.

The English government was well aware that its harsh policies toward the Indians had almost cost it the war with France. Learning from past mistakes, the English issued the Proclamation of 1763 in an attempt to improve colonial-Indian relations. The proclamation reserved the western portion of the previously claimed French area for Indian use. Colonies and private individuals were forbidden to survey, purchase, or settle on any of these lands. Settlers already in the area were ordered to leave. This was the first attempt by any European power to limit the growth of settlements, thereby protecting Indian titles. As it turned out, however, the terms of the proclamation were soon abandoned, and this was not the last time Indians were promised perpetual title to lands they were later expected to cede. In fact, such promises were consistently made, and never fulfilled, for the next two hundred years.

And whereas it is just and reasonable, and essential to our interest, and the security of our colonies, that the several nations or tribes of Indians, with whom we are connected, and who live under our protection, should not be molested or disturbed in the possession of such parts of our dominions and territories as, not having been ceded to, or purchased by us, are reserved to them or any of them, as their hunting grounds; we do therefore . . . declare it to be our royal will and pleasure, that no governor . . . do presume, upon any pretense whatever, to grant warrants of survey, or pass any patents for lands beyond the bounds of their respective governments, . . . or upon any lands whatever, which not having been ceded to, or purchased by us, as aforesaid, are reserved to the said Indians, or any of them.

Royal Proclamation, 1763

CHAPTER 4

A CENTURY OF DESTRUCTION

Britain's Proclamation of 1763, which had granted tribes perpetual rights to lands west of the British colonies was never upheld. Instead the American Revolution (1775–83) intervened. Once again, the Indian nations found themselves caught in a dispute of European making. And once again, both sides—the British as well as the colonial revolutionaries—courted the Indian nations, especially the powerful Iroquois League, as allies.

In 1775 the Continental Congress created three departments of Indian affairs: a northern, a middle, and a southern department. Staffed by eleven commissioners, including Patrick Henry and Benjamin Franklin, the departments were assigned the task of treating "with the Indians . . . to preserve peace and friendship with the said Indians and to prevent their taking part in the present commotion."

The "commotion" presented most tribes with a choice between two evils. Although England's record in dealing with the tribes was not unblemished, most tribes realized that English policy, however imperfect, gave them some protection from land-hungry colonists. Most tribes of the Iroquois and Muscogee confederacies, and the Cherokees, Shawnees, and others, sided with the British.

The colonists did, however, win the neutrality of the Oneidas and the Tuscaroras, both members of the Iroquois League. By splitting the force of the Iroquois League, the colonists may have guaranteed their eventual victory in their war of independence.

Another fortunate alliance for the colonists was with the Delaware Nation. In 1778, three years after the war's onset, the United States signed its first Indian treaty with the Delawares, who agreed to allow colonial troops to pass through their territory. The Delawares also agreed to sell corn, meat, horses, and other supplies to the colonies and to allow their braves to enlist in the colonial army. The treaty also stated that if the Delawares so decided, they could "invite any other tribes who have been friends to join the present confederation and form a state whereof the Delaware Nation shall be the head and have a representative in Congress." But neither the Delawares nor any other Indian nation was ever admitted as a state, although Congress continued to consider the idea for the next hundred years.

More than sixteen hundred warriors fought with British forces, attacking colonial settlements and causing considerable fear and loss in the frontier regions. Tribes allied with both sides suffered heavy casualties. Gen. George Wash-

This is a family quarrel between us and old England . . . we desire you to remain at home, and not join on either side, but keep the hatchet buried deep.

Message from George Washington to the Iroquois League, 1775

That a perpetual peace and friendship shall from henceforth take place, and subsist between the contracting parties aforesaid, through all succeeding generations: and if either of the parties are engaged in a just and necessary war with any other nation or nations, that then each shall assist the other in due proportion to their abilities, till their enemies are brought to reasonable terms of accommodation; and that if either of them shall discover any hostile designs forming against the other, they shall give the earliest notice thereof, that timeous measures may be taken to prevent their ill effect.

Article II, Treaty with the Delawares, 1778

CLAIMS TO TRIBAL TERRITORIES
1776-1803

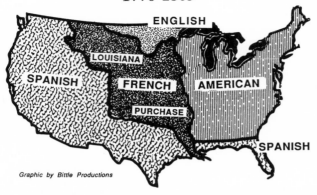

Graphic by Bittle Productions

European claims to tribal lands changed continuously throughout the seventeenth, eighteenth, and nineteenth centuries. As the map above indicates, during the early years of the American Republic, the United States possessed claims to only the eastern portion of the present-day United States.

ington ordered Gen. James Clinton and Gen. John Sullivan to engage in a scorched-earth policy against the Iroquois to retaliate for destruction of colonial food supplies. Sullivan's troops burned more than forty Iroquois towns, destroyed sixteen hundred bushels of corn and vegetables, and chopped down orchards of apple, pear, and peach trees. From then on the Iroquois referred to Washington as Ha-no-da-ga-nears, "Town Destroyer." By the time the Revolutionary War ended, in 1783, its ravages had broken the strength of the Iroquois League. Mohawk leader Thayendanegea Joseph Brant led most of his people to Canada, where the British provided them with land.

THE BEGINNINGS OF A FEDERAL POLICY

After the Revolutionary War ended, Indian-white relations remained in chaos. Under its Articles of Confederation (1781–89), the United States comprised a loose political union with a weak central government and powerful states. In fact, Benjamin Franklin had modeled the new country's structure on that of the Iroquois League. The system that had proved so effective for the league, however, was ineffective for the United States. The powerful states and weak central structure presented problems in relations with Indian nations. The Articles of Confederation granted each state the right to handle its own Indian relations. Unfortunately, treaty violations, unfair trading practices, fraudulent land cessions, and illegal settlements became common. Ongoing hostility intensified between states and tribes, and all too often it erupted into warfare.

In 1791, after a two-year ratification process, the U.S. Constitution replaced the Articles of Confederation. The Constitution provided for a stronger central government. Indian relations, like foreign affairs, became the exclusive authority of the federal government. Articles I and II granted the president and Congress the authority to declare war and make treaties. Article III gave Congress sole authority to regulate commerce with foreign nations, Indian tribes, and between the states. Indians were not otherwise mentioned in the Constitution, except in a passage about census taking (article I, section 2). Neither the federal government nor the states had jurisdiction over Indian tribes. Indians were citizens of their own nations, not of the United States.

It was hoped that the new Constitution would assist the new American Republic with its most pressing national and international problem—its relationship with the Indian nations. The 1783 Peace of Paris, which had ended the Revolutionary War, established the western boundary of the new republic at the Mississippi River. The continued growth and progress of the young country depended on the government's ability to obtain these westernmost lands from the Indians for settlers. The young country also needed to keep the Indians from allying with the English and Spanish competitors surrounding it on three sides. Obtaining land from the Indians and maintaining peaceful relations with them, however, were contradictory objectives.

President George Washington sought early to define a national Indian policy. In 1789 one of his first actions was to ask Secretary of War Henry Knox to prepare a detailed report on the status of Indian affairs. The secretary responded with a lengthy document in which he analyzed the tribes' legal rights and discussed what he thought were the best procedures for dealing with the tribes.

In his report Knox emphasized that Indians had a right to their land and that their land could not be taken without their consent except in a war with a just cause. Knox warned that obtaining land through war would be costly in terms of men and materials. He proposed instead that the federal government help the tribes make a transition from a hunting to an agricultural life-style. Tribes could then support themselves on less land and cede their surplus portions to the federal government. Knox insisted above all that if there was to be peace on the frontier, the government must stop citizens from settling illegally on Indian lands.

In response to Knox's report, Congress passed a number of regulatory acts, known as trade and intercourse acts, between 1790 and 1834. These acts protected against fraudulent land deals by prohibiting states and individuals from purchasing land directly from tribes. Only the federal gov-

> Brother: We are of the same opinion with the people of the United States; you consider yourselves as independent people; we, as the original inhabitants of this country, and sovereigns of the soil, look upon ourselves as equally independent, and free as any other nation or nations. This country was given to us by the Great Spirit above; we wish to enjoy it, . . . The great exertions we have made, for this number of years, to accomplish a peace, and have not been able to obtain it; our patience, as we have already observed, is exhausted, and we are discouraged from persevering any longer. We, therefore, throw ourselves under the protection of the Great Spirit above, who, we hope, will order all things for the best. We have told you our patience is worn out; but not so far, but that we wish for peace, and, whenever we hear that pleasing sound, we shall pay attention to it.
>
> Joseph Brant, Mohawk, 1794

> No purchase, grant, lease, or other conveyance of lands, or of any title or claim thereto, from any Indian nation or tribe of Indians, shall be of any validity in law or equity, unless the same be made by treaty or convention entered into pursuant to the Constitution.
>
> 1802 Trade and Intercourse Act

ernment could buy Indian lands. To control unfair trading practices and ensure the quality of trade goods, the government required all traders to obtain government licenses, and, until 1822, Congress owned and operated a governmental system of trading houses. Another act required citizens traveling in Indian country to obtain passports.

Congress also passed laws authorizing funds for the distribution of goods and services owed to tribes as a result of various treaties and land cessions. Trading goods to tribes in exchange for land and other concessions was a common government practice. The government also gave goods outright to tribes to gain their friendship and maintain their alliance against the British, the French, and the Spanish. Small services were also provided in the same spirit. Gradually Indians began regularly to negotiate for services as well as for goods. For example, the Muscogee Nation, in one of its treaties, arranged for blacksmiths to live in tribal villages. By 1802, education for Indian children and some adults had become one of the services Congress offered in exchange for land.

Knox's report and the trade and intercourse acts contained two contradictory policies, however. On the one hand, Indian tribes were recognized as nations with treaty-making powers and rights to their land. On the other hand, Knox was urging the federal government to "civilize" and ultimately assimilate the tribes. The government's policy has continued to waver between the conflicting policies of respect for tribal sovereignty and attempts to assimilate Indians into the American mainstream.

To cope with the government's increasingly complex involvement in Indian affairs, Congress created the Indian Office in 1824. The office operated through agents who, in reality, were ambassadors with broad powers of negotiation. They concluded treaties with the Indian nations, delivered trade goods, and tried to maintain peace with the tribes. (The history of the Indian Office, which later became the Bureau of Indian Affairs [BIA], is discussed in more detail in chapter 12.)

THE LOSS OF THE INDIANS' ENGLISH AND SPANISH ALLIES AND THE WAR OF 1812

In 1787, just a few years before it passed the first trade and intercourse acts, Congress had passed the Northwest Ordinance. This ordinance outlined a plan and a schedule for turning the Northwest Territory (the present-day states of Ohio, Illinois, Indiana, Michigan, and Wisconsin) into states. Since much of this land was occupied by Indian tribes, the ordinance contained assurances to the tribes that they would not be treated unfairly:

The utmost good faith shall always be observed towards the Indians, their lands and property shall never be taken

And it be further enacted, that in order to promote civilization among the friendly Indian tribes, and to secure the continuance of their friendship, it shall be lawful for the President of the United States to cause them to be furnished with useful domestic animals and implements of husbandry, and with goods or money, as he shall judge proper . . .

1802 Trade and Intercourse Act

The United States, immediately upon the ratification of this convention, or as soon thereafter as may be, shall cause to be furnished to the Kansas Nation, three hundred hogs, five hundred domestic fowls, three yoke of oxen, and two carts, with such implements of agriculture as the Superintendent of Indian Affairs may think necessary; and shall employ such persons to aid and instruct them in their agriculture, as the President of the United States may deem expedient; and shall provide and support a blacksmith for them.

Article 4,
Treaty with the Kansa
Indians, 1825

from them without their consent; and in their property, rights and liberty they never shall be invaded or disturbed, unless in just and lawful wars authorized by Congress. . . .

But as was often the case in Indian affairs, a wide gap existed between promise and practice. Gen. Arthur St. Clair, the first governor of the territory, ignored both the promise of the ordinance and the warnings of Secretary Knox. St. Clair told his negotiators to do everything necessary—no matter how unscrupulous—to gain possession of Indian lands. The tribes met St. Clair's tactics with force. In 1791 an alliance of the Miami, Delaware, Shawnee, Chippewa, Potawatomi, and Ottawa nations, led by Chief Little Turtle, handed General St. Clair one of the worst defeats in U.S. history. Almost nine hundred of St. Clair's fourteen hundred men were either killed or wounded.

St. Clair's tactics were employed by others as well. William Henry Harrison, governor of Indiana from 1801 to 1811 (and later president) negotiated fifteen treaties with various tribes and thereby gained title to almost all of Illinois and Indiana and parts of Michigan and Wisconsin. Harrison obtained Indian signatures to treaties through bribery, treachery, and fraud. The total payments made to tribes for this vast, fertile area amounted to only about one cent per acre.

Harrison's unscrupulous tactics and illegal dealings enraged Tecumseh, a great Shawnee warrior from central Ohio, and his brother Tenskwatawa, also known as "the Prophet." An engaging orator and statesman, Tecumseh campaigned throughout the country, meeting with different tribal councils and preaching that the land belonged to all Indians and that no tribe could sell any portion of the common, sacred resource.

Taking advantage of one of Tecumseh's absences, Harrison bribed a few unauthorized chiefs with alcohol and negotiated a treaty that ceded three million acres of land, including land from tribes not even represented at the council. In retaliation, Tecumseh stationed one thousand warriors at Prophet's Town, one of the areas ceded, to prevent settlement of the land. When Tecumseh left the area again to counsel with some southern tribes, Harrison once again took advantage of his absence and sent troops against the warriors. This attack was the opening battle of what became a general frontier war. The frontier war itself merged the next year with the War of 1812 between Britain and the United States.

The causes of the War of 1812 evolved from American anger over British impressment of American seamen and seizure of American goods on the high seas, British commerce and economic restrictions, and opposition to British incitements of Indian attacks. As in the Revolutionary War, most of the tribes in the upper Mississippi Valley and half of the tribes in the South sided with England. Indian auxiliaries

The way, the only way to stop this evil is for the red men to unite in claiming a common and equal right in the land, as it was at first, and should be now—for it was never divided, but belongs to all. No tribe has the right to sell, even to each other, much less to strangers. . . . Sell a country! Why not sell the air, the great sea, as well as the earth? Did not the Great Spirit make them all for the use of his children?

Tecumseh (Shawnee),
protesting land sales to
Gov. William Henry Harrison,
1810

Where today are the Pequot? Where are the Narragansett, the Mohican, the Pocanet, and other powerful tribes of our people? They have vanished before the avarice and oppression of the white man, as snow before the summer sun. . . . Will we let ourselves be destroyed in our turn, without making an effort worthy of our race? Shall we, without a struggle, give up our homes, our lands, bequeathed to us by the Great Spirit? The graves of our dead and everything that is dear and sacred to us? . . . . I know you will say with me, Never! Never!

Tecumseh's speech
urging southern Indians
to unite into a
confederation, 1811

Tecumtha (Tecumseh), or One Who Passes Across Intervening Space From One Point to Another (1768–1813). Pencil sketch by Pierre Le Dru, a French trader at Vincennes, Indiana. (Courtesy Smithsonian Institution, National Anthropological Archives, Bureau of American Ethnology Collection.)

played a large role in the war, fighting in all major northern battles. Tecumseh, said to have been a brigadier general in the British Army, successfully defended the important Detroit region until the American offensive of August, 1813. The U.S. victory on September 10, 1813, in the decisive Battle of Lake Erie cut off British supply lines to the East. The British then retreated from the area, despite Tecumseh's protests, thereby breaking their promise to the tribes that the "King their Great Father always true to his promises is resolved not to lay down the [tomahawk] until the Indians are restored to their rights and their future secured." Tecumseh's death on October 5, 1813, during the Battle of Thames sealed American control of the old Northwest Territory.

During negotiations to end the War of 1812, Britain argued for an independent Indian buffer state between Canada and the United States. The United States steadfastly refused, agreeing only to restore tribal rights to their 1811 status. The War of 1812 and its aftermath ended forever the Indian tribal alliances with Great Britain, and soon afterward the Indian nations lost their Spanish ally as well.

Gen. Andrew Jackson had commanded the American forces in the South during the War of 1812. His two most difficult and important victories occurred at New Orleans, where he defeated the British, and at Horseshoe Bend, Alabama, where he defeated the Red Sticks, a militant faction of the Muscogee Confederacy (see chapter 7). Spurred by his successes against the British and the Muscogees, Jackson invaded Florida in 1818 with the objective of clearing both the Seminoles and the Spanish from the area. Jackson was successful in routing the Spanish, and three years later Spain sold Florida to the United States. This agreement set off a new rush of settlers to the area, and the Seminoles, forced to retreat into the interior swamplands, began a series of three long and costly wars in defense of their homeland.

With the removal of England and Spain as potential tribal allies, and with the idea of an independent Indian state dead, tribal-federal relations entered a new phase. The opportunity to align themselves with the European powers had given Indian nations more strength against the United States than their own military could supply. Now tribes had to deal on their own with a rapidly expanding nation interested in obtaining Indian lands as quickly as possible.

THE MARSHALL DECISIONS: THE FIRST LEGAL DEFINITION OF INDIAN STATUS

After the War of 1812 immigration to the United States increased steadily, causing further pressure on Indian lands. The tribes of the Southeast, especially the Cherokees, Choctaws, Chickasaws, Muscogees, and Seminoles (called the Five Civilized Tribes by the whites), sought to counteract this pressure by adopting some white practices while still maintaining their own cultures. By the late 1820s the five tribes had become remarkably successful in agriculture and political and educational development. In 1821 the brilliant Cherokee linguist, Sequoyah, who neither spoke nor read English, produced a written syllabary for the Cherokee language. This syllabary, which was later adopted by the other four tribes, was taught in Cherokee schools established by the Moravian Brethren Church. Within a short time most of the tribe was literate.

The tribes also began to alter their political systems, hoping that doing so would enable them to better confront the demands of the dominant society. In 1828, for example, the Cherokees elected delegates to a constitutional convention. The resulting government, patterned after that of the United States, consisted of an elected chief (analogous to the U.S. president), a bicameral council (like the U.S. Congress), and a judicial system. The Cherokee Constitution guaranteed in-

In the present state of our country one of two things seems to be necessary. Either that those sons of the forests should be moralized or exterminated. . . . Put into the hands of their children the primer and the hoe, and they will naturally, in time, take hold of the plow.

House Committee on Appropriations, 1818

Sir, to these remarks we beg leave to observe and remind you that the Cherokee are not foreigners but original inhabitants of America, and that they now inhabit and stand on the soil of their own territory and that the limits of this territory are defined by the treaties which they have made with the government of the U.S., and the states by which they are now surrounded have been created out of land which was once theirs, and they cannot recognize the sovereignty of any state within the limits of their territory.

Cherokee Memorial to President James Monroe, 1823

Sequoyah's syllabary, 1835. Sequoyah, a silversmith by profession, perfected his eighty-six–character syllabary (a set of symbols, each representing a syllable) in 1821, because of his conviction that a written language would greatly benefit his people in a rapidly changing world. By 1828 old and young alike were reading in Cherokee, neighbor having taught neighbor by writing the "talking leaves," as the characters were called, on backyard fences and on the walls of their houses. By 1843, the year of Sequoyah's death, more than four million pages of books, articles, and newspapers had been published using his alphabet. (Courtesy Library of Congress.)

dividuals many of the same rights American citizens had under the Bill of Rights. The major exception was that Cherokee land was to be held communally.

The tribes' progress did not pacify the southeastern states. When gold was discovered on Cherokee lands in 1828, the states' determination to rid themselves of their Indian populations intensified. Shortly thereafter, Georgia, followed by Alabama and Mississippi, passed a series of laws intended to remove the five tribes from their own lands. These laws redistributed tribal lands to various counties, declared all Indian laws and customs void after 1830, and forbade the testimony of Indians against whites in court. These measures permitted the wholesale confiscation of Indian property. The stage was set for a major legal confrontation between the

tribes and the states. Two resulting Supreme Court decisions, written by Chief Justice John Marshall, established for
the first time a legal statement on the status and rights of the
Indian nations. These decisions provided the foundation for
all future federal-tribal relations.

The states' unfair behavior alarmed not only the Cherokees but also many U.S. congressmen, including Daniel Web-
ster. With the encouragement of these friends, the Cherokees sought an injunction against the state of Georgia. The
Cherokees wanted the injunction to stop the state from
applying laws intended to "annihilate the Cherokees as a
political society and to seize for the use of Georgia the
lands of the nation which have been assured to them by the
United States in solemn treaties." A former U.S. attorney,
Gen. William Wirt, served as the tribe's lawyer. He argued
before the Supreme Court that the Cherokees were in fact a
foreign nation and that, therefore, Georgia's laws were inap-
plicable to them. The Cherokees, Wirt stated, had been a
sovereign nation from time immemorial, "acknowledging no
earthly superior."

The Cherokees' case was strong and logical. But Chief
Justice John Marshall ruled in 1831 that the Cherokees were
not a foreign state within the meaning of the U.S. Constitution. He denied their motion for an injunction. The Cherokees, Marshall ruled, were neither citizens of a foreign nation nor state citizens nor conquered subjects. Instead, the
Cherokee Nation was a *domestic dependent nation*, one whose
relationship to the United States was like that of "a ward to
a guardian." Marshall's decision, while disappointing to the
Cherokees, was actually a clever (if temporary) solution to a
complex problem.

Legally, the *Cherokee Nation* v. *Georgia* case was about
Cherokee sovereignty and rights. But politically, it involved
the future of the Supreme Court. President Andrew Jackson
had campaigned for office on a pledge to move the tribes
westward. But a Supreme Court ruling that the Cherokees
were a foreign state would have prevented the government
from moving the tribes. President Jackson made it clear that
he intended to ignore the Court if it ruled in favor of the
Cherokees. Marshall realized that a president's refusal to enforce a Supreme Court decree would seriously harm the future of the Court. He was, however, unwilling to sacrifice the
Cherokees by leaving them at the mercy of the states. So he
chose a third and politically ingenious alternative. By ruling
that the Cherokees could not sue as a foreign nation, Marshall avoided a direct confrontation between the Supreme
Court and President Jackson. And by defining the Cherokees
as a domestic dependent nation, Marshall left open the possibility of the Cherokees receiving federal protection against
individual states.

The Cherokees and their non-Indian supporters understood the political realities behind Marshall's decision. They
tried again, this time through a test case aimed at probing

The title of the Cherokee
people to their lands is the most
ancient, pure and absolute known
to man; its date is beyond the
reach of human record; its va-
lidity confirmed by possession
and enjoyment antecedent to all
pretense of claim by any portion
of the human race.

The free consent of the Cherokee people is indispensable to a
valid transfer of the Cherokee
title. The Cherokee people have
neither by themselves nor their
representatives given such consent. It follows that the original
title and ownership of lands still
rests in the Cherokee Nation, un-
impaired and absolute. The
Cherokee people have existed as
a distinct national community for
a period extending into antiquity
beyond the dates and records and
memory of man. These attributes
have never been relinquished by
the Cherokee people, and cannot
be dissolved by the expulsion of
the Nation from its territory by
the power of the United States
Government.

Cherokee Memorial to
Congress prior to
their removal west

the legality of Georgia's actions. Two missionaries sympathetic to the Cherokee cause, Samuel Worcester and Elizur Butler, deliberately broke a Georgia law requiring a state license to live on Indian lands. When they refused to obey Georgia laws, they were tried by a Georgia court and sentenced to four years of hard labor. The two appealed their conviction to the U.S. Supreme Court on the grounds that Georgia's laws did not apply on Cherokee lands. William Wirt, representing the Cherokees once again, pointed out that the U.S. Constitution granted "the regulation of intercourse with the Indians" exclusively to the federal government. States were therefore barred from passing any laws infringing on the special and exclusive federal-tribal relationship.

Marshall agreed with Wirt and the Cherokees. He declared the Georgia laws an unconstitutional interference with existing treaties between the United States and the Cherokees. In writing his decision, the chief justice also elaborated on his previous description of the Cherokees as a domestic dependent nation. Marshall explained that the United States, like Great Britain, traditionally recognized Indian nations as "distinct political communities, having territorial boundaries within which their authority is exclusive and having right to all the lands within their boundaries." He pointed to all the treaties made between the United States and the Cherokees as proof that the United States "considered the Cherokees as a nation."

In the *Cherokee Nation* case, Marshall had written that the relationship between the Indian nations and the United States was like "that of a ward to his guardian." In the *Worcester* v. *Georgia* decision Marshall explained this relationship more fully. Although Indian nations, according to the chief justice, were somewhat like wards of the federal government, the United States' protection of the tribes did not reduce Indian sovereignty. The relationship between the Cherokees and the United States, Marshall stated, was that "of a nation claiming and receiving the protection of one more powerful, not that of individuals abandoning their national character, and submitting as subjects to the laws of the master." This description is of a *protectorate* relationship. Marshall referred to international law to prove that a weaker power does not surrender its independence or right to self-government by associating with a stronger state. And he emphasized that protection meant the "supply of their essential wants and protection from lawless and injurious intrusions into their country." Most important, protection did not imply the destruction of the protected.

REMOVAL

The *Worcester* decision was a legal victory for the Cherokees. But unfortunately it did little to prevent the tribe's removal. Government officials had proposed for some years to solve

The Cherokee nation, then, is a distinct community, occupying its own territory, with boundaries accurately described, in which the laws of Georgia can have no force, and which the citizens of Georgia have no right to enter, but with the assent of the Cherokees themselves, or in conformity with treaties, and with the acts of Congress. The whole intercourse between the United States and this nation, is, by our Constitution and laws, vested in the government of the United States.

Worcester v. *Georgia,* 1832

The Commissioners Plenipotentiary of the Chickasaws, do hereby acknowledge the tribes and the towns of the Chickasaw nation, to be under the protection of the United States of America, and of no other sovereign whosoever.

Article II,
Treaty with the Chickasaws,
1786

DISLOCATION of the (UNAMI) DELAWARE NATION

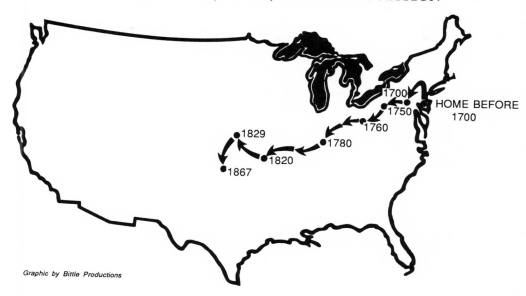

Graphic by Bittle Productions

The Unami majority of the Delaware Nation was one of many tribes relocated to Indian Territory. This map depicts the tortuous route by which they arrived there. Forced to resettle over and over again in response to white demands for land, the Delawares, and other tribes whose experiences were similar, splintered into a number of distinct groups. Descendants of Delawares who stayed in the various areas of occupation still live there today, and Delaware communities exist in New Jersey, southern Ontario (Canada), Wisconsin, Kansas, and Oklahoma.

the "Indian problem" by establishing a "permanent Indian frontier" in the Louisiana Territory, which had been purchased from France in 1803, and moving all eastern tribes into that region. In 1830, President Andrew Jackson asked Congress to pass the Indian Removal Bill, a bill to set aside lands west of the Mississippi River for the tribes. Despite protests that the bill violated previous treaties and laws recognizing Indian sovereignty, it was passed by five votes. The bill gave some individual tribal members a choice: they could stay in the South and submit to state laws, or they could move west.

The Mississippi Choctaws were the first to leave. They were promised that they would never again be asked to cede any of their new land, and that no state or territory would ever have the right to pass laws over the Choctaw Nation. In the early 1830s, tribal members left their ancestral home for the West. More than one-third of the Choctaws remained in Mississippi, believing that they would be given individual land allotments as stipulated by treaty. These Choctaws waited more than one hundred years for the government to fulfill its promise (see chapter 1).

The Muscogees, Cherokees, and Seminoles were among the next to be removed. After several years of resistance, including a civil war, the Muscogee Nation moved west during the late 1830s. Along the way almost one-half died of starvation, exposure, disease, and despair. The Cherokees, who had fought with Andrew Jackson to defeat the Red Sticks, also resisted removal, so in the summer of 1838, Jackson sent Gen. Winfield Scott with seven thousand soldiers to round them up, place them in stockades, and forcibly remove them. Of the estimated eighteen thousand Cherokees who traveled west on what became known as the Trail of Tears, more than four thousand died. The Seminoles presented a vigorously organized resistance to removal throughout the end of the Third Seminole War, in 1858. The Seminole wars extracted a great toll on the United States in money and lives, and finally, in the face of such determined opposition, the government relented. The Seminoles never signed a peace treaty, and in 1858 the United States decided that those Seminoles still in Florida could remain there.

Tribes such as the Potawatomi and the Miami in the Midwest also fell victim to removal. The region's non-Indian population had grown from less than five thousand at the

> I saw the helpless Cherokees arrested and dragged from their homes, and driven by bayonet into the stockades. And in the chill of a drizzling rain on an October morning I saw them loaded like cattle or sheep into wagons and started toward the west. . . . Chief Ross led in prayer and when the bugle sounded and wagons started rolling many of the children . . . waved their little hands goodbye to their mountain homes.
>
> U.S. Army private who served during Cherokee removal

TRIBAL RELOCATION TO INDIAN TERRITORY

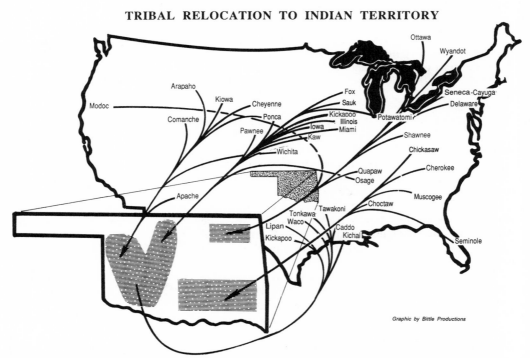

Graphic by Bittle Productions

More than thirty tribes were moved from throughout the United States to Indian Territory. The tribes were originally promised that they would never be asked to cede any of this new land and that they would have the opportunity to organize an Indian state. Congress broke these promises in 1907 when it admitted Oklahoma to statehood.

The Cherokee's removal from their homeland to Indian Territory on the Trail of Tears. Painting by Robert Lindneux. (Courtesy Woolaroc Museum, Bartlesville, Oklahoma.)

end of the Revolutionary War to more than three million by 1830. Land was at a premium. Despite spirited resistance by some tribes, such as the Sac and Fox in Black Hawk's War (1832), the tribes were eventually moved. All in all, between 1832 and 1842, the federal government relocated nineteen tribes, more than fifty thousand people, to the area shown on the map on page 62 as Unorganized Indian Territory.

THE OPENING OF THE WEST

Although the Indian Removal Bill guaranteed that tribes would never be asked to surrender their new lands, it soon became clear that no tribe would be secure on lands west of the Mississippi River. The government knew that selling the western lands to white settlers would help immensely toward paying off the national debt and underwriting the future expenses of the national government. "Manifest Destiny," the notion that the land from the east coast to the west coast was meant to be one country, had become the catchword of the day. Expansion and progress were the primary American values, and the tribes and their lands presented a barrier to both. Within twenty-five years after passing the Indian Removal Bill, the government had apparently forgotten all its promises.

In the 1840s and 1850s, America grew faster than ever before. Congress annexed Texas in 1845, and a year later it

Say, to them, their father, the President, will lay off a country of equal extent. . . . He will establish landmarks for them never to be moved, and give them a fee simple title to their lands. You must be prepared to give assurances of permanency of title and and dwell upon the idea that they will never be asked to surrender an acre more . . .

President Andrew Jackson to
agents negotiating
Indian removal treaties, 1830s

UNORGANIZED INDIAN TERRITORY

Graphic by Bittle Productions

Congress guaranteed to the eastern Indian nations that originally agreed to move westward possession of the large section outlined above as Unorganized Indian Territory. Responding to pressure for land, Congress later reduced this area, forcing tribes into the much smaller Indian Territory and onto various reservations.

added the Oregon Territory. In 1848 the entire Southwest became American territory as a result of the Mexican War. Five years later the Gadsden Purchase completed the present boundaries of the continental United States. In ten years the country's non-Indian population increased by almost one-third and its land area by 70 percent.

To open this vast new area to white settlement, however, the federal government needed to solve the Indian problem. The government decided to accomplish this by settling tribes on reservations. This procedure had first been used in Connecticut in 1638 (see chapter 3). Now, two hundred and some years later, the government negotiated fifty-three "reservation" treaties with various tribes. Between 1853 and 1857 the United States thereby acquired more than 174 million acres for settlement. Although they had been promised the entire region between the Mississippi River and the Rocky Mountains, tribes in Arkansas, Iowa, and Missouri were moved farther west to Kansas, Nebraska, and Oklahoma. In 1854, Congress admitted Kansas and Nebraska as territories to the Union, thereby diminishing further the area reserved to tribes. This ended the government's promise that the Indians would be provided a permanent and unorganized territory west of the Mississippi.

In the latter half of the nineteenth century the Indians, acutely aware that their lands and resources were being seriously threatened by the increasing influx of white settlers, reacted fiercely to protect their own existence.

THE INDIAN WARS OF THE WEST

Between 1866 and 1891, western tribes fought more than one thousand battles with the U.S. Army. The Indian tribes

And when the last Red Man shall have perished, and the memory of my tribe shall have become a myth among the White Men, these shores will swarm with the invisible dead of my tribe, and when your children's children think themselves alone in the field, the store, the shop, upon the highway, or in the silence of the pathless woods, they will not be alone. In all the earth there is no place dedicated to solitude. At night when the streets of your cities and villages are silent and you think them deserted, they will throng with the returning hosts that once filled them and still love this beautiful land. The White Man will never be alone.

Let him be just and deal kindly with my people, for the dead are now powerless. Dead, did I say? There is no death, only a change of worlds.

Chief Seattle, Suquamish, 1853

As the photos above show, councils between government representatives and the Indian nations became a frequent occurrence in the late nineteenth century as the government sought to convince tribes to cede more and more of their lands. Shown here are a treaty signing by William T. Sherman and the Lakotas at Fort Laramie, Wyoming, 1868 (top, left; Courtesy Newberry Library); a Paiute tribal council, with non-Indians in attendance, held in the 1870s near the Grand Canyon of the Colorado (top, right; Courtesy Smithsonian Institution, National Anthropological Archives, Bureau of American Ethnology Collection); a Grand Council between friendly and hostile chiefs at Pine Ridge Agency, South Dakota, January 17, 1891 (bottom, left; Courtesy Smithsonian Institution); and a large tribal delegation with several Indian agents and other officials on the White House grounds, circa 1870 (bottom, right; Courtesy National Archives).

were fighting desperately for physical and cultural survival against a growing nation motivated in part by land hunger and racial arrogance and in part by a sincere belief in Manifest Destiny and the perceived superiority of their civilization.

One of the earliest spurs to westward migration had been the discovery of gold in California in 1848. The two following years saw the non-Indian population of California explode from 15,000 to 93,000. In 1850, California became a state, and it entered the Union with a virulent anti-Indian policy. Early California laws permitted indenturing Indian women and children, a practice tantamount to slavery. The state also unofficially permitted the outright extermination of the tribes. Originally one of the most densely populated

> The more [Indians] we can kill this year the less will have to be killed the next war, for the more I see of these Indians, the more convinced I am that they all have to be killed or be maintained as a species of paupers.
>
> **Gen. William T. Sherman, 1867**

Indian areas, with a tribal population in excess of 150,000, by 1890 the state had an Indian population of only 17,000, a decrease of almost 90 percent. Hoping to reduce hostilities, the federal government negotiated a number of treaties with Indians in California in the 1850s. The tribes ceded half the state, reserving for themselves eight million acres in perpetuity. Under pressure from Californians, however, the Senate did not ratify the treaties, and the tribes lost all their lands. Not until the early 1900s were California tribes granted rights to some of their former lands, when Congress purchased 117 small rancherias for Indian use.

White populations in the Northwest did not grow as quickly as in central California, and Northwest tribes met with more success in their resistance. The Cayuses (Cayuse War, 1847–48), the tribes of the Rogue River (Rogue

You said that you wanted to put us upon a reservation, to build us houses and to make us Medicine lodges. I do not want them.

I was born upon the prairie where the wind blew free, and there was nothing to break the light of the sun. I was born where there were no enclosures, and where everything drew a free breath. I want to die there, and not within walls. I know every stream and every woods between the Rio Grande and the Arkansas. I have hunted and lived over that country. I lived like my fathers before me, and like them, I lived happily.

Ten Bears, Comanche, 1867

Schonchin John and Captain Jack, leaders of the Modoc War, being held in chains. Both were hanged at Fort Klamath, Oregon, on October 3, 1873. (Courtesy Smithsonian Institution, National Anthropological Archives.)

River War, 1853–55), and the Yakimas (Yakima War, 1855) battled federal troops before finally accepting reservations. And in the lava beds of northern California, fifty Modoc warriors, under the leadership of twenty-four-year-old Kentipoos (called Captain Jack by the whites), held off one thousand U.S. Calvary soldiers for seven months. They were fighting to gain a reservation in their homeland instead of being placed on the reservation of their traditional enemies, the Klamaths. A Modoc reservation might have cost the government ten thousand dollars. The war with the Modocs cost over one-half million dollars.

In 1877, five years after the Modoc War, Thunder Rolling in the Mountain, chief of the Nez Percés (known as Chief Joseph to the whites), led his people from Oregon across Idaho and Montana in a flight from removal. For two and a half weeks, the Nez Percés defeated and eluded two thousand troops over thirteen hundred miles of the most difficult terrain in the country. Gen. William Tecumseh Sherman described the campaign as "one of the most extraordinary wars of which there is any record." When Chief Joseph and his band were finally captured in Montana, near the Canadian border and freedom, the government exiled them to Indian Territory, where most died of malaria. A year after Chief Joseph's capture, the Bannocks in Utah and Nevada similarly resisted removal, in their case an illegal removal resulting from a clerk's error in transcribing a treaty. The Bannock War, which was brief and costly, signaled the end of the northwestern tribes' fight against forced removal to reservation life.

In the Texas region, home to some 25,000 Indians, the Southern Comanche, Kiowa, Cheyenne, Lipan, and Kickapoo tribes had been fighting white settlement with vengeance since the 1840s. A Comanche could shoot twenty arrows in the minute required to reload the muzzle-loading rifles carried by federal troops, and the Kiowas, in proportion to their numbers, killed more whites in war than any other tribe west of the Mississippi River. Texas had refused to recognize any form of Indian land title and pursued a policy of extermination. To subdue the Kiowas and Comanches, the War Department, in 1874, turned to Gen. William Tecumseh Sherman. Uncertain whether his troops could defeat the tribes in an all-out confrontation, Sherman invited Kiowa chiefs Satanta and Satank to a council at Fort Sill, in Indian Territory. Violating the flag of truce, Sherman imprisoned the unarmed chiefs and their men and sentenced them to hang. Realizing that Sherman's flagrant disregard for honor and fair play could provoke a general Indian uprising, the government freed Satanta and Satank. The army's war against the tribes, however, continued until the Indians were finally subdued in Texas in the early 1880s.

Attempts to settle the Rocky Mountains and the Southwest met with similar resistance from the Utes, Comanches,

Tell General Howard I know his heart. What he told me before I have in my heart. I am tired of fighting. Our chiefs are killed. Looking Glass is dead. Too-hul-hulsote is dead. The old men are all dead. It is the young men who say yes or no. He who led on the young men is dead. It is cold and we have no blankets. The little children are freezing to death. My people, some of them, have run away to the hills, and have no blankets, no food; no one knows where they are—perhaps freezing to death. I want to have time to look for my children and see how many of them I can find. Maybe I shall find them among the dead. Hear me, my chiefs. I am tired; my heart is sick and sad. From where the sun now stands I will fight no more forever.

Surrender speech of Chief Joseph, Nez Percé, 1877

Arapahos, Paiutes, Shoshonis, Apaches, and Navajos. Bitter experience had taught them not to trust whites. On November 29, 1864, Col. John Chivington, a Methodist minister and a ruthless Indian hater, with a troop of seven hundred men, surprised an encampment of peaceful Cheyennes and Arapahos at Sand Creek, Colorado. Having previously made peace, Chief Black Kettle and his band met the troop with an American flag and a white flag of truce. Chivington's men began firing to kill; they chased the fleeing Indians for more than five miles. At the end of the massacre the ground lay covered with the bodies of more than five hundred horribly mutilated corpses, over four hundred of them women and children.

Three years later, in 1867, the government negotiated the Treaty of Medicine Lodge with representatives of the 86,000 members of the Southern Plains tribes, the Kiowas, the Comanches, the Southern Cheyennes, and the Southern Arapahos. After inducements ranging from feasting to bribery to threats, the tribes agreed to accept reservations in western Indian Territory on land taken from the Five Civilized Tribes after the Civil War.

The Navajos fared little better. Initial reports incorrectly indicated that the Navajos' and Apaches' homeland contained large deposits of gold and silver. The Navajos refused to cede their land. In 1863, the army, in desperation, turned to Indian fighter Kit Carson. Carson was ordered to round up the Navajos and resettle them on the Bosque Redondo Reservation in what is now eastern New Mexico, far from their home. Using Mexican scouts to find the Navajo settlements, Carson and his troops moved into their communities one by one, burning crops, destroying orchards, and scattering livestock. Finally, after more than one hundred engagements, Carson succeeded in trapping 7,000 Navajos at the bottom of Canyon de Chelly, in present-day northwest Arizona. Soon afterward, more than 8,000 men, women, and children were forcibly marched more than 350 miles, on what has become known as the Long Walk. Approximately 10,000 Navajos were interned at Bosque Redondo. In four years of captivity, some 2,500 died from starvation, malaria, and dysentery. In 1868 the United States concluded another treaty with the Navajos and allowed them to return to their homeland, west of the Rio Grande.

The Apaches, whose reputation for fierceness and stealth was justly earned, were nearly the last tribe to be subdued. The Apache wars cost the government one thousand lives and forty million dollars and lasted almost twenty years. Throughout the 1860s and 1870s Apache bands were hunted down one by one and confined to reservations as prisoners of war. Among the last to succumb were the Chiricahua Apaches, led by Geronimo. Some years before his capture, Geronimo's first wife and three young children had been murdered by Mexican authorities who had lured the Apaches

They were scalped, their brains knocked out; the men used their knives, ripped open women, clubbed little children, knocked them in the head with their guns, beat their brains out, mutilated their bodies in every sense of the word.

Eyewitness to Sand Creek Massacre, 1864

Geronimo's "other life" as husband and father. Taken around 1895–96, this photo shows Geronimo with his wife and children in his melon patch at Fort Sill, Oklahoma. (Courtesy Museum of the American Indian, Heye Foundation.)

to a feast under a flag of truce. Deeply distrustful and hateful of whites, Geronimo refused to bow to the demands of the American government. Time and again, Geronimo and his band left the parched bottomlands of the San Carlos Reservation, in present-day Arizona, to resume their life of raiding. Finally, in 1886, after sixteen months of pursuit, some five thousand U.S. troops captured Geronimo and his band of twenty warriors and eighteen women and children.

As discussed more fully in chapter 8, the Lakotas, or Sioux, and their allies, the Northern Cheyennes and Northern Arapahos, fought the army more successfully, and for a longer time, than any other tribes. In 1851 the Plains Indian wars came to an end when the government convened the largest treaty council ever held. Perhaps ten thousand Plains Indians from the Lakota, Cheyenne, Arapaho, Crow, Arikara, Mandan, and other nations attended. After more than two weeks of negotiations, the tribes signed the Treaty of Fort Laramie. The tribes established tribal boundaries (some accepted reservations), promised peace with one another and with whites, and agreed to allow the construction of forts and roads in their country in return for a fifty-year annuity.

This peace, however, was short-lived. In 1862 the Santee Sioux of Minnesota, angered over a series of fraudulent treaties, revolted and killed some five hundred white settlers before being driven out of Minnesota. In 1862, the government hanged 38 Sioux leaders of the revolt. President Abraham Lincoln pardoned another 268 Sioux, stating that they should be held as prisoners of war, instead of being executed for fighting for their cause. Many Santee Sioux fled to Canada, where their descendants live today.

By the mid-1860s tensions on the Plains had increased to the breaking point, primarily because of the movement of settlers across the Bozeman Trail—a road constructed across land promised to the Sioux in the Fort Laramie Treaty of 1851. In 1866, Lakota leaders Red Cloud, Crazy Horse, Sitting Bull, and Gall retaliated in what became known as the Powder River War.

In 1868 the United States agreed to negotiate another treaty with the Lakotas. The Fort Laramie Treaty of 1868 has been described as the only peace treaty the United States has negotiated in which it has agreed to all of the other party's demands and received nothing in return. The 1868 treaty promised the Powder River country, including the Black Hills, to the Lakota Nation forever, and ordered that the Bozeman Trail be closed.

In 1873, however, gold was discovered in the Black Hills. The Lakotas and the Cheyennes, led by Crazy Horse and Sitting Bull, battled the miners, settlers, and troops swarming into the area. In 1876 the government sent Lt. Col. George Armstrong Custer and Gen. Alfred Terry to the Powder and Bighorn rivers in Wyoming to round up the Lakotas and return them to their reservation. As the country at large was celebrating its centennial and marveling over inventions such as the telephone, Crazy Horse and his warriors were annihilating Custer and 267 of his men at the Battle of Little Bighorn. The Sioux wars continued unabated until Crazy Horse was taken prisoner and murdered in 1877 and Sitting Bull surrendered in 1881.

Although sporadic Indian revolts continued until 1915, tribes could offer little active resistance to the federal government after about 1885. They had been defeated not so much by armies as by the unstoppable westward migration

> Greed and avarice on the part of the Whites—in other words, the almighty dollar, is at the bottom of nine-tenths of our Indian troubles. I have never yet seen [an Indian] so demoralized that he was not an example in honor and nobility compared to the wretches who plunder him of the little our government appropriates for him.
>
> **Gen. George Crook, 1860s**

> We took away their [the Sioux's] country and their means of support, broke up their mode of living, their habits of life, introduced disease and decay among them and it was for this and against this that they made war. Could anyone expect less?
>
> **Western commander Brig. Gen. Philip Sheridan, 1878**

Indian Peace Commission distributing presents to Crow Indians at the Treaty Council of 1868, Fort Laramie, Wyoming. (Courtesy Smithsonian Institution, Bureau of American Ethnology Collection.)

Custer's wagon train on the prairies, traveling in four columns near the North and South Dakota line. (Courtesy of South Dakota State Historical Society.)

Shown here are some of the few buffalo remaining in 1894. The buffalo occupied the center of Plains Indian culture, religion, and existence. In 1871, the great buffalo herds numbered fifteen million, but over the next few years, white hunters killed three to four million a year. It made no difference that many of these herds belonged to tribes in protected treaty areas. The plains became a sea of stinking, unused carcasses. Even before 1871, large numbers had been killed annually for sport. In 1871, when buffalo hides became profitable, the massacre escalated unbelievably. Within six years the beast was virtually extinct, and in 1903 only 34 animals remained. The extermination of this great animal was the single most important factor in the subjugation of the Plains Indian tribes. (Courtesy Newberry Library.)

of settlers, the extermination of the buffalo, and the intrusion of new technology. The construction of the transcontinental railroad encouraged the growth of settlements, and the buffalo, a major food source, was driven to the brink of extinction by whites. The invention of the Gatling gun (a machine gun) and the telegraph tipped the balance further against the Indians. These developments, along with diseases brought by

Arapaho Ghost Dance worshipers praying. (Courtesy Smithsonian Institution, National Anthropological Archives.)

settlers, did more to defeat the tribes than did the military. In fact, recent studies estimate that more whites than Indians lost their lives during the Indian wars, and for each Indian killed, the government spent close to $2 million. The wars with the Navajos, Lakotas, and Cheyennes between 1862 and 1867 cost the government $100 million. The United States was most successful militarily when it used Indians of hostile tribes as scouts and auxiliary troops.

The result of the Indian wars and white settlement was devastation of the Indian way of life. In the midst of the tribes' widespread misery, an Indian prophet appeared. Wovoka, a Nevada Paiute, preached the Ghost Dance religion. He predicted that whites would disappear and that an Indian messiah would resurrect the Indian dead and restore the buffalo. The Ghost Dance religion spread like wildfire across the Plains. Its popularity frightened the whites, who were afraid it might lead to a united Indian revolt. Three days after Christmas in 1890 the Seventh Cavalry (Custer's former unit), fearing an uprising, herded together about 350 refugee Sioux. The following morning the troops opened fire on the Sioux camp. Within a short time more than three hundred Sioux were dead, some of them women who were chased for over three miles before being caught and killed. More than four hundred years after the Europeans had arrived, American Indians finally had been subdued through battle, disease, and loss of land. The Indian people did not abandon their struggle, however. They continued it in a new setting. In the twentieth century the battle for Indian autonomy has taken place with the Congress and in the courts.

The best way to get rid of the Indian is to destroy the buffalo by which he lives. The more buffalo killed, the better and what good is a buffalo anyway except for slaughter?

Brig. Gen. Philip Sheridan, 1870s

Our land is more valuable than your money. It will last forever. It will not even perish by the flames of fire. As long as the sun shines and the waters flow, this land will be here to give life to men and animals. We cannot sell this land. It was put here for us by the Great Spirit and we cannot sell it because it does not belong to us. You can count your money and burn it within the nod of a buffalo's head, but only the Great Spirit can count the grains of sand and the blades of grass of these plains. As a present to you, we will give you anything we have that you can take with you; but the land, never.

Chief of the Blackfeet Tribe on being asked to sign a treaty ceding land

CHAPTER 5

A CENTURY OF CONFUSION

In 1867, Congress appointed a peace commission to recommend how best to end the Plains Indian wars. The commission's report indicated that the government's failure to keep treaty commitments and its repeated demands for tribal land cessions were the main causes of continuing Indian hostilities. The government's reaction to the report echoed an argument that had been heard in federal circles for several years—that the government ought to stop negotiating with the tribes as sovereigns and instead assimilate them into the dominant society.

ASSIMILATION OF INDIANS INTO MAINSTREAM AMERICA

Before assimilation could take place, the government needed to establish a new relationship with the tribes. Under the old relationship the United States had recognized Indian nations as independent sovereigns and signed treaties with them. By doing so, the federal government had acknowledged the tribes as distinct political communities with full authority and rights to manage their own affairs. Assimilation meant dissolving the tribal entity and integrating individual Indians into mainstream society. This was no easy task and certainly not a process likely to occur naturally, since 150 years of contact with Euro-American civilization had not convinced Indians to give up their tribal identity, culture, or heritage. To bring about assimilation, the federal government needed to gain legal control over the tribes through legislation.

An 1871 act ending treaty making provided the first legal groundwork necessary to begin assimilationist lawmaking. The treaty process, by recognizing tribal autonomy, directly contradicted the goals of assimilation. So, in 1871, the House of Representatives, intent on initiating assimilation, and also jealous of Senate control of the treaty process, passed a law specifying that "hereafter, no Indian nation or tribe within the territory of the United States shall be acknowledged or recognized as an independent nation, tribe or power with whom the United States may contract by treaty."

The government's goal of assimilation was further assisted by a series of Supreme Court decisions between 1880 and 1910. The first came in the *Crow Dog* ruling of 1883.

In 1883, Crow Dog, a well-known Lakota medicine man, killed Spotted Tail, another popular leader of the tribe. Federal authorities removed Crow Dog from the reservation and tried him for murder. Crow Dog argued that the federal government had no right to try him because federal courts had

We see nothing about Indian nationality or Indian civilization which should make its preservation a matter of so much anxiety to the Congress or the people of the United States. The fundamental idea upon which our cosmopolitan republic rests is opposed to the encouragement or perpetuation of distinctive national characteristics and sentiments in our midst.

We see no reason why the Indian should constitute an exception. . . . If the Indian cannot learn to forego such of habits as are peculiar to savage life, and such of his political opinions and sentiments as are not in harmony with the general policy of our Government, then he cannot, beyond a limited period, exist among us, either as a nation or as an individual.

Senate Report by Senator
James Warren Nye of
Nevada, 1871

No Indian nation or tribe within the territory of the United States shall be acknowledged or recognized as an independent nation, tribe, or power with whom the United States may contract by treaty; but no obligation of any treaty lawfully made and ratified with any such Indian nation or tribe prior to March third, eighteen hundrd and seventy-one, shall be hereby invalidated or impaired.

Act of March 3, 1871

Chief Spotted Tail of the Lakotas. Spotted Tail was killed by Crow Dog in 1883, and the murder became the impetus for the important *Crow Dog* case. (Courtesy National Archives.)

no jurisdiction over Indian activities on the Lakota Reservation. In killing Spotted Tail, Crow Dog acknowledged that he had broken Lakota law and claimed that he should be tried and punished by the Lakotas. (Under tribal law, Crow Dog would have been made responsible for the care and protection of Spotted Tail's family.) The court agreed with Crow Dog's argument, ruling that the federal government had passed no legislation giving it criminal jurisdiction over the tribes and that criminal disputes involving tribal members were to be settled according to tribal law.

Congress reacted to the *Crow Dog* ruling with disbelief and anger. It quickly moved to gain jurisdiction by passing the Major Crimes Act of 1885. Under this act the federal courts claimed jurisdiction over the following seven crimes committed between Indians on Indian land: murder, manslaughter, rape, assault with intent to kill, arson, burglary, and larceny.

One year later, in *U.S.* v. *Kagama*, the Supreme Court looked again at Congress's claim to criminal jurisdiction in Indian affairs. Two Indians, Kagama and Mahawaha, had killed another Indian on the Hoopa Valley Indian Reservation in California. The government, arguing that the commerce clause of the Constitution gave Congress the authority to claim jurisdiction over crimes between Indians, arrested and tried the two men. Although the Supreme Court rejected this argument, it did uphold the government's claim to jurisdiction by virtue of its authority as guardian to the tribes. Writing for the Court, Justice Samuel Miller acknowledged that the United States had always recognized the tribes as semi-independent entities, "not as States, not as nations, but as separate people, with power of regulating their internal social relations and thus not brought into the laws of the Union or of the States within whose limits they resided."

Yet, Miller went on to explain, despite this recognition and despite the government's history of relating to the tribes by treaties, Congress was entitled to determine the new approach of governing tribes by legislation. This change, according to Justice Miller, was permissible because of the tribes' dependent condition:

> These tribes are the wards of the nation. They are communities dependent on the United States. Dependent largely for their daily food. Dependent for their political rights. . . . From their very weakness and helplessness, so largely due to the course of dealing of the Federal Government with them and the treaties in which it has been promised, there arises the duty of protection, and with it the power. This has always been recognized by the Executive and by Congress and by this court, whenever the question has arisen.

The *Kagama* decision was based on an unusual interpretation of the treaty power. The Court argued that the federal government, because of the treaties it had signed with the tribes, was legally obliged to protect them. From the duty to protect the tribes came the power to protect them.

Although the government had indeed promised "protection" in exchange for land, that "protection" meant protecting the tribes' remaining land and their tribal existence from unwanted intrusion by white settlers. The *Kagama* decision changed all that. In effect it meant that the government had absolute authority to define how it would "protect" Indian tribes. In the 1880s, "protection" took the form of assimilation rather than the protection of tribal autonomy that had originally been promised. All the treaties that had been negotiated by the tribes in good faith ceased to function as protection against federal intrusion and became instead licenses for federal intervention. The *Lone Wolf* decision of 1903, discussed below, gave some indication of the extent of the guardianship authority (as it was called) that had been granted to the federal government in the *Kagama* case.

The relations of the Indian tribes living within the borders of the United States both before and since the Revolution, to the people of the United States has always been an anomalous one and of a complex character.

U.S. v. *Kagama*, 1886

I know what the misfortune of the tribes is. Their misfortune is not that they are red men; not that the are semi-civilized, not that they are a dwindling race, not that they are a weak race. Their misfortune is that they hold great bodies of rich lands, which have aroused the cupidity of powerful corporations and of powerful individuals. . . . . I greatly fear that the adoption of this provision to discontinue treaty-making is the beginning of the end in respect to Indian Lands. It is the first step in a great scheme of spoliation, in which the Indians will be plundered, corporations and individuals enriched, and the American name dishonored in history.

Senator Eugene Casserly of California commenting on the reasons behind the 1871 Act

Lone Wolf, a Kiowa chief who sought to protect his tribe's land and force the federal government to uphold its treaty commitments by taking the case to the Supreme Court. Photo circa 1868–74. (Courtesy National Archives.)

A 1903 Supreme Court case, *Lone Wolf* v. *Hitchcock*, established that Congress had absolute authority over Indian relations, including the right to pass laws that violated treaties. In 1867 the Kiowa and Comanche tribes had signed the Treaty of Medicine Lodge with the United States. Article XII of this treaty guaranteed that the United States would not take any of the tribes' lands without the consent of three-fourths of the adult males. In 1892 the government allotted the tribes' land and sold the surplus without obtaining tribal approval.

On behalf of himself and other members of the Kiowa and Comanche tribes, Lone Wolf, a Kiowa, charged the government with disposing of tribal property in violation of both the Treaty of Medicine Lodge and the Fifth Amendment to the Constitution, which guarantees that no person shall be deprived of private property without due process of law and that private property shall not be taken for public use without just compensation.

The Supreme Court ruled against Lone Wolf and the tribes. The Court pointed out that, by basing their case on the terms of their treaty, the tribes had overlooked their dependent status and the government's role as their guardian. To hold Congress to the treaty would be to limit the government's authority to care for and protect the Indians. The Court conceded that the tribes' rights to their lands had been described as "sacred." But the Court went on to "clarify" that such a "sacred" right extended only to protecting the lands against states or individuals, not against the federal government. The Court asserted that federal control over Indian lands had to be absolute, because of the federal government's guardianship duty to the Indians. Government authority over Indian lands was limited only by those "considerations of justice as would control a Christian people in their treatment of an ignorant and dependent race."

PATERNALISM AND INCREASED IMPORTANCE OF THE BIA AND FEDERAL SERVICES

Indian life in the 1880s was already dramatically different from what it had been even a few decades earlier. Game depletion and tribal relocation to unproductive regions had forced radical changes in life-style, accompanied, in many instances, by profound poverty, suffering, and even starvation. Many reservations resembled prison camps, surrounded by barbed wire. Tribal members needed special passes to leave their reservations and were required to work for rations, even though the rations were actually payments in return for land ceded to the United States.

Beef being issued at the Pine Ridge Agency, South Dakota, 1892. Meat and other rations were often of inferior quality, causing starvation and sickness. (Courtesy Nebraska State Historical Society.)

The economic hardship on reservations compelled the government to provide food and other necessities. The realities of this situation, coupled with the government's assimilationist policies, constituted an enormous increase in federal control over tribal affairs. Unfortunately, the expanded government role only accelerated the tribes' worsening situations and deprived them of the freedom to manage their own affairs.

During the assimilation era, the Bureau of Indian Affairs (BIA) literally took charge of Indian life. The BIA looked upon itself as the parent and regarded Indians as children, deciding what was best for them and forcing their compliance. Many BIA agents, who were often corrupt and greedy, impeded whatever benefits the BIA policies might have had. The agents were generally poorly educated, had little relevant experience, and were ignorant of tribal values and beliefs. Few were committed to improving Indian life. Many retired wealthy, having taken advantage of the opportunity to sell to the Indians rations and annuities promised to them in treaties.

Another strong alien force on many reservations was the school. The federal government had gradually turned responsibility for running reservation schools over to non-Indian church organizations. Having decided to assimilate the Indians, however, the government took an increased interest in Indian education. Congress had first appropriated money for Indian education in 1819. Many treaties signed after that date had promised education in exchange for land. Not until 1879, however, did Congress establish an off-reservation Indian boarding school, and then the move was made to assist assimilation. As the school's director told Congress, "We accept the watchword, let us by patient effort kill the Indian in him and save the man."

The government favored boarding schools over day schools, realizing that assimilation would occur more rapidly if a child were separated from his or her family, tribe, and culture. While boarding schools never outnumbered reservation schools, they did represent the trend of the 1880s. BIA agents often forcibly removed children from their homes and sent them to boarding schools. When the students eventually returned to their reservations, they were virtual strangers, unable to speak their own language or understand the ways of their own people. In 1887 more than fourteen thousand Indian students were enrolled in 227 schools. The BIA operated 163 of these schools, while private agencies and missionary societies operated the rest.

The government also established the first Indian healthcare and law-enforcement services during the late 1800s. Health care was especially needed as Indians were aptly identified as "vanishing Americans." As the chart indicates, their population suffered a dramatic decline as a result of war, malnutrition, and disease. By 1880 the death rate exceeded

Some time about the middle of the winter a large vat was constructed of cotton-wood lumber, about six feet square and six feet deep, . . . Into this vat was thrown beef, beef heads, entrails of beef, some beans, flour and pork. I think there was put into the vat two barrels of flour each time, which was not oftener than one in twenty-four hours. This mass was then cooked by the steam from the boiler passing through the vat. When that was done, all the Indians were ordered to come there with their pails and get it. . . . The Santees and Winnebagos were fed from this vat; some of the Indians refused to eat it, saying they could not eat it, it made them sick. . . . The Indians reported several deaths from starvation. . .

Army surgeon commenting on the early days of the Crow Creek Reservation, South Dakota

Indian dances and so-called Indian feasts should be prohibited. In many cases these dances and feasts are simply subterfuges to cover degrading acts and to disguise immoral purposes. You are directed to use your best efforts in the suppression of these evils.

Commissioner of Indian Affairs, 1901

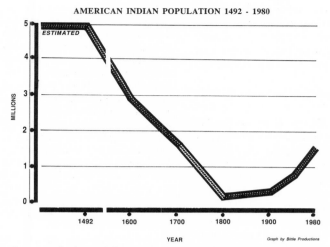

AMERICAN INDIAN POPULATION 1492 - 1980

ESTIMATED

MILLIONS

5
4
3
2
1
0

1492 1600 1700 1800 1900 1980

YEAR

Graph by Bittle Productions

At the time of white settlement, an estimated 5 million Indians lived in what is now the United States. By 1850, after three hundred years of white contact, their population had diminished by 95 percent, to only 250,000. Non-Indian immigration brought death from disease, starvation, and war, as tribes fought to protect their lands and food sources. In recent years the Indian population has increased due to improved health care and higher birth rates. Today there are over 1.5 million Indians, Inuits, and Aleuts in more than six hundred Indian nations, tribes, and bands.

the birth rate for American Indians, and their total population numbered only 125,000. Despite considerable improvements since that time, even as late as 1969 the average life expectancy for an Indian was a shocking forty-four years, compared to sixty-five years for a non-Indian.

THE DAWES ALLOTMENT ACT

In 1887, Congress passed its most assimilative law, the Land in Severalty Act, also known as the Dawes Act or the Allotment Act. The act's aim was to assimilate Indians into white society by teaching them the techniques of farming and the values of individualism and private property ownership. Reservation lands were to be allotted, or divided among individuals for farming or livestock raising. Generally, heads of families received 160 acres and single persons over eighteen years of age received 80 acres. All other tribal members received 40 acres. The government held the allotments in trust for twenty-five years. At that time individuals acquired title to their land and could dispose of it freely. The Dawes Act also provided for federal purchase of land left over after the allotment process. This surplus land was then sold to settlers.

The allotment process proved disastrous for tribes culturally, politically, and economically. First, the notion of private ownership seriously conflicted with the deeply held tribal

The head chief told us there was not a family in that whole Nation that had not a home of its own. There was not a pauper in that nation and the nation did not owe a dollar. It built its own capitol . . . and it built its schools and its hospitals. Yet the defect of the system was apparent. They have got as far as they can go, because they own their land in common . . . and under that there is no enterprise to make your home any better than that of your neighbors. There is no selfishness, which is at the bottom of civilization. Till this people will consent to give up their lands, and their citizens so that each can own the land he cultivates, they will not make much more progress.

Senator Henry Dawes, 1883

belief that land was a sacred resource to be used communally. Second, while many eastern tribes were traditionally agriculturalists and could indeed take credit for teaching farming techniques and introducing new crops to the first settlers, farming represented a completely alien way of life for most western Indians.

Politically, the allotment process seriously eroded the role and authority of tribal government. In earlier times the federal government had dealt with tribal leaders and tribal governments when providing goods and services to tribes. After passage of the Dawes Allotment Act, the government furnished supplies, food, and payments directly to individuals, ignoring tribal governments. Tribal governments subsequently declined in importance, the vacuum that was left being filled by the BIA agent on the reservation.

Economically, the allotment process brought further poverty and loss of land to the tribes. By 1934 the government had allotted more than one hundred reservations, and tribes had lost ninety million acres, approximately two-thirds of the land they had held in 1887. Sixty million acres of this lost land had been sold as "surplus" in accordance with the Dawes Act. Government officials often intentionally allotted poorer land to Indians and labeled more desirable parcels "surplus" for sale to settlers. (In fact, in terms of real land value, not just total acreage, tribes lost more than 80 percent of their land wealth.) Since their land was often unsuitable for agriculture and since the government's promises of money, supplies, and technical advice rarely materialized,

> The real purpose of this bill is to get at the Indian lands and open them up to settlement. The provisions for the apparent benefit of the Indians are but the pretext to get at his lands and occupy them. . . . If this were done in the name of greed, it would be bad enough; but to do it in the name of humanity, and under the cloak of an ardent desire to promote the Indian's welfare by making him like ourselves whether he will or not, is infinitely worse.

> Minority opinion on the
> Dawes Act,
> Committee on
> Indian Affairs, 1880

Formerly a part of Indian Territory, the Cherokee Strip, in Oklahoma Territory, was opened to white settlement in the 1893 Land Run, shown above. (Courtesy Kansas State Historical Society.)

INDIAN LAND CESSIONS

1660

1780

1840

1880

Graphic by Bittle Productions

Indians could not compete with their white neighbors, who were beginning to use machines to farm large areas. Unable to farm, many Indians leased or sold their lands to whites, some of whom were not above taking advantage of individuals in desperate need of money. Between 1903 and 1933, two million acres of Indian lands passed into white hands each year. Of the ninety million acres lost after 1890, only three million have been restored to Indian ownership.

THE INDIAN CITIZENSHIP ACT OF 1924 AND THE MERIAM REPORT OF 1928

Following the Civil War, in 1868, Congress passed the Fourteenth Amendment, which granted citizenship to former slaves in language that permitted wider interpretation: "All persons born or naturalized in the United States, and subject to the jurisdiction thereof, are citizens of the United States and of the States wherein they reside." In 1884, John Elk, an

Indian, filed a lawsuit charging the state of Nebraska with violating his Fourteenth Amendment rights by refusing him the right to vote. Elk argued that, as an Indian born in the United States, he was a U.S. citizen and, therefore, a state citizen. The Supreme Court ruled that Nebraska was correct in denying John Elk the right to vote. Indians, the Court ruled, were not American citizens but members of a distinct and alien nation. Their allegiance was not to the United States but to their tribe.

The federal government occasionally had granted citizenship to Indians, but usually at the expense of their tribal citizenship. For example, a treaty with the Ottawas in 1862 gave American citizenship to all Ottawas following the complete allotment of their reservation and the dissolution of the tribal entity. Other treaties and special statutes granted citizenship to certain tribes upon proof that tribal members had adopted "the habits of civilized life," become self-supporting, and learned to read and write English. By and large, however, Indians were not accorded U.S. citizenship until after World War I.

World War I, which the United States entered in 1917, affected tribes mainly in two ways. First, as the government turned its attention to the war, it neglected Indian affairs. Indian health, education, and welfare services were cut back, and tribes became even more impoverished. Second, an estimated ten thousand young Indian men were in active service in the U.S. armed forces. Largely in response to this patriotic contribution, Congress passed the Indian Citizenship Act of 1924 to provide "that all noncitizen Indians born within the territorial limits of the United States be, and they are hereby, declared to be citizens of the United States: *Provided*, That the granting of such citizenship shall not in any manner impair or otherwise affect the right of any Indian to tribal or other property."

As provided for by this law, tribal members did not lose their tribal citizenship or rights when they became American citizens. Indians, therefore, are citizens of three sovereigns— the United States, the state of which they are residents, and their tribe—and they have the rights and privileges of each. As federal citizens, Indians are required to register for the draft and are protected by the Bill of Rights. As state citizens, they are eligible to vote and to receive state services. And as tribal citizens, they may receive certain federal benefits as required by the federal government's trust relationship with Indian tribes.

Two years after passing the citizenship act of 1924, the government asked the Institute for Government Research (today called the Brookings Institution) to thoroughly study Indian economic and social conditions. The resulting report, known as the Meriam Report of 1928, revealed an existence filled with poverty, suffering, and discontent. Indians suffered from disease and malnutrition, had a life expectancy of only forty-four years, and had an average annual per capita income of only one hundred dollars. The report reached two basic conclusions: (1) The BIA was inadequately meeting the needs of Indians, especially in the areas of health and education; and (2) Indians were being excluded from the management of their own affairs.

The Meriam Report signaled a change in federal philosophy toward Indians. It recognized the value of Indian economic, social, religious, and ethical concepts and recommended that the government develop and build on Indian values rather than trying to destroy them. The impact of this report and the influence of John Collier, who became BIA commissioner in 1932, led to the reorganization of the BIA and the passage, in 1934, of the Indian Reorganization Act (IRA), discussed below. These changes reflected a change in national philosophy and attitude that occurred in the 1930s. The Great Depression made people question the predominant values of eighteenth- and nineteenth-century America: individualism, expansionism, resource exploitation, and unlimited growth. Reformers argued that resources should be

Children on the Mescalero Apache Reservation, April, 1936. The 1928 Meriam Report discussed the severe poverty and substandard living conditions throughout Indian country. (Courtesy Library of Congress.)

conserved and that the government had an obligation to provide for the minimum needs of its citizens. President Roosevelt's New Deal, a system of welfare and economic programs, reflected the same changes in attitude that had been hinted at in the Meriam Report of 1928.

THE INDIAN REORGANIZATION ACT OF 1934: THE STRENGTHENING OF TRIBAL GOVERNMENTS

BIA policymakers in the 1930s and early 1940s initiated and implemented far-reaching new policies. Their leadership contributed greatly to bringing about a new philosophy toward Indians and their tribal rights and lands. Secretary of the Interior Harold Ickes, BIA Commissioners C. J. Rhoades and John Collier, and Associate Solicitor Felix Cohen were reformers who believed fervently in reviving Indian culture and sovereignty. Collier, an anthropologist who had lived with Pueblo Indians and been active in the Indian Defense Association, was the leading force behind the Indian Reorganization Act. Believing that Indian cultures and values had much to offer non-Indian society and that Indian problems were best solved by Indians, Collier lobbied for a bill that would: (1) strengthen tribal governments and restore the bilateral relationship between the federal government and tribes; (2) stop the sale of allotments and restore tribal lands to communal holdings; (3) provide procedures and funds for tribal economic development; (4) grant preferential hiring of Indians in the Bureau of Indian Affairs; and (5) recognize and aid tribes in maintaining and developing their cultures, especially their language, religion, and crafts.

Despite Collier's good intentions the IRA has often been termed a "disaster" for tribes. Ironically, it has also been acclaimed as the most important piece of Indian legislation in the twentieth century. It was probably both. The IRA had three main advantages: (1) it stopped the allotment process; (2) it ended the loss of Indian lands (tribal landholdings actually increased somewhat); and (3) it reestablished tribal governments. In the first ten years after passage of the IRA, tribal governments took new steps toward self-management of property and resources. They established tribal business cooperatives, passed law-and-order codes, began public-works programs in health, education, and welfare, and raised funds for land, equipment, and livestock.

But critics of the IRA point out that it was written without tribal input, that its ratification was highly irregular, and that the tribal governments it created imposed an alien form of government on the tribal cultures. Although the IRA seemed to provide for tribal ratification of its terms, it did so in a way that effectively negated tribal wishes. Tribal members could vote either to accept or reject the IRA, but all abstentions (that is, the "votes" of anyone who did not vote) were counted as votes in favor of the IRA.

On several reservations, such as the Nez Percé and the

Coeur d'Alene, the majority of those voting voted against the act, but since abstentions were counted as votes in favor of the act, it was ratified. On the Hopi Reservation, for example, traditionalists simply refused to recognize the BIA's authority, and thus most Hopis boycotted the election. Refusing to recognize the mass abstention for what it was—absolute nonacceptance of the act—the BIA counted the Hopi vote as favoring the act. Any tribe that failed to hold an election automatically came under the act's provisions.

Today about half of all tribes have IRA constitutions, all of which are, in general, very similar. A typical IRA constitution establishes a governing board, often called the tribal council. Unlike federal and state governments, most IRA constitutions do not provide for the separation of powers. The executive, legislative, and, in many instances, judicial functions are performed by the governing board. Council members are elected at large or by district by all voters. The chairperson and other officers who form the executive committee are members of the council, elected either by the people or by the council from among its membership. The judicial function may be performed either by the council itself or by tribal members appointed by the council. In some instances, tribal members may elect judges, allowing for a greater separation of powers.

Critics of IRA constitutions charge that the governments they establish impose an alien political system on tribal culture, that the powers given to the tribal council by the constitution may be less than those possessed inherently by the tribe, and that the required secretarial approval clause continues the BIA's domination. The secretarial approval clause empowers the secretary of the interior to approve or veto new tribal laws, to overrule certain tribal council actions, to call elections and settle election disputes, to oversee the tribe's economic affairs, to review the taxation of nonmembers, and to approve the hiring of legal counsel.

In recent years the secretary of the interior's practice has been to respect tribal sovereignty and not meddle in tribal affairs. As many tribes work toward self-determination, however, they come to regard the secretarial approval clause as an unwarranted intrusion upon their sovereignty. Some tribes have subsequently amended their IRA constitutions to remove the clause.

THE TERMINATION ERA: THE END OF TRUST STATUS

Less than fifteen years after passing the IRA in 1934, Congress reversed its decision to strengthen Indian sovereignty and tribal governments. Once again it decided to implement new assimilation policies. The assimilation policies initiated in the late 1940s and early 1950s had two related aims: to terminate government responsibilities to the tribes and to integrate Indians into the white communities of their resident states. To bring about these goals, Congress implemented several measures, one of which was the Indian Claims Commission.

In 1855, Congress had established the court of claims to hear suits brought by individuals, including Indians, against the federal government. During the Civil War, however, Congress, angered by the support of some tribes for the Confederacy, barred tribes from presenting claims to the court. Finally, in 1946, Congress established the Indian Claims Commission. Through the claims commission tribes could sue for lands illegally taken from them by the United States. Between 1946 and 1952, the cut-off date for filing claims, tribes filed 370 petitions representing some 850 claims. The commission had actually been established for two purposes: to repay tribes for lands illegally taken but also to clear the slate of tribal claims, thereby allowing the government to express a new orientation in Indian affairs.

Criticisms against the claims commission's guidelines have been many. Tribes could not regain their old lands or acquire new ones. They could be granted only financial awards, which were computed on the market value of the land at the time it was taken, not on its current value. In general, no interest was paid. Any gratuitous expenditures made by the federal government for the tribes were subtracted from the overall award, thereby penalizing the tribes for unrequested services. The average interval between filing a claim and receiving an award was fifteen years.

Despite these criticisms, the Indian Claims Commission represented an important recognition by Congress that tribes were entitled to restitution by the federal government for the unfair confiscation of their lands. The commission, which is now defunct, awarded more than $800 million overall to various tribes, and while it did help Indians by providing a mechanism for settling their claims, it often settled the claims to the disadvantage of the tribes involved. In the last analysis it was yet another structure designed to help the government get out of the Indian business.

Congress followed the Indian Claims Commission Act with a series of bills in the early 1950s designed to diminish the status of Indians as a separate group. The last vestige of discriminatory Indian legislation was removed in 1953 when Congress ended the prohibition against selling liquor and firearms to Indians. (Until the late 1920s and early 1930s, even more prohibitive legislation had forbidden the practice of Indian religion, curtailed Indian freedom of speech, and provided for military control on reservations.) Again, this was an assimilationist reform aimed at removing distinctions between Indians and non-Indians. So too was Congress's decision in 1954 to shift the obligation for Indian health services from the BIA to the Department of Health, Education and Welfare (now the Department of Health and Human Services), which oversaw the health and welfare of all U.S. citizens. Congress also directed the BIA to begin transferring its responsibility for Indian education to the states. All these changes integrated Indian affairs into the general federal administration rather than administering them separately.

An even greater threat to Indian sovereignty came in 1953 with the approval of House Concurrent Resolution 108. This measure provided that Congress, "as quickly as possible, move to free those tribes listed from Federal supervision and control and from all disabilities and limitations specially applicable to Indians." For the more than one hundred groups involved, representing ten thousand Indians, termination meant the end of the government's trust relationship with Indian people and their tribes. In most cases reservation lands were sold, with the proceeds going to the tribes. For some tribes the termination legislation provided that their lands be placed in private trust. For all terminated tribes federal protection and aid ended. Termination also meant the end of all special tribal programs, the removal of state tax exemptions, and the imposition of state civil and criminal authority. The federal government could not deprive tribes of their inherent sovereignty, but the termination process made it extremely difficult for tribes to exercise their sovereignty. The termination process was actively pursued until the early 1960s. The legislation remained on the books until its repeal by the House of Representatives in 1988.

Another piece of legislation—Public Law (P.L.) 280—gave five states judicial control over resident Indians, thereby se-

In view of the historic policy of Congress favoring freedom for the Indians, we may well expect future Congresses to continue to endorse the principle that as rapidly as possible we should end the status of Indians as wards of the Government and grant them all the rights and prerogatives pertaining to American citizenship. With the aim of equality before the law in mind our course should rightly be no other. Firm and constant consideration for those of Indian ancestry should lead us all to work diligently and carefully for the full realization of their national citizenship with all other Americans. Following the footsteps of the Emancipation Proclamation of 94 years ago, I emblazon the letters of fire above the heads of the Indians—"These people shall be free!"

Senator Arthur V. Watkins of Utah speaking on House Concurrent Resolution 108, 1953.

Today approximately 75 percent of the Indian population lives in urban areas. To provide services and support, many cities have established urban Indian centers, such as the one shown here in west Los Angeles. (Courtesy Donald L. Fixico.)

riously eroding Indian autonomy. Passed in 1953, P.L. 280 empowered California, Minnesota, Nebraska, Oregon, and Wisconsin to assume complete civil and criminal jurisdiction over most tribes within their borders. The tribes in these states were not given the opportunity to decide whether they wished to fall under state control. The implications of P.L. 280 are discussed in more detail in chapter 13.

Congress also used economic incentives to promote assimilation and urbanization. Public Law 959, passed in 1956, provided funds for institutional and on-the-job training for Indians, both of which were greatly needed. The act, however, did not make these opportunities available on the reservation. To obtain training, Indians had to relocate to urban areas often far away from their homes. Until recently, once they were living in the urban community, Indians were ineligible for federal services. Although an estimated 35,000 individuals relocated in the late 1950s, the act's goal of abolishing Indians' ties to their reservations and cultures was not realized. More than one-third returned home within a few years.

SELF-DETERMINATION: AN ATTEMPT TO END PATERNALISM

The 1960s and early 1970s in America were a time of inquiry, self-awareness, social upheaval, and experimentation as the nation sought to solve problems of discrimination and social injustice. During this time the federal government and several private foundations undertook studies of Indian affairs, including Indian administration, education, and health standards. The reports include the Study of the United States Senate Select Committee on Indian Affairs (1961), the Report of the Commission on the Rights, Liberties and Responsibilities of the American Indian (1961), the Coleman Report (1966), the White House Task Force on Indian Health (1966), the Report of the Special Senate Subcommittee on Indian Education (1969), and the American Indian Policy Review Commission Report (1975).

All of these studies found that Indian social, educational, and health conditions had improved little since Congress's last review of the situation, published in the Meriam Report of 1928. Termination policies had clearly failed to "liberate" Indian people or to solve the "Indian problem." If anything, the policies of the 1950s had increased suffering and despair among Indians. The new studies characterized health conditions as "deplorable" and services as "totally inadequate." Indian education was a "national tragedy." These findings caused President Lyndon B. Johnson to refer to Indians as "the forgotten Americans." The major recommendation of each report was that Indians be given greater self-determination, that is, greater control in governing their reservations and greater participation in planning federal Indian policy.

Like other Americans, urban and reservation Indians par-

> The protection of our land and water and other natural resources are of utmost importance to us. Our culture not only exists in time but in space as well. If we lose our land we are adrift like a leaf on a lake, which will float aimlessly and then dissolve and disappear.
>
> Our land is more than the ground upon which we stand and sleep, and in which we bury our dead. The land is our spiritual mother whom we can no easier sell than our physical mother. We will resist, to the death if necessary, any more of our mother being sold into slavery.
>
> . . . .
>
> We are the products of the poverty, despair, and discrimination pushed on our people from the outside. We are the products of chaos. Chaos in our tribes. Chaos in our personal lives.
>
> We are also products of a rich and ancient culture which supersedes and makes bearable any oppressions we are forced to bear. We believe that one's basic identity should be with his tribe. We believe in tribalism, we believe that tribalism is what has caused us to endure.
>
> Policy Statement,
> National Indian Youth
> Conference, 1961

ticipated intensely in the awareness and activism of the 1960s. Proud of their heritage and determined to protect their political, cultural, and land rights, Indian people across the nation organized, demonstrated, and protested. In 1961, five hundred Indians representing sixty-seven tribes met at the University of Chicago and adopted a Declaration of Indian Purpose. Later that year several of the younger participants from the Chicago conference formed the National Indian Youth Conference (NIYC). This group demonstrated against the denial of Indian rights, staged "fish-ins" to support Northwest tribal fishing-rights claims, published studies and newspapers, and lobbied Congress. Five years later, the native peoples of Alaska formed the Alaskan Federation of Natives to protect and preserve Alaskan native culture, land, and resources.

The founding of the American Indian Movement (AIM) in 1968 ushered in a new period of Indian militancy in the United States. AIM was first organized by Clyde Bellecourt, a Chippewa, and other Indians to help Indians in Minneapolis-Saint Paul. AIM chapters soon spread to other urban areas and to reservations. In every section of the country Indian militants staged demonstrations, take-overs, and sit-ins, protesting the destruction of tribal culture and government, the loss of tribal lands and resources, and the denial of Indian civil rights.

In 1969, a group of Indians occupied Alcatraz Island in San Francisco Bay. Abandoned by the government in 1963, Alcatraz Island had previously been a maximum-security federal prison. The activists claimed the island as Indian property under the terms of the Fort Laramie Treaty of 1868, which permitted any male Indian over eighteen years of age whose tribe was a party to the treaty to file for a homestead on abandoned federal lands. The protesters, who offered to buy the island with beads worth twenty-four dollars, also proposed a "Bureau of Caucasian Affairs" to guide whites in the correct way of living.

In 1972 participants in a protest march named the Trail of Broken Treaties occupied the BIA headquarters in Washington, D.C., for six days to protest the bureau's policies. In 1975, Indian militants took over the tiny hamlet of Wounded Knee, on the Pine Ridge Reservation in South Dakota, to demand the return of tribal lands lost through 250 years of broken treaties and to protest the federal government's control of an allegedly corrupt tribal government. For more than two months, two hundred Indian activists and three hundred FBI agents and U.S. marshals faced each other in a tense standoff that left two FBI agents and one Indian dead. Indians and non-Indians alike questioned whether the relationship between the two societies had progressed at all since the earlier Wounded Knee confrontation in 1890.

The federal government responded to national demands for social justice and civil rights with laws and programs

We will give to the inhabitants of this island a portion of the land for their own to be held in trust by the Amerian Indian Affairs and by the Bureau of Caucasian Affairs to hold in perpetuity—for as long as the sun shall rise and the rivers go down to the sea. We will further guide the inhabitants in the proper way of living. We will offer them our religion, our education, our life-ways, in order to help them achieve our level of civilization and thus raise them and all their white brothers up from their savage and unhappy state. We offer this treaty in good faith and wish to be fair and honorable in our dealings with all white men.

Proclamation to United States
by Indians who seized
Alcatraz Island, 1969

The Longest Walk protest march in Washington, D.C., July 1978, symbolized an era of militancy among American Indians during the 1970s. (Courtesy *Akwesasne Notes.*)

aimed at combating poverty and racial discrimination. A number of these efforts benefited Indians both on and off reservations. The 1968 Indian Civil Rights Act guaranteed civil rights to tribal members on reservations and provided funds for development of tribal judicial systems. The Economic Opportunity Act gave tribal governments funds to run Head Start, Upward Bound, Vista, and other economic and social assistance programs. Other legislation provided economic assistance for housing (the Public Housing Act of 1961), vocational facilities and training programs (the Manpower Development and Training Act of 1962), improved health services (the Indian Health Care Improvement Act of 1966), business ventures (the Indian Financing Act of 1972), and education (the Indian Education Act of 1972).

Another important act passed during the early 1970s was the Alaskan Native Claims Settlement Act (ANCSA) of 1971. This act cleared the way for the federal government's construction of the Alaska pipeline by providing approximately 44 million acres of land and $964.5 million to the eighty thousand Eskimos, Aleuts, and Indians living in Alaska who relinquished their aboriginal title to nine-tenths of Alaska. The cash settlement was given to approximately 225 state-chartered village corporations and twelve regional corporations and was earmarked for development. Each native received one share of stock in both a village and a regional corporation. Under the terms of the original legislation, individuals were entitled to sell their stock in 1991. In 1988, after intense lobbying by Alaska natives, who argued that this provision would result in an effect similar to that of the Dawes Act—loss of land and corporate shares—Congress revised the act. Under the revision each corporation was allowed to decide as a whole whether to allow members to sell their stocks in 1991. Despite the amendments, many Alaska natives remain concerned that non-Indians will ultimately buy all the land and stocks from the natives, thereby weakening native cultural identity and bringing it closer to extinction.

With the 1975 passage of the Indian Self-Determination and Educational Assistance Act, Congress demonstrated its acceptance of tribal autonomy. In a 1970 speech to Congress, President Richard M. Nixon had presented a special message on Indian affairs. He denounced termination and pledged federal government resources "to strengthen the Indian's sense of autonomy without threatening his sense of community." On January 4, 1975, Congress implemented Nixon's promise with the Indian Self-Determination and Education Assistance Act. The act allows the secretary of the interior and the secretary of health and human services to contract directly with tribal governments to administer BIA or Indian Health Service programs. This means that tribal governments can now manage their own housing, law-enforcement, education, health, social service, and community development programs.

Two other laws, the Indian Child Welfare Act and the American Indian Religious Freedom Act, passed in 1978, further solidified the government's attempt to recognize and respect tribal cultural rights. State child-custody laws, to which tribes were subject, allowed non-Indian state employees with little understanding of Indian culture to make decisions about when to remove children from their families. Once a decision to remove a child had been made, other Indian families usually could not qualify to become adoptive or foster parents because of guidelines restricting placement with relatives and requiring certain living standards. These guidelines conflicted with the cultural practice of many tribes, in which children were frequently raised by relatives other than their parents. Although some tribes had attempted to reverse these state laws for years, by 1977, 25 to 35 percent of all Indian children had been taken from their homes by bureaucratic authorization.

In 1978, "recognizing that there is no resource that is more vital to the continued existence and integrity of Indian tribes than their children," Congress passed the Indian Child Welfare Act. This act gave tribes authority over all Indian child custody proceedings unless parents specifically requested state jurisdiction. It also appropriated money to tribes for child- and family-service programs. Since then many tribal governments have adopted juvenile codes and established juvenile courts, group homes, and foster and adoptive-care programs.

The passage of the American Indian Religious Freedom Act (AIRFA), while less successful in its implementation, similarly recognized the government's obligation to maintain tribal cultural existence. The AIRFA acknowledged that the First Amendment had not adequately protected Indians' rights to practice their religions. Indeed, federal officials, had often worked actively to suppress and destroy Indian religions. The Religious Freedom Act promised to "protect and preserve for American Indians their inherent right of freedom to believe, express and exercise [their] traditional religions" and instructed federal agencies to review their regulations for possible interference with Indian religious practices. Unfortunately, as has often been the case with federal legislation, the act has provided little assistance to tribes in the protection of their religious rights. Few federal agencies changed their regulations and few courts have upheld tribal suits to protect their first amendment rights and the right of religious freedom guaranteed by the AIRFA. Hence, ignorance about religious beliefs, especially regarding the sanctity of certain lands, still results in Indians being denied the right to practice their own religions.

FEDERAL CLASSIFICATION OF TRIBES

The federal government today classifies tribes into the following four categories according to the type of political relationship the tribe has with the federal government or the state: (1) federally recognized tribes; (2) state-recognized tribes; (3) terminated tribes; and (4) unrecognized tribes.

Of the more than 600 tribes in the United States, 502 are federally recognized. These tribes maintain a special political relationship, usually one established by treaty, or sometimes, as with the 200 Alaskan communities, by congressional legislation, with the federal government. The federal government is obligated to protect the tribal lands and resources of federally protected tribes and to provide them with health care, education, and economic-development assistance.

There are twenty-six state-recognized tribes, many of which live on state reservations and receive some state funding. Most state-recognized tribes, like the Shinnecocks of New York, the Mattaponis of Virginia, and the Lumbees of North Carolina, are located in the eastern United States.

The remaining tribes are classified either as terminated or as unrecognized. Terminated tribes had their special relationship with the federal government ended by Congress during the termination era of the 1950s and early 1960s. These tribes are without reservations and are no longer eli-

In a mass society, which presses at every point toward conformity, the protection of a self-expression, however unique, of the individual and the group becomes ever more important. The varying currents of the subcultures that flow into the mainstream of our national life give it depth and beauty. We preserve a greater value than an ancient tradition when we protect the rights of the Indians who honestly practice an old religion in using peyote one night at a meeting in a desert hogan near Needles, California.

People v. *Woody* (1964)

gible for the special services and benefits granted to federally recognized tribes. Unrecognized tribes, of which there are more than two hundred, have no political relationship with the federal government because they have never made a treaty with the United States, nor have they ever received federal recognition through executive or congressional action. Like terminated tribes, unrecognized tribes have no tribal land and receive none of the special services or benefits given to recognized tribes. Many unrecognized tribes and some terminated tribes are working to obtain or regain federal recognition so that they can take advantage of special programs to help their people.

MODERN TRIBAL GOVERNMENTS AND THEIR POWERS

Part 2 demonstrated how the coming of whites dramatically altered the Indians' world. Part 3 will examine in more detail the effect that the U.S. government has had on the structures and powers of tribal governments and will look closely at the powers of tribal governments today.

The first major change the United States brought about in Indian tribal governments came during the treaty-making era. Through its efforts to simplify and speed treaty negotiations, the United States often pressured tribes to centralize their governments. Traditional tribal governments incorporated guards against concentration of power to preserve values of freedom, respect, and harmony. Decisions generally required the approval of leaders of several bands, each of whom needed the consensus of all band members. This democratic nature inconvenienced and exasperated the U.S. government, which urged tribes to select a principal chief with the authority to make decisions on behalf of the tribe.

In some tribes the pressure to centralize and streamline was internal, because certain tribal leaders recognized that the system of strong local governments facilitated the U.S. government's "divide and conquer" tactics. Stronger central governments gave tribes more control over their leadership and helped prevent land cessions by weak leaders. By the early reservation period many tribes had strengthened their tribal or national governments at the expense of local systems.

When the United States changed its national Indian policy from treaty making to assimilation, the federal government set about actually to destroy traditional tribal governments. BIA agents gradually gained near total control of rationing, land allocation, tribal judicial systems and tribal law-enforcement systems.

By the 1930s, when the Indian Reorganization Act (IRA) was passed, traditional tribal governments had almost ceased to exist on over half of all reservations. BIA Commissioner John Collier tried to reverse this process by using the IRA to return tribal affairs to tribal control.

Most tribes today have a governing council of some sort, although these governing bodies vary widely in their titles, structures, and powers. Approximately half of all federally recognized tribes have organized themselves under the guidelines of the Indian Reorganization Act (1934), the Oklahoma Indian Welfare Act (1936), or the Alaskan Reorganization Act (1936). Tribes organized under these acts have constitu-

5. The source of sovereignty, self-government and nationhood of the Navajo Nation is its own independent status as a state under international law, and the source of such powers is not the United States.

6. The Navajo Nation has plenary authority over its people, lands and affairs, and that plenary authority cannot be removed or eroded without consent of the Navajo People.

7. The Navajo Nation retains and will not compromise or surrender its fundamental right of self-determination and it will guard and protect its right to fully control its own lands and resources.

8. The Navajo Nation retains and will exercise all governmental powers and authority which it does not specifically give up to another nation or government with the consent of the Navajo People.

From Philosophy of Principles, adopted by the Select Committee of the Department of Justice, Navajo Nation, 1983

Installation of officers at Gila River Indian Reservation in Arizona.
(Courtesy Arizona State Museum, University of Arizona.)

tions similar in structure to state constitutions, with the
exception that the tribal council frequently exercises the executive, legislative, and judicial functions of government.
Several tribes, including some Pueblo groups, the Onondaga
and Tonawanda Senecas of New York, most native communities of Alaska, and many smaller bands in California, have
retained their traditional forms of government and still operate in much the same manner described in chapter 2. Other
tribes, including the Crows and the Yakimas, operate their
governments according to rules and procedures established
in tribally agreed upon resolutions.

Chapters 6–10 will examine the modern governments of
the five tribes discussed in chapter 2. Chapter 6 covers the
Senecas of New York; chapter 7, the Muscogees (Creeks) of
Oklahoma; chapter 8, the Cheyenne River Sioux of South

Dakota; chapter 9, the Isleta Pueblo of New Mexico; and chapter 10, the Yakimas of Washington. To understand the historical pressures that have helped transform tribal governments, it is important to review and expand upon the history discussed in part 2. Thus, the historical evolution of each tribe's government is covered here, followed by discussion of how each tribe currently meets the political, social, and economic needs of its members.

Chapter 11 then examines the powers possessed by tribal governments—the rights to determine membership, administer justice, regulate property and commerce, protect the environment, and provide services to their members, for example—showing how those powers have changed and evolved, explaining their current status, and providing examples to show how tribes are carrying out those powers at present.

The Papago Council, subject to the guarantees contained in Article VI of this Constitution, reserves the right and is hereby confirmed in the right to use its old laws and customs in its religious ceremonials, in its social life, and in its local self-government. This includes the manner of selecting headmen and councils and of deciding matters affecting the welfare of individuals and the communities.

Article V, Section I,
Constitution and bylaws
of the Papago Tribe of
Arizona

CHAPTER 6

THE SENECA NATION OF INDIANS

The Seneca Nation of Indians Tribal Council is meeting in the tribal hall on the Cattaraugus Reservation in New York State. The president of the Seneca Nation calls the meeting to order and asks one of the Allegany Reservation council- lors to lead the council in prayer. Then the minutes from the last meeting are read and approved. Next the president turns to the first order of business on the agenda—the lease agreement between the Seneca Nation and the city of Sala- manca, "the only leased city on an Indian reservation." Sala- manca has leased its land from the Seneca Nation since 1890. The present lease will expire on February 19, 1991. Under the terms of this lease the city pays the nation forty thousand dollars—less than four dollars per city resi- dent—per year. The Seneca Nation and the city of Sala- manca must agree on several items before a new lease agreement can be successfully concluded. For example, should lease payments be negotiated for a set amount or on a sliding scale that would increase as property values go up? Should the lease be for twenty years or ninety- nine years or in perpetuity? Which governments—local, state, or federal—should be responsible for payment of the lease money? The General Lease Committee, charged with working out the agreement, is asked to explain to the coun- cil the terms of the proposed lease.

The 5,400 members of the Seneca Nation live in the for- ested Allegheny River Valley region of western New York State. Once the owners of half of New York State, the Seneca Nation now holds title to 52,100 acres divided into three reservations: the Allegany (although named after the river, the name of the Seneca reservation is spelled *Alle- gany*), the Cattaraugus, and the small, unpopulated Oil Springs Reservation.

In addition to the Seneca Nation, there are three other set- tlements of Seneca Indians in the United States and Canada. The Tonawanda band occupies a 7,549-acre reservation near Akron, New York. Considered the most traditional of all the U.S. Senecas, the Tonawandas have continued their tradi- tional system of government and have retained their mem- bership in the Iroquois League, which meets on the Onon- daga Reservation in north-central New York.

Another group of Senecas lives on the Six Nation, or Grand River, Reserve near Brantford, Ontario. This group also has retained a traditional government. Included in this group are descendants of the Senecas and other pro-British Iroquois who moved to Canada after the Revolutionary War and a second group of Senecas that migrated to this reserve from New York in 1838 after their Buffalo Creek Reservation was sold.

The third Seneca group, the Seneca-Cayugas of Oklahoma, has a five-thousand-acre reservation in northeastern Oklahoma. These Senecas originally lived along the Ohio River. In 1838 they ceded their Ohio lands to the United States and relocated to Indian Territory. Today a chief and a five-member council, organized under the IRA, govern the six hundred tribal members.

HISTORY

The Senecas called themselves "Djiionondo-wanenaka," (People of the Hill). To their enemies they were the "Nation of Snakes," a name befitting their reputation as the most ambitious and warlike of all the Iroquois tribes. As members of the Iroquois League the Senecas contributed over half of its fighting force and, at the height of the league's power, in the mid-1600s, were its most populous nation, numbering approximately eight thousand. This large membership resulted in part from the tradition of adopting captives into the tribe. More than twenty tribes made up the Seneca Nation during the early colonial period. The Senecas originally inhabited the western portion of present-day New York State and a part of present-day Pennsylvania.

The Revolutionary War

As discussed in chapters 3 and 4, the Iroquois League, because of its size and power, represented a valuable ally to European colonists. Consequently, the league found itself at the center of competition, first between the English and the French and later between the English and the Americans. Throughout the French and Indian War, the league officially maintained neutrality, although unofficially it lent aid to England.

The Revolutionary War (see chapter 4) brought about a split in the Iroquois League. At a league council meeting on August 25, 1775, the league adopted an official position of neutrality, but only after much discussion and disagreement. This tenuous agreement broke apart on May 20, 1776, when a combined force of British and Mohawk warriors engaged and defeated the Americans in the Battle of the Cedars. A few days later a contingent of Oneidas, Tuscaroras, and members of a smaller tribe called the Stockbridge Christians formed an Indian auxiliary under American command. The league council reconvened to discuss the situation. The Mohawks remained determined to support the British; the Senecas continued to argue for neutrality; and the Oneidas and the Tuscaroras, having decided to support the American side, were absent. At the end of a long, tense, and impassioned

Brother! Listen to what we say. There was a time when our forefathers owned this great land. Their seats extended from the rising to the setting of the sun. The Great Spirit has made it for the use of Indians. He had created the buffalo, the deer, and other animals for food. He made the bear and the deer, and their skins served us for clothing. He has scattered them over the country, and had taught us how to take them. He had caused the earth to produce corn for bread. All this he had done for his red children because he loved them. If we had any disputes about hunting grounds, they were generally settled without the shedding of much blood.

But an evil day came upon us. Your forefathers crossed the great waters and landed on this island. Their numbers were small. They found friends and not enemies. They told us they had fled from their own country for fear of wicked men, and had come here to enjoy their religion. They asked for a small seat. We took pity on them, granted their request and they sat down amongst us. We gave them corn and meat. They gave us poison [spiritous liquor] in return. The white people had not found our country. Tidings were carried back and more came amongst us. Yet we did not fear them. We took them to be friends. They called us brothers. We believed them and gave them a large seat. At length their numbers had greatly increased. They wanted more land. They wanted our country. Our eyes were opened, and our minds became uneasy. Wars took place. Indians were hired to fight against Indians, and many of our people were destroyed. They also brought strong liquors among us. It was strong and powerful and has slain thousands.

Red Jacket, Seneca Chief, 1792

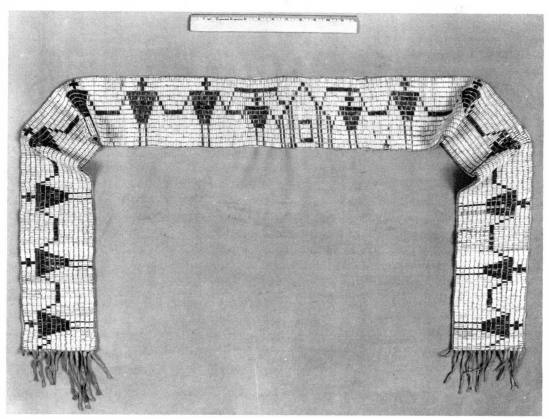

The Washington Covenant Belt, containing approximately ten thousand purple and white beads, dates from either 1775 or 1789. It commemorates an agreement of peace between the Iroquois League and the Thirteen Colonies. Friendship between the two sides is represented on the belt by thirteen figures, symbolizing the colonies, and two different figures, representing the Six Nations of the Iroquois League, joined by a long-house. Wampum belts had great political, ceremonial, and economic importance in the Iroquois League. They were often woven in duplicates and given to each party as records of treaties. Others symbolized the authority and sanctity of political offices, as the crown did in European monarchies. Wampum was also used as a medium of exchange by the Dutch and the English in the fur trade. Wampum beads were usually made of clam shells gathered from the New Jersey and Long Island beaches. The boring and shaping of each shell required precision and dexterity and was done with a hand bow and a simple grinding stone. (Courtesy New York State Museum.)

council meeting, the Senecas reluctantly agreed to join the Mohawks and support the British.

As discussed in chapter 4, the Revolutionary War proved disastrous for the Iroquois League as a whole and for the Senecas in particular. Their homes and crops destroyed by the Americans, hundreds of Senecas died of starvation and in the smallpox epidemic of 1781–82.

At the war's end General Washington announced that he regarded Iroquois land as "conquered provinces," and in treaty negotiations at Fort Stanwix in 1794, the United States demanded cession of all Iroquois League lands west of New

Cornplanter. (Courtesy Smithsonian Institution, National Anthropological Archives.)

York (this land belonged primarily to western tribes under Iroquois control). Most league chiefs refused to accept their status as conquered subjects and declined to sign the treaty. Only twelve of the required forty-nine chiefs signed, making the treaty, in the eyes of the league, null and void.

The western tribes, especially the Shawnees and the Miamis, continued to agitate over the loss of their lands for the next several years. They threatened war and repeatedly asked the league to join them in hostilities against the new U.S. government. But the Revolutionary War had finally broken the unity of the league, and at a joint council meeting held in 1791, urged by Seneca Chief Gaiantwaka, or Cornplanter, the Iroquois formally refused to support the western tribes.

Cornplanter continued to serve as peace negotiator between the Ohio tribes and the United States for the next three years. In appreciation for his services, the Commonwealth of Pennsylvania bestowed upon Cornplanter and his heirs three tracts of land on the Allegheny River. Today most of that land is submerged under the artificial lake created by

Joseph Brant. (Courtesy Smithsonian Institution, National Anthropological Archives.)

the construction of the Kinzua Dam in the 1960s, discussed later in this chapter.

Meanwhile, President Washington, hoping to prevent future Indian alliances, moved to strengthen the country's new friendship with the Iroquois. In 1794 the United States agreed to renegotiate the Treaty of Fort Stanwix. The result was the Canandaigua, or Pickering, Treaty, in which the United States offered its friendship to the league and recognized Iroquois sovereignty and land rights. In doing so, the United States repudiated its conquest argument of previous years. Furthermore, the United States agreed to distribute $4,500 to each of the league's member nations annually and to provide a one-time bonus of goods worth $10,000 to aid in "civilizing" the Iroquois.

Changes and the Loss of an Aboriginal Land Base

By 1800 the Senecas' life had changed dramatically from what it had been during the Revolutionary War. The split within the league during the war had badly reduced its mili-

Now, the United States acknowledge all the land within the aforementioned boundaries, to be the property of the Seneca nation; and the United States will never claim the same, nor disturb the Seneca nation, nor any of the Six Nations, or their Indian friends residing thereon and united with them, in the free use and enjoyment thereof: but it shall remain theirs, until they choose to sell the same to the people of the United States, who have the right to purchase.

Article III, Treaty of Canandaigua (Pickering Treaty), 1794

tary and political power, and disease, war, and starvation had killed half of its population.

It was at about this time that the Society of Friends—the Quakers—began an association with the Senecas that further changed Seneca culture. The Quakers stressed education and encouraged tribal members to fence their lands and build sawmills and other businesses for personal profit. With the fencing of land and the establishment of businesses, the notion of private property began to compete with, and then to dominate, the traditional system of communal ownership. The Senecas' subsistence economy changed to one based on profit. Log cabins began to replace traditional longhouses, and this change in turn affected traditional family relationships. The smaller, nuclear family of husband, wife, and children replaced the extended family.

The Quakers and other Christian denominations also changed the religious composition of the tribe. By 1820 half of all Senecas, including many of the principal chiefs, were at least nominally Christian. Over the next several decades religion played a prominent role in tribal politics, with the Christian faction usually favoring the sale of tribal lands and the adoption of white practices and traditions.

The greatest dislocation in Seneca life, however, was caused by population shifts that resulted from a decreasing land base. In 1787 land speculators began to exert intense pressure on the New York tribes to sell their lands. Eagerness for Iroquois lands was intensified by an agreement made between New York and Massachusetts in 1786 as to within which state Iroquois lands fell. According to the agreement, Massachusetts held *preemptive rights* to the lands—that is, it had the right to buy land from the tribes and resell it, thereby reaping profits. Once the lands had been resold, however, they became part of New York State. Two years after this agreement, Massachusetts sold its preemptive rights to a land company for $1 million. That same year the Senecas sold what was to be the first of several land cessions to a succession of land companies.

Other New York tribes were also being pressured by land companies around this same time. In 1795 the Cayugas sold their New York lands. Some Cayugas subsequently moved to the Senecas' Cattaraugus Reservation, where their descendants still live. Others moved west and joined the Ohio Senecas.

In 1816, President James Madison approved a plan to move all New York tribes, including the Senecas, west. Anticipating this removal, Congress, in 1823, bought lands from the Menominee Nation of Wisconsin for the resettlement of the New York tribes. Between 1823 and 1838 approximately 650 Oneidas settled in Wisconsin with dreams of establishing a western Iroquois empire. In 1831 the Ohio Senecas, with their Cayuga contingent, ceded their last forty

The first subject to which we would call attention of the governor, is the depredation daily committed by the white people upon the most valuable timber on our reservation. . . . This has been the subject of complaint for many years. . . .

Our next subject of complaint is the frequent thefts of our horses and cattle by the whites, and their habit of taking and eating them when they please, and without our leave.

Another evil arising from the pressure of the whites upon us, and our unavoidable communication with them, is the frequency with which our Indians are thrown into jail . . . and for the most trifling causes.

In our hunting and fishing, too, we are greatly interrupted. Our venison is stolen from the trees where we have hung it to reclaim it after the chase. . . . The fish which, in the Buffalo and Tonnewanto creeks, used to supply us with food are now—by the dams and other obstructions of the white people—prevented from multiplying, and we are almost entirely deprived of that accustomed sustenance.

The greatest source of all our grievances is, that the white men are among us.

Red Jacket, Seneca Chief, in a letter to DeWitt Clinton, Governor of New York, listing the grievances of the Iroquois, 1821

thousand acres in Ohio and moved to the Indian Territory; today they are known as the Seneca-Cayugas of Oklahoma.

In 1826 the Senecas remaining in New York sold all five of their remaining Genesee River reservations, most of their Tonawanda Reservation, and parts of their Buffalo Creek and Cattaraugus reservations. This sale, like the previous ones to land companies, technically violated the Trade and Intercourse Act of 1790 (see chapter 4), which forbade the purchase of Indian lands by anyone except the federal government. This cession, which relinquished 85,000 acres for $48,260, badly divided the nation, and afterward the Senecas took a firm stand against either selling more land or moving west.

To ensure that the sale would be their last, the Senecas adopted their first written constitution in 1833. The constitution gave legislative and executive power to the nation's chiefs and headmen and specifically stated that any leader favoring removal would be relieved of office. To make their position clear, the council forwarded a memorial, or petition, to President Andrew Jackson stating their decision to cede no more land.

Unfortunately, these precautions proved ineffective against lies and deceit. In 1838 the Ogden Land Company signed a highly questionable treaty with the Senecas for their remaining 125,000 acres of New York land. The treaty, which also required the tribe's removal to Kansas, was blatantly illegal; only forty-three chiefs, a minority of the total number, had signed it, and sixteen of those had been bribed. Others had been threatened and intimidated, and some signatures had been forged. Under the terms of the treaty the Senecas were paid $202,000 for land appraised at $2 million.

The U.S. Senate voted on the treaty's ratification three times. Each time the vote was tied. Finally, in 1840, President Martin Van Buren proclaimed the treaty in force even

SENECA NATION LAND: PAST AND PRESENT

Tribal Lands Today

Aboriginal Area

Graphic by Bittle Productions

though the Senate had not approved it by the constitutionally required two-thirds majority. The Senecas, aided by the Quakers, protested vigorously. Finally the United States agreed to negotiate a compromise treaty. Signed in 1842, this treaty confirmed the loss of the Tonawanda and Buffalo Creek reservations but returned the Allegany, Cattaraugus, and Oil Springs reservations.

The Constitution of 1848 and Political Separation from the Tonawanda Senecas

The disastrous treaty of 1838 and other intratribal disagreements led to increasing dissatisfaction with the tribal government. In response to the dissatisfaction, the nation convened a special convention on the Cattaraugus Reservation in December, 1848. At that meeting tribal members abolished their traditional system of chiefs and created the Seneca Republic, adopting a written constitution that mandated an annually elected council of eighteen members and an executive branch consisting of a president, a clerk, and a treasurer.

The 1848 constitution also mandated the separation of church and state and universal male suffrage. These changes altered basic tenets of Seneca culture. Traditional Seneca culture had not distinguished between political and religious functions, and women had traditionally enjoyed great respect and power in tribal matters. (Seneca women did not regain an active vote or the right to hold office until 1964 and 1966, respectively.) In 1849 the commissioner of Indian affairs formally recognized the Seneca Nation as a new government.

The five hundred Tonawanda Senecas, however, had not adopted the new constitution, and they remained distinct from the Seneca Nation. Throughout the 1840s and 1850s they struggled to retain control of their own reservation. They argued that the 1842 treaty affirming the loss of the Tonawanda Reservation was not binding on them, since their chiefs had not signed it. Afraid that any change in their established government would invalidate their claims, they retained their traditional system. In 1857 they signed a new treaty with the United States, permitting them to buy back, at twenty dollars an acre, one-tenth of their former reservation, for which the Ogden Land Company had paid twenty cents an acre in 1838. To this day the Tonawandas maintain their participation in the Iroquois League and are governed by sixteen hereditary chiefs selected by clan mothers in consultation with other women of their clan.

The major problem facing the newly constituted Seneca Nation in the first two decades of its existence was factionalism created within the tribe by differing opinions on how to govern the tribe, administer its land base, and meet the cultural changes and pressures of the outside world. The factionalism grew so severe at several times that it threatened to divide the nation into two politically distinct reservations.

Some former chiefs, ousted by the new system, formed the Old Chiefs' party and worked against the New Government party, which supported the new, elective system. The Old Chiefs' party won office in 1851, 1854, and 1864, but efforts to reinstate the traditional system of chiefs failed repeatedly. The U.S. government, which had lent its support to the new system, suggested a division of the reservations as a compromise measure, but the nation always declined the idea. Eventually the New Government party achieved steady majority support, and the Old Chiefs' party took on its role as an opposition party.

As the two factions settled into an uneasy truce, the nation turned its attention to fine tuning the structure of its new government. In 1854 the Senecas adopted their first written civil code. In 1855 the constitution was amended and the number of councillors reduced from eighteen to twelve, seven from the Cattaraugus and five from the Allegany Reservation. In 1862 voting rights were restricted to Seneca males instead of all male Indian residents, and in 1868 the constitutional provision was omitted that had allowed residency to "any member of the Ancient Confederacy of the Iroquois." For all their complexity, these intratribal and intertribal squabbles soon receded to the background as the nation turned its attention to stopping the threat posed by the state of New York and the influx of white settlers to Seneca lands.

> **The power of making treaties shall be vested in the council, subject to the approval of at least three-fourths of the legal voters and the consent of three-fourths of the mothers of the Nation.**
>
> Section V, Amended Constitution of the Seneca Nation of Indians, 1898

The State and the Railroads Move In

The Senecas, like most eastern tribes in the original thirteen colonies and unlike the tribes in the West, had always maintained a strong relationship with the state government. In the East the tribal-state relationship had existed before the tribal-federal relationship, and the states had always jealously guarded it. The tribal-federal relationship in the eastern states, on the other hand, was quite weak in the 1800s. Involved with Indian wars in the West, the federal government had little money for, or interest in, the smaller and more peaceful eastern tribes. Except for a yearly government distribution of calico, required by the 1794 Canandaigua Treaty, and the presence of Indian agents and superintendents, the federal government provided few services to eastern tribes.

On the one hand, this lack of federal involvement suited the Senecas well, since, like all the Iroquois, they jealously guarded their sovereignty. On the other hand, the lack of a strong federal relationship allowed the state to assume increasing control over Seneca affairs.

New York State had first provided services to Indians in 1795, when the state legislature had appropriated money for the care of Indian orphans. And throughout the eighteenth and early nineteenth centuries the New York legislature, and not Congress, was the guiding force behind the Seneca land

sales. By the 1840s, New York State was making serious attempts to exert general control over the New York reservations. In 1845, three years before the Senecas adopted their
own constitution, the New York state legislature had illegally
but successfully insisted on changes in the Senecas' government, calling for an elected clerk, a treasurer, and the creation of "peacemaker courts," whose function was to hear
disputes involving amounts under fifty dollars. The legislature also called for the election of a chief council president
from among the chiefs and provided for the allotment of
tribal lands to tribal individuals.

In 1855, in a move that ultimately resulted in a landmark
Supreme Court case, the state of New York opened the Thomas Asylum for Orphan and Destitute Indian Children on
the Cattaraugus Reservation. Although many Senecas supported the school, many traditionalists wanted all mission-
ary-run schools removed from the reservation. At any rate,
the school's presence soon extended beyond the education it
offered. From the state's viewpoint the school's existence and
the state's sponsorship of it gave the state the right to impose
its laws and taxes on the Seneca Nation. The state also argued that because the reservations had been state lands between 1838 and 1842, they were therefore taxable. The state
government tried to collect "overdue" state taxes from the
Seneca Nation, and when the nation refused to pay, the state
attempted to sell 13,300 acres of tribal land. The nation sued
in 1866 and won one of the earliest federal decisions holding
that a state has no authority to tax tribal lands.

Unfortunately the Seneca Nation's success in protecting its
land and controlling its use was short-lived. In 1836 the New
York legislature had granted railroad companies permission
to lease lands from the tribes. The original leases were for
short periods and had caused little disruption. By the 1850s,
however, the situation had changed. An 1851 Seneca council
report voiced concern that the construction of the New York
and Erie railroads had introduced to the reservation "a large
number of unknown workmen of low character and loose
habits." More important, the railroad's "temporary" settlements had a way of turning into permanent villages. By the
1860s, whites were asking the federal and state governments
to change their five-year leases into permanent titles.

The Seneca Nation was able to defeat several congressional bills that would have done this. But in 1875, Congress
did authorize establishing six "congressional villages." These
"villages" occupied 5,465 acres, or one-third of the Allegany
Reservation. In 1890, Congress ordered that the villages'
leases run for ninety-nine years instead of the original twelve
and that the state have jurisdiction within village boundaries.
This, in effect, gave the state authority over one-third of the
Allegany Reservation. Within sixty years, the state had expanded its jurisdiction to include all the New York Seneca
reservations.

Original signers of the city of Salamanca lease in 1892. This lease is currently being renegotiated by the tribes and the city. (Courtesy Seneca Iroquois National Museum.)

The congressional village leases continued to be of serious concern to the Seneca Nation, and in the 1940s the nation canceled several leases in the city of Salamanca for nonpayment of back rent. The villages and the state took the tribe to court, arguing that state law prevented the tribal government from taking such action. The Supreme Court disagreed, however, and upheld the Seneca Nation's authority to control its own property. The Court also emphasized that New York law was not applicable to the Senecas. The decision infuriated state officials, who continued to argue that providing state services to the tribe gave them the right to exert control over the tribe. In retaliation the county passed legislation urging the state to cancel all social services to the nation. After the Court's decision, the state began a federal lobbying effort to obtain criminal and civil jurisdiction over the New York reservations. In 1948 and 1950, without Indian consent and despite tribal efforts to defeat the bills, Congress approved the necessary legislation. Soon after the bill's passage, the Bureau of Indian Affairs closed its New York agency and turned educational and health services over to the state.

Kinzua Dam

The Canandaigua Treaty of 1794, discussed earlier in this chapter, recognized and guaranteed the Senecas' right to their land:

> Now the United States acknowledge all the land within the aforementioned boundaries, to be the property of the Seneca nation; and the United States will never claim the same, nor disturb the Seneca nation . . . but it shall remain theirs, until they choose to sell the same to the people of the United States, who have the right to purchase.

In 1928, however, without the Senecas' knowledge or approval, the Army Corps of Engineers began surveying the Allegany Reservation with the aim of building a large reservoir. The reservoir was to be part of the Kinzua Dam project to reduce flooding on the Allegheny River and to provide recreational facilities to the citizens of Pennsylvania and New York. The Great Depression and World War II intervened, and the plan was shelved. Then, in 1956, the Seneca Nation learned that Congress, without the Senecas' input or consent, had appropriated money for the construction of a large reservoir on the Senecas' reservation. Greatly alarmed, the nation tried various avenues in an attempt to stop the project. Using the guarantees of the 1794 Canandaigua Treaty as a basis, the Senecas' went to court and sought an injunction against the dam's construction. With Quaker assistance they hired two eminent engineers to report on the feasibility of alternate sites.

The nation's efforts were in vain, however. The federal court ruled that the U.S. government's actions were legal under the domestic law of eminent domain. The Senecas' treaties offered no protection. The federal government had the authority to make treaties and the authority to break them. And despite evidence from several sources that the dam could be built more cheaply and with less human suffering elsewhere, neither Congress nor President John F. Kennedy intervened to halt construction.

The reservoir created by the dam flooded 10,000 acres of the Allegany Reservation. This left residents with only 2,300 acres flat enough for use. When the Kinzua Dam was completed, in 1965, the nation's ancestral lands, farms, hunting and fishing sites, cemeteries, and homes lay under water. More than one-third of the reservation's members were forced to move from their homes, and three thousand graves had to be relocated.

The Kinzua Dam not only altered the reservation's landscape but changed its living and social patterns as well. Two new communities, Jimerstown and Steamburg, were established. Relocated residents were given new housing in these communities, but the living arrangements were unsatisfactory to many Senecas, who were not accustomed to relatively dense, suburbanlike living. Before the dam's construction, tribal members typically had lived in isolated rural areas surrounded by woods and game.

The dam also destroyed the cultural heart of the Seneca Nation. The Army Corps of Engineers had unceremoniously unearthed the remains of Cornplanter and three hundred of his descendants, moved them to a newly constructed Indian-white cemetery, and flooded the old burial ground. Desecrating this land was equivalent to moving Abraham Lincoln's tomb or flooding Bethlehem to build a skating rink.

Unable to block the dam's construction, the Seneca Nation tried at least to get compensation for its lost lands. Congress eventually, in 1964, appropriated $15 million to the Seneca Nation. The reparation bill itself brought near disaster, however, because included in its provisions was the requirement that, to qualify for the reparations, the nation submit a plan for terminating its relationship with the federal government. Fortunately, by the time the plan was submitted, in 1967, the termination policy had been discredited, and the plan was ignored.

The nation concentrated on putting its reparation settlement to good use for education, economic development, and construction. Realizing that the best insurance for the future lay in educating its members, the nation established a $1.8 million scholarship fund. It also worked on increasing its economic self-sufficiency by developing a sixty-acre industrial park on the Cattaraugus Reservation. Community halls and tribal office complexes were built on each reservation. The following sections examine these accomplishments in greater detail.

MODERN TRIBAL GOVERNMENT

The Seneca Nation's legal status and political system are both unique. The Senecas have a long history of treaty relations with the United States and are a federally recognized tribe. They also maintain a close relationship with the state of New York. As discussed previously, these two relationships have often threatened the nation's existence, but in every instance the nation has fought to protect its sovereignty—whether

Maintaining good relations between the state of New York and their own nation has been a priority of the Senecas. Shown here, in 1977, are U.S. Representative Jack Kemp and Seneca Nation of Indians President Calvin E. Lay. (Courtesy Seneca Iroquois National Museum.)

by resisting the imposition of state taxes, fighting against allotment, or vetoing acceptance of the Indian Reorganization Act.

The Senecas' success has come in large part from their traditional interest in the political life of their community. A community's strength depends greatly upon its government's ability to solve its internal disputes peaceably, to alter its structure to meet new challenges, and to maintain the support of its constituents. In 1848 the Senecas established an elective system of government—a change needed to better protect the community from outside threats. As mentioned, the change in government was not universally accepted and the ensuing disputes were worked out slowly through the development of a party system of politics. This party system remains in operation today on both the Cattaraugus and the Allegany reservations.

Every two years, the People's party and the New Deal party meet throughout the summer to draw up their respective platforms and their slates of candidates for tribal office. In general, any tribal member may place himself or herself on the party ballot. A primary election is held each August to vote on each party's candidates. The primaries are open, meaning that all eligible voters may vote in each party's election.

Seneca national elections are held on the first Tuesday of November in even-numbered years. All tribal members over the age of twenty-one may vote. Tribal membership in New York State follows the traditional matrilineal system—all children of enrolled Seneca mothers are eligible for enrollment. During the Seneca national election, voters elect tribal members to the three branches of government: executive, legislative, and judicial. Unlike the federal system, the Seneca government is made up of three interdependent, not independent, branches.

> . . . the right to enrollment . . . depends upon the laws and usages of the Seneca Nation and is to be determined by that Nation for itself without interference or dictation from the supreme courts of the state. . . . The conclusion is inescapable that the Seneca tribe remains a separate nation, that its powers of self-government are retained with the sanction of the state, that the ancient customs and usages of the nation, except in a few particulars, remain, unabolished, the law of Indian land; that in its capacity as a sovereign nation, the Seneca Nation is not subservient to the orders and directions of the courts of New York State, that above all, the Seneca Nation retains for itself the power of determining who are Senecas, and in that respect is above interference and dictation.
>
> *Patterson v. Council of Seneca Nation, 1927*

SENECA NATION GOVERNMENT

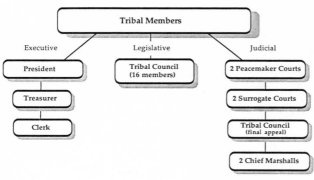

Graphic by Bittle Productions

Seneca Nation of Indians Council, 1984–86. (Courtesy Seneca Iroquois National Museum.)

The Legislative Branch

The legislative branch is the most important and powerful branch of Seneca government. A sixteen-member council, eight elected from each reservation, forms the legislative arm. The councillors, who are elected to four-year terms, must be at least twenty-one and have lived on the reservation for at least one year. The council meets once a month and is responsible for passing the nation's laws, establishing programs and services to meet the needs of its citizens, and appropriating funds to run the programs and the government itself.

According to the Seneca constitution, tribal law must be consistent with federal and state law. That is, it must not violate state or federal law, although it need not be identical. The constitution also empowers the council to make treaties with other governments, subject to the approval of three-fourths of the legal voters and three-fourths of the "Mothers" of the nation. The constitution also stipulates that all constitutional changes must be approved by a majority of those eligible to vote, not just of those voting.

The Executive Branch

The president, clerk, treasurer, and chief marshal, as well as various appointed officers, make up the executive branch. The president's function, like that of the U.S. president, is to execute faithfully the laws of the Seneca Nation, to bring important issues to the council's attention, and to represent the nation in its dealings with other governments. The president also has important appointive powers. He or she ap-

points a highway commissioner (who oversees tribal roads),
an assessor (who assesses the value of tribal and individuals'
lands), an overseer of the poor (who distributes funds to help
poor tribal members), and committee members. The committees assist the executive and legislative branches by reviewing areas of concern and issuing reports and proposals
for the council's consideration.

The treasurer keeps the nation's financial records and fills
in for the president in case of illness or death. The clerk, who
serves as the nation's secretary, records the minutes of council meetings and maintains the nation's records, including the
tribal membership rolls and tribal lease arrangements with
Indians and non-Indians. Historically, the Senecas recorded
their important political transactions on wampum belts. Today the nation's records and files are stored in the tribal government's computer system. This modern system provides an
instantly accessible and accurate accounting of the nation's
membership, finances, employees, and tribal programs.

The Judicial Branch

The Seneca Nation's judicial branch is made up of two peacemaker courts, two surrogate courts, the council (in its role
as Court of Final Appeal), and two chief marshals. Each
reservation elects three peacemaker judges, one surrogate
judge, and a chief marshal. The chief marshals assist the
president by keeping order at council meetings and other
tribal functions.

Since the passage of the 1948 law, discussed earlier, giving
the state jurisdiction over New York tribes, state courts have
held concurrent, or shared, jurisdiction with Seneca tribal
courts. In practice, the state courts refer all disputes between
tribal members to the Seneca Nation's courts for settlement.
The peacemaker court, which meets as needed during the
evenings, settles land disputes, performs marriages and divorces, and imposes fines for fishing violations. The surrogate courts handle deeds, powers of attorney, wills, adop-
tions, and guardianship cases.

The peacemaker and surrogate courts may apply tribal,
federal, or state law to the case they are hearing, depending
upon the circumstances. Traditional law is still honored by
the Senecas, especially in the regulation of property. For instance, individuals can own only surface property rights, "a
plowshare deep." Resources below that depth, such as minerals and oils, belong to the nation. In the case of gravel,
which lies close to the surface, any sales profits are divided
evenly between the individual owner and the nation.

Unlike Anglo-American courts, which are formal and
based on an adversarial system of justice, the peacemaker
and surrogate courts are informal and conciliatory, aiming at
restoring harmony—a traditional Seneca value. Individuals
can be represented by a lawyer, but most often a relative or
friend acts as a spokesperson. There are no prosecutors.

Rather, the peacemaker or surrogate judge questions the parties involved and then makes a decision.

The Seneca court system differs from the American judicial system in two other important ways. First, the tribal courts have no right of judicial review over council actions—that is, they have no authority to rule on the constitutionality of a tribal law or decision—and second, they are not independent of the legislative branch. According to the Seneca constitution, the tribal council functions as a "supreme court" and hears appeals from the peacemaker and surrogate courts. All decisions of the tribal council are final and cannot be appealed to state or federal courts.

Social Services

Using the reparation money from the Kinzua Dam along with funds from tribal awards, leases, businesses, and state and federal grants, the Seneca Nation has set up a variety of educational, cultural, social, health, public-safety, and housing programs for its citizens. Some of these are discussed below.

Education of the Youth and Care for the Elderly

The Seneca Nation has survived thanks to the determination and strength of its older members and ancestors. Its future depends upon the well-being and commitment of its youth. With these thoughts in mind, the Senecas devote a significant portion of their resources to educating their youth and caring for their elderly.

Since the 1950s, all Seneca students in both elementary and high school have attended nearby public schools off-reservation. The nation's focus today is on supplementing the state's basic educational program. Both reservations offer Head Start programs that prepare preschool children for elementary school. Both reservations also run day-care centers for children of working parents. The Allegany Day Care Center uses the progressive Montessori system of education. Tribal buses pick older children up after school and take them to the tribal library or to the recreation buildings, where they read, study, or play until their parents pick them up at 5:30.

The nation has set up a scholarship fund for Seneca high-school graduates who want to attend college or vocational school. Adults who did not complete high school can take advantage of an adult education program leading to a high-school diploma. The adult education program also offers classes in typing, shorthand, income-tax assistance, and speed reading.

During the summer months the tribe's Health Department runs a recreational-educational program for youth. About twenty students in their midteens attend the half-day program during each of its month-long sessions. The students discuss youth-related issues such as alcohol abuse, sexuality, child rearing, communication, health, and social skills.

The Seneca Iroquois National Museum is devoted to the preservation of the prehistory, history, and contemporary culture of the Seneca Indians and the Iroquois people. (Courtesy State of New York, Department of Economic Development.)

Two of the most important educational endeavors sponsored by the nation are the Seneca Nation libraries and the Seneca-Iroquois National Museum. The libraries provide educational, cultural, and recreational services to the residents of the Allegany and Cattaraugus reservations. Funded by the New York state legislature, the libraries offer general library services as well as cultural exhibits and demonstrations of such arts as splint-basket making, ribbon-shirt making, stone carving, and indoor and outdoor snow-snake demonstrations. The tribally owned Seneca-Iroquois National Museum is run by a trained Seneca director and staff. The outside of the museum is decorated with traditional symbols and designs. Displays inside include a wide range of exhibits and artifacts depicting early Iroquois culture and traditions. The museum also houses wampum belts and historically significant documents, making it the Seneca Nation's repository of the past and link to the future, a place where younger and older generations, both Indian and non-Indian, can learn about traditional Seneca ways.

The nation has worked hard to ensure that the lives of its elderly are as comfortable as possible. Four days a week the elderly are brought together for a hot lunch prepared by tribal members. For those who live some distance from the community this provides a time to visit and exchange information. Many of the nation's elderly continue to live in their own homes or with family members. Others live in the nation's elderly housing unit in Salamanca, which is open to Indians and non-Indians alike. A tribal bus transports the elderly to their noon meals, to the health clinic, or to doctor's appointments in nearby towns.

Health Care

The health-care needs of the Senecas are met by the Seneca Department of Health. This department operates two medical clinics on each reservation in addition to the important Human Services Division. The clinics offer general medical and dental care to tribal members and are open during both daytime and evening hours to allow all tribal members to obtain medical care. Specialists including a gynecologist, a psychiatrist, and a podiatrist visit the clinics twice a month. The clinics run their own pharmacies. Transportation is available to the clinics and to the human services office. The Human Services Division offers alcohol, drug-abuse, and mental-health counseling, including programs in juvenile delinquency and child abuse. The division also helps needy tribal members obtain public assistance, food stamps, or Medicare and Medicaid benefits.

Public Safety

Maintaining public safety and order is an important obligation of all governments. This task in the Seneca Nation is carried out by the Seneca Security Force, the Seneca Game

Commission, and the volunteer fire department. Each reservation has its own fire truck, staffed by about forty volunteers, and its own ambulance, staffed by trained paramedics. An agreement with nearby local governments has led to cooperation in fighting fires and providing ambulance service. Cooperation, although more informal, also exists between the Seneca Security Force and local municipal and county police forces. Organized in 1976, the four-member tribal security force receives the same training as state-certified-off-reservation forces.

The two game wardens employed by the Seneca Game Commission are responsible for issuing fishing permits to non-Indians and for ensuring that tribal fishing laws are obeyed. Although tribes cannot exercise criminal jurisdiction over non-Indians, the Senecas have passed a tribal law that violators of Seneca game laws will have their catch and equipment confiscated by the game warden. After appearing in tribal court and paying a civil fine, the equipment is returned.

Economic Development

The Seneca Nation tribal government has worked aggressively over the past two decades to increase the tribes' economic self-sufficiency. The unemployment rate of the Sen-

Seneca ironworker. The Iroquois are renowned as construction workers on high-rise buildings in the metropolitan areas of the eastern United States. (Courtesy Seneca Iroquois National Museum.)

Groundbreaking ceremony for the Seneca Nation Sports Arena, Cattaraugus Reservation. Members of the Seneca Nation Indian Council and the New Town Lacrosse Team are present. (Courtesy Seneca Iroquois National Museum.)

eca—approximately 30 percent—is much lower than that of many other tribes. Still, it is far higher than the national average—and it is growing. Decreased federal funding in the early 1980s reduced reservation programs and cost many jobs. The poor reservation economy has also meant that many tribal members have been forced to move to find work; almost half of all tribal members live off the reservation. Economic development would give tribal members job opportunities and provide the tribal government with increased funds for programs to meet the social and cultural needs of tribal citizens.

Using money from the Kinzua Dam settlement, the tribe built a sixty-acre industrial park on the Cattaraugus Reservation but has so far failed to attract major industry to the site. The tribe has met with more success in its efforts to develop the reservation's recreational potential. In the mid-1970s the nation built a sixteen-lane bowling alley in Salamanca. A sports arena on the Cattaraugus Reservation is also used for the nation's lacrosse games. In the late 1970s, deciding to make the best of the forced flooding of their lands by the Kinzua Dam project, the nation began construction of the Highbanks Campgrounds on the banks of the Allegheny Reservoir. Fifty cabins and more than one hundred campsites are available for daily or weekly rental. The campgrounds, which are open year round, offer visitors cross-country skiing and ice fishing in the winter and camping, swimming, boating, and fishing in the summer. In 1986 the nation constructed a mini-mart and gas station, selling gas and cigarettes at discount prices.

Highbanks Campground, which overlooks the Allegheny River Reservoir, on the Seneca Reservation. The camp has several kinds of cabins, a swimming pool, a playground, and boat docks. (Courtesy State of New York, Department of Economic Development.)

The nation's most successful enterprise to date is its bingo operation. Games are held in the tribal community halls—four nights a week on the Cattaraugus Reservation and two nights a week on the Allegany Reservation. Unlike other tribal bingo games, which are partially owned by outside businesses, the Senecas' enterprise is entirely Seneca owned and operated. Approximately six thousand people from on and off the reservation attend the games each week. Profits from the games help underwrite such tribal efforts as the day-care center, recreational programs, and building-repair projects.

Seneca economic plans for the future include exploring for oil and gas and completing a hotel and restaurant near a new highway running through the reservation. Construction funds for the hotel and restaurant will come in part from a $2 million cash settlement the nation won from the state of New York in the mid-1970s in a battle to obtain just compensation from the state for Seneca lands used to build the highway.

CHAPTER 7

THE MUSCOGEE (CREEK) NATION OF OKLAHOMA

The twenty-two members of the House of the Muscogee Nation, many newly elected under the terms of a recently adopted reapportionment plan, have gathered in the tribal council chambers in Okmulgee, Oklahoma. Designed along traditional lines, the building rises from the earth, a circular, mound-shaped structure. The house speaker, chosen from among the council members, calls the meeting to order. The new council members are welcomed and procedures of the meeting explained. The speaker then yields the floor to the principal chief, who delivers his state of the nation address. The principal chief details the progress made in the previous year and the main objectives for the coming year. High on the government's list of priorities is the continued development of the nation's judicial system. Emphasis on local control is a tradition among the Muscogees and one the present government seeks to continue, in part by setting up eight district courts to hear local criminal and civil disputes.

Today, the thirty-four organized rural and small urban communities of the once-powerful Muscogee Confederacy (see chapter 2) are scattered throughout the towns and rural areas of central Oklahoma. Two groups still inhabit the Muscogees' aboriginal homeland, the area that now encompasses the states of Georgia, most of Alabama, and the panhandle of Florida. Approximately four hundred eastern Muscogees live in southwest Alabama, descendants of tribal members who refused to move to Indian Territory. This group has recently been granted federal recognition. Another six hundred Muscogees live in northwest Florida. Federally unrecognized, this group is organized under the Northwest Florida Creek Indian Council and has received state support since 1975. Other groups formerly in the confederacy include the Seminole tribes of Oklahoma and Florida, the Coushatta of Louisiana, and the Alabama-Coushatta of Texas.

HISTORY

Hernando de Soto invaded Muscogee lands in 1540 and was followed by numerous other explorers, traders, and settlers. At first all faced opposition from the Muscogees, but by the 1600s a fairly peaceful relationship existed between the confederacy and the European powers. The Muscogees quickly adopted horses, guns, metal utensils, and cloth brought by the colonists, and for the first two hundred years of white contact the Muscogees skillfully played one European nation off against another, successfully using their own strength and political skills to win favorable trading concessions and military alliances.

Serious threats to the confederacy's security began in 1733, when the Lower Creeks, a group within the confederacy, permitted Gen. James Oglethorpe to establish the colony of Georgia. A formal agreement specified that colonial settlements were to be confined to areas not needed by the Muscogees and that Oglethorpe was to establish a licensed trader in each *talwa* to increase the Muscogees' access to trade goods. Chief Tomochichi of the Lower Creeks even traveled to England and presented King George II with a bundle of eagle feathers, explaining that "these feathers are a sign of peace in our land and have been carried from town to town there and we have brought them over to leave with you, 0 Great King, as a sign of everlasting peace." England, in return, promised friendship and protection and acknowledged that the area "doth by ancient right belong to the Creek [Muscogee] Nation." The Muscogees soon learned, however, that the king's words and Oglethorpe's promises were meaningless. The Muscogee word for the immigrants soon became "Ekvn-Anoksvlke," meaning "People Greedily Grasping after the Lands of the Red People." Instead of barring or removing settlers from unceded areas as promised, the colony allowed and even encouraged homesteaders to settle in such areas. Then it would demand the area from the tribe. Since the coming of the settlers had ruined the hunting, the tribe often agreed.

The Relationship with the New Nation

During the late 1700s, Alexander McGillivray, son of a Scottish trader and a Muscogee woman, assumed leadership of the Muscogee Confederacy. Knowing both cultures well, McGillivray clearly understood the changes threatening the Muscogee Nation, and he realized that the Muscogees' decentralized government would be difficult to defend against the organized, "divide and conquer" politics of the colonists. Accordingly, McGillivray worked to change the Muscogee Great Council from a loose association of town governments to a more centralized, forceful, and active institution. To effect this change, however, required that the *talwas* relinquish their control over local Muscogee political and cultural life (see chapter 2). This change came only after many decades.

In the meantime, McGillivray attempted to counter Georgia's threat by strengthening the Muscogees' alliances with Spain, England, and, later, the United States. This tactic proved effective for several years. A military alliance with Spain brought arms to use against the Georgians, and a trade alliance with England meant less dependence on colonial traders. After the Revolutionary War, McGillivray negotiated with the U.S. government to obtain federal recognition and protection of Muscogee lands. In 1790 a treaty was signed in which the United States recognized Muscogee holdings and promised to protect them, and the Muscogees extended peace and friendship to the United States. This treaty was one of McGillivray's final acts. In 1793 he died, at the age of thirty-four.

For the next several years the Muscogees continued to strengthen and centralize their national council. Each town sent five or six delegates to the council, which, in turn, appointed the principal chief and passed laws of national concern. Towns were grouped into districts, and each district was governed by one man responsible for enforcing the nation's laws. By 1818 these laws had been codified into a written document.

Changes in farming patterns, in addition to the changes brought about by the district plan, also diminished the traditional power of the towns. Benjamin Hawkins, Indian agent for the Muscogees in 1796, was determined to bring "civilization" to the nation. He encouraged the Muscogees to give up their communal farm plots and establish individual farms outside of the *talwas*. He also introduced new crops and increased the use of the steel plow. When cotton became a cash crop, several Muscogee families began farming for profit rather than for subsistence. This innovation led to the formation of a wealthy class. Many Muscogee farms, like those of their white neighbors, were worked by black slaves.

By becoming more like whites, however, the tribes were not trying to assimilate into white society but to strengthen and preserve their traditional existence, hoping that they would be left in peace. No amount of assimilation, however, could alter the fact that Indian tribes occupied lands coveted by whites. The Georgians' hunger for land, especially after the invention of the cotton gin, became insatiable. In 1802 and again in 1805, the Muscogee Nation ceded portions of its land to whites.

In 1811 the Muscogees met with Tecumseh, the famed Shawnee leader and himself the son of a Muscogee woman. As discussed in chapter 4, Tecumseh believed that the future of all Indian nations lay in uniting and driving the Americans from their shores. The decision by some Muscogees to join Tecumseh's alliance soon embroiled the nation in a bloody war. Tecumseh's followers, known as the Red Sticks because of the red war clubs they carried into battle, successfully conquered several non-allied Muscogee towns and then marched on Fort Mims, near Mobile, Alabama. Caught by surprise, three hundred soldiers, settlers, and non-allied Muscogees died in the attack. Gen. Andrew Jackson counterattacked and laid waste to loyal, neutral, and hostile parts of the Muscogee Nation. During the last battle of this campaign, at Horseshoe

Bend, Jackson and his Choctaw, Cherokee, and Muscogee allies killed over five hundred Red Sticks.

After the war Jackson showed no gratitude to his Muscogee warriors, demanding instead that the nation cede 22 million acres to the United States in return for $195,000 in damages. Congress sold the land to white settlers for over $11 million, but the payment owed to the Muscogees was not completely paid off until forty-one years later.

Removal

As discussed in chapter 4, when England and Spain left the Southeast, the Muscogees lost useful allies. Facing no competition, the southern states stepped up their demands for Indian removal to the Louisiana Territory.

The Muscogee Nation repeatedly refused to negotiate land cessions and even passed a law, in 1818 or 1819, declaring that no tribal lands could be sold without approval of the national council, under penalty of death. Federal negotiators, however, ignored the nation's refusal to negotiate and concluded a series of illegal treaties. In 1825 federal officials bribed William McIntosh, Speaker of the Lower Towns, and a handful of his followers into signing the Treaty of Indian Springs, which ceded all Muscogee lands in Georgia and two-thirds of their Alabama lands in return for new land in what is now Oklahoma.

> No person shall permit a White into the Nation to live except the whole Nation agree to it.
>
> Law 49,
> Muscogee Constitution, 1824

When the national council learned of this treaty, it declared McIntosh a traitor and sentenced him to die. On May 1, 1825, a duly appointed execution party surrounded McIntosh's house and set it on fire. As he appeared in a doorway of the burning house, McIntosh died in a hail of bullets. The execution helped convince President John Adams that the Treaty of Indian Springs had been fraudulent. He ordered new negotiations. The Muscogees were forced into a compromise, and, in the Treaty of Washington, they agreed to cede their Georgia lands.

The state of Alabama was also determined to rid itself of the tribe, however, and passed a series of illegal laws outlawing tribal government and denying tribal members basic rights. Shortly after these laws were passed, the U.S. Congress passed the Indian Removal Bill of 1830 (see chapter 4).

> And be it further enacted if any person or persons should employ a White Man to work, after work done he shall go back into his own country, shall not stay no longer than the work done.
>
> Law 41,
> Muscogee Constitution, 1824

In response, the Muscogee Nation, in March, 1832, reluctantly signed a second Treaty of Washington, in which it ceded more than 3 million acres to the United States and divided its remaining 2.2 million acres among individual tribal members. The treaty provided that tribal members wishing to join McIntosh's followers, who had moved west after signing the Treaty of Indian Springs, could do so, but only 630 of the 21,792 tribal members chose to leave. The Muscogees hoped that, by making the compromises they did in the second Treaty of Washington, they would at least be allowed to remain in their homeland, on the lands they loved.

William McIntosh. (Courtesy Smithsonian Institution, National Anthropological Archives.)

Instead, the greed, fraud, and deception escalated. Overnight, whites appeared with fistfuls of counterfeit deeds. Forbidden by state law to testify in court, the Muscogees were legally powerless to protect their lands. Hostilities erupted, leading eventually to an uprising known as the Creek War of 1836. In retaliation the U.S. Army rounded up the Muscogees and forced them west. In 1836 and 1837 approximately 20,000 tribal members made the 1,200-mile trip to Indian Territory under military guard. Many—estimates range from 3,500 to 7,000—were buried along the way.

Rebuilding in Indian Territory

The Upper Creeks (the more traditional faction of the Muscogees), under the leadership of Opthleyaholo, settled along the territory's Canadian River after their trek west. The Lower Creeks, many of whom had belonged to the faction led by William McIntosh, clustered near the Arkansas River. Both groups had left behind prosperous farms, comfortable homes, and well-established political and social systems. In their new location they encountered starvation, sickness, demoralization, abysmal living conditions, increased factionalism, and harassment by the tribes indigenous to the area. More than one-fourth of the population died during the first twelve months in Indian Territory.

The Muscogees set about rebuilding a life for themselves. They reestablished approximately forty-five of their towns, which continued to function as the basic unit of government. A head chief, or *micco*, two second chiefs, and from four to forty-five lawmakers governed each town. The last vestiges of Red and White clan designations disappeared with removal and were replaced by the increasingly important distinction between Upper and Lower towns. The Upper Creeks were highly traditional and had many full-blooded members. While many of the mixed-blood Lower Creeks readily adopted aspects of white culture, Upper Creeks did not. For years the Upper Creeks outlawed wearing non-Indian attire and attending Christian religious services. Since each faction was governed by its own principal chief, the nation in effect had a three-tiered system of government. Both chiefs, sitting side by side, jointly ran the annual council meetings. The council was made up of representatives from all the towns. The council passed national laws, subject to the final approval of the chiefs.

The Muscogees in Indian Territory continued to hold education in high esteem. By the time of the Civil War, the Five Civilized Tribes boasted a higher literacy rate and a higher educational level than their surrounding white neighbors. Children and adults read books and newspapers in their own language, using the Cherokee syllabary invented by Sequoyah or the alphabet of Muscogee missionaries and interpreters.

Agriculture remained the Muscogees' primary source of income. The nation owned six million acres of land, which was held communally. Individuals were given the right to cultivate as much land as they needed or wanted. Tribal law protected an individual's rights of occupancy and to any improvements made on the property. Within ten years after removal, Muscogee farmers were producing surplus crops. In 1846 the nation exported 100,000 bushels of corn, most of it sent to Ireland to help relieve the hardships of the potato famine.

The Civil War

A generation after their removal, the Muscogees found themselves involved in yet another white man's war. And once again the repercussions included death, destruction, and a deepening division within Muscogee society. This time the Lower and Upper factions wore the colors gray and blue, siding respectively with the Confederacy and the Union.

When the first white man came over the wide waters, he was but a little man . . . very little. His legs were cramped by sitting long a little man . . . very little. His legs were cramped by sitting long in his big boat, and he begged for a little land. . . .

When he came to these shores the Indians gave him land, and kindled fires to make him comfortable. . . .

But when the white man had warmed himself at the Indian's fire, and had filled himself with the Indian's hominy, he became very large. He stopped not at the mountain tops, and his foot covered the plains and the valleys. His hands grasped the eastern and western seas. Then he became our Great Father. He loved his red children, but he said: "You must move a little farther, lest by accident I tread on you."

With one foot he pushed the red men across the Oconee, and with the other he trampled down the graves of our fathers. . . .

On another occasion he said, "Get a little farther; go beyond the Oconee and the Ocmulee [Indian settlements in South Carolina and Georgia]—there is a pleasant country." He also said, "It shall be yours forever."

Now he says, "The land you live upon is not yours. Go beyond the Mississippi; there is game; there you may remain while the grass grows and the rivers run."

Will not our Great Father come there also? He loves his red children, and his tongue is not forked.

Brothers! I have listened to a great many talks from our Great Father. But they always began and ended in this—"Get a little farther; you are too near me." I have spoken.

Speckled Snake, Muscogee Chief, in 1829, when the Muscogees were considering the move west of the Mississippi River

The Indian agent for the Muscogees was an ardent seces-
sionist who worked actively to bring the tribe to the Confederacy's side. In July, 1861, the mostly mixed-blood Lower
Creeks signed a treaty with the Confederacy, which recognized tribal sovereignty and guaranteed that Muscogee lands
would never be allotted and tribal members never placed under the authority of a territorial government. The Confederacy also promised to pay the annuities owed to the nation
by the United States but unpaid in recent years. The treaty
also legalized slavery and provided for the election of a Muscogee and a Seminole delegate to the Confederate Congress.

The Upper Creeks opposed this treaty, arguing that it violated the nation's prior treaty commitments to the United
States. In August, 1861, the largely full-blood Upper Creeks
established a separate government loyal to the United States.
For four years the two factions fought against each other. By
the war's end, Muscogee lands and property, especially those
of the Upper Creeks, lay destroyed.

After the war the United States, overlooking its own broken treaty commitments and heedless that many Muscogees
had died fighting for the Union, charged the Muscogee Nation with treason. In 1866 the Muscogees were forced to negotiate a new treaty in which they ceded almost half their
lands, abolished slavery, and accepted the "freedmen," their
former slaves, as members of the tribe with full property
rights. The treaty also allowed construction of railroads
through the Muscogee Nation and outlined the eventual goal
of a unified Indian government for all tribes in the Indian
Territory. The three million acres sold by the Muscogees for
thirty cents an acre became home to the Cheyennes, Arapahos, Kickapoos, Sacs and Foxes, and the Iowas.

For the second time in less than forty years, the Muscogee
Nation had to rebuild following destruction by forces generated in the white, "civilized" world. The obstacles to rebuilding were great. Almost one-fourth of the nation's population
had died. Its land base was reduced by half, and its economy
was in shambles. Land had to be cleared, crops planted, livestock rounded up, and houses rebuilt. Muscogee schools, a
model system before the war, were closed. Most important,
the nation's social fabric had been torn apart, and the nation
had been divided against itself.

A Second Rebirth

The Muscogees made a surprisingly rapid economic and
social recovery. Within five years after the war the nation
had reestablished its school system, now with a unified
school board that had full responsibility for teacher contracts, school curriculum, and school construction. The new
system included three boarding schools, five day schools,
three orphanages, and thirty-one neighborhood schools, six
of which were for children of former slaves. Older students

were sent to colleges and seminaries in the states at the nation's expense. In the 1870s, in perhaps the first piece of social-welfare legislation in the United States, the national council passed a bill allotting thirty dollars a year to handicapped and elderly citizens with no means of support.

Political unification of the full-blood and mixed-blood factions remained a difficult and pressing problem. After the war the two sides met and signed an agreement stating that the Muscogee people should "unite and live as one Nation . . . There was to be no North and no South among the Muskogee people, but peace and friendship." In October, 1867, the nation unanimously adopted a new constitution and code of laws aimed at healing internal divisions through governmental changes. Okmulgee was designated the nation's capital, and a new council house was constructed.

The new government was patterned after the U.S. system. The legislative branch, or national council, was made up of a House of Kings (like the Senate) and a House of Warriors (like the House of Representatives). Each of the forty-eight towns (forty-five Indian towns, three freedmen towns) elected one representative to the House of Kings and at least one representative, plus an additional delegate for every two hundred people, to the House of Warriors.

Muscogee Nation Council House, Okmulgee, Oklahoma. The tribe completed this capitol in 1878. It housed council sessions, political meetings, religious services, and also served as a school. Unable to maintain it, the tribe eventually sold the building to the city of Okmulgee for $100,000, less than half its estimated value. The Council House is probably the scene of the execution of Timmie Jack. (Courtesy Donald L. Fixico.)

Council room of the Muscogee Nation Council House, Okmulgee, Oklahoma. The large chair is for the principal chief; others are for assistants and council members. (Courtesy Donald L. Fixico.)

The executive branch consisted of a principal chief and second chief, elected by male citizens over the age of eighteen, and a treasurer and a national interpreter chosen by the council to serve during each administration's four-year term. In addition, the constitution authorized the principal chief to hire a private secretary (usually a tribal member who was fluent in English), an office reminiscent of the traditional Speaker.

The judicial branch consisted of a national Supreme Court composed of five judges chosen by the council, six prosecuting attorneys appointed by the principal chief, and a law-enforcement agency, or "lighthorse company," of one captain and four privates elected by each district. Civil cases involving more than one hundred dollars were handled by the Supreme Court, and the district courts were responsible for all criminal cases and minor civil cases. National officers held office for four years; district officers served for two years.

Penalties in criminal cases included the death penalty for murder, fifty lashes for the first rape offense and death for the second, restitution to the victim and fifty lashes for the first theft offense, one hundred lashes for the second, and death for the third. Selling and drinking liquor were prohibited, and the lighthorsemen were authorized to "search, find and spill" intoxicants. Any cases involving U.S. citizens or violations of federal liquor laws were handled by the federal courts.

One of the greatest changes brought about by the 1867 constitution was the system of voting by secret ballot. Under the traditional system nominations had been made from the floor at council meetings. Nominees then stood in different areas of the council grounds, surrounded by their supporters. Hence, openness and responsibility for one's opinions were important elements of traditional Muscogee society. Many Muscogees considered the secret-ballot system a serious departure from traditional practice.

In 1871, four years after the secret-ballot system was adopted, Muscogee traditionalists occupied the council house to protest it. Known as the Sands Rebellion, this protest ended quickly, but differences between progressives and traditionalists continued to fester. Confrontations broke out again ten years later, in 1881, in what became known as the Green Peach War (in reference to the season of the year). The dispute consisted of a series of rather serious skirmishes that went on for several months and ended formally in 1883 when Samuel Checote, leader of the mixed-blood, progressive faction, and Isparhecher, leader of the full-blood, traditional faction, signed an agreement to abide by the constitution.

Statehood and the Near Loss of a Nation

The nation had barely begun to rebuild and reunify after the Civil War when it was again buffeted by outside forces. In 1870 construction of railroad lines through the nation began. With the railroad came disorderly crews who squatted on tribal lands and established shantytowns. The council quickly passed a series of ordinances to try to control this influx of outsiders. All noncitizens had to obtain residence permits to live on Muscogee lands, and Muscogee citizens hiring noncitizens needed permission from the chief. Noncitizens could hire only citizens as employees. The council repeatedly asked federal agents to remove squatters from the nation's lands. Although the United States was required by law to protect tribal lands from trespass, the council's requests remained largely unanswered.

By 1890 the population within Muscogee Nation lands had reached 17,912, only slightly more than half of whom were Muscogee citizens. As settlers and corporations closed in, eager for a piece of this last frontier, Congress increasingly proposed legislation to dispossess tribes of their lands and eliminate tribal governments. The nation attempted to counteract these proposals by maintaining permanent delegates in Washington to lobby against adverse bills. Closer to home, the nation worked to unite the tribes of the Indian Territory through a series of intertribal councils.

In 1870, Okmulgee became the official meeting place of the general council of Indian Territory. In a move at first encouraged by the United States, this council adopted the Okmulgee Constitution. Meant as the governing document for a proposed Indian state, the constitution provided for the federal union of all territory tribes to be governed by a governor, a house of representatives, and senate. Although the plan was never adopted, the council continued to meet for the next ten years.

The Execution of Timmie Jack

A sense of honor and of the sanctity of one's word: these had high value in tribal society. They were important and pervasive enough to influence the structure of traditional tribal justice systems. As the story of Timmie Jack demonstrates, jails were not a necessary part of traditional society. Timmie Jack had given his word.

In 1896 Timmie Jack, an Euchee Indian of the Muscogee Nation, was convicted and sentenced to death by a Creek jury for the murder of James Brown. He was sentenced to be publicly executed (the last such execution in the Muscogee Nation). Between his conviction and the date of his execution, however,—a period of nearly five months—he was free to attend to his business and spend time with his family.

After his trial in January, Timmie Jack returned home to arrange his affairs. On May 1, he and his wife returned to Okmulgee for his execution. After inspecting and trying his coffin for size, Timmie Jack went to the Council House grounds where his execution was to take place. As was the Creek custom, the sentenced man selected one of his closest friends to execute him. Then, seated upon a box with his eyes covered and a white piece of cloth pinned over his heart, he faced his execution. He had earlier donned a new suit of clothes. After the shot, Timmie Jack's body was delivered to his wife for burial.

Pleasant (Duke) Berryhill,
Captain of Lighthorse Company
of Okmulgee District

Delegates from thirty-four tribes, representing ten thousand Indians, meeting at the Muscogee Council House, circa 1880. The tribes in Indian Territory met periodically to consider methods of maintaining the promised area as Indian Territory. (Courtesy Smithsonian Institution, National Museum of Natural History.)

By the late 1880s, the federal government, as discussed in chapter 5, was pursuing the goal of Indian assimilation, and Congress's desire to terminate the tribal governments of the Indian Territory had assumed a momentum impossible to stop. In 1889 an agreement with the Muscogee Nation allowed the western half of the Indian Territory to be opened for homesteading and established as the Oklahoma Territory. Three years later, Congress created the Dawes Commission to negotiate with tribes for the allotment of their lands and the eventual creation of the state of Oklahoma.

In 1895 the Muscogees, united in their opposition to allotment, elected the full blood Isparhecher as principal chief. Vehemently opposed to allotment, Isparhecher steadfastly refused to accept the division of Muscogee lands. The Muscogee National Council passed memorials requesting that Congress respect the treaties. The federal government, however, was determined to accomplish allotment with or without tribal consent. It directed the Dawes Commission to compile the tribe's membership rolls as the first step toward allotment. An intertribal council of the Five Civilized Tribes again petitioned Congress to allow them to retain their lands.

Congress answered the request by passing the Curtis Act, which provided for allotting tribal lands by force if necessary,

SEC. 56. It is the sense of this body that any change in the present status of the Indian Territory that would include the Muscogee Nation within the limits of an organized State of the American Union, would be contrary to the best interests of the citizens of the Nation, and any proposition of Congress to effect such a change or to include this nation in any State or Territory of Oklahoma shall be a component part is greatly to be depreciated and resisted by all proper means.

Muscogee Law, approved
November 1, 1893

dissolving tribal courts, putting tribal funds under the control of the secretary of the interior, and requiring presidential approval of all tribal laws. The Muscogee National Council appropriated twenty thousand dollars for lawyers' fees to test the act's legality. President William McKinley nullified the nation's attempt to protect itself by vetoing the tribal law appropriating the lawyers' fees.

In 1900 the Muscogees, hoping through compromise to save their government from extinction, finally agreed to the division of their lands. The final rolls indicated 6,858 full bloods, 5,094 mixed bloods, and 6,809 freedmen in the population for a total of 18,761 citizens. Out of the Muscogees' total holdings of over 3 million acres, more than 2.9 million were allotted. The remaining 82,000 acres of tribally owned land were eventually sold.

Many full bloods refused to accept their allotments and attempted to establish a separate government dedicated to traditional life. This attempt became known as the Crazy Snake Rebellion. These tribal members, like all the rest, were

SEC. 120. We still believe that the Government of the United States will prove true to her many pledges and keep perfect faith with our people and will aid instead of obstruct our present form of government to the end that we may enjoy peace and happiness in our sacred home, for which we have paid full compensation.

Muscogee Tribal Council
Resolution
in Response to
Dawes Commission,
approved November 5, 1894

Muscogee Nation Lighthorse Company bringing in Crazy Snake's band in 1901. (Courtesy Museum of the American Indian, Heye Foundation.)

MUSCOGEE LAND: PAST AND PRESENT

Graphic by Bittle Productions

eventually forced to accept their allotments—and they eventually lost them. According to the provisions of a 1906 act, full bloods were not even allowed to sell their allotments for twenty-five years. Mixed bloods were allowed to sell their allotments immediately. Many tribal members were quickly cheated out of their lands. Kidnapping and forgery were commonplace, and murder was not unknown. Guardians were appointed to handle the allotments of full bloods and orphans, and many guardians became wealthy while their wards lived in poverty.

In 1904 the Five Civilized Tribes met again, drew up a new constitution, and requested that the Indian Territory be admitted to the Union as an Indian state to be named Sequoyah. Land speculators, railroad corporations, and oil interests lobbied against the request, and Congress refused to consider it. In 1907 the Oklahoma and Indian territories were united and admitted to the Union as the state of Oklahoma, a Choctaw word meaning "Land of the Red People." On the day of Oklahoma's admission to the Union, the former tribal lands became a sea of wagons and buggies as homesteaders raced to claim the land the Muscogees had fought so hard to retain. Oklahoma's statehood violated the promises made to the tribes upon removal and again in the 1829 and 1835 Cherokee treaties, the 1830 Choctaw treaty, and the 1856 Creek and Seminole treaty.

The Restoration of Tribal Government

The United States, through the BIA, remained steadfast in its determination to control and eventually destroy Muscogee government. Beginning in 1907 the nation could no longer elect its own head of government but was forced to accept the bureau's choice. Bureau officials also refused to allow vacant council seats to be filled by election. These federal actions were patently illegal and denied the nation's inherent

As a people we have kept our faith with the U.S. government. . . . Knowing your intense honesty, your hatred of shams . . . we turn to you, Mr. President, feeling that you will understand us better than Congress. . . . You know the West—you know our hopes and our ambitions; and we appeal again to your sense of justice and fair dealing.

Letter from Muscogee Tribal Council to President Theodore Roosevelt, 1904

rights of sovereignty. The Muscogees refused to concede the end of their tribal government. In 1909 the towns elected delegates and convened the Creek Convention. Although unrecognized by the federal government, which continued to deal only with its illegally appointed chief, the convention held regular meetings to discuss and decide tribal issues.

The condition of Oklahoma tribes was no exception to the general conditions described in the Meriam Report of 1928. The Senate Select Committee on Indian Affairs visited the Five Civilized Tribes in the 1930s, finding near starvation the rule in many of the full-blood communities and an illiteracy rate of 25 to 30 percent—much higher than it had been under the tribal school system. The Muscogees had been dispossessed of all of their original lands except for 1 acre that remained in tribal hands and 100,000 acres in individual allotments.

In response to these conditions, Congress passed the Oklahoma Indian Welfare Act on June 26, 1936. Similar in objectives to the Indian Reorganization Act (IRA), this bill encouraged Oklahoma tribes to adopt constitutions and charters of incorporation and provided funds for the purchase of tribal lands lost through allotment. Eventually the Muscogees were able to buy back five thousand acres of their former lands.

The Muscogees chose not to adopt a new constitution but did petition BIA Commissioner John Collier to allow them to elect their own principal chief and second chief. Collier agreed, and in 1934 delegates of forty-two tribal towns elected their first principal chief in thirty-one years.

Nine years later the Muscogee General Convention did adopt a new constitution and bylaws. Under the new constitution the executive and legislative branches were merged into one body, the Muscogee Indian Council. A business committee was established to handle tribal affairs when the council was not in session. Although the council and the constitution never received BIA recognition because of the Muscogees' refusal to grant tribal membership rights to their freedmen's descendants, this governing structure continued for approximately fifteen years.

Political infighting erupted again in the 1950s and led to the principal chief's repudiation of the constitution and council. In place of the elected council the chief appointed his own council of advisers. The elected council continued to meet until their terms expired in 1955. When the principal chief's term ended in the mid-1950s, the termination era was in full swing. The BIA, once again aiming to destroy tribal government, refused to allow the Muscogees to elect a new chief. The office was filled by BIA appointees until 1970, when the country's policies moved toward self-determination. In 1970, Congress passed a law allowing the Five Civilized Tribes to select their own principal officers.

For several hours on October 10, 1904, I watched these dusky warriors conferring in their bare and grimy chambers, sensing in their voices the sadness of a vanishing race whose history was fading into myth. Their procedure was a curious mingling of town meeting and campfire. They had a presiding officer who put the resolutions to vote quite as a state legislative official might have done, and a clerk recorded the result.

Hamlin Garland
describing last Muscogee
Tribal Council meeting,
October, 1905

MODERN TRIBAL GOVERNMENT

The Muscogees, as their history has shown, are masters at the art of survival and rebuilding. United by their heritage and determination, they have survived adversity and remained a nation. Today the Muscogee Nation once again is undergoing a period of rebirth and rebuilding.

In 1973, Principal Chief Claude Cox appointed a committee to draft a new constitution. In 1979 the nation adopted this new constitution as the successor to the 1867 constitution. The nation's new governing structure, which is organized under the Oklahoma Indian Welfare Act, is made up of three separate and independent branches of government.

A principal chief and second chief are elected by all citizens over eighteen years of age for four-year terms. The principal chief's responsibilities include organizing the executive department, overseeing tribal programs, preparing the annual budget, and informing the national council about the state of the nation's affairs. The principal chief, with council approval, also appoints a five-member election board, a five-member citizenship board, and six Supreme Court judges.

The election board oversees all national elections, while the citizenship board maintains the nation's membership rolls. The constitution provides for two kinds of citizenship. Any individual whose name appears on the nation's 1906 roll, or who is a descendant of a Muscogee Indian whose name appears on that roll, may claim tribal citizenship if not enrolled with another tribe. Full citizenship is granted to tribal members who have at least one-quarter Muscogee blood. Only full citizens may hold the offices of principal chief, second chief, or representative.

Unlike the Muscogee government of the 1860s, which had a bicameral legislature, today's system vests legislative authority in a single body. Representatives to this council are no longer elected from each town but from eight districts. Each district is entitled to one representative plus an addi-

The vitality of our race still persists. We have not lived for naught. We are the original discoverers of this continent, and the conquerors of it from the animal kingdom, and on it first taught the arts of peace and war, and first planted the institutions of virtue, truth and liberty. The European Nations found us here and were made aware that it was possible for men to exist and subsist here. We have given to the European people on this continent our thought forces—the best blood of our ancestors having intermingled with [that of] their best statesmen and leading citizens. We have made ourselves an indestructible element in their national history. We have shown that what they believed were arid and desert places were habitable and capable of sustaining millions of people. We have led the vanguard of civilization in our conflicts with them for tribal existence from ocean to ocean. The race that has rendered this service to the other nations of mankind cannot utterly perish.

**Pleasant Porter, Muscogee
chief, 1906**

MUSCOGEE NATION GOVERNMENT

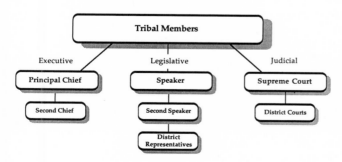

Muscogee tribal complex in Okmulgee, Oklahoma. The building reflects the mound-building tradition of historic times. (Courtesy Donald L. Fixico.)

tional representative for every thousand citizens. A Speaker and a Second Speaker, chosen from among council members, preside over council meetings. Laws passed by the council are forwarded to the principal chief for his or her approval or veto. The national council may override the chief's veto with a two-thirds majority vote.

A Supreme Court and a system of lower courts make up the judicial branch. The six Supreme Court justices are appointed by the principal chief and approved by the council for six-year terms. The Supreme Court rules on tribal ordinances and traditional law and interprets the Muscogee constitution. A judicial code passed in 1983 governs Supreme Court procedures. Other tribally approved codes include an election code, a citizenship code, and a juvenile code. Future plans call for establishing district courts, a juvenile court, and a real-estate court (to settle land disputes).

The constitution guarantees the government's responsiveness to its citizens. National council members can be removed from office upon the signed petition of 20 percent of the registered voters in the representative's district and a subsequent majority vote of that district. The principal chief, second chief, and Supreme Court judges may be removed by a petition signed by 20 percent of all voters and a subsequent three-fourths vote of the council.

Tribal Administration, Programs, and Services

The principal chief's main job is to oversee tribal programs. The executive branch includes several offices, divisions, and agencies. The services provided by these agencies are funded by federal grants, judicial awards, mineral royalties, and revenues from tribal businesses.

The Office of Justice, similar to the federal government's Office of the Attorney General, is headed by a lawyer who advises the chief and council on the tribe's rights, powers, and obligations. The treasurer and his or her staff manage and monitor the nation's budget. In addition to the election and citizenship boards already mentioned, three other citizen advisory boards function as independent agencies. The Housing Authority has overseen the construction of more than thirteen hundred new homes since 1965. The Board of Health works closely with the Division of Community Services to administer a thirty-nine-bed hospital in Okemah. Purchased by the nation in 1977, the hospital is the only medical facility in the county and serves both Indians and non-Indians. It was the first tribally administered hospital in the United States. The hospital's services are supplemented by three Indian Health Service (IHS) clinics and two IHS dental clinics. A mobile health clinic enables the tribe to bring routine medical services to members who live far from medical facilities.

The Board of Economic Affairs works with the Division of Tribal Affairs to develop tribal and individual business projects. The cornerstone of the nation's plan for a thriving tribal economy is an agribusiness complex. Established with an Economic Development Administration (EDA) grant, this farming and livestock business occupies over 2,000 acres of tribal lands. A 557-acre dairy farm sells milk produced by the tribe's herd of 250 Holstein cows. More than 300 head of cattle and 250 hogs are raised yearly for sale to meat processors. One thousand acres are cultivated to grow feed for the livestock. Another 500 acres produce a variety of row crops. The whole complex, established in 1976, is just the first phase of a twenty-five-year plan, which will employ approximately 300 people when completed.

Some of the milk, meat, and vegetables produced by the tribal farm are sold to the tribal grocery and discount store. Open only to Muscogee citizens, the store allows members to buy food and goods at discounted prices. A 1 percent tribal sales tax generates a small revenue which is used for funding other tribal programs. Since November, 1984, the Muscogees have operated three bingo halls under the direction of the Office of Public Gaming. Drawing more than one thousand visitors, some from as far away as Saint Louis, the halls offer jackpots as high as twenty thousand dollars, employ over one hundred people, and have provided the tribe with much-needed revenue for tribal programs.

The Office of the Administration, with four subdivisions, is responsible for the general operation of governmental services. The Administrative Support Service supervises budget and personnel matters and is a central clearinghouse for information. It also maintains the tribal archives. The Communications and Graphic Services Department publishes the *Muscogee Nation News*, the official newspaper of the Musco-

Front page of the *Muscogee Nation News*. Over 475 tribes have published their own newspapers. (Courtesy Donald L. Fixico.)

gee Nation, and has produced several videos on such subjects as the Green Corn Ceremony, the annual Muscogee festival and rodeo, and Muscogee art. It has also taped a series of programs on tribal government. A sixty-minute documentary entitled "The Creek Nation: A Tribal Success" was produced in cooperation with a local television station. The newspaper, archives, and video productions are crucial for preserving the Muscogees' rich heritage and educating tribal citizens and their neighbors about the nation's history and current situation.

Three agencies—the Division of Tribal Affairs, the Division of Community Services, and the Division of Human Development—operate programs protecting and enhancing tribal life. The Division of Tribal Affairs has designed and operated such undertakings as the agribusiness complex, the discount store, and the bingo games. This division also oversees the Lighthorse Law Enforcement Agency, which protects tribal lands and facilities. The fifteen employees of the Lighthorse, named after the Muscogees' traditional law-enforcement system, patrol and protect tribal lands. Since the tribal government has not yet authorized the Lighthorse to make arrests, violators are currently reported to county and city law enforcement officers.

The Division of Community Services oversees tribal health and housing needs and provides care to the elderly. The Environmental Services Agency has rehabilitated more than 170 substandard homes and built 4 community centers. Community activities such as meetings, library services, and recreational and educational programs are held in these centers. The Muscogees regard the well-being of their elderly as an important community responsibility. The nation has built 100 housing units for the elderly and physically handicapped. Legal services, health care, recreational activities, and lunch programs are also provided for the elderly. The community services division also maintains relations with twenty-seven organized Muscogee communities, six of which now have tribal charters to determine their own affairs.

CHAPTER 8

THE CHEYENNE RIVER SIOUX

A handful of early arriving Cheyenne River Sioux council members wait for the remainder of their members to appear. Some of them must travel more than one hundred miles along rural roads from their districts to Eagle Butte, South Dakota, for the meetings. As they wait, council members chat about such topics as the progress of the tribal beef and buffalo herds, the new equipment needed for the phone company, the loss of a respected elder, and the upcoming Sun Dance. When all eighteen council members have assembled, the newly elected chairperson calls the meeting to order. The chairperson asks each of the fourteen committees to report on any problems or needs in the various programs under their jurisdiction. Of high priority to the education committee is the threatened cutoff of all funds for the reservation's small community college. Operated under the sponsorship of Black Hills State College, the Cheyenne River Sioux Community College offers freshman and sophomore courses to the reservation's residents. In an area where education levels are as far below average as unemployment rates are above the norm, the opportunity for education and training of all types is crucial. The school's closing would mean a step backward in the tribe's quest for control and self-determination.

The Lakotas, or Teton Sioux, as they were known to whites, were established on one large reservation encompassing part of the states of North and South Dakota in 1868. Fierce and determined warriors, they long defied American attempts at intimidation, but finally, in 1889, as discussed in chapter 5, after the murder of several of their leaders and having been virtually starved into submission, they agreed to divide their land and accept six separate reservations in North and South Dakota: the Cheyenne River, Crow Creek, Lower Brule, Pine Ridge, Rosebud, and Standing Rock reservations.

The 2.8-million-acre Cheyenne River Sioux Reservation is located in north-central South Dakota. It is roughly 85 miles long and 94 miles wide and located within the boundaries of the original, large reservation. The landscape is a gently rolling range covered by carpets of prairie grass that are green in spring and brown in late summer. It is a land of long, hard winters and hot, dry summers. It is also a land of deep spirituality, where the Sun Dance is still held and the keeper of the sacred buffalo pipe still lives. To the southwest

For many tribes the eagle is the most sacred of all birds. Feathers
are used in virtually all ceremonial occasions. Because eagles today
are an endangererd species, the government has made special provisions for tribal religious leaders to obtain and use eagle feathers.
(Courtesy National Congress of American Indians.)

of the reservation lie the sacred Black Hills and the craggy,
ethereal buttes of the Badlands. Sparsely settled, the reservation's nine thousand Indian and non-lndian inhabitants
live in twenty-seven small towns that dot the reservation.

HISTORY

The Lakotas originally inhabited the forests and grasslands
of central Minnesota, where they sustained themselves by
hunting and gathering the wild rice of the region. As French
fur trappers moved into the region in the early 1600s, the
Lakotas moved onto the Plains, leaving their eastern brethren, the Dakotas, or Santee Sioux, to compete with the Ojib-
was for the fur trade. As they moved west, they acquired
horses from the tribes of the Southern Plains and guns from
trade with the Santees. By the late 1700s the Lakotas' horse-
manship and shooting skills had earned them a wide reputation as fierce hunters. They controlled the Northern Plains,
winning territory from the neighboring Kiowas, Poncas,
Cheyennes, Arikaras, Mandans, and Crows. The early 1800s
were a time of peace and prosperity for the Lakotas. Game
was plentiful, and French traders frequently married into the
tribe, keeping the bands well supplied with guns, ammunition, knives, and other goods.

Known to the Lakotas for more than three thousand years,
the rugged granite cliffs known as Paha Sapa, the Black Hills,

Approximately twenty of the Plains tribes practice the Sun Dance. Participants in the Sun Dance pierce their flesh and insert a stick or eagle claw through the skin. A rope is tied to the stick and secured to the Sacred Tree. The pledge prays and pulls back on the rope until the skin breaks and the stick is released. (Drawing by Fernando Dreaming Bear.)

and the eerie white and sandy buttes known as the Badlands became central in their culture and religion. Here they bred and traded their large pony herds, hunted buffalo, and returned each year to celebrate the sacred Sun Dance.

In the late 1820s conditions began to change. American traders, disregarding demands by the tribal leadership that they remove themselves, filtered into the region, using liquor as a trade good to compete with the French-Canadian traders. At the same time, immigrants along the Oregon Trail were killing and running off the buffalo and bringing cholera, smallpox, and measles into Indian country. With no natural resistance to these imported diseases, Plains tribes lost up to half of their populations. In 1849 the gold rush in California increased the number of settlers flowing through the region. That same year, Minnesota, the eastern door to the Lakotas' homeland, became a territory. After nearly two hundred years of indirect and direct white contact, the Lakotas began to fear for their existence.

The 1851 Treaty of Fort Laramie

Several of the Lakota bands had signed friendship and trade treaties with the United States in 1825. Dissatisfied with the terms of those treaties, the BIA began pressuring the government to negotiate new treaties with the Plains tribes. In 1851, at Fort Laramie, Wyoming, federal officials convened the largest treaty council ever held. More than ten thousand Plains Indians from the Lakota, Cheyenne, Arapaho, Crow, Arikara, Mandan, Assiniboine, and Hidatsa nations attended. For eighteen days these tribes, many of them traditional enemies, "smoked and feasted together; exchanged presents and adopted each other's children according to their own traditions."

In exchange for fifty thousand dollars a year for fifty years, the nations agreed to allow the United States to construct roads and military posts through their country (the yearly payment was reduced to fifteen thousand dollars by the Senate upon ratification, without the tribes' consent). The tribes also established the boundaries of their territories and agreed to maintain peaceful relations with one another and with the United States. In addition, several of the tribes, including the Mandans, Gros Ventres, Crows, Blackfeet, and some bands of the Cheyennes and Arapahos, accepted reservations.

The peace was short-lived. In 1854 a young lieutenant, determined to bring to justice a few Indians who had stolen a cow, killed a chief, Bear that Scatters, while discussing payments for the cow. A battle followed, and the chief's tribesman killed the lieutenant and his twenty-nine men. Ordered to punish the "hostiles" for this deed, Brig. Gen. William Selby Harney killed eighty-six people. Relations between the Lakotas and the whites continued to deteriorate. In 1862 the Oglalas and the Brules found themselves drawn into hostilities on behalf of their cousins, the Santee Sioux. The Santees were infuriated by a fraudulent treaty that displaced them from their homeland. They retaliated. At the end of the killing more than five hundred settlers and soldiers and a greater number of Sioux lay dead. Hysterical reports from neighboring states that the entire Sioux Nation was poised to attack forced the federal government to send troops to posts on the Platte and Missouri rivers. The tribes in this area, previously friendly to whites, watched with concern as their homeland filled with soldiers—soldiers who were bored and eager to fight.

The Powder River War

Tensions increased to the breaking point in April, 1864, when Col. John Chivington and his troops massacred more than five hundred Cheyennes under a flag of truce at Sand

Creek, Colorado. At the same time, a large influx of immigrants started moving along a new trail, the Bozeman Trail.
As news of the Sand Creek massacre filtered out to the
various camps, destroying all hopes of peace, chiefs who
had been attempting to hold their young warriors in line
now nodded their assent. The Platte and Powder river regions erupted into full-scale war. Expecting to quell the hostilities quickly, the federal government constructed three
new forts and moved in new troops, confident after their
Civil War victory. In battle after battle the tribes (led by Lakota leaders Sitting Bull, Red Cloud, and Crazy Horse and the
Cheyenne leader Roman Nose) defeated or held the troops
to a draw. Traffic along the Bozeman Trail came to a complete halt—forcing mail to California to be shipped via
Panama.

Its military effort a failure, the government eventually
changed tactics. President Ulysses S. Grant appointed a
peace commission to negotiate with the tribes for permis-

Sitting Bull, 1885. (Courtesy National Archives Trust Fund Board.)

sion to run the trail through their country. In October, 1865, the federal government won agreement from a handful of the more peaceful bands. In June, 1866, it held further meetings with Sitting Bull, Red Cloud, and other hostile leaders. As the chiefs sat in council with government agents, they received word that the United States was at that moment moving troops into the disputed area and building roads there without the tribes' approval. Indignant over the government's deceit, the chiefs and their followers left for home, vowing they would fight all white intrusion into their country.

For the next two years Indian war parties made life in the region extremely dangerous as the tribes fought to protect their land. In February, 1867, an investigative peace commission sent to the area recommended that the Bozeman Trail be abandoned. The chiefs and their warriors had won. The following year the government proposed a new treaty with the Lakotas. Red Cloud, the holder of over one hundred coups (battle feats), stuck to his demands that all whites leave the country and refused to participate in any negotiations until the troops had left and the forts had been destroyed.

The Treaty of 1868

In the Treaty of 1868, which ended the Powder River War, the United States recognized the western half of the present state of South Dakota as the Great Sioux Reservation. The government also agreed that the Powder River and Bighorn countries were unceded Indian territory where the Lakotas and their allies, the Cheyennes, could hunt undisturbed by white intrusions. The treaty promised that no unauthorized person "shall ever be permitted to pass over, settle upon, or reside in [this] territory." In return for peace, the United States agreed to remove all troops and forts from Indian areas, establish schools and agencies where the bands could obtain food and clothing for four years, and provide agricultural aid and blacksmiths, carpenters, millers, and engineers on the reservation. Finally, the treaty provided that all further land cessions would require the approval of three-fourths of the adult male tribal members.

For the next several years Lakota-federal relations were a tense tug-of-war, with each side having a different understanding of the treaty and a different set of objectives. What had not been explained to the bands during negotiation was that the treaty contained a clause that they relocate northward away from the Platte River basin, their best hunting grounds, and away from Fort Laramie, where they traded. A further point of disagreement concerned the location of the agencies. The United States wanted the agencies built as far north of white settlements and the partly constructed Union Pacific Railroad as possible. The government hoped that the bands, once settled under the influence of their "father," the agent, would gradually shift from a nomadic life to a life of farming.

The Lakotas wanted the agencies established close to areas of white settlement so they could protect their lands from the settlers. Far from viewing the agent as their master, they saw him more as a servant responsible for distributing the goods owed them under the treaty. Nor had they any intention of adopting an agricultural life-style. To a people accustomed to the free and independent life of the buffalo hunt, farming was an impossible alternative. In any case—as everyone knew—farming was out of the question in an area of constant drought and grasshopper plagues.

As tensions mounted, the government invited Red Cloud, Spotted Tail, and several other chiefs to Washington, D.C. The United States hoped that the chiefs, who had never seen a city or a train, would be so impressed by the might and power of the whites that they would give in. Totally unimpressed, Red Cloud, in meeting after meeting, patiently repeated that the treaty gave his people the right to remain in their present locations and the right to trade at Fort Laramie. Now, for the first time, the treaty's true provisions were explained to the chiefs.

Furious and despondent, but not beaten, the Indian delegation returned home by way of New York City. Again the government wanted to impress the delegation with the advancements of the white world. Once again the government's strategy backfired. Not only were Red Cloud and the other chiefs unfazed, but in an impassioned, dignified speech to hundreds of New Yorkers, Red Cloud spoke of the government's duplicity and of his people's desire to live in peace and be left alone to raise their children. The speech gained many eastern supporters for the Lakotas, supporters who continued for years to lobby on behalf of Lakota rights.

Invasion of the Paha Sapa (Black Hills)

In the midst of this uneasy atmosphere came reports of gold in the Black Hills. In 1874, in direct violation of the 1868 treaty, the government ordered Lt. Col. George Armstrong Custer and twelve hundred men to explore the Black Hills and to report on the extent of the gold deposits. As newspapers headlined the reports of a major new gold discovery, settlers streamed into the Lakotas' sacred Paha Sapa. The white intruders laid out towns and demanded that the army, whose job it was to enforce the 1868 treaty, protect them from the Indians, on whose lands they were trespassing.

The following spring, Red Cloud, Spotted Tail, and other chiefs were again brought to Washington. Bluntly, the government announced that the whites wanted the Black Hills. The tribes could either sell the area or have it taken. The chiefs refused to sell. Again that spring a treaty commission

We came to Washington to see our Great Father that peace might be continued. The Great Father that made us both wishes peace to be kept; we want to keep peace. Will you help us? In 1868 men came out and brought papers. We could not read them, and they did not tell us truly what was in them. We thought the treaty was to remove the forts, and that we should then cease from fighting. But they wanted to send us traders of the Missouri. We did not want to go to the Missouri, but wanted traders where we were. When I reached Washington the Great Father explained to me what the treaty was, and showed me that the interpreters had deceived me. All I want is right and just. I have tried to get from the Great Father what is right and just. I have not altogether succeeded. . . . Look at me. I am poor and naked, but I am the Chief of the nation. . . . I wish to know why Commissioners are sent out to us who do nothing but rob us and get the riches of this world away from us? I was brought up among the traders, and those who came out there in the early times treated me well and I had a good time with them. They taught us to wear clothes and to use tobacco and ammunition. But, by and by, the Great Father sent out a different kind of men; men who cheated and drank whiskey; men who were so bad that the Great Father could not keep them at home and so sent them out there. I have sent a great many words to the Great Father but they never reached him. They were drowned on the way, and I was afraid the words I spoke lately to the Great Father would not reach you, so I came to speak to you myself and now I am going away to my home.

Red Cloud (Oglala Sioux),
Visit to New York, 1870

was sent to the reservation. It offered the nation $6 million for the land. The chiefs, aware of the hills' vast mineral resources, demanded $70 million. The negotiations reached a deadlock, and the government responded by sending troops to the reservation. The message was clear. Cede your land or face war. Orders were issued for all bands who were hunting in the unceded area reserved for them by the treaty to return to their agencies, but few did. Travel at the time was difficult, because it was the dead of winter, but few bands had any intention of obeying illegal orders given them in their own land anyway.

As U.S. troops moved in, warriors of the more peaceful bands, led by Spotted Tail and Red Cloud, left in increasing numbers to join the war camps of Sitting Bull and Crazy Horse. In June, 1876, Crazy Horse and Sitting Bull defeated General Crook at the Battle of Rosebud and turned their attention to Custer and the Seventh Cavalry. Arrogant and self-assured, Custer disobeyed orders and found himself trapped at the Little Bighorn River. His plans for personal glory ended with the loss of his entire company of 267 men.

Unable to win a military victory, the government played its trump card. For several years it had encouraged the killing of buffalo, the staple food of the Plains tribes. By the late 1870s the buffaloes were virtually extinct, a situation that made the tribe dependent on its treaty rations of beef. The Sioux Appropriation Bill, passed by Congress in 1876, stated that unless the Lakotas sold the Black Hills and Powder River and Bighorn countries, no further funds and rations would be forthcoming. This meant starvation. The treaty commission again traveled to the reservation. It offered the nation the following choice: cede the Black Hills and Powder River and Bighorn countries or face starvation and federal troops.

The Agreement of 1876

Realizing that without food they could not hold off the army for long, the chiefs reluctantly signed the agreement. The principal provision of this treaty was that the Lakotas would relinquish their rights to the Black Hills and their right to hunt in unceded lands to the north in exchange for subsistence rations. In violation of the 1868 treaty, the agreement was signed by only 10 percent of the adult male Lakota population. By the spring of 1877 the majority of Crazy Horse's and Lame Deer's followers had surrendered. Sitting Bull and his camp refused to submit to military authority and fled to Canada, where they remained until 1881. Crazy Horse, who had never given up hope of returning to his free life in the Bighorn country, was murdered the following fall while under arrest at Fort Robinson, Nebraska. Crazy Horse, perhaps the greatest military strategist and most militant of all Sioux chiefs, was thirty-three.

In 1878 military rule was withdrawn, and the agencies re-

We had buffalo for food, and their hides for clothing and for our teepees. We preferred hunting to a life of idleness on the reservation, where we were driven against our will. At times we did not get enough to eat, and we were not allowed to leave the reservation to hunt.

We preferred our own way of living. We were no expense to the government. All we wanted was peace and to be left alone. Soldiers were sent out in the winter, who destroyed our villages.

Then "Long Hair" [Custer] came in the same way. They say we massacred him, but he would have done the same thing to us had we not defended ourselves and fought to the last. Our first impulse was to escape with our squaws and papooses, but we were so hemmed in that we had to fight.

Crazy Horse (Oglala Sioux),
1877

turned to civilian control. Gradually the bands, exhausted and miserable, settled around the agency locations chosen by the government.

The United States had finally won. The Treaty of 1868 had promised that the Paha Sapa, the sacred heartland of Lakota land and culture, would forever belong to the Lakotas unless the tribe agreed to sell it. When the tribe later refused to sell the land, the government launched an outright war and virtually starved the nation into submission. It was an immoral and illegal victory—won through trickery, deceit, war, and starvation. (In 1980 the Supreme Court ruled that the United States had illegally taken the Black Hills and awarded the nation $122 million in restitution. Even then, one hundred years after the loss of the Paha Sapa, most Lakota voted to refuse the award and instead to seek the return of their land.)

Great Sioux Agreement of 1889

The settlers and Congress were not satisfied with the Black Hills and the land obtained in the agreement of 1876. Almost immediately, plans were initiated to divest the Lakotas of their remaining land. In 1882, Congress established a commission to win the Lakotas' acceptance of separate reservations and the cession of more than half their reservation. To obtain the Lakotas' agreement, the commission lied, neglected to explain that the agreement meant loss of lands, and threatened the bands with military control and removal to the Indian Territory. Even with these tactics, the commission gathered just 384 signatures, far fewer than the several thousand required. And when news of the commission's tactics leaked out, the Senate was forced to disavow the agreement.

The 25,000 members of the Lakota Nation were no match, however, for the half million whites in the Dakotas who wanted the Lakotas' lands. Within another five years Senator Henry Dawes introduced a new land bill in Congress. This bill provided that six separate reservations be established and allotted to individual tribal members and that nine million acres of "surplus" Lakota land be sold to whites for from $.50 to $1.25 an acre, with the proceeds held in trust for the tribe. In addition the nation was to receive 26,000 head of cattle and have its educational benefits extended for thirty years.

Once again the chiefs were united in their opposition to ceding their lands; once again they were brought to Washington; and once again they refused to sell. Unable to obtain an agreement honestly, the government appointed Gen. George Crook to travel to the agencies and "persuade" the nation. Having their old enemy General Crook as the chief negotiator told the Lakotas what to expect: agree to the cession or have all your land taken. Finally, in 1890, after using fraud, misconduct, intimidation, and bribery, General Crook was able to report to Washington that he had secured an "agreement."

I am a red man. If the Great Spirit had desired me to be a white man he would have made me so in the first place. He put in your heart certain wishes and plans, in my heart he put other and different desires. Each man is good in his sight. It is not necessary for eagles to be crows. Now we are poor but we are free. No white man controls our footsteps. If we must die we die defending our rights.

Sitting Bull (Oglala Sioux) responding when asked why he did not surrender and move to a reservation even when his people were starving, 1876–77

We understand that over 80 percent of the Black Hills is still under the control of the United States. This must be immediately returned to the Lakota people and negotiations must begin for the remainder in individual ownership. We know the white people living in the hills now love it. We love it for many of the same reasons and more importantly because they are sacred grounds. So these white people should understand why we will not sell. The Oglala Lakota have always been the caretakers of the Black Hills and it is appropriate that I have been allowed to talk here today defending the sale of these hills for my people and other Lakota people from our other Lakota tribes.

Testimony of Frank Crow and Matthew Kills Enemy, of the Lakota Treaty Council, to the House Interior Subcommittee on Indian Affairs, September 10, 1976

From Wounded Knee to the Depression: Assaults
on a Proud Tradition

For years Congress had been decreasing the Lakotas' appropriations. By 1890 they were receiving less than half their promised rations. Malnutrition and poor living conditions made the Lakotas vulnerable to measles and whooping cough. These diseases spread throughout the reservations, taking the lives of hundreds of children.

The loss of their land combined with semi-starvation and disease brought about complete demoralization among the Lakotas. Into this state of despair came news of a new religion that promised hope and a return to the old ways. Wovoka, a Nevada Paiute, founded the Ghost Dance religion. Wovoka preached a message that foretold the return of the buffaloes, the disappearance of the whites, and the reincarnation of deceased Lakotas. Desperately wanting to believe the message, the people flocked to learn the dances, songs, and prayers. The Ghost Dance Ceremony required fasting, purification in the sweat lodge, and four consecutive nights of dancing. The dances had a highly hypnotic effect and often caused the dancers to fall into a trance. Waking later, they told joyful tales of meeting and talking with their dead relatives and friends.

The Ghost Dance religion did not teach hostility toward whites. Instead it promised that its followers would be protected from attacks by whites, especially if they wore a "ghost shirt" painted with sacred symbols. The government was ignorant of the religion's peaceful teaching, however. Threatened and fearful of a general Indian uprising, the government again placed the Lakota agencies under military control in November, 1890. The troops, which included Custer's old unit, the Seventh Cavalry, were ordered to return the scattered Ghost Dance camps to the agencies.

The Cheyenne River Reservation was the center of the Ghost Dance religion. There the military sought out Hump, chief of the Minneconjous. Considered more dangerous than Sitting Bull, Hump had led his band against Crook and Custer and had stubbornly clung to the old traditions after coming to the reservation. Hump agreed to return to the agency and to arrange the return of Spotted Elk's band as well. Having succeeded with Hump and Spotted Elk, the military turned its attention to Sitting Bull, who had returned from Canada with most of his band in 1881 and was camped at the southeastern end of the Standing Rock Reservation. On December 14, 1890, Agent James McLaughlin of Standing Rock ordered the Indian police to arrest Sitting Bull. The troops and the police surrounded Sitting Bull's camp at dawn. A battle ensued in which Sitting Bull, seven of his followers, and seven Indian policemen were killed. Most of Sitting Bull's band surrendered, and the rest fled, joining Hump's and Spotted Elk's bands.

The Lakota . . . loved the earth and all things of the earth, the attachment growing with age. The old people came literally to love the soil and they sat or reclined on the ground with a feeling of being close to a mothering power . . . the old people liked to remove their mocassins and walk with bare feet on the sacred earth. Their tipis were built upon the earth and their altars were made of earth. The birds that flew in the air came to rest upon the earth and it was the final abiding place of all things that lived and grew. The soil was soothing, strengthening, cleansing and healing.

What law have I broken? Is it wrong for me to love my own? Is it wicked for me because my skin is red? Because I am a Sioux; because I was born where my father lived; because I would die for my people and my country?

Sitting Bull

In the meantime, another band, under the leadership of
Big Foot, was making its way to Pine Ridge when it was surrounded by Major S. M. Whitside's troops. This band was
forcibly marched to Wounded Knee, on the Pine Ridge Reservation, where it was placed under the guard of the Seventh Cavalry. On the morning of December 29, 1890, the
men and youths were separated from the women and children and ordered to disarm. As the weapons were collected,
Yellow Bird, a medicine man, began to chant. Following his
lead, the other men began to sing their death song. A shot
was fired—whether by one of the troops or a Ghost Dancer
remains unclear. The troops responded with a rapid hail of
bullets. Most of the men and youths, who had been huddled
together in a close semicircle, were killed immediately. The
captain then ordered the hotchkiss, an early machine gun,
fired on the women and children. Eighty-four men, forty-
four women, and eighteen children were killed, many of
them hunted down as they attempted to flee and killed more
than a mile away from where the shooting first began.

Sporadic fighting continued for another month until starvation and despair forced the bands' return to the agencies.
Thirty U.S. soldiers were awarded the Congressional Medal

Members of Big Foot's band at a Grass Dance on the Cheyenne River. From left to right, they are Bear That
Runs and Growls, Warrior, One Tooth Gone, Sole, and Make It Long. This photo was taken in 1890, three
months before the Wounded Knee massacre, where most of those pictured met their deaths. (Courtesy
Smithsonian Institution, National Anthropological Archives.)

Above is an Indian killed at Wounded Knee, his body frozen in the snow. (Courtesy Smithsonian Institution, National Anthropological Archives.) The photo below shows the mass burial of victims at Wounded Knee. (Courtesy of Museum of the American Indian, Heye Foundation.)

of Honor for their performances at Wounded Knee. The few survivors of Big Foot's band returned to the Cheyenne River Reservation, where their descendants live today in the communities of Red Scaffold, Bridger, Cherry Creek, and Pine Ridge.

The following year, 1891, the army moved the Cheyenne Agency from Fort Bennett to Charger's Camp. Shortly after the move, the army restored the agency to civilian control, and the BIA agents promptly resumed with renewed fervor their objectives of destroying the traditional Lakota political, cultural, and economic systems.

For several years the Lakotas' traditional political system had been assaulted and undermined. Interior Department officials had used favors and trips to Washington to try to increase the stature and authority of a few of the more peaceful chiefs. It was much easier to deal with one or two friendly leaders than with a large group of often hostile leaders. The United States eventually named Spotted Tail principal chief of the Lakota Nation. To most Lakotas, however, Spotted Tail remained one of several headmen, none of whom had significantly more authority than the others.

As the Interior Department tried to strengthen the authority of its preferred leaders, BIA agents tried to undermine the authority of all Lakota leaders. The courts of Indian offenses and the Indian police, established in 1883, began slowly to take over the peacekeeping roles of the chiefs and the akicita societies. The agents' direct control of food and goods distribution to individual tribal members took away another important role traditionally held by band leaders. When agents also took over land management during the allotment process, they almost completely usurped the chiefs' direction of Lakota economic life.

The effects of these changes on Lakota culture and society were far reaching. The courts and codes of Indian offenses, by strictly forbidding all traditional ceremonies, aimed straight at the center of the Lakotas' spiritual and cultural life. The Sun Dance (until its revival in the 1930s) was held infrequently and in secret, away from the eyes of the agent. The Wounded Knee massacre effectively ended the Ghost Dance religion. On the social level, when families moved to the newly allotted lands, they were forced to abandon the traditional living pattern of the *tiyošpaye* and the extended family and bands. Children were forced increasingly to attend schools where they were forbidden to practice their religion, speak their language, and wear their hair long.

By the turn of the century the government had accomplished half of its goal of persuading the Lakotas to give up their nomadic hunting life and become farmers. A hunting life was no longer possible—tribal hunting lands had been severely diminished by a series of illegal agreements, the buffaloes were near extinction, and the majority of the Lakotas were disarmed. Turning the Lakotas into farmers, however, was less successful. Ranching and farming in north-central South Dakota required large tracts of productive land and large amounts of capital, neither of which the Lakotas had.

Once the railroad routes through the Dakotas were completed, more settlers flocked into the states, demanding land for farms and ranches. In 1908 a congressional statute opened 1.7 million acres of the Cheyenne River Reservation, roughly half its acreage, to homesteading. This move, along with the Interior Department's earlier decision to lease Indian allotments to non-Indian ranchers, meant that, within

Fourth: The "sun dance," and all other similar dances and so-called religious ceremonies shall be considered "Indian offenses" and any Indian found guilty of being a participant in one or more of these offenses shall, for the first offense committed, be punished by withholding from him his rations for a period not exceeding ten days; and if found guilty of any subsequent offense under this rule, shall be punished by withholding his rations for a period of not less than fifteen days nor more than thirty days, or by incarceration in the agency prison for a period not exceeding thirty days.

. . . .

Sixth: The usual practice of so called "medicine men" shall be considered an "Indian offense" cognizable by the court of Indian offenses, and whenever it shall be proven to the satisfaction of the court that the influence of a so-called "medicine man" operates as a hindrance to civilization of a tribe, . . . or shall adopt any means to prevent the attendance of children at the agency schools, or shall use any of the arts of the conjurer to prevent the Indians from abandoning their heathenish rites and customs, he shall be adjudged guilty of an "Indian offense," and upon conviction of any one or more of these specified practices, or any other, in the opinion of the court, of an equally anti-progressive nature shall be confined in the agency guardhouse for a term not less than ten days, or until such time as he shall produce evidence satisfactory to the court, and approved by the agent, that he will forever abandon all practices styled "Indian offenses" under this rule.

Rules of the Court of
Indian Offenses, Pine
Ridge Reservation, 1908

CHEYENNE RIVER SIOUX LAND: PAST AND PRESENT

Aboriginal Area

Tribal Land Today

Graphic by Bittle Productions

a short time, non-Indians controlled the best reservation lands.

By the late 1920s, Lakota lands were dangerously over-grazed. A severe drought had caused widespread crop failure. Livestock herds were wiped out and the land was severely eroded. The once lush and serene beauty of the Plains had, in fifty years of white control, become a barren, desolate, and dusty landscape. The Depression forced some Lakotas to sell their allotments to survive. The once fiercely independent and self-sufficient Lakotas were again forced to either accept rations or face starvation.

The New Deal and the IRA

President Roosevelt's New Deal, with its public-works pro-grams and conservation projects, extended to Indian reser-vations as it did to all of rural America. For the Cheyenne River Sioux, these programs made possible the survival of the people and the land. For the first time, many young men were able to find jobs, working for one of the various public-works projects on the reservation. Between 1933 and 1936, the Indian Civilian Conservation Corps built dams and dug wells, strung fences, planted gardens, constructed roads and telephone lines, and established a tribal ranching program.

The New Deal had a political as well as an economic com-ponent. Employed in Roosevelt's administration as BIA com-missioner was John Collier, father of the Indian Reorganiza-tion Act (IRA). In 1934 the BIA proposed to the Cheyenne River Sioux that they accept the IRA and a new constitution drafted primarily by bureau employees. The tribe decided by a narrow margin to adopt the IRA and the new constitution. Those in favor believed that the IRA would give the tribe more control over its day-to-day life, in addition to the op-portunity to use IRA revolving loan funds. The reservation was in the depths of its own economic depression and des-perately needed funds for land consolidation and economic development. The revolving loan funds were available only to those tribes accepting the act. Opponents of the IRA

We, the Sioux Indians of the Cheyenne River Reservation in the State of South Dakota in or-der to establish our tribal organi-zation, to conserve our tribal property, to develop our common resources, to establish justice, and to promote the welfare of ourselves and our descendants, do hereby ordain and establish this constitution and by-laws for our tribal council as a guide to its deliberations.

Preamble, Constitution and Bylaws, Cheyenne River Sioux Tribe of South Dakota, 1935

feared that the required constitution, which gave the secretary of the interior authority over certain areas of tribal affairs, unnecessarily limited the tribe's inherent sovereignty.

MODERN TRIBAL GOVERNMENT

As discussed in chapter 2, the Lakotas traditionally operated under what today would be called a federal system of government, with government units existing at the band, tribal, and national levels. A headman governed each band and represented that band's interest at the tribal level. Each summer the various bands met in the Greater Sioux Council to discuss matters of interest to the entire Sioux Nation. In accepting the IRA constitutions, the Lakotas retained their federal structure, although in a modified form.

The national-level government structure is the National Sioux Council, composed of delegates from the Cheyenne River, Standing Rock, Lower Brule, Crow Creek, Pine Ridge, Rosebud, Santee, and Fort Peck reservations. Each year the council meets to discuss matters affecting the entire Sioux Nation. The most pressing issue in recent years has been whether or not to accept the Supreme Court's 1980 award of $122 million as compensation for the nation's loss of the Black Hills.

Tribal courts should have jurisdiction over non-Indians and over all crimes because everyone should be subject to the laws of the locale he is in. If I go to Denmark, I'm subject to the laws there, so if someone comes here he should be subject to our laws. . . . [This] is nationalism at its most basic. . . . It is our land and we should be in control.

Trudell Guerue, Chief
Judge, Rosebud Sioux
Tribal Court, 1988

The Tribal Level

At the tribal level, each reservation is governed by an elected tribal council. On the Cheyenne River Reservation, an eighteen-member council, composed of a chairperson, secretary, treasurer, and fifteen representatives, serves as the tribe's official governing body. The chairperson, secretary, and treasurer are elected at-large. The fifteen representatives are elected by the reservation's six local districts according to their population size. Council representatives elect a vice-chairperson from among their own number.

The tribal council, as the tribe's supreme governing body, is constitutionally empowered to enter into negotiations with federal, state, and local governments on the tribe's behalf; to employ attorneys and to protect tribal land and political rights; to appoint tribal officials, boards, and organizations; to evict nonmembers whose presence may be injurious to the tribe; to administer the tribal budget; to regulate property and to pass laws and establish courts for the administration of justice. Although the Cheyenne River Sioux Constitution provides the council with considerable authority, it does stipulate (as it must by law) that the secretary of the interior has the authority to approve or disapprove certain actions by the tribal council.

The chairperson, vice-chairperson, secretary, and treasurer form the tribe's executive branch. They and the other council members work with fourteen committees of four to six members to carry out their responsibilities. Appointed by the chairperson, the committees oversee the work of various tribal programs and make recommendations to the council about problems and goals.

Council representatives report directly to their district councils. Each of the six districts is governed by a locally elected president, secretary, treasurer, and council. Local officials are elected for two-year terms. The district councils meet at least once a month to conduct business, hear reports from the district's tribal council representatives, and pass resolutions to be taken to the tribal council.

The judicial branch of the Cheyenne River Sioux is composed of a lower-court system as well as an innovative appeals court procedure. The Cheyenne River Sioux lower-court system consists of one court and a panel of three judges responsible for hearing criminal, civil, and juvenile cases. A magistrate handles arraignments, and a tribal prosecutor is responsible for arguing cases on the tribe's behalf. Defendants may present their own case, ask a friend or family member to speak for them, or hire a lawyer at their own expense.

In 1978 the tribal governments of the Cheyenne River, Sisseton, Lower Brule, Fort Thompson, and Standing Rock reservations formed an intertribal appeals court. Located on the Crow Creek Reservation, this court decides cases filed from any one of the five member reservations. The intertribal appeals court is made up of the chief judges from the five member reservations. Decisions require a majority vote of the judges. All decisions are final and may not be overturned by the tribal council or any federal or state court. This court has the advantages of providing individuals with an independent avenue of redress and of promoting closer interrelation and cooperation between member tribes of the Lakota Nation.

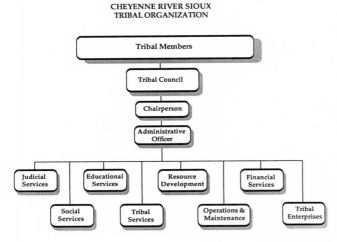

CHEYENNE RIVER SIOUX
TRIBAL ORGANIZATION

Graphic by Bittle Productions

Requirements for Office and Enrollment

To be a member of the Cheyenne River tribal or district council, or to vote in tribal and district elections, one must be enrolled as a tribal member, meet either a one-year (to hold office) or thirty-day (to vote) residency requirement, and be at least twenty-five years of age. Individuals may run for tribal office from their district upon presenting a petition signed by 10 percent of the district voters. A district election board supervises each district's election.

Enrollment in the tribe is open to those with one-quarter or more Cheyenne River Sioux Indian blood and whose parents were residents of the reservation. Individuals of Cheyenne River Sioux blood who do not fulfill the blood quantum or residence requirement may be admitted to membership upon a two-thirds vote of the tribal council.

A constitutional provision for recalls and referendums gives the Cheyenne River Sioux a system of checks on governmental authority. A council representative is subject to a recall election if 40 percent of the district voters sign a petition so directing and if the tribal council agrees. A proposed or enacted ordinance or resolution must be put to a vote of the entire tribe if the tribal council receives a petition so requesting signed by three hundred qualified voters. Constitutional amendments need majority approval in an election in which at least 30 percent of eligible voters cast a ballot.

Economic Development and Land Management

The Cheyenne River Sioux tribal government operates more than fifty programs designed to protect and manage the land and resources, to promote economic self-sufficiency, and to improve the living conditions and educational skills of its citizens. Since income from leased land and federal funds are the tribal government's main sources of money, the dramatic funding cutbacks under the Reagan administration ended several programs and increased unemployment.

For the last thirty years the tribal government has given high priority to buying back and consolidating reservation lands. Until the mid-1960s, non-Indian farmers and ranchers were purchasing and leasing Indian allotments at below-market prices. Because checkerboarding (dividing land between Indian and non-Indian owners) and fractionated heirship holdings (Indian allotments owned by numerous heirs) made it difficult for tribal members to use the land profitably on their own, many sold or leased their allotments, often at cut-rate prices. Land worth two to three hundred dollars an acre was often sold, with the BIA approval, for eight to thirteen dollars an acre or leased for ten cents to thirty-three cents an acre. An estimated 90 percent of the reservation's farmland and 75 percent of its grazing land was under non-Indian control.

In 1954 the tribe received $10.5 million from the federal

The Moreau River Irrigation Project was completed in 1987. It irrigates slightly over one thousand acres of both tribally and individually owned land. A special government appropriation funded the $1.6 million project. (Courtesy Helen Clausen, *Eagle Butte News,* South Dakota.)

government for reservation land required for construction of the Oahe Dam on the Missouri River. With this money the tribe established a tribal land consolidation program. By purchasing land from non-Indians and tribal members and exchanging it with others, the tribe began a still-active program of reclaiming and organizing tribal lands in the large tracts necessary for ranching and farming.

Today approximately 47 percent of the 2.8-million-acre reservation is still non-Indian owned. Of the remaining acreage, 444,620 acres are allotted to tribal members, and 950,703 are tribally owned. Tribal members who have no allotment may obtain leases or land assignments from the tribal council. Once a request has been filed with the tribal council's secretary, copies of it are posted at the agency's office and in three other places for at least twenty days. If there are no objections, the tribal council is authorized to lease the applicant up to 160 acres for a period of twenty-five years, renewable for another twenty-five-year period. By law, Indian cooperative associations and individual tribal members must be given first priority for all land before it can be leased to nonmembers.

Some of the reclaimed and reorganized land has been used by families and cooperatives to establish cattle herds through a unique payment-in-kind program set up with money from the Oahe Dam settlement. The program "lends" interested families one hundred head of cattle. As their herds increase in size, the families pay off their loan in cattle, thereby allowing the tribe to extend the program to other families. Today the tribe operates both a beef herd and a buffalo herd.

The Cheyenne River Sioux Tribe is in the process of rebuilding the once vast buffalo herds of the Great Plains. (Courtesy South Dakota Department of Tourism.)

Despite great improvements in land management, the Cheyenne River Sioux still face high unemployment and a low annual per capita income. More than five thousand Indians live on the reservation. Their unemployment rate is roughly 80 percent, with 65 percent of all families living on less than three thousand dollars per year. In its ongoing efforts to improve the tribe's economic status, the tribal government has attempted with varying success to establish local businesses and to attract labor-intensive and light-industrial factories. One of the tribe's most successful enterprises is its tribally owned telephone company. Purchased in the mid-1950s with Oahe Dam money, it is the only telephone company owned and operated by an Indian tribe. In the late 1970s, the tribe constructed an industrial park and funded several small business concerns. A laundromat, a grocery store, and a printing shop are leased by the tribe to Indian and non-Indian individuals. Currently under consideration are proposals to construct a pottery factory, to establish a mail-order service selling traditional Lakota crafts, to explore for oil and gas, to develop the reservation's recreational resources, and to construct an airfield in a joint venture with the town of Eagle Butte.

Social Services

In the early days the Lakotas trapped the sacred eagle at a place called Wanbli Paha, "Eagle Butte." The highest flying of all animals, the eagle is the messenger between the Great Spirit and earthly creatures. Eagle feathers are prized for use in headdresses and plumes; the wing bone is used for whistles blown by Sun Dance participants; and the claws are used for necklaces. Today, Wanbli Paha is the seat of the Cheyenne River Sioux government and the location of the BIA agency. The government headquarters were established at Wanbli Paha in 1959, when the Oahe Dam Reservoir placed the former headquarters under water. Also located at Wanbli Paha are the IHS hospital, the high school, the tribally operated swimming pool, and the youth recreation program, as well as the offices of the tribal government's education, housing, health, and elderly programs.

The BIA operates six elementary and junior-high schools on the reservation. High-school students attend either the joint BIA-public high school in Eagle Butte or one of the BIA's boarding schools in other states. A number of tribal educational programs, including a Head Start program and a basic education skills program, supplement and enhance the basic education received by tribal members.

The Cheyenne River Sioux are one of eighteen tribes to have established a community college on their reservation. Cheyenne River Sioux Community College, a branch of Black Hills State College, offers students an opportunity to obtain an associate of arts degree. The Harry Johnson Me-

Billy Mills, an Oglala Sioux from the Pine Ridge Reservation, winner of the 10,000 meter race in the 1960 Olympics, serves as a role model for Cheyenne River youngsters when he visits the reservation. Mills, now an insurance executive in California, has not forgotten his roots, and he visits South Dakota often to help instill a sense of pride in Indian youths. (Courtesy Helen Clausen, *Eagle Butte News,* South Dakota.)

More than 115 new, low-rent housing units have been completed at Eagle Butte in the No Heart Housing area. This brings the total of low-rent housing units on the Cheyenne River Reservation to 689 since the program's inception in 1965. In addition to these, there are 77 small apartments in a manor for the elderly. (Courtesy Helen Clausen, *Eagle Butte News,* South Dakota.)

morial Cultural Center, established by the tribal council in the 1970s, houses a small museum, a crafts shop, and a meeting room. Transmitting Lakota history and culture is the primary objective of the center. Included among its displays are several murals by local artists depicting tribal history.

In 1963 the Cheyenne River Reservation established the Cheyenne River Housing Authority to help improve the housing situation on the reservation. In the last two decades, several housing units for families and for the elderly were constructed in various communities across the reservation. A weatherization program helps families install insulation, while an energy assistance program helps those who cannot afford the full cost of heat during the long, harsh winters.

Health care is provided by a thirty-bed IHS hospital in Eagle Butte. Four outlying field clinics are served by a traveling medical team from the hospital. The tribal government's Community Health Department supplements the medical and dental care provided by the IHS. One of the Health Department's most important services is a halfway house for recovering alcoholics. A trained staff provides counseling and a supportive setting to help individuals combat their disease.

As in other tribes, honoring and caring for the elderly are respected traditions. In fact, the Lakota word for "beautiful woman" metaphorically means "old woman." Like many other tribal members, the elderly on the Cheyenne River Reservation often live in isolation and poverty. Their houses are often poorly heated and have marginal or no plumbing. Few have phones. Roads, if they exist, are often impassable in rain and during the winter. For the few who can even get to the often-distant markets, fresh fruits and vegetables are unaffordable luxuries. At home, lack of refrigeration and efficient cooking facilities further contribute to poor nutrition. More than half of the reservation's elderly suffer from serious health problems such as heart and kidney disease, arthritis, and diabetes.

In 1973 the tribal council established the Elderly Nutrition Program to help improve the diet of its elderly members. Today the program serves as a model throughout the state. Its benefits are available to all reservation inhabitants—both Indian and non-Indian—over the age of fifty-five. A nine-member board, made up of three Indians and three non-Indians over the age of fifty-five and three individuals under fifty-five, directs the program. The board works closely with the tribal council's health committee. The Elderly Nutrition Program is supported by federal, state, and tribal funds. The elderly themselves also contribute money from bazaars and other fund raising events they hold throughout the year.

The core of the program is nutritious midday meals prepared five days a week and served in six nutrition centers scattered across the reservation. These facilities, which also serve as community centers, contain modern kitchens and dining and meeting areas. Five of the six centers have vans that transport the elderly to the center for meals and to town for shopping trips, doctor's appointments, or other outings. During blizzards, the centers use snowplows and sleds to ensure that the elderly have sufficient food.

Since it has been in operation, the program has expanded to provide more than meal service and transportation. Each center schedules periodic talks by specialists on nutrition, health care, and legal rights. An information-and-referral ser-

Two Cheyenne River elders, Harvey Horn and Amy Fiedler, officiated at the groundbreaking ceremony in 1985 for the Teton Mall, which houses several businesses and the state social services office. (Courtesy Helen Clausen, *Eagle Butte News,* South Dakota.)

Dancers of all ages enter the contests at the annual tribally sponsored Cheyenne River Fair and Rodeo, held on Labor Day weekend each September. (Courtesy Helen Clausen, *Eagle Butte News,* South Dakota.)

vice directs the elderly to specific social-service agencies. A phone reassurance program run by senior volunteers periodically checks on those seniors with telephones. To increase the seniors' general mental and physical health, the centers hold exercise classes and dances and have instituted a "Walk a Mile" program. Seniors and staff members who complete the program's goal of walking one mile a day are honored at an awards ceremony held each summer. A cultural awareness program staffed by the seniors provides speakers for elementary, junior, and high schools. Senior citizens teach youngsters traditional dances and show them how to prepare Indian foods and perform the crafts of beading, quill work, moccasin making, and star-quilt making.

Each center is directed by a committee of local seniors. The committee members help to decide menus, oversee the building's maintenance, plan trips, hold bazaars and other fundraisers, organize birthday parties and celebrations, and determine future needs and goals.

In 1980 several seniors at the Eagle Butte Center proposed that they plant a large "Back to Basics" garden, which would allow them to increase their access to traditionally grown and prepared foods. The idea grew into a reservationwide effort. Community members donated tillage equipment and labor; the BIA contributed seeds and fencing; the local water authority opened a fire hydrant for irrigation; and planting, hoeing, and weeding were all done by the seniors, working at dawn to avoid the broiling summer midday sun. A harvest festival of thanksgiving, with prayers and a feast, is now a yearly tradition at the Eagle Butte Nutrition Center. In 1983 the Elderly Nutrition program expanded its highly successful and acclaimed Back to Basics project with the construction of a large greenhouse. Solar-heated and wind-powered, the greenhouse has enabled the seniors to extend their growing season and to experiment with a variety of new crops.

CHAPTER 9

THE ISLETA PUEBLO

It is unusually cool even for a desert night in New Mexico. The Isleta Tribal Council has gathered in the adobe administration building for its monthly meeting. An elder council member, a farmer on a small plot of land, offers a prayer in the native language. It will be a long night for the council, with several important items to discuss. For one thing, there are the tribal programs affected by federal funding cuts. And the council will also consider leasing requests from several families who want to enlarge their holdings to increase their ranching operations. Most important, the council will hear a status report on New Mexico v. Aamodt. *The case is being pursued by four of the northern pueblos—Nambe, San Ildefonso, Tesuque, and Pojoaque. The case's outcome will decide the water rights of the nineteen pueblos throughout New Mexico. The Pueblos' side is supported by the federal government and by laws stretching back to the reign of Ferdinand and Isabella. The future of Pueblo water rights and, therefore, Pueblo development, depends on the case's resolution.*

The Pueblo Indians today live on twenty reservations, nineteen of which are clustered along the Rio Grande Valley in New Mexico. The Hopis, who have experienced a slightly different history of Spanish and American relations, live farther west in Arizona. Despite their similar appearance, the Pueblos are diverse, with different languages, social organizations, and beliefs. They do share, however, a general cultural orientation.

The nineteen New Mexico Pueblos speak three distinct languages. The Acoma, Cochiti, Laguna, San Felipe, Santa Ana, Santo Domingo, and Zia Pueblos speak Keresan. The Taos, Picuris, Sandia, and Isleta Pueblos speak Tanoan, which itself has three dialects: Tiwa, Tewa, and Towa. The Zunis, of western New Mexico, who have the largest population of all Pueblos, speak the Zuni language.

Although the Pueblos have integrated elements of Hispanic and Anglo culture into their lives, their overall culture remains uniquely their own. Pueblo society is traditional and conservative yet highly adaptive. Traditional institutions have been modified but not abandoned. Although a cash economy and wage work have replaced subsistence farming, an individual's bond to the land remains strong. The nuclear family exists side by side with the traditional extended family. Many families attend Catholic mass and par-

We have lived upon this land from days beyond history's records, far past any living memory, deep into the time of legend. The story of my people and the story of this place are one single story. No man can think of us without thinking of this place. We are always joined together.

Taos Pueblo Man

Historical photo showing image of the Southwest. (Courtesy National Congress of American Indians.)

ticipate in the celebration of saints' days, but the rich ceremonial calendar of the traditional religion continues to guide and solidify Pueblo life.

HISTORY

The first settlers in the Southwest other than the Pueblos were the Navajos and the Apaches. Nomadic by nature, the latter two tribes moved into the area from Canada in the early 1400s. Some years later—in the early 1530s—members of the Zuni Pueblo came upon four men of strange complexion wandering through their lands. The only survivors of a Spanish vessel that had sunk in the Gulf of Mexico, these four Iberian sailors roamed the Southwest for eight years before finding their way back to colonized Mexico.

Theirs and other stories led the Spanish viceroy to sponsor
Francisco Coronado's exploration of the region in 1540. Expecting to find the riches of another Aztec empire, Coronado
arrived in the area with several hundred well-armed soldiers.
He responded to the Pueblos' hospitality by occupying Tiwa
villages and waging military campaigns against those who
resisted. Coronado returned to Mexico two years later, disil-
lusioned and empty handed, his expedition a failure. Fifty-
eight years passed before the Pueblos were disturbed again.

In 1598, approximately thirty years after the founding of
Saint Augustine, Florida, Juan de Oñate came north from
Mexico, leading a group of colonists into what is now the
state of New Mexico. De Oñate claimed more than 150,000
acres near the San Juan Pueblo in the name of Spain and
imposed a system of tribute and forced labor on the northern
Pueblos. Under the encomienda system (see chapter 3), each
individual was required to produce an annual fixed tax, such
as two bushels of corn and a square yard of cloth. The Spanish colonists, in turn, provided missionaries and schools. In
these missions, built with forced Indian labor, the Indians
learned to weave textiles, work leather, and forge metal
goods for the Spanish. Many of the women and children
were exploited as household servants. The men were required to tend the Spaniards' crops and livestock.

By 1630, De Oñate reported to Spanish authorities that
some ninety chapels and missions had been constructed with
Indian labor. The Indians were compelled to attend mass and
receive instruction in Catholic doctrine. Accompanying this
forced conversion was a systematic persecution of the native
religion. The Catholic priests encouraged raiding of kivas,
destruction of religious objects, and harassment or imprisonment of spiritual leaders. The Spanish also required that
the Pueblos establish a secular local government modeled on
Spanish colonial rule. This imposed government was headed
by a village governor who represented the community in all
its dealings with Spanish officials. The Spanish government
bestowed on each Pueblo governor a silver-headed cane en-
graved with a cross as a symbol of its recognition of his political authority.

For the Pueblos to give up their religion was to give up life
itself. As discussed in chapter 2, Pueblo religion was based
on a belief in the role of natural order and harmony in daily
activity. A rich ceremonial life offered prayers and thanksgiving to spirit guardians of these forces. The Pueblos believed that if these rituals and dances were not performed,
life itself would become unbalanced. Consequently the Pueblos "accepted" their imposed government—not as a replace-
ment but as a means of shielding their traditional leaders and
practices from Spanish view. Their religious societies and kivas continued to perform their functions in secret.

The long-term effect of Spanish colonization on the Pueblos was devastating. Overgrazing by Spanish livestock re-

sulted in soil erosion, water shortages, and a serious lack of food. Any Pueblo resistance to Spanish rule was met with brutal repression. When the Acoma Pueblo staged an insurrection against De Oñate's government, Spanish soldiers burned the pueblo, executed a large number of men, and amputated one foot of all survivors. The Pueblo population before Coronado's expedition was estimated at sixty thousand inhabitants housed in some eighty pueblos. By 1643 the number of pueblos had dropped to forty-three and their total population to forty thousand. Forced labor, smallpox, and Apache and Navajo raids further reduced the Pueblo population to fourteen thousand by 1690.

The Revolt of 1680

After eighty-two years of unabated harassment, cruelty, and enslavement by the Spanish, the Pueblos rebelled. The revolt was traced by the Spanish to Popé, a medicine man of the Opi society from San Juan. Five years before the revolt, Popé had been one of forty-seven religious leaders publicly whipped in Santa Fe by colonial authorities. In 1680 he led a coalition of all but two of the pueblos in an effort to expel the Spanish. By the end of the three-week rebellion, 21 missionaries and 375 colonists were dead, and 2,000 colonists were fleeing south toward Mexico. Fearing reprisals for not having taken part in the revolt, remnant villagers of the Manzano, Tiwas, and some Isletas accompanied the Spanish, making new homes at Tortugas and Ysleta, Texas. The fleeing colonists resettled and founded the city of El Paso, Texas.

Once rid of the colonists, the Pueblos destroyed all that had been built and every object and relic of the Spanish era. Baptisms were "washed off" in the rivers. Peace, however, was not forthcoming. Interpueblo disputes surfaced, spurred by continuing famines and raids by Apaches and Navajos. In 1692 a group of Pueblo men from Jemez, Zia, Santa Ana, San Felipe, Pecos, and Tanos, seeking protection from the Navajo and Apache raids, traveled to Guadalupe del Paso and invited the Spanish to return. The following year, Don Diego de Vargas reestablished colonial rule in Pueblo lands. Not all the Pueblos were in favor of the Spaniards' return, however, and minor revolts continued for the next several years.

Following Spanish recolonization, some aspects of the earlier Spanish-Pueblo relationship were abandoned. The encomienda system was disbanded in favor of land grants, by which Pueblo land rights were recognized. Non-Indians were forbidden to live on Pueblo lands, a law enforced by Spanish authorities. Although Pueblos still had to practice their traditional religion in secret, the leadership in the Catholic church became far less coercive and corrupt. For the most part the final one hundred years of Spanish-Pueblo relations were uneventful, with differences between the two groups mediated at annual meetings.

> We were told by Masauwu, The Creator: This is your Land. Keep it for me until I come back.
>
> Thomas Benyacya, Hopi Elder

Mexican Rule

In 1821, Mexico declared its independence from Spain. At that time, the ten thousand Pueblo Indians constituted one-fourth of the population of New Mexico. Relations between the new, Mexican government and the Pueblos were generally cordial. Pueblo Indians were regarded as citizens of Mexico and protected against discrimination by the Plan of Iguala, the Mexican Declaration of Independence, adopted in February, 1821. The two governments disagreed only on land rights. Although Pueblo land rights were officially recognized by Mexico, the Mexican government, unlike Spain's, did little to keep squatters out of Pueblo lands.

In 1837 and again in 1847 the Pueblos joined with local Spanish populations to overthrow unpopular regimes. In the first uprising the provocation was Mexico's appointment of Albino Perez as governor. Resented as a manipulative outsider, Perez was assassinated by several Taos Indians. A mixed-blood Indian from Taos, José Gonzales, was installed as territorial governor until his arrest by Mexican authorities six months later on charges of insurrection. In 1847 the Pueblos again joined forces with local Hispanics to overthrow the newly imposed American territorial regime. The American-appointed governor, Charles Bent, was killed. This time the U.S. Calvary retaliated quickly, laying a barrage of mortar fire and killing more than 150 Taos Indians who had taken refuge in the Taos Pueblo mission.

American Rule

New Mexico came under American rule on August 18, 1846, following a three-month war between Mexico and the United States. Two years later, on May 10, 1848, the two countries signed the Treaty of Guadalupe Hidalgo. In this treaty Mexico ceded California, Nevada, Utah, and parts of Arizona, New Mexico, Colorado, and Wyoming to the United States. Under Article 8, all inhabitants, including the Pueblos, of the newly ceded territory were granted full rights of U.S. citizenship. Residents who wished to retain their Mexican citizenship were given one year to do so.

From the Pueblos' perspective, American rule at first brought certain advantages. The military was generally more effective than the Mexicans had been in containing Navajo and Apache raids. The establishment of numerous American forts brought welcomed prosperity to the Pueblo livestock raisers of New Mexico. The newly formed New Mexican legislature recognized the Pueblos as independent units of government with full rights to their lands as established by the laws of Spain and Mexico; sixteen years later Pueblo rights were similarly recognized by the federal government. In 1864, President Abraham Lincoln issued land grants to the majority of the Pueblos, acknowledging that they possessed title to their lands, which totaled approximately 700,000 acres. In May of the same year, BIA Superintendent Michael Steck, continuing the tradition established by the Spanish and Mexican governments, presented "Lincoln canes" to each Pueblo governor. The Spanish, Mexican, and Lincoln canes, which signify more than three centuries of sovereign Pueblo authority, are still used today in inauguration ceremonies of Pueblo secular and traditional leaders.

By the 1870s, however, the Pueblos' status under American law had become unclear and complex. The Pueblos were Indians and had been receiving BIA services since 1872. Under the American law of the time, Indians were considered wards of the federal government, not citizens; the Pueblos, however, *were* citizens. They had been viewed as citizens under Mexican law and had been given American citizenship under the Treaty of Guadalupe Hidalgo. Moreover, they had been recognized by Spanish, Mexican, and American law as holding full title to their lands.

In 1876 the Supreme Court ruled in *United States* v. *Joseph* that the Pueblos, because of their "civilized" nature (unlike their seminomadic neighbors, the Pueblos were a settled people who had farmed their lands for centuries), were not Indians in the legal sense. This meant that federal law that applied to other tribes did not apply to the Pueblos. Paradoxically, this decision was not in the Pueblos' interest, since it removed the government's obligation to protect Pueblo lands. Without federal intervention, homesteaders began encroaching on Pueblo lands in droves.

After the railroads were completed in the 1880s, the squatters were accompanied by tourists, traders, and adventurers—all bringing great changes to the Pueblos' pastoral and

Isleta Pueblo circa 1880. (Courtesy Braun Research Library.)

isolated life. Access to new markets and goods brought about a change from a subsistence-trade economy to an one based on cash and credit. Pueblo artisans began selling their jewelry, baskets, and pottery. Some Pueblos began migrating to local towns for wage employment, a trend that was encouraged by U.S. government officials and missionaries. Pueblo households gradually changed from the traditional multi-family, apartmentlike dwellings into smaller, nuclear-family housing units.

Many traditional Pueblos strongly disapproved of these changes, and their dissent led to factions within villages. At Laguna, for example, the Pueblos split into pro- and anti-American factions. About fifty of the more traditional Lagunas, facing prosecution from Protestant missionaries and their own tribal government, eventually relocated to Isleta. Isleta, too, experienced serious problems with factionalism, which at times paralyzed the government and led in the early twentieth century to a change in the government's structure.

In 1913 the U.S. Supreme Court overturned the *Joseph* decision. The Pueblos, the Court now ruled, were, like other Indians, wards of the federal government. Like the 1876 *Joseph* decision, this new definition had both advantages and disadvantages. The Pueblos were now clearly eligible to receive federal assistance. Irrigation ditches and tools provided by the BIA improved agricultural production, for example. But with BIA assistance came paternalism and oppression.

Unprotected by the U.S. Constitution's First Amendment guarantee of religious freedom, the Pueblos were a special target of the Religious Crimes Code, a series of BIA regulations forbidding tribes from practicing their traditional religions. As Spanish colonial rulers had done, BIA officials confiscated and burned religious objects and imposed fines and jail sentences on Pueblos who practiced traditional religious ceremonies. Once again the Pueblos were forced to practice their cherished religion in secret. Even today many Pueblos forbid outsiders from viewing their religious ceremonies.

BIA oppression extended into education as well. The BIA had been operating day schools at Zuni, Isleta, Santa Clara, San Juan, Laguna, and Jemez since 1885. There, and at Indian boarding schools, which many children were virtually kidnapped and forced to attend, teachers degraded Pueblo culture and prohibited Pueblo children from speaking their native languages.

Also during this time, non-Indian cattle and sheepherding enterprises began seriously to encroach upon and destroy Pueblo lands. Overgrazing and extensive logging and mining operations in the central Rio Grande Valley led to serious soil erosion and flooding. By the early 1900s, the Pueblos had lost virtually one-half of their productive lands and were facing a seriously diminished water supply as a result of upstream diversion.

> The people of the Pueblos, although sedentary rather than nomadic in their inclinations and disposed to peace and industry, are nevertheless Indians in race, customs and domestic government, always living in separate and isolated communities, adhering to primitive modes of life, largely influenced by superstition and fetishism, and chiefly governed according to the crude customs inherited from their ancestors. They are essentially a simple, uninformed, and inferior people.
>
> *U.S. v. Sandoval,* 1913

This nineteenth-century photo shows an Isleta Pueblo footrace, a ritual contest symbolizing the ongoing movement of natural forces. (Courtesy Maxwell Museum, University of New Mexico.)

In 1922, nine years after the *Sandoval* decision, a Congressional investigation revealed that more than three thousand non-Indian families were squatting on Pueblo lands. More than 10 percent of the Pueblos' richest and most irrigable lands were threatened. That same year, Senator Holm O. Bursum of New Mexico introduced a bill to "remedy" the situation. The "remedy" was to grant title to nearly sixty thousand acres of Pueblo land to the squatters. Mainly through the efforts of the writer Mabel Dodge Luhan and later appointed BIA Commissioner John Collier, the Pueblos were made aware of this bill, and as they had done in 1680, the Pueblos united to protect their lands. The All-Indian Pueblo Council (discussed more fully in chapter 11), a long-standing organization of governors from the nineteen Pueblos, met at Santa Domingo and drafted a protest to be taken by a delegation to Washington, D.C. With the support of many non-Indian organizations, they lobbied vigorously to defeat the Bursum Bill and were successful. In place of the Bursum Bill, Congress passed the Pueblo Lands Bill on June 7, 1924. This bill forced many squatters to leave and provided monetary compensation to the Pueblos for 4,685 parcels of lost land.

Group of Isleta men. Photo taken around the turn of the century.
(Courtesy Library of Congress.)

MODERN TRIBAL GOVERNMENT

Isleta Pueblo has stood at its present location, fifteen miles
south of Albuquerque, since before Coronado's visit in the
early 1540s. At one time the Isleta Pueblo occupied a hill on
the banks of the Rio Grande, and the standing water surrounding the village gave it the appearance of an island;
hence the name Isleta Pueblo, from the Spanish word for
islet. With an enrollment of 3,020, Isleta is one of the most
populous pueblos. In total land area it covers 210,974 acres
and is the fourth largest of the nineteen New Mexico pueblos. Isleta enjoys a diverse and beautiful setting. The forested

Manzano Mountains sit to the west, and the land slopes in an alluvial plain east from the mountains onto the tree-lined and fertile river bottom of the Rio Grande. The reservation continues onto the mesa land on the west slope and ends at the Puerco River wash. The village of Isleta is located on the bank of the Rio Grande; it is the pueblo's main settlement. Other, smaller settlements include Los Charos and Oraibi. Isleta's mission church, constructed in the early 1600s and surrounded by old, adobe homes, dominates the community's historic plaza. A modern tribal office complex, an arts and crafts shop, and a meeting hall form the nucleus of the pueblo's growing administration sector.

As already discussed, the structure of Pueblo government has altered over the years to meet changing demands. At Spanish insistence the Pueblos installed a secular government headed by a governor and his staff. But instead of allowing the new government to replace their traditional system, the Pueblos used it to protect their traditional leaders. This dual system of government, one religious and one secular, continues today to some degree in all the pueblos and reflects, to varying degrees, the acceptance of some distinction between the religious and secular worlds.

At Isleta, the secular government is elected by all eligible adult voters. The secular government is responsible for handling the business of the modern world. The governor functions, in essence, as a foreign minister, representing the pueblo in its dealings with other governments and with the business world. This arrangement frees the cacique and the other religious leaders to attend to and preserve the community values upon which the traditional culture is based.

Few details are available about the structure and operation

In the past our people were very fond of a race in which a piece of flint or obsidian was kicked and we were called Tsug-waga, "Kick–flaking stone place people." From our knowledge about our ancestors we know there are old sites below the mountain to the east where they had lived. The people "got crazy" talking about how the yellow and red faced people with red hair came; then they ran away and crossed the river and made Isleta.

Isleta creation story

Isleta Pueblo church. (Courtesy Mark Nohl, New Mexico Economic and Tourism Department.)

PUEBLO LAND: PAST AND PRESENT

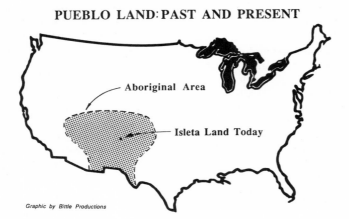

Graphic by Bittle Productions

of the Pueblos' present religious system and structure. The past five hundred years of domestic interference have convinced the Isletans that openness can lead to disrespect and disregard of their traditions by the outside world. Although Isleta no longer has a taikabede (cacique), its moieties and other ceremonial associations remain strong. The Isleta moieties are called Winter and Summer (also called the Black Eye, or Shifun, and the Red Eye, or Shure, moieties). A war captain and two or three assistants head each moiety. Each moiety is responsible for the coordination and performance of one major dance a year. The Black Eyes are responsible for the preplanting spring dance, which is a prayer for rain, good crops, and fertility. The Red Eyes have charge of the water turtle dances, held in the fall.

Isletans belong to their mother's corn group (a ceremonial association whose traditional role was to pray, sing, and dance for successful corn harvests) in addition to one of the two moieties. Isleta has five corn groups: White Corn, Black Corn, Yellow Corn, Blue Corn, and All-Colors Corn. Each group has one or more corn chiefs, or Fathers, and at least three assistants. A women's auxiliary is attached to each group and is responsible for performing certain duties and dances. Together the moieties and corn groups are responsible for coordinating the pueblo's various ceremonial activities. Ceremonies are performed in either the large, round communal house or in one of six smaller ceremonial structures.

Other groups are also integral to maintaining Isletan community life. Hunting associations offer prayers for hunting success, and two groups of clowns participate in important ceremonies associated with each season. The clowns, or *koshares*, provide comic relief and exercise social control during ceremonies.

An Isletan may also be dedicated to, and later initiated into, one of two curing societies. Anyone who has been cured or assisted by one of the medicine societies is eligible for membership. Final acceptance into the society may take several years and occurs only after a person has received instructions in secret curing techniques and fulfilled the initiation requirements.

Historical Development of the Modern Isleta Government

Until the late nineteenth century, Isleta's taikabede, or cacique, was chosen from each of the corn groups in succession and served for life. His duties were demanding and exacting. He was never permitted to leave the pueblo and spent his entire time attending to religious matters. The taikabede was aided in his ceremonial responsibilities by several assistants, including a war chief and a hunt chief. In return for the taikabede's work for the community, pueblo members, under the direction of the war priest, planted and harvested food for him and his family. The community also provided his family with firewood, clothing, and other necessities.

Isleta, like other pueblos, established a secular government in 1620 as decreed by Spanish authorities. Basically this government consisted of a governor chosen by the religious leaders to deal with non-Indians. The cacique and the council of principals (all religious leaders, heads of organizations, and first assistants) met in the kiva to discuss the best candidates for governor. This name was put forth by the cacique at a public meeting of the pueblo. Other nominations

Pueblo Indian Council meeting, November 17, 1926, Santa Fe, New Mexico. (Courtesy Braun Research Library.)

could be made from the floor. After a discussion of merits, a standing vote was taken. Traditionally, the man elected repeatedly declined the honor, claiming his unworthiness. After much argument, the governor-elect reluctantly agreed to serve and was subsequently installed by the cacique. The governor then appointed his own two lieutenant governors and two sheriffs.

This dual system of government worked well until the late 1800s, when Isleta, like several other pueblos, began experiencing disagreements over the operation of the government and the adoption of Anglo traditions and practices. The factions in the pueblo were represented by those who wished to maintain the traditional ways and those who, influenced by Anglo and Spanish ideas, wished to alter Pueblo society. For a society that greatly valued harmony and cooperation, this situation was disturbing and serious. Historically, unsolvable disagreements were worked out by one faction leaving and founding a new community or joining another pueblo. In recent times the limited availability of land has not made this possible.

The factor precipitating Isleta's political crisis began in 1896, when the last traditionally installed cacique died. According to custom, the war chief installed the cacique, and the cacique installed the war chief. Through a series of coincidences and deaths, the pueblo was left without either a cacique or a war chief in 1896. For the next several decades the pueblo was divided as to how the problem should be solved. The more conservative members believed strongly that the old ways and customs should be carried out as fully as possible. They sincerely believed that without adherence to the age-old rituals and ceremonies, the power necessary for success would not be forthcoming. The more acculturated members of the pueblo pushed for a change in the pueblo's governing system. They argued for less control by religious leaders and more control by the general population. For a time, during the 1940s, two governors, representing the two main factions, claimed to hold office. In an effort to solve the problem, the BIA, in 1946, proposed that a delegate from each of the major factions jointly draft a constitution to govern the pueblo. This constitution was accepted by the people the following year. In 1970 the pueblo replaced the 1947 constitution with a new one. The government set up by the new constitution is rather different from that of most tribal governments. While most tribal governments stress a strong legislative branch, with the tribal council as the dominant element, Isleta gives greatest power to the executive branch, which is, in turn, responsible for choosing the legislative branch.

The Executive Branch

Isleta's constitution provides for an executive branch of five officers: governor, first lieutenant governor, second lieu-

Isleta Pueblo Council circa 1984. (Courtesy Isleta Pueblo.)

tenant governor, sheriff, and under-sheriff. The governor directs the pueblo's civil affairs and represents it in dealings with other governments, outside businesses, and individuals. The governor supervises pueblo employees but does not attend council meetings. The two lieutenant governors assist the governor and replace him or her in case of absence, death, resignation, or removal. The sheriff and the under-sheriff also assist the governor in the pueblo's general administration.

All enrolled members over twenty-one are eligible to vote in the general election for governor, held every two years. Enrollment requirements at Isleta are strict, requiring one-half or more Isletan blood. In addition, the council may naturalize or adopt persons of one-half or more other Indian blood. Isletan law specifically forbids membership of non-Indians.

The general election takes place on December 30 of even-numbered years. It is actually a nomination process. Each person casts a secret ballot nominating an eligible enrolled member as a candidate for governor. The three persons receiving the greatest number of votes form the election slate. A second vote is held in which the candidate receiving the most votes is elected governor; the second highest, president of the council; and the third, vice-president of the council. To hold the positions of governor and lieutenant governor, which are full-time jobs, a person must be an enrolled member of the Pueblo, be at least thirty-five years old, and have been a resident for at least five years. Enrolled five-year residents may hold all other government positions at the age of twenty-five.

The Legislative Branch

A twelve-member council, which meets weekly, forms the legislative branch of Isletan government. The governor appoints four council members and the president and vice-president of the council each appoint three. The council's secretary and treasurer are chosen by the council itself at its first meeting. The council is directed by the constitution to employ legal counsel; to protect and manage pueblo lands; to negotiate and enter into agreement with federal, state, local, and other pueblo and tribal governments, businesses, and individuals; to enact tribal laws; to set and collect taxes; to allocate funds for the pueblo's health, safety, and welfare; to establish committees and commissions; and to regulate trade. Isleta's constitution was written under the terms of the Indian Reorganization Act, so Isleta council actions are subject to the approval of the secretary of the interior and an affirmative vote by 30 percent or more of eligible Isletan voters.

Members of the legislative branch, like the executive branch, hold office for two-year terms. The council may remove appointed officials accused of misconduct by a two-thirds vote of the full council. Elected officials can be recalled by a vote of 50 percent of the registered voters.

The Judicial Branch

The three judges of the Isleta Court are appointed by the governor and must be approved by at least two-thirds of the

ISLETA PUEBLO (SECULAR) GOVERNMENT

Graphic by Bittle Productions

council. Judges serve for two-year terms. Court is held every Monday and Wednesday evening from six to nine o'clock. The court hears all criminal and civil cases in which the defendant is an Indian. In 1976 the tribal council adopted the Pueblo of Isleta Code, which includes a law-and-order code, livestock ordinances, a traffic code, and rules concerning jury trials and professional attorneys. Civil cases are decided according to tribally adopted ordinances or custom, unless prohibited by federal law. The Pueblo council functions as the appellate court in Isleta's judicial system. All appeals must be referred to the council within five days of the lower court's ruling. The council's appellate decisions are final.

Article III of the Isleta Constitution is similar to the U.S. Bill of Rights and explicitly defines the rights of individual Pueblo citizens. Defendants have many of the same protections found in the Anglo-American judicial system, including the right to a jury trial, the right to confront witnesses, and the right to be represented by an attorney at their own expense.

However, the Isleta Court does not operate according to a strict adversarial system of justice. Isletan judges are far more interested than are their Anglo-American counterparts in understanding why a member has broken the law and what can be done to repair the breach. Defendants are often accompanied by an older relative or friend who speaks on the defendant's behalf. Together, these participants seek a solution to whatever problem made the legal proceedings necessary. Emphasis is on rehabilitation and the establishment of harmony rather than on punishment. Although judges can sentence an individual to up to a year in jail and/ or a one thousand dollar fine, many sentences require community work or service. Young offenders are frequently referred to counseling or alcohol and drug rehabilitation programs. Violators who are required to serve jail terms are housed under agreement with county officials in the county jails, located in nearby towns.

A six-member police force maintains law and order in the pueblo. Three members of the Isletan force are tribally employed and are responsible for handling misdemeanors. The other three police officers are BIA employees trained to handle felonies.

Economic Development and Protection of Land and Water Rights

Unemployment at Isleta, as at many of the pueblos, stands at approximately 50 percent. Except for the few families who farm or produce traditional crafts, finding jobs means commuting daily to Albuquerque or other major employment centers. But for many Pueblos, who are closely tied to their land and community, moving to the city is unacceptable. In the 1960s many Pueblo men acquired a national reputation as skilled firefighters. Specially trained firefighting units were flown to fire sites throughout the West. But these units alone cannot bring significant improvement to Pueblo unemployment problems. The pueblo's leaders realize that, to improve Pueblo economic life, they must develop a local economy with local employment opportunities, and that doing this depends on protecting and effectively managing the land base and water supply of the region.

In fact, protecting Pueblo land and water lies at the heart of Isletan survival—politically, culturally, and economically. In an area where rainfall averages only fifteen inches a year, water is precious. Without water the land will die physically. Without land the people will die spiritually. Today about 20 percent of those employed at Isleta have jobs in commercial farming and ranching. Others farm small plots for their personal use. The governor assigns land to individual pueblo members, usually in tracts of ten to fifteen acres. Roughly six thousand acres are presently under cultivation. The Isleta Pueblo Tribal Enterprise, operated by the pueblo's government, owns a tractor, grader, and other equipment, and assists farmers with plowing, cultivating, and maintaining irrigation ditches. With improved irrigation techniques and sufficient water, the tribe's plan is to consolidate small holdings into larger ones and thereby enhance the land's productive use. But as the city of Albuquerque grows, siphoning off more groundwater and increasing the river's pollution, Isleta's water supply will become increasingly endangered.

Besides preserving the land and water for future generations, the Isletan government is working to increase on-reservation employment opportunities. In 1975, the pueblo government received a federal economic development grant to construct a small supermarket and gas station. A few years later, Isleta took its first step toward capturing the tourist trade that could potentially be attracted by the pueblo's natural recreational opportunities and scenic beauty. The pueblo government developed a small fishing park with camping facilities and trailer hookups. A gift shop near the tribal office building sells local crafts. Other funds, some of which help underwrite social programs, are raised by cigarette sales and the sale of hunting and fishing licenses to nonmembers.

Social Services

Given their small populations and close cultural ties, the Pueblos have established the All-Indian Pueblo Council (AIPC) to facilitate cooperation and effectiveness in providing social services. Housed in Albuquerque, the AIPC is a coalition of the nineteen Pueblo governments. It works with the federal and state governments to protect Pueblo culture and improve the well-being of all Pueblo tribal members. The first recorded meeting of a council of all Pueblos was actually held in 1598, making the AIPC, like the Iroquois League, one of the oldest mutual alliances in the world. During the early years of this century, the AIPC functioned mainly as a lobbying organization to protect Pueblo land rights, working actively to defeat the Bursum Bill in 1924.

In the mid-1960s the AIPC began its transition into a sophisticated administrative organization. In 1965 it adopted a constitution and bylaws and began actively to develop economic, educational, and health programs and to take the lead in protecting Pueblo land and water rights and preserving Pueblo culture. From a small office with four employees, the AIPC grew by the mid-1970s to an enterprise with over two hundred employees and a budget of $6 million. The AIPC constructed and now occupies a new office called the Pueblo Indian Cultural Center. Complete with a computer system and library, the offices also house the Pueblo Cultural Museum, whose extensive holdings illustrate Pueblo history, art, and dress. A restaurant serves traditional Pueblo foods to thousands of visitors each year. Programs and grants administered by the AIPC include a scholarship fund, a public-employment program, a consumer-education project, a youth-corps fund, mental-health and alcohol programs, and a speech-and-hearing program. Currently the AIPC operates Isleta's housing, manpower, and CETA programs.

Other Isleta programs, such as its education, health, social-services, and law-enforcement programs, are operated by Isleta's own government or by the BIA. The BIA, for example, is responsible for running the pueblo's elementary school. A local Isletan advisory school board, appointed by the Isleta governor, advises the BIA's director of education for the Southern Pueblo Agency (SPA), the branch of the BIA that serves the seven southern pueblos, including Isleta. The Isleta Head Start program serves students aged three to five. It is designed to boost in-school readiness and social skills and help with good nutrition and health care. A tribal board oversees the federal funds allocated to surrounding public schools for Indian education. These funds go to public junior high and high schools in south Albuquerque and Los Lunas, which Isletan students attend.

The Isleta Pueblo also operates a youth counseling program in cooperation with the courts and the schools. The program provides counseling to troubled youths and their families. When alternative living arrangements must be found for a youngster, the pueblo's child-welfare program may assume jurisdiction over the child to place him or her in a foster, adoptive, or group home. During the summer the pueblo operates a recreational program for children and young adults. Baseball, basketball, and football leagues operate year-round. The year is also filled with traditional dances, foot races, and ceremonies that bring together the entire community.

Isleta's health-care needs are met by the Indian Health Service (IHS) at a small clinic owned by the pueblo. Here residents receive basic medical, dental, and emergency care. A pueblo-owned ambulance service operated by the Commu-

nity Health Representative Program (CHRP) transports pa-
tients to the clinic or, for more serious cases, to nearby hospitals. The CHRP is one of the most important and valuable
programs operated by the tribal government. CHRP workers
are pueblo residents trained to perform a variety of health-
care functions. CHRP workers are also trained in family
planning and basic maternal and child care and nutrition.
They assist in the clinic and provide counseling and referral
to specialized health agencies in the surrounding area.

CHAPTER 10

THE YAKIMAS

It is a brisk fall day in September at the longhouse in White Swan. The Yakimas' annual general council meeting is called to order by the council's chairperson. A respected tribal elder opens the meeting with a prayer sung in Yakima. His song asks the Creator to lead the council to wisdom. A practitioner of the traditional weshat *religion, he rings a bell three times as he sings. Following the prayer, the chairperson calls upon the BIA superintendent of the Yakima Agency for a report. The BIA official summarizes the federal government's efforts during the previous year to protect Yakima treaty rights. The council then turns its attention to its business agenda. The first item is a big one: the problem of the salmon depletion in area rivers caused by pollution, irrigation projects, and the damming of the Columbia River. The tribal council has proposed that the nation build and operate a fish hatchery and stock young salmon in the streams in an effort to increase the fish runs.*

The Yakima Reservation today covers 1.4 million acres, an area one and one-half times the size of Rhode Island. Thirty-six miles long and seventy miles wide, it is a land rich in timber, fertile soil, and water. On the western side of the reservation, Pahto (or Mount Adams, as the whites call it) rises to a height of 12,307 feet. Sacred to the Yakimas, the mountain was lost to the nation for several decades because of a surveying error. Finally, in 1972, after years of protests and lobbying efforts, the mountain was returned to the nation by the federal government.

Eastward from Mount Adams lie the forested and sagebrush-covered foothills of the Cascades Mountains. The Yakima River Valley forms the easternmost boundary of the reservation. Irrigation from the river has turned the land for several miles on either side into one of the most important agricultural areas in the Northwest.

Here in this rich valley the majority of the reservation's population lives. As a result of allotment, however, the Yakimas today are a minority in their own homeland. Of the more than 27,000 people who reside on the reservation, only 6,800 are Yakimas—approximately one-quarter. The remaining 75 percent include roughly 10,000 whites and 10,000 Mexicans, migrant farm laborers who pick the crops grown on the reservation. Providing a stable and responsive government for all reservation residents, preserving and developing the reservation's rich resources, and protecting the nation's treaty rights are the challenges and responsibilities facing the Yakima tribal government.

HISTORY

The Yakimas first encountered white people when they met explorers Meriwether Lewis and William Clark in the eastern Cascades one October morning in 1805. The United States, which was in dispute with England over ownership of what is now Oregon and Washington, had commissioned Lewis and Clark to find an overland trade route to the area. The route was needed to protect American interests in the Northwest and to break England's monopoly over the lucrative fur trade.

For several decades following Lewis and Clark's expedition, the western coastal bands and tribes bore the brunt of white intrusion. The homeland of the Yakimas and other eastern bands lay outside the major routes used by fur traders, missionaries, and wagon trains, making their contact with non-Indians minimal. The contact that did occur took place at the trading houses scattered along the coastline and the Columbia River. Here tribes traded their pelts and horses for cattle and seeds, enabling some of the bands to supple-

Traditional Yakima tipi. (Courtesy Eastern Washington State Historical Society.)

ment their traditional diet of fish, roots, and berries with potatoes, melons, beans, and beef.

The peace and freedom enjoyed by the eastern bands drew to a close with the passage of the Donation Act, in 1850. This act opened lands west of the Cascades to homesteading. Single persons were given 320 acres of land and married couples 640 acres. The availability of free land dramatically increased the stream of settlers making their way across the Yakimas' homeland.

The Treaty of 1855

Within three years of the Donation Act's passage, Washington was admitted as a territory, and Isaac Stevens was appointed governor and superintendent of Indian affairs. Stevens's primary objective was to acquire tribal lands for white settlement. Within two years of taking office, Stevens had negotiated treaties with the coastal tribes, obtaining their lands for settlement and resettling the bands on reservations. As the coast filled with settlers, Stevens turned his attention to the interior. He sent Capt. George McClellan to visit the inland tribes and assess their attitudes toward land cessions.

Since the 1840s, Kamiakin, headman of the Yakimas, had been recognized as a regional leader among the bands east of the Cascades. He was the first chief since Wa-ow-wicht in the 1700s to unite the bands of the Yakima Valley. Respected for his generosity, wisdom, and daring, he had earned a reputation as an orator, counselor, and organizer. Originally friendly and hospitable to the whites, Kamiakin's attitude changed when it became clear that the whites were determined to take over Yakima lands.

In 1854, Kamiakin called for a council of the Nez Percé, Umatilla, Palouse, Walla Walla, Cayuse, Warm Springs, Wenatchi, Columbia, Chelan, Okanogan, Colville, Spokane, and Coeur d'Alene bands. He sought tribal unity against cession of tribal lands. Meeting in the Grand Ronde Valley of eastern Oregon, the tribes agreed upon the boundaries of their territories and reaffirmed their refusal to sell their lands.

Despite these declarations, Governor Stevens continued to press the bands and tribes to attend a council meeting. On May 29, 1855, a council of six thousand Indians convened at Camp Stevens in the Walla Walla Valley. Governor Stevens proposed that the tribes cede all their lands in return for annuities and two reservations—one for the bands of the upper and lower Yakima Valley and the other for the Nez Percés. With the exception of the Nez Percés, all the tribes opposed the proposal.

Stevens then offered to establish a third reservation for the Walla Walla, Cayuse, and Umatilla tribes. After several more days of threats, bribery, and persuasion, all the bands agreed. The Nez Percé reservation was established in eastern Idaho. The Umatillas, Cayuses, and Walla Wallas agreed to a small

We have listened to all you have to say, and we desire you to listen when any Indian speaks. . . . In one day the Americans have become as numerous as grass. I know the value of your speech from having experienced it in California. . . . We had not seen in the true light the object of your speeches. . . . You have talked in a round-about way. Speak straight! Goods and the earth are not equal. Goods are for using on earth. I have ears to hear you and here is my heart. . . . You have spoken in a manner partly tending to evil. Speak plain to us.

Peopeo Moxmox, Yakima Chief at Camp Stevens Treaty Council, June 2, 1855

reservation in northern Oregon. Kamiakin, of the Yakima band, and the chiefs of a dozen other tribes and bands agreed to unite as the Confederated Tribes and Bands of the Yakima Nation. This confederation numbered approximately 2,500 people and included speakers of the Sahaptian, Salishan, and Chinookan languages.

The treaty that the Yakimas signed contained ten articles. Article I provided for the cession of 10.8 million acres of Yakima land (one-third of the present state of Washington) for $200,000 (two cents an acre) and the establishment of a 1.2-million–acre reservation (an area one-tenth the size of the bands' original homeland). Originally known as Fort Simcoe, this reservation was renamed the Yakima Reservation in 1922.

Article II guaranteed that the reservation would be held for the "exclusive use and benefit" of the bands and promised that no "white man, excepting those in the employment of the Indian Department," would be permitted to reside on the reservation "without the permission of the tribe and the superintendent and agent."

Article III promised the bands exclusive fishing rights on the reservation as well as "at all usual and accustomed places, in common with citizens of the Territory." The bands were also guaranteed the right to hunt, gather roots and berries, and pasture their horses and cattle upon open, unclaimed land. Article IV, added at Kamiakin's insistence, specifically gave tribes the right to fish at their traditional off-reservation fishing site, known as the Wenatshapam Fishery.

Article V obliged the federal government to open and supply two schools, one of which was to be an agricultural and industrial school, and to hire teachers. The United States was to build two blacksmith shops, a sawmill, a flour mill, and a staffed-and-equipped hospital. This article also recognized Kamiakin as head chief and provided that the chief would receive a salary of five hundred dollars per year for the next twenty years.

In Article VI the confederated tribes and bands acknowledged their dependence on the United States, agreed to deliver fugitives from U.S. law to federal authorities, and promised not to make war on other tribes except in self-defense. The article also made possible the future allotment of the reservation, but only to those tribal members who were "willing to avail themselves of the privilege."

Article X stipulated that the Yakimas' lands were to remain in their control, free of white settlement, until the treaty's ratification. It was Governor Stevens's violation of this article that precipitated the Yakima War. Within a month after the treaty's conclusion, but prior to its ratification, Stevens announced in local newspapers that the interior Plateau region of Washington Territory was open to settlement. Settlers rushed in immediately, illegally taking tribal grazing lands

Tell them [the soldiers] we are quiet friends of the Americans, that we are not thinking of war. The way the governor has talked to us has irritated us.

He has taken us and thrown us out of our country in a strange land in a place where its people do not even have enough to eat. . . . Now we know perfectly the heart of the Americans. They hanged us without knowing if we were right or wrong; but they have never killed or hanged one American, though there is no place where an American has not killed savages. . . .

You want us to die of famine, little by little. It is better for us to die at once.

Kamiakin (Yakima) 1850s

and farmlands before the Indian owners could even move their livestock or harvest their crops.

The Yakima War

The tension created by illegal white settlement led to the killing of trespassing miners in the summer of 1855. Soon afterward, Indian Agent A. J. Bolon, who had been sent by Governor Stevens to investigate the murders, was killed by several Yakimas in retaliation for the killing of an Indian in Oregon. Two weeks later, Maj. Granville Haller arrived in the Yakimas' territory with 102 men and a howitzer to avenge Bolon's death. Determined to protect Yakima rights, Kamiakin and 700 warriors attacked and easily defeated Haller. Within a few weeks the Plateau had become the setting of a full-scale war.

Kamiakin quickly formed a confederation of various Yakima bands and the Columbia bands. The Walla Wallas, Palouse, and Umatillas united in a second alliance. In 1856, with orders to secure the Yakima Valley, Maj. Robert Garnett built and manned Fort Simcoe. Hostilities continued for two years, the outnumbered Indians finally surrendering on September 17, 1858. In 1859, Congress ratified the Treaty of 1855, four years after its negotiation. In May, 1859, the army withdrew from Fort Simcoe and turned the buildings over to the BIA. The fort served as the Yakima Indian Agency until the agency's relocation to Toppenish in 1922.

Reservation Life

The war and resettlement on the reservation left the Yakimas dispirited and demoralized. Kamiakin never forgave the whites for their treatment of his people. When offered his annual salary as provided in the treaty, he replied, "Sir, I am a poor man, but too rich to receive anything from the United States." Kamiakin also refused to settle on the reservation.

YAKIMA NATION LAND: PAST AND PRESENT

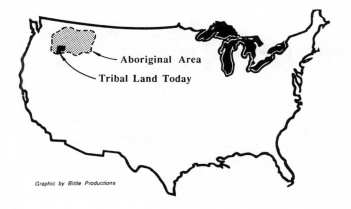

Aboriginal Area

Tribal Land Today

Graphic by Bittle Productions

His absence created a power vacuum that was quickly filled by Dr. R. H. Lansdale, an Indian agent unfamiliar with Yakima tribal culture and needs. Unable to gather, fish, and hunt on their former lands and cheated out of the full amount of rations and goods promised in the treaty, the Yakimas' general well-being and prosperity declined.

In 1865 the BIA appointed the Reverend James Wilbur as agent of the reservation. Wilbur was a Methodist minister who had served as an instructor at the Yakima reservation school—the first federal school constructed on an Indian reservation—since 1860. Although unswerving in his conviction that the Yakimas should become Christians, Wilbur had great respect for the Yakimas and dedicated his life to helping them make the transition to reservation life.

Believing that farming and ranching would bring the nation self-sufficiency, Father Wilbur, as the Yakimas called him, encouraged tribal members to plant crops and orchards, to fence land, to exchange traditional dwellings for frame houses, and to work in the new tribal lumber and ranching businesses. By 1871 the Yakimas had three thousand acres under cultivation and four thousand acres fenced. They owned fourteen hundred head of cattle and twelve thousand horses. Wilbur oversaw the construction in 1873 of a sawmill capable of producing ten thousand feet of lumber in twelve hours. By the early 1880s, according to Wilbur's estimate, one-fourth of the reservation residents had made the transition to farming and ranching. The rest continued to depend upon the seasonal patterns of hunting, gathering, and fishing.

Wilbur was equally tireless in his determination to convert the tribe to Methodism. He preached continually against

The coming of the pale-face changed all things as a cloud obscures the mid-day sun. They took our country and drove us from the homes we loved so well. The bones of our ancestors lay buried among those mountains and streams, which to us were both the cradle and the grave.

Lo-Kout (Yakima)

Gathering of Yakima men around 1900. (Courtesy Smithsonian Institution, Anthropological Archives, Bureau of American Ethnology Collection.)

the evils of the native religion as well as against competing forms of Christianity. In exchange for Sunday attendance at church, Wilbur often "bribed" his parishioners with promises to till their lands. One of his first acts as agent had been to journey to Washington, D.C., and demand the removal of the Catholic Saint Joseph Mission, which had been established on the banks of Ahtanum Creek since the 1850s. Wilbur was successful in his plea. President Ulysses S. Grant forced the Catholics to relocate outside the reservation's boundaries. But only in the area of religion was Wilbur so small minded. In all other areas he supported the Yakimas in the maintenance of their rights and worked unremittingly for their welfare.

Allotment, Railroads, and Irrigation

With the 1880s began two decades of profound political, economic, and social change for the Yakimas. Following his appointment as agent in 1864, Wilbur had held an election to fill the vacancy left by Kamiakin. Joe Stwire, or White Swan, was elected as the nation's chief and served until his death. Local government, as was the tradition, remained in the hands of each band's headman and council. In 1883, the Reverend Robert Milroy, first in a series of less-than-knowledgeable and incompetent agents, succeeded Wilbur. Milroy tried to destroy the Yakimas' traditional government by splitting the reservation into three districts and appointing a tribal policeman whose function was to insist that the people forget their old ways and become "civilized." Even more destructive was Milroy's support for the allotment of Yakima lands.

Since signing the Treaty of 1855, the Yakimas had carefully guarded their rights to "exclusive use and benefit" of reservation lands. The treaty had further guaranteed that whites would not be allowed access without tribal approval and that any division of the land into individual plots would be voluntary. They had enforced this provision by requiring all non-Indians (except those married to members) to leave the reservation.

The Dawes Allotment Act, discussed in chapter 5, violated the spirit, if not the letter, of the Yakimas' treaty. Although a few of the families Wilbur had converted to farming were in favor of allotment, most tribal members were not. To divide the land, they argued, was to divide the people's unity of thought and action.

The U.S. government's reply was that, treaty or no treaty, unless allotment occurred, the reservation would be opened to white homesteading. Left without a choice, the nation accepted allotment. From 1892 to 1914, when the rolls were finally closed, 440,000 acres were allotted to 4,506 members in tracts of up to 160 acres. (In addition, several families had accepted off-reservation allotments under the provision of the Homestead Act of 1884, which allowed Indians allotments on public lands.) After allotment, 780,000 acres remained under tribal ownership. The government offered to buy this land from the tribe for $1.4 million. Due largely to the efforts of the tribe's full-blood faction, the tribe refused to sell this land or the additional 357,879 acres added to the reservation in 1900 to correct a surveying error.

As on all allotted reservations, tribal members could sell their allotments after twenty-five years, and many, unable to pay their taxes or just in need of money, did so. In effect, then, the allotment process became a means by which non-Indians could obtain Indian lands. And Yakima lands were especially attractive because of railroads and irrigation projects established on the reservation.

In 1885 the Northern Pacific Railroad completed its line through the Yakima Reservation. This important transportation link meant that the reservation's produce and livestock could be quickly moved to commercial points throughout the Northwest. In 1906 and 1907 several families who had envisioned the potential benefits of owning allotments near the railroad sold their allotments for the townsites of Toppenish (formerly Fort Simcoe) and Wapato. Toppenish immediately boomed and was incorporated in 1907. Other white settlements followed, including the unincorporated towns of Parker, Harrah, and White Swan.

The value of irrigation in the Yakima Valley had first been recognized by Chief Kamiakin. Digging a quarter-mile ditch from a summer spring, Kamiakin had grown potatoes, melons, squash, barley, and corn for his people. Later, Wilbur had constructed the reservation's first true irrigation system, using the labor of five hundred northern Paiute prisoners of war to dig the ditches.

In 1899 the Yakimas sold the Wenatshapam Fishery to finance an irrigation project bringing water to 30,000 acres near the Yakima River. Congressional funds totaling $2 million allowed for the construction of a dam in the northwestern corner of the reservation, a 26-mile main canal, and 735 miles of lateral canals. The Wapato Project, as it was called, eventually brought 150,000 acres under cultivation.

A mad flurry of land sales followed this project's completion. By 1913 practically all agriculturally productive land on the reservation had been leased to or bought by white farmers for a fraction of its true value. Residential centers like Toppenish and Wapato flourished as the valley became a center of farming and ranching. By 1905 towns and settlements occupied more than fifteen hundred acres of reservation land. In spite of their treaty, which had guaranteed them exclusive use and benefit of reservation, tribal members became a minority on their own reservation, living off their meager lease money or working as day laborers picking crops and freighting produce to transportation points.

The Wapato Project and other reclamation projects on and off the reservation changed reservation life in ways other

God created this Indian country and it was like He spread out a big blanket. He put the Indians on it. They were created here in this country, truly and honestly, and that was the time this river started to run. Then God created fish in this river and put deer in these mountains and made laws through which has come the increase of fish and game. Then the Creator gave us Indians life; we awakened and as soon as we saw the game and fish we knew that they were made for us. For the women God made roots and berries to gather, and the Indians grew and multiplied as a people. When we were created we were given our ground to live on, and from that time these were our rights. This is all true. We had the fish before the missionaries came, before the white man came. We were put here by the Creator and these were our rights as far as my memory to my great-grandfather. This was the food on which we lived. My mother gathered berries; my father fished and killed the game. These words are mine and they are true. It matters not how long I live, I cannot change these thoughts. My strength is from the fish; my blood is from the fish, from the roots and the berries. The fish and the game are the essence of my life. I was not brought from a foreign country and did not come here. I was put here by the Creator. We had no cattle, no hogs, no grain, only berries and roots and game and fish. We never thought we would be troubled about these things, and I tell my people, and I believe it, it is not wrong for us to get this food. Whenever the seasons open I raise my heart in thanks for the Creator for his bounty that this food has come.

Chief Menenock's testimony in court case to protect Yakima hunting and fishing rights, 1920

than economic. The irrigation projects caused major changes in the delicate balance of the Yakimas' environment. As farmers cleared land and ranchers increased their herds, traditional Yakima foods—roots, tubers, and bulbs—gradually disappeared. Wild horses, once the pride of many Yakimas, were slaughtered in huge numbers by ranchers who considered them competitors with their cattle for grazing lands.

Most important, as water was diverted for irrigation, the levels of the rivers were lowered, and it became impossible for salmon to return to their spawning grounds. By 1925 the salmon runs in the Yakima River had been virtually eliminated. Depletion of the salmon runs not only diminished a primary food source but also caused families to leave their traditional fishing villages and move to their allotments. This in turn caused a change in the traditional reliance on the extended family group. What is more, in all of these projects, Indian water rights were completely ignored. Water from the Yakima River and other streams was used primarily to benefit non-Indian farmers and ranchers.

MODERN TRIBAL GOVERNMENT

The Yakima Nation is an example of a tribe that has successfully adapted its traditional form of government—the general council—to the needs of the modern world. As the chart indicates, the Yakimas' tribal government combines a traditional structure with modern organizational practices. The government is divided into three levels, each with its own functions. The tribal council is responsible for establishing policy and preserving treaty rights. The administrative level supervises the administration and planning of the government. The operations level directs the actual programs designed to meet the needs of the tribal citizen.

The general council oversees the entire government structure. Like New England town meetings, the general council meetings represent the purest form of democracy. All important matters, including the election of the tribal council, are voted on by the general council. The nation has no written constitution or bylaws but is governed by a series of resolutions passed by the general council at its annual meetings. The general council retains all government authority except what it has delegated to the tribal council and committees and retains the authority to repeal or annul all acts, resolutions, ordinances, laws, or rules of procedure passed by the tribal council.

General council meetings are held in the last week of November. Voting in all council meetings is done in the traditional manner, by standing. Four counters and two alternates are elected at each meeting to count the votes. They are the final judges of a person's qualifications to vote (a voter must be at least eighteen and an enrolled member of the tribe). To be enrolled a person must have at least one-quarter Yakima blood and be a member of one of the fourteen original bands.

From the very beginning of this nation, the chief issue around which federal Indian policy has revolved has been, not how to assimilate the Indian nations whose land we usurped, but how to transfer Indian lands and resources to non-Indians.

U.S. v. *Aktanum Irrigation District,* 1956

Section 1—Objectives: It shall be the objective of the Confederated Tribes and Bands of the Yakima Nation to:

a. Establish and enforce such rules and procedures as may be necessary to safeguard individually and tribally owned property and resources for the use of present and future generations and to promote social welfare of its members.

b. To safeguard, protect and secure rights, privileges and benefits, guaranteed to the members of the Yakima Indian Nation by the Treaty of June 9, 1855 for all time.

Yakima General Council Resolution, 1944

Children do not have to be born on the reservation, but parents are required to establish residency by returning to the reservation once every five years for feasts or ceremonies.

Two hundred and fifty people represent a quorum, with 175 necessary to transact business. It is possible for meetings to last several days if there is a great deal to discuss. Everyone is granted the right to speak on all issues and accorded the respect to speak for as long as he or she wishes. Four officers (a chairperson, vice-chairperson, secretary-treasurer, and a sergeant-at-arms) are responsible for organizing and running the meetings. These are positions of great respect that an individual holds for life.

The Tribal Council

In 1944 the general council created a fourteen-member tribal council, which meets monthly to enforce the general council's directives. Originally, each of the fourteen bands chose its representatives to the tribal council. In 1947 the general council voted to make the election process at-large. Every two years the general council elects seven members who serve for four years. By electing the councillors in staggered years, a continuity in knowledge is maintained.

The tribal council elects three people from among its membership to serve as the executive committee—a chairperson, vice-chairperson, and secretary-treasurer. The executive committee has the power to act on behalf of the tribal council in certain matters and possesses important appointive powers. Seven committees—legislative, timber grazing and economic development; housing, employment and welfare; enrollment; law and order and fish and wildlife; lands; and education and housing—exert considerable power by overseeing the programs under their jurisdiction. The ex-

Hereafter the Tribal Council, a body of fourteen Chiefs, is hereby empowered to transact all business of the Tribe, provided that any measures of great importance may be referred back to the People.

Yakima General Council
Resolution, 1944

Yakima tribal council table, in the shape of an arrow. (Photo from the author's collection.)

Salmon provided the staple food of the Yakimas. While the tribe still retains some important fishing rights, several other important fishing sites have been destroyed by dams. Shown here is Celio Falls, now under water. (Courtesy Eastern Washington State Historical Society.)

ecutive committee appoints councillors to serve on these committees.

As stated in an important general council resolution, the tribal council's primary responsibilities are to protect tribal property, to promote social welfare, and safeguard the nation's treaty rights. With these directives in mind, the tribal council carefully studies every resolution, grant, and proposal to ensure that it will not conflict with Yakima tradition or treaty rights.

The Treaty of 1855 is a sacred document to the Yakima Nation. Written on blue, lined, legal-sized notebook paper, this treaty represents a solemn agreement and set of guarantees concluded between two sovereigns more than one hundred years ago. In modern times the Yakimas have turned to the ballot box and courts to force the United States to honor its commitments in this treaty. The nation voted two-to-one against the Indian Reorganization Act, fearing that it would jeopardize and limit its treaty rights and traditional government by requiring secret balloting and other changes. Over the last one hundred years the nation has sued the federal government more than fifteen times. Its legal victories have

I,   , do solemnly swear to support and uphold the constitution and laws of the United States of America, the laws of the Yakima Indian Nation, and above all, the Yakima Treaty of 1855 and the rights thereof; and to faithfully, honestly, and unselfishly serve the Yakima Indian Nation as a Yakima Tribal Councilman under the laws, resolutions and documents pertaining thereto.

In the eyes of the Creator, I take this Oath freely and voluntarily with no mental reservations whatsoever.

Oath of Office,
Yakima Indian Tribe

forced the federal government, among other things, to recognize and protect the off-reservation gathering, hunting,
and fishing rights reserved by the nation in the 1855 treaty,
to protect the nation against state attempts to tax trust lands,
and to recognize and enforce tribal water rights.

Tribal Administration

In 1976 the tribal council undertook changes to provide for
a more efficient and responsive government. It separated
its legislative and policy-making functions from its administrative and operational roles. The tribal council hired an administrative director and assistant and a tribal comptroller
(or accountant) to oversee the government's administration.
This left the tribal council free to direct its attention to the
larger issues facing the nation: the protection of Yakima sovereignty, treaty rights, and culture and the establishment of
goals and programs to meet the social and economic needs
of all tribal members.

Tribal council members keep themselves informed about
tribal programs, problems, and needs through biweekly
meetings with administrative heads and program directors.
These program directors run a variety of programs directed
toward meeting the social-welfare, resource, and economic
needs of the Yakima Nation and Reservation.

Economic Development and Natural Resource Management

The Yakima Reservation is blessed with timber, water, fertile
soil, and wildlife. Preserving and developing the tribal land
base and its resources is viewed by the tribal government as
one of its most sacred responsibilities. Currently one-half of
the reservation is devoted to timber, one-third to grazing,
and one-eighth to agriculture.

The Yakimas possess the largest stand of timber, including
ponderosa pine, Douglas fir, western larch, hemlock, and ce-
dar, of any reservation. Ninety percent of all tribal revenue
is derived from logging, making timber the most important
resource and enterprise on the reservation. Five privately
owned off-reservation mills and three Indian logging companies harvest the timber on a sustained-yield basis. The
BIA, which employs approximately two hundred people,
many of them Yakimas, helps the tribe manage this important resource. Foresters and biologists trained in the latest
techniques of planting, harvesting, disease control, and re-
forestation monitor and oversee the forests.

In addition to protecting and expanding their timber
yields, the Yakimas are investigating means by which to
take advantage of the area's rich fishing and agricultural potential. A tribal fish hatchery is restocking streams with steelhead trout. The Yakima Valley, which forms the eastern
boundary of the reservation, is one of the most productive
crop-producing areas in the country. Commercial production of sugar beets, hops, potatoes, apples, and other crops

Whereas, in the absence of any
Constitution or By-Laws, the enrolled members of the Yakima
Tribe living on the Yakima Reservation believe that voting and
elections should be held in the
same manner since time immemorial and since the signing of
the Yakima Treaty of June 9,
1855. . . .

Yakima General Council
Resolution, 1944

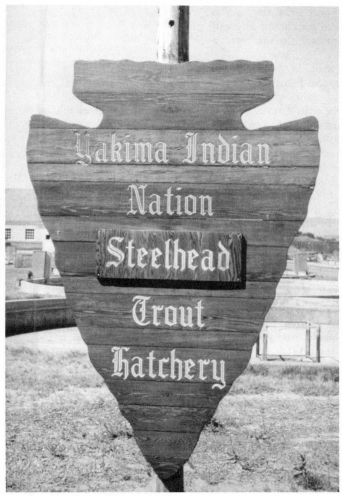

The steelhead trout hatchery on the Yakima Indian Reservation, in Washington, is one of more than sixty fish hatcheries located on Indian reservations throughout the country. (Courtesy Gary Rankel.)

is a multimillion-dollar industry. Because of the allotment process, however, the Yakima Nation receives less than 1 percent of the profits from crops grown on the reservation. Non-Indians own 40 percent of the irrigated lands on the reservation, much of it bought very cheaply from needy tribal members at the turn of the century. Yakimas who still own allotments in the valley find their shares too small (some allotments are owned by as many as 120 people) and the needed capital investment too great to enter the agricultural business.

The nation has attempted to meet these obstacles by consolidating and enlarging the tribal land base and by better utilizing existing tribal lands. Since 1954 the nation, through its Land Enterprise Office, has purchased all available Indian and non-Indian allotments within the reservation's boundaries.

To better protect and use existing tribal lands, the nation has adopted zoning and water codes and has established a soil survey program to analyze the soil composition and water needs of all reservation lands. Once the survey is complete, the tribe will use the information to develop a comprehensive land-management program that will pinpoint the areas most suitable for agriculture, grazing, and other uses.

The Yakimas' traditional reverence for the land has also made them leaders in the fight against nuclear pollution. In 1979 the Yakima Tribal Council became the first tribal council to adopt a resolution barring the transport of nuclear wastes, residues, fuels, and by-products "by land, rail, air or water across the Yakima reservation." The Handford Nuclear Reservation lies thirteen miles south of the reservation on ceded lands to which the Yakimas still possess hunting, fishing, and gathering rights. Nearly one-half of the entire United States' nuclear wastes are stored here. Fearful that construction of two nuclear power plants in the area would interfere with and damage the nation's treaty rights by increasing the radiologic, chemical, and thermal pollution of the entire Columbia River Basin, the nation is working to prevent their construction.

The Yakimas are also involved in a number of smaller but expanding enterprises. The Mount Adams Furniture Company, located in the nation's industrial park, near Wapato, manufacturers recliners, rockers, love seats, and sleepers. Highly successful, the furniture is sold by Sears and Roebuck in their stores throughout the Northwest. The Tobacco Warehouse sells cigarettes to reservation members. The tribal tax collected on these cigarettes provides additional funds for the tribe's elderly and youth programs.

Another successful enterprise and one unique among tribes is Yakima Executive Aircraft. Executive Aircraft owns and/or leases several aircraft, including twenty-six helicopters. Services provided by the tribally owned company include airplane rentals, air ambulance service, aircraft maintenance, and a cessna pilot-training program. Licensed by the Federal Aviation Administration, the pilot-training program has achieved a reputation for quality and efficiency, graduating well-trained pilots at three-quarters the time and cost of other schools.

The Yakima Cultural Heritage Center is the nation's most recent enterprise. Located in Toppenish, the structure is a modern, million-dollar complex dedicated to the preservation of Yakima culture. Central to the center is a museum of Yakima artifacts and photographs depicting and explaining traditional Yakima culture. Visitors to the museum can eat in

WHEREAS, the establishment of nuclear facilities and nuclear waste facilities on the Hanford Reservation will affect the lives, the health and safety of the Yakima Indian Nation and its members and will affect the use and enjoyment of the Yakima Indian Reservation; and

WHEREAS, the Yakima Indian Nation is a Sovereign Nation, by right of the Treaty of June 9, 1855, over the Totally Reserved Lands, and in its Reserved Usage Rights over all Ceded Land; and

WHEREAS, the Yakima Indian Nation has the right and obligation to protect from environmental harm all Yakima Indian Nation Ceded and Totally Reserved Lands; and

WHEREAS, said nuclear facilities and nuclear waste facilities will have a detrimental effect on the Treaty reserved hunting, fishing and gathering rights together with sacred and archaeological sites within the area Ceded in the Treaty of 1855;

NOW, THEREFORE, BE IT RESOLVED by the Yakima General Council meeting in its annual session, at the Wapato Longhouse, Wapato, Washington, a quorum being present, does take a stand against the establishment of nuclear facilities and nuclear waste facilities on the Hanford Reservation.

Yakima General Council
Resolution, December 7, 1982

The Yakima Cultural Heritage Center houses a museum, restaurant, and shops. (Photo by Jane Levin.)

its restaurant, which specializes in salmon, the traditional Yakima food, and visit the museum shop, which sells beaded crafts, Indian jewelry, and books on Yakima history and life. The museum complex also contains a media center, which publishes the *Yakima Nation River*—one of the most informative and highly acclaimed tribal newspapers in the country—as well as a theater for the performing arts, meetings, and films and a commercial radio station.

Education and Community Services

In Article V of the 1855 treaty, the federal government promised the Yakimas it would establish, maintain, and supply two schools, one of which was to be an agricultural and industrial school, on the reservation. In 1860 the first school on any reservation opened at Fort Simcoe. In 1922 the BIA's offices and the school were moved to Toppenish, and children attending the Simcoe school were integrated into the public school system.

In recent years the Yakimas, like the other tribes discussed here, have turned their attention to supplementing the basic educational program provided by the state. Like many other tribes, the Yakima operate a Head Start program for preschoolers and an adult education program that offers adults an opportunity to obtain their high-school diplomas and receive training in other areas, such as secretarial skills.

In addition the nation operates two unique programs to assist children with special educational needs. Project Palatisha offers special education services, including assistance with language, speech, motor coordination, and socialization to children from birth to eight years. This program is offered both through the school and in the home. During the summer, students from grades three through nine may take remedial courses in a variety of subjects at Camp Chaparral. The camp, constructed and operated by the nation and located in the forested western foothills of the reservation, al-

We must stand side by side, not back to back or face to face. We must stand together to face these issues. You must go out into the melting pot and learn to compete so we can uphold our rights—our aboriginal rights to our language and our culture and our treaty rights—to uphold these rights which have been handed down from generation to generation.

Leonard Tomaskin,
Yakima leader, 1982

The white man never sleeps. We must be ever vigilant, for he will change the laws.

Russell Jim (Yakima), 1982

lows children to learn in a beautiful and quiet environment.

The preceding five chapters have illustrated that tribal governments vary in their structures, programs, resources, and needs. All tribes, however, possess governing powers that are theirs not because the federal government has granted them to the tribes but because, as inherent sovereigns, the tribes possess inherent powers of government. In fact, all tribes possess all inherent powers of a sovereign government unless they have ceded such powers in treaties, the powers have been extinguished by congressional legislation, or the courts have found certain powers to be inconsistent with the tribe's status as a dependent nation.

The preceding discussion has also revealed, however, that the federal and state governments have periodically attempted to alter, or to extinguish, tribal existence, powers, and lands. The continuing viability of tribal governments is an indication of the tenacity of Indian sovereignty and culture. Chapter 11 will examine the powers exercised by tribal governments and give examples of how tribes are carrying out those powers for the good of their people.

CHAPTER 11

THE POWERS OF TRIBAL GOVERNMENT

In 1895 the Cherokee Tribal Court found a member of the Cherokee of Oklahoma tribe guilty of murdering another tribal member. The Major Crimes Act of 1885 did not restrict the Cherokee Tribal Court in this case, because treaties negotiated with the United States gave Indian nations in Oklahoma Territory exclusive jurisdiction over crimes committed by tribal members in Indian country. But the defendant in this case, known as *Talton* v. *Mayes*, appealed his conviction to the Supreme Court, claiming that it was illegal because the Cherokee jury had five members instead of six, as required by the U.S. Constitution.

The Supreme Court ruled against the defendant on the grounds that the U.S. Constitution did not apply to the Cherokees. Tribal governments were dependent sovereigns and had full authority to structure their governments, including their court systems, as they chose. They were not bound by the guidelines established by the U.S. Constitution.

This Supreme Court decision underscored the fact that the tribal governments that exist today are continuations of governments in existence for thousands of years. Unlike state governments, tribal governments were not created by the U.S. Constitution. Rather, they sprang from a power, or sovereignty, in existence before the Constitution and the federal government existed. Tribal governments were recognized as sovereign nations by the Spanish, French, Dutch, and English colonists who first settled in North America, and treaties concluded over two hundred years ago testify to Congress's long-standing recognition of tribal governments. This relationship is based not on American Indians' status as a racial group but on individual tribes' status as political entities with executive, legislative, and judicial powers.

While it is true that the United States, especially from the 1880s through the 1920s, sought to destroy tribal life, times have changed. Indian people have demanded control of their own affairs and are making major advances in taking charge of their own governments. Tribes are making the transition from dependency to self-determination. Although the structure and laws of tribal governments have changed over the centuries, their purpose has not. Tribal governments still exist to meet the social, physical, and cultural needs of their people.

This chapter examines how tribes today exercise some of their governmental powers to protect their land and resources, improve the social and economic well-being of their

Section 1. No provision of this constitution shall be construed as a limitation of the inherent residual sovereign powers of the Zuni Tribe. Any such powers, not delegated to the representative tribal government by this constitution, are retained for direct exercise by the people through referendum, as provided for herein, or for exercise by the tribal government following amendment of the constitution.

Article XVIII—Inherent Powers of the Zuni Tribe, Constitution of the Zuni Tribe, 1934

[Indian sovereignty] is the principle that those powers which are lawfully vested in an Indian tribe, are not, in general, delegated powers granted by express acts of Congress, but rather inherent powers of a limited sovereignty which has never been extinguished. Each Indian tribe begins its relationship with the federal government as a sovereign power, recognized as such in treaty and legislation.

Felix Cohen, *Handbook of Federal Indian Law* (1942)

people, and preserve and maintain their culture and traditions. At the core of these efforts is the issue of jurisdiction.

JURISDICTION

Jurisdiction is the power of a government to make and enforce its own laws. Jurisdictional questions—whether or not a tribal government has the authority to act in a certain area—lie at the heart of tribal sovereignty. As a government's jurisdiction decreases, its strength and power decline. The smaller a government's territory, the fewer its citizens, and the more limited the kinds of behavior it can control, the less independence or sovereignty it may have and, as a result, the less able it may be to meet the needs of its people adequately.

Jurisdiction is defined in terms of territory, personnel, and subject matter. Territorial jurisdiction refers to the geographic area over which a government's authority extends. Tribal geographic jurisdiction generally encompasses what is known as "Indian country," the land within a reservation and land outside the reservation that is owned by tribal members or by the tribe and held in trust by the federal government. An example of an issue regarding tribal geographic jurisdiction is the extent to which tribes may enforce their laws on non-Indian-owned land within their reservation. Many tribes, for example, have passed zoning ordinances for non-Indian-owned reservation land, and non-Indians have challenged the tribes' right to do so.

Personnel jurisdiction refers to the individuals over whom a sovereign may legislate and enforce its laws. In general, these personnel include a government's citizens, wherever they live, as well as any aliens within the sovereign's territory. The U.S. government, for example, can require its citizens to pay federal income tax even if they live and work abroad, and citizens of other countries traveling in the United States are subject to the laws of the United States. A crucial issue of personnel jurisdiction for tribal governments is the extent to which they may enforce their laws against non-Indians living or working on their reservations.

Subject-matter jurisdiction defines the subjects, or topics, about which a sovereign can make laws. The U.S. Constitution, for example, gives the federal government exclusive control over bankruptcy and the operation of the post office, among other subjects. States have no jurisdiction in those areas and are forbidden to pass and enforce any laws on those topics. Similar issues apply to tribal governments. Are laws regulating bingo or severance taxes, for instance, within their jurisdiction?

Limitations on Tribal Jurisdiction

Before white settlement, tribal governments enjoyed full jurisdictional powers within their territories. Today their jurisdiction is no longer total. Two hundred years of tribal-federal contact have greatly reduced tribal authority in certain areas.

The governmental powers of the Menominee Indian Tribe of Wisconsin, a federally recognized sovereign Indian Tribe, shall, consistent with applicable federal law, extend to all persons and subjects, to all lands and other property including natural resources, and to all waters and air space, within the exterior boundaries of the Menominee Indian Reservation, including any land which may hereafter be added to the Reservation under any law of the United States. The governmental power of the Menominee Indian Tribe shall, consistent with applicable federal law, also extend outside the exterior boundaries of the Reservation to any person, subjects or real property which are, or may hereafter be included within the jurisdiction of the Tribe under any law of the United States or of the Tribe.

Constitution of the Menominee
Indian Tribe
of Wisconsin

Tribal governments are restrained in their autonomy by their treaties, their constitutions, their dependent status, and by congressional statutes. The *Kagama* decision, discussed in chapters 5 and 12, held that when tribes accepted the protection of the United States, they also submitted to its legislative control; thus, Congress has full, or plenary, authority to legislate Indian affairs. In 1978 the courts added a new test to be used in determining the extent of Indian sovereignty: tribes may not exercise powers that are inconsistent with their dependent status. Finally, tribal governments may act only in those areas dictated by their tribal constitutions. This automatically limits the sovereignty of tribes with IRA constitutions, because the secretarial approval clause requires that tribes obtain the approval of the secretary of the interior for tribal ordinances, amendments, and contracts.

Tribal governments today retain *exclusive* jurisdiction only in certain areas; they have *concurrent* jurisdiction in yet other areas; and in some very important areas they have no authority at all. Exclusive jurisdiction means that the tribe has the authority to act and that no other entity has the authority to overrule that action—in defining membership, for example. Concurrent jurisdiction means that the authority to act is shared with another government. Tribes in Public

In June, 1942, Chief Jesse Lyon and other members of the Iroquois League declared war against the Axis powers on the steps of the Capitol in Washington, D.C. (Courtesy Dr. Laurence Hauptman and the National Archives.)

Law (P.L.) 280 states (see chapter 5 and 13) have concurrent criminal and civil jurisdiction with the states. Tribes have lost all criminal jurisdiction over non-Indians as a result of the *Oliphant* decision (see chapter 5), which stated that the tribes' dependent status was inconsistent with the authority to exert criminal jurisdiction over non-Indians.

Despite such reductions in their power, tribes continue to be recognized as sovereign governments with the inherent authority to govern the affairs of their people. Before a local city government can pass and enforce laws, it must determine whether it is authorized by state law to do so. Tribal governments, in contrast, do not require this delegation of authority to act. Their source of power comes from within. The question is not whether tribes are *permitted* to act but whether they are *prevented* from acting in a given instance.

MEMBERSHIP

The authority to define membership, or citizenship, is an important power, for membership determines who may enjoy a community's rights and privileges. According to federal law, for example, any individual born in the United States is a U.S. citizen, and only U.S. citizens may vote. Tribes, as sovereigns, also possess the authority to determine their own membership. Generally they do so according to one or a combination of four methods: descendancy, residency, blood quantum, or birth to an enrolled mother or father.

The Cherokee Nation of Oklahoma, for example, emphasizes descendancy. Anyone descended from individuals listed on the Dawes Commission rolls of 1906 is eligible for membership. Tohono O'Odham, or Papago, tribal membership, on the other hand, is defined primarily by residency. All children born to members who reside on the reservation automatically become members. Many tribes define membership according to blood quantum. The Unitah-Ouray tribe of Utah requires one-half tribal blood; the Fort McDermitt band of Paiutes and Shoshonis requires one-fourth Paiute/Shoshoni blood, and the Citizen Potawatomi band, one-eighth tribal blood. Other tribes trace membership through the mother or the father. The Santa Clara Pueblo restricts membership to persons born to an enrolled father. The Onondaga and Seneca tribes restrict membership to persons born to an enrolled mother. Many tribes prohibit dual enrollment, or membership in two tribes. Many tribal constitutions also provide for adoption, or naturalization into the tribe, of certain individuals who do not meet the established requirements.

The right of tribes to determine their own membership was reaffirmed by the Supreme Court in the 1978 *Martinez* case. The case was brought by Julia Martinez and her daughter, of the Santa Clara Pueblos. According to tribal law, children of male tribal members who married nonmembers were eligible for membership but children of female members who

> The lineal descent of the people of the Five Nations shall run in the female line. Women shall be considered the progenitors of the nation. They shall own the land and the soil. Men and women shall follow the status of the mother.
>
> Ne Gayaneshagowa,
> The Great Binding Law
> (Constitution of the
> Iroquois League)

married nonmembers were ineligible. Martinez, a member herself but married to a nonmember, brought the suit against the tribe. She argued that the tribal law violated her daughter's rights to equal protection under the Indian Civil Rights Act. The tribe maintained, however, that its membership laws were culturally based. The Santa Clara Pueblo was a patriarchal society in which membership traditionally was defined through the father. Most important, the tribe argued, definition of tribal membership was a matter for the tribal government—not the federal government—to decide.

The Supreme Court agreed with the tribe. While the Indian Civil Rights Act did protect the civil rights of individuals from unjust actions by tribal governments, its overriding purpose was to promote Indian self-government and self-determination. The Court reasoned that allowing federal courts to apply the dominant culture's standards of equal protection and due process to tribal disputes would undermine the tribe's status as a "culturally and politically distinct entity." The Indian Civil Rights Act authorized federal courts to act only in cases involving a writ of habeas corpus (that is, illegal imprisonment) against the tribe. All other issues, including membership and election disputes, were to be handled by tribal courts, where, the Court noted, such disputes could be settled according to Indian values and traditions.

ADMINISTRATION OF JUSTICE

Looking at Indian culture through European eyes, some early explorers and colonists erroneously believed that Indian societies were without laws. All tribes, however, had laws and customs regulating behavior, domestic relations, and intertribal relations. Non-Indians simply did not understand that traditional Indian societies had different ideas about law than did Europeans.

Within the Anglo-American political tradition, law is seen as a set of secular, or civil, rules. The purpose of law is to protect individuals' "inalienable rights"—their rights to hold property, speak freely, read a free press, and so forth. Laws protect individuals from the government and from each other. Justice is obtained through an adversary system. In such a system each party makes its case according to strict rules of procedure (about what evidence may be used, for instance), and then a judge or jury decides which side has best proved its case. Individual freedom is considered the greatest right in such a system, and imprisonment, the denial of freedom, is considered the appropriate punishment for breaking the law.

Traditional Indian Law and Its Demise

Traditional Indian law originates in the spiritual, or religious, world. Since traditional Indian societies placed little emphasis on personal rights, their legal systems were not

Among us we have no prisons, we have no pompous parade of courts, we have no written laws, and yet judges are as highly revered among us as they are among you, and their decisions are as highly regarded.

Property, to say the least, is well guarded, and crimes are as impartially punished. We have among us no splendid villains above the control of our laws. Daring wickedness is never suffered to triumph over helpless innocence. The estates of widows and orphans are never devoured by enterprising sharpers. In a word, we have no robbery under color of the law.

Joseph Brant, Mohawk leader
(1742–1807)

based on protecting such rights. Indeed, the Iroquois languages had no word for "rights." Traditional Indian law emphasized responsibility and the maintenance of harmony within oneself, the community, and the environment. There was no adversary system of justice, and there were few formal procedures. Violators were questioned and a punishment determined. Civil disputes were typically settled by mediation and compromise. There were no jails, since confinement did not serve to reestablish harmony. All penalties were enacted with the aim of reestablishing balance and harmony. Compensation reestablished relationships. Whipping and teasing shamed individuals into reforming their behavior, while exile and the death penalty removed the disruptive presence from the community. Sentences were carried out quickly. Once the punishment had been met, the crime was considered erased, the violator cleansed, and harmony restored.

The Cherokees were one of the first tribes to adopt and integrate a western concept of law into their government, but before colonization they already had a highly developed legal system, summarized here as an example of traditional Indian law. In Cherokee traditional law, a crime, depending on its nature, might fall under the jurisdiction of the priests, the Council of Seven Clans (composed of elders from each of the seven Cherokee clans), or the victim's clan itself. The Council of Seven Clans determined punishments for such crimes as repeated assaults or refusal to work and contribute to the community welfare. Punishment was usually a whipping or scratching on the legs by a priest. The council also considered charges of witchcraft, a crime punished by death by an execution squad representing the seven clans.

Individual clans had the greatest responsibility for dispensing justice in the Cherokee system. Murder, whether deliberate or accidental, was considered an offense against the victim's clan. It was believed that the spirit of the murdered individual could not pass to the spirit world until his or her soul had been avenged. Vengeance required the death of the murderer or of a close relative. So deeply held was this tradition that it was not uncommon for the murderer's clan, not the victim's, to execute the offender. If a killing was accidental the murderer could flee to one of four "free" towns or to the holy ground of the local priest and there receive protection. In some cases the wronged clan might accept a captive or an enemy scalp in retribution.

An annual renewal ceremony also served an important purpose in the Cherokee legal system. Each year at the Busk Ceremony all sins and wrongs (except murder) from the previous year were erased, and harmony was restored. At this ceremony the tribal orator, dressed in fine clothes and wearing raven's wings in his hair, recited the Cherokee Nation's history and laws, chided the people for their past wrongs, and urged them to repent and reform and look into the sa-

Criminal Jurisdiction
Residents

19. Whoever shall live on the Ottawa land must be dealt with if he shall violate any of these laws. He shall also be permitted to prosecute others if he shall be in any way wronged.

Theft

2. If any person shall steal an article of property, when it is known the stolen article must be taken back. If the owner, upon seeing it, shall discover that it has not been injured, he must take it back. If it be injured, the thief shall pay the price and a half of the article. The full price must be paid to the owner, and the half price into the treasury.

Ottawa Laws, 1850

cred fire and receive forgiveness. This ceremony signified the nation's renewal and rebirth.

During the early reservation period, the Cherokees continued to make and enforce their own laws. Indeed, the federal government urged tribes to relocate to reservations by using the argument that there they would be free to manage their own affairs. By the 1870s, however, all tribes, wherever located, had begun increasingly to lose control over their own lives. BIA agents, and in many cases the military, had gained economic, political, and judicial control of the reservation. By the 1880s, the U.S. government had set about to destroy traditional tribal governments by removing their authority to dispense justice. In 1879, Congress appropriated money for reservation-based Indian police forces to be directed by BIA agents. Generally viewed as turncoats, the Indian police were eventually accepted by tribes as a lesser evil than the U.S. military.

In 1883 the BIA created "courts of Indian offenses" and appointed leading tribal officials, such as Comanche Chief Quanah Parker, as judges in an effort to win tribal support. In one sense, these courts were beneficial, since tribal judges understood their people better and were fairer in their judgments and punishments than BIA agents, who previously had the authority to impose penalties and who frequently dictated cruel sentences. The new courts, however, had the negative effect of pushing aside tribal traditions in favor of Anglo-American notions of law.

The courts of Indian offenses were charged with enforcing the Code of Federal Regulations (CFR), which was written to "civilize" and assimilate Indians. Under the code, dancing, polygamy, shamanism, destroying the property of the dead, and neglecting to "adopt habits of industry or to engage in civilized pursuits or employment" became criminal acts punishable by fines, loss of rations, or imprisonment.

Having established this system of Indian police and courts, the government then severely reduced funding for it during the termination era. A few tribes did have funds to maintain some level of service, but many tribes, their traditional systems essentially destroyed, were forced to go without law enforcement. In the mid-1950s the government addressed the problem it had created by turning criminal and civil jurisdiction over to some states under P.L. 280, but few states were willing to stretch their already tight budgets further. As a result, many reservations continued to suffer from a serious lack of judicial enforcement.

Modern Tribal Courts

Conditions began to improve during the late 1960s and 1970s, when an availability of funds and the advent of self-determination gave tribes both the opportunity and the means to reestablish their own legal systems.

Today more than 140 tribes have their own court systems.

Indian people are thirsty to make their own laws and live by them.

James Iosty, Judge of
Intertribal Sioux
Appeals Court

Of these, about twenty-five have retained the Code of Federal Regulations and have BIA-appointed judges. Most tribes, however, have established their own tribal courts and enacted their own laws and codes. A few tribes, including twelve of the nineteen Pueblo groups in New Mexico, use only a strict traditional system of law. At the San Juan Pueblo, defendants may choose to appear before either a more Anglo-oriented tribal court or the more traditional tribal court.

A recent innovation is the intertribal court, a court system created by and shared among neighboring tribes. For example, the Intertribal Court of Appeals of South Dakota, at Crow Creek, presently serves five Lakota tribes: Crow Creek, Lower Brule, Sisseton, Wahpeton, and Cheyenne River. Eighteen tribes in western Oklahoma share a single court system with offices in four communities.

Tribal courts vary greatly both in appearance and in the laws they apply. Some tribes have spacious new courtrooms, bound volumes of tribal laws, and the capability to establish courts of special jurisdiction, such as juvenile and conservation courts. The court officials for these tribes may include a judge, a court reporter, a bailiff, a tribal prosecutor, and police who use the most up-to-date methods to gather evidence. The Navajos, for example, have six district courts (and a seventh, "floating" judge, who is used in all areas as needed), a Supreme Court, and a police force of approximately two hundred members.

Other tribes make do in cramped, sometimes unheated, quarters that may also serve as offices or conference rooms. The "court reporter" may be a tape recorder. In many Indian courts the judge also acts as prosecutor, risking an obvious conflict of interest, simply because no funds are available to hire a prosecutor. Sometimes smaller tribes contract with larger tribes for the use of their legal systems.

Most tribal judges are Indians and members of their tribes. Few are actually lawyers, although most have received some training from the National American Indian Court Judges Association or the National Indian Justice Center. Judges are either elected or appointed, depending on their tribal constitutions. Court proceedings may be held in either the tribal language or in English, with interpreters available as needed.

The role and status of lawyers varies by tribe. A few tribes have established their own bar examinations. Others require lawyers to be members of the state bar. In an effort to keep their courts from becoming overly legalistic, some tribes do not allow outside attorneys to participate in court proceedings unless they are tribal members. In general, however, defendants usually represent themselves or are represented by a tribal paralegal or a friend. Although a few tribal courts operate by strict rules of procedure, the orientation is usually in keeping with the tribal desire to keep the legal process informal. The courts' primary interest is in serving as

S1-3-7. Oath of Office of Judge. (1) Every Judge prior to taking office or acting in such office shall take the following oath of affirmation:

I,   , do solemnly swear (affirm) that I will support, defend and uphold the Constitution, Bylaws and Treaties of the Menominee Indian Tribe and support and defend the best interests of the Menominee Indian Tribe; that I will support, uphold, and enforce the Law and Order Code of the Menominee Indian Tribe and the resolutions and ordinances duly passed by the Menominee Legislature of the Menominee Indian tribe, and that I will faithfully and impartially discharge the duties of my office to the best of my ability.

General Provisions,
Title I,
Menominee Tribal Code

forums for arbitration and conciliation. In this sense modern tribal courts have retained the essence of traditional tribal courts—emphasis continues to be on reestablishing social harmony, not on punishment.

Tribal Codes

Tribal courts apply the laws or codes that have been adopted by the tribal government. A code is a series of laws or statutes arranged by subject. Tribal governments usually adopt both criminal and civil codes. Tribal courts handle more than seventy thousand cases a year. Approximately 70 percent of all cases heard by tribal courts are criminal misdemeanors, such as disorderly conduct, juvenile cases, traffic violations, public intoxication, and assault. The other 30 percent are civil cases, such as divorces, probate, property disputes, debts, adoption, child custody, and suits for damages and broken contracts. Tribes possess civil jurisdiction over both members and nonmembers, although not all tribes have chosen to hear cases involving nonmembers.

When tribes started replacing the Code of Federal Regulations with their own codes, few had the expertise or the resources to do a professional job of establishing new tribal laws. As a result the codes in operation on many reservations today look much like the federal code they replaced: they are outdated, Anglo-oriented, and poorly reflective of tribal philosophy and culture.

Having recognized these problems, many tribes are currently revising their codes and restructuring their courts to better suit the needs of their ever-changing and complex societies. The Hualapai Civil and Criminal Law and Order Code, for instance, was adopted in 1975 and contains laws dealing with court procedure, civil action, domestic relations, custody and conciliation, heirship and probate, crimes, juveniles, removal of nonmembers, health and sanitation, taxes, animal control, tribal elections, alcoholism, narcotics, mental health, and traffic laws. The Navajo Tribal Code, the most extensive tribal code, contains rules and regulations covering more than twenty different areas. In 1986 the Navajo Nation became the first tribe to adopt a uniform commercial code, designed to promote and govern business transactions. Most tribal laws pertain only to actions committed on the reservation, although Hopi law states that it is a crime to conduct religious services off-reservation for profit. Tribal members accused of this offense are prosecuted when they return to the reservation. The Kickapoo tribe of Oklahoma has drafted a Child Welfare Code that incorporates traditional tribal values and philosophy with modern legal terms and concepts.

The Jurisdictional Maze

The jurisdiction of Indian tribal courts is limited geographically to "Indian country" (land within the exterior bounda-

Code of the Papago Tribe
Chapter 4—Sentences
Nature of Sentences

Sec. 1. Any Indian who has been convicted by the Papago Tribal Court or any District Court of violation of a provision of the Code of the Papago Tribe shall be sentenced by the Court to work for the benefit of the tribe for any period fixed or found by the Court to be appropriate . . .

Southern Ute Penal Code
Chapter 6

Sec. 5. Any Indian who shall take the property of another person, with intent to steal, shall be deemed guilty of theft and upon conviction thereof, shall be sentenced to labor for a period not to exceed 6 months.

Beaded gavel and block used by the Sac and Fox tribal court (above). Sac and Fox Supreme Court docket book, tribal code of laws, and flag (below). (Courtesy Sac and Fox National Public Library.)

ries of an Indian reservation as well as land outside those boundaries owned by Indians and held in trust by the federal government). Tribal legal jurisdiction in Indian country is no longer total, however. In certain instances tribes have concurrent, or shared, jurisdiction with the federal and state governments. In other situations, depending on the state, the type of crime, and the race of the individual involved, state or federal law may take precedence. As discussed in chapters 5 and 13, Public Law (P.L.) 280 gave some states criminal and civil jurisdiction over "Indian country" within their boundaries.

If a state has jurisdiction under P.L. 280 and a tribal legal system is also present, concurrent jurisdiction exists, meaning that both governments have jurisdictional rights. In this situation a case involving a tribal member may be filed in either the state court or the tribal court. Once filed, a case may not be refiled in or appealed to the other court system.

If any citizen of the United States, or other person not being an Indian, shall attempt to settle on any of the lands hereby allotted to the Indians to live and hunt on, such person shall forfeit the protection of the United States of America, and the Indians may punish him or not as they please.

Article IV,
Treaty with the Choctaws, 1786

THE LAW-ENFORCEMENT JURISDICTIONAL MAZE

Misdemeanors

Accused	Victim	Agency	Court
Non-Indian	Non-Indian	State or County	State
Non-Indian	Indian	FBI	Federal
Indian	Non-Indian	FBI	Federal
Indian	Indian	Tribal	Tribal

Major Crimes

Accused	Victim	Agency	Court
Non-Indian	Non-Indian	State or County	Federal
Non-Indian	Indian	FBI or BIA	Federal
Indian	Non-Indian	FBI or BIA	Federal
Indian	Indian	Tribal	Tribal

This chart illustrates the complexities involved in determining the appropriate court in which to try crimes involving Indians and Indian country.

The Major Crimes Act

The Major Crimes Act, passed in 1885, gave the federal government jurisdiction over Indians who committed any of seven major crimes while in Indian country. The original list of crimes has since been expanded to fourteen and now includes murder, manslaughter, kidnapping, rape, carnal knowledge of any female not the perpetrator's wife and who is under sixteen years of age, assault with intent to commit rape, incest, assault with intent to commit murder, assault with a dangerous weapon, assault resulting in serious bodily injury, arson, burglary, robbery, and larceny. Indians accused of these crimes are tried and sentenced in federal court, while those accused of lesser crimes are tried in tribal court. Tribal courts' authority to sentence those found guilty of crimes originally was limited by the Indian Civil Rights Act to a maximum sentence of six months in jail and/or a five-hundred–dollar fine per crime. In 1986, these penalties were increased to one year in jail and/or a five thousand dollar fine. Tribal courts usually sentence offenders to pay compensation to the victim or community or to participate in community work. Among some Pueblo groups, a ritualistic whipping, symbolizing a spiritual cleansing, is still used to punish some crimes.

The Oliphant Decision

In 1978 the Supreme Court handed down a decision that dealt a major blow to tribal sovereignty. The situation that led to the *Oliphant* decision arose during the annual Chief Seattle Days celebration on the Port Madison Reservation of the Suquamish tribe in Puget Sound, Washington. Earlier that same year the Suquamish tribal council had adopted a law-and-order code that gave the Suquamish court criminal jurisdiction over non-Indians who violated tribal law. During the course of the celebration, two non-Indian reservation residents, Mark Oliphant and Dan Belgarde, were arrested by

tribal police. Oliphant was arrested for assaulting a tribal police officer and resisting arrest; Belgarde, whose car collided
with a tribal police car after a high-speed chase, was charged
with recklessly endangering another person and damaging
tribal property.

The two white defendants took their case to federal court,
arguing that the Suquamish Tribe had no criminal jurisdiction over non-Indians, and in a surprise ruling, the Supreme
Court agreed with the defendants. Before the *Oliphant* case,
U.S. courts had held that tribes possessed all aspects of their
original sovereign powers unless specifically extinguished by
treaty or congressional act or specifically forbidden by the
tribal constitution. The Suquamishes had made no cessions
of sovereignty by treaty, nor had any congressional act ever
specifically canceled the right of the Suquamishes to punish
all lawbreakers within Suquamish territory. The Supreme
Court reasoned, however, that exercising tribal criminal jurisdiction over non-Indians was inconsistent with a tribe's
dependent status. In practical terms this ruling created serious and important law-and-order problems on reservations.
If tribes could not control non-Indian violators, who would?

After the *Oliphant* ruling, tribal governments immediately began to seek solutions to the problem of controlling
non-Indian behavior in Indian territory. The Confederated
Salish and Kootenai Tribe of the Flathead Reservation in
Montana has provided its tribal court with the authority to assess civil fines against non-Indians for the violation of tribal
hunting and fishing laws. Another solution has been cross-
deputization with local and county police officers. Other
tribes have arranged for non-Indians on the reservation to
submit voluntarily to tribal legal jurisdiction. Such an agreement was worked out between the Colville tribe and the
AMAX Corporation. In 1980 the Colvilles and AMAX signed
a preliminary agreement for molybdenum mining on tribal
lands. The mining operation, which was delayed, would have
created a large influx of new workers to the reservation. Not
wishing to lose control over a large part of the reservation's
activities, the Colvilles included as part of the AMAX agreement that all AMAX workers would abide by tribal law.
Workers who violated tribal law were to be subject to disci-
plinary action and dismissal by the company. The AMAX
agreement also stipulated that all business disputes between
the corporation and the tribe would be resolved in tribal
court.

REGULATING DOMESTIC AND FAMILY RELATIONS

Stable domestic and family relations are important elements
in overall social harmony. Like other sovereigns, tribes have
the authority to regulate such matters as marriage, divorce,
inheritance, and the welfare of children, including adoption,
foster care, and juvenile counseling. In earlier times family

> We must either hold that there
> can be no valid Indian marriage,
> or we must hold that all mar-
> riages are valid which by Indian
> usage are so regarded. . . . They
> did not occupy their territory by
> our grace and permission, but by
> a right beyond our control. They
> were pleased by the Constitution
> beyond our jurisdiction, and we
> had not more right to control
> their domestic usage than those
> of Turkey or India.
>
> *Kobogum v. Jackson Iron Co.,* 1889

relations were regulated within the extended family or clan according to tribal laws and customs.

Marriage and Divorce

Traditional marriage practices varied widely. Among the central Eskimos and some Northwest Coast tribes, for example, marriages were often arranged while children were young. Arranged marriages strengthened tribal welfare by cementing relations between groups; most individuals accepted them. Other tribes allowed youths to choose their own mates. Among the Muscogees, elopements were forgiven if the couple was able to elude the posse sent after them until after the Busk Celebration, which involved a symbolic cleansing and forgiveness of all past wrongs and crimes (except murder).

Many tribes, especially Plains tribes, practiced polygamy. In many tribes it was the custom for a man to marry his brother's widow. This arrangement ensured that women and children were cared for, an important consideration in societies with a high male death rate from hunting and warfare. The Iroquois and their neighbors, on the other hand, were monogamous. Many tribes had strict laws governing whom one could marry. The Tlingits and Haidas of southeastern Alaska, for example, prohibited marriage between members of the same moiety. The Mohave tribe forbade marriage between clan members, and the Blackfeet refused to allow members of the same village to marry each other.

Among the Lakotas a man frequently had to prove his qualifications as a husband before his marriage could take place. The prospective groom often lived for a year with his future bride's family, helping her father to hunt and provide for the family. Only after the man had demonstrated his ability to care for the daughter did the marriage take place. Among the Hupas and some other tribes, a marriage was not considered final until after the birth of the first child.

Divorce procedures also varied. A woman's failure to bear children, adultery, cruelty, and incompatibility were acceptable grounds for divorce among many tribes. An Apache man whose wife was guilty of adultery had the right to cut off the end of her nose and divorce her. Among the Pueblos and Iroquois a woman divorced her husband by setting his clothes outside the door of their home. Today, many tribes are adapting to a changing world by establishing civil codes and social-service programs to help families handle their domestic problems.

Whether tribal marriage and divorce law follows tradition, state law, or both, the federal courts have ruled that state courts must give "full faith and credit" to tribal marriages. Full faith and credit means that state law must recognize marriages performed according to tribal law as valid—just as they do marriages performed in neighboring states.

Title V—Ute Indian Domestic Relations Code

I. Marriage

5-1-1. Marriage License.
(1) No marriage shall be performed under authority of this Code unless the parties have first obtained a marriage license from the Clerk of the Ute Indian Tribal Court.

5-1-4. Who May Perform Marriages.
(1) A marriage may be solemnized on the Reservation by any of the following:
(a) recognized clergyman or person recognized by his religion as having authority to marry;
(b) a judge of the Ute Tribal Court;
(c) the Chairman of the Tribal Business Committee;
(d) any person recognized by Utah State Law as having authority to marry.

5-1-5. Marriage Ceremony.
No particular form of marriage ceremony is required, provided, however, that the persons to be married must declare in the presence of the person performing the ceremony, that they take each other as husband and wife, and he must thereafter declare them to be husband and wife.

The Hopi Marriage Ceremony

Many tribes, for instance the Utes and the Hopis, recognize marriages performed according to either traditional custom or state law. The 8,500-member Hopi tribe of Arizona is among the most traditional tribes in the United States. The Hopi Constitution, adopted in 1935, maintains the traditional system of twelve autonomous villages. Today each village is governed either by a *kikmongwi* (a hereditary village leader) or by an elected governor. A nineteen-member tribal council composed of a chairperson, vice-chairperson, and representatives from the villages, is the official governing body of the tribe. Each village sends one or two representatives, depending on its population. Council representatives must speak the Hopi language fluently and must have the approval of the village's *kikmongwi* or governor to serve as a government official.

Like other Pueblo Indians, the Hopis have a complex religion and a rich ceremonial life, and Hopi tribal law,

Hopi bride leaving her mother-in-law's house wearing the traditional wedding dress, woven by the male relatives of the groom. Photo taken in 1932. (Courtesy Museum of Northern Arizona.)

like that of many tribes, is a mixture of traditional and Anglo-influenced law. According to the Hopi civil code, marriages performed according to traditional law are as valid as those performed according to state law. Many young Hopis are married first in a civil ceremony and later, sometimes months later, in a traditional ceremony.

The traditional marriage ritual lasts several days and involves celebration, revelry, and prayer. The ceremony begins when a young woman takes a tray of white cornmeal to her future mother-in-law's home. The young woman remains with her future mother-in-law for several days, grinding corn. At some point prior to the final ceremony, the groom's father engages in a good-natured and fun-filled mud fight with other family members and the bride's family in the village plaza. Just before the final ceremony the bride's mother washes the groom's hair and his mother washes the bride's hair, both mothers using the free-sudsing pounded roots of the yucca plant. At the final ceremony the bride wears a beautiful cotton robe edged in black, green, and red, specially woven by the groom's male relatives. In her arms she carries another handwoven robe, wrapped in a mat of reeds. (She will wear this robe at the name-giving ceremony of her firstborn child, and, eventually, she will be buried in it.) At the ceremony's conclusion the newlyweds take a pinch of the sacred cornmeal the bride and her mother-in-law ground and walk to the eastern part of the mesa. Here they pray, blow on the cornmeal, and throw it to the rising sun. After the ceremony a great feast is held for friends and relatives.

Child Welfare

Indian society is traditionally child oriented. Infants were rarely left alone, usually strapped instead to their mothers' backs or hung in their cradleboards from nearby trees while their mothers worked. Childhood was a time of freedom and gentle discipline. Illegitimacy was an unknown distinction. Children belonged not just to their biological parents but to the extended family and clan. Children were frequently raised by grandparents. Education in many tribes was the responsibility of the uncle.

White society had little understanding of the Indian concept of the extended family. State welfare agencies and state courts, applying non-Indian standards of child care, regularly removed Indian children from their homes and placed them with non-Indian families, away from their relatives, reservations, and cultures. State agencies paid little attention to the important role of the extended family in Indian society and made little effort to place children with extended family members or other families on the reservation.

Eventually tribes realized that they were in danger of losing their most precious resource, their children, and they worked vigorously to regain their right to handle custody matters for tribal children. In 1978 tribes successfully ob-

Red Lake Band of Chippewa Indians, Juvenile Court Code Sec. 1—Title, (1965) Intent, and Construction, Ordinance No. 1-65,

Sec. 1 (2) Purpose of this Code of Laws relating to juvenile courts is to secure for each child under the jurisdiction of the court the care and guidance, preferably in his own home, as will serve the spiritual, emotional, mental, and physical welfare of the child and the best interests of the Red Lake Indian reservation; to preserve and strengthen the child's family ties whenever possible removing him from the custody of his parents only when his welfare or safety and protection of the public cannot be adequately safeguarded without removal; and, when the child is removed from his own family, to secure for him custody, care and discipline as nearly as possible equivalent to that which should have been given by his parents. The laws relating to Juvenile Courts shall be liberally construed to carry out these purposes.

Oglala Sioux Tribal Code, Chap. 8, Indian Custom Adoption, Section 113, Adult Indian Custom Adoption

Any Indian or Indians wishing to adopt an adult according to Indian Custom (Waliyacinpi) shall appear before the Superior Court of the Oglala Sioux Tribe with the party to be adopted and all other parties concerned and declare their intentions.

tained passage of the Indian Child Welfare Act, which acknowledged the tribe as the best agency to determine custody issues for Indian children. The act reaffirmed that tribes possessed jurisdiction over child-custody proceedings for all Indian children living on the reservation. The act also specified that when an Indian child lived off-reservation or in a P.L. 280 state, the state court was required to transfer jurisdiction to the tribal court unless the parents objected. If child-custody proceedings remained in state court, the state court was required to place the child with members of his or her extended family or with another Indian family living on or near the reservation. State courts and welfare agencies were allowed to place an Indian child with a non-Indian family only if no suitable tribal families or facilities existed. Since the passage of this act, many tribes have developed comprehensive child welfare codes and juvenile-care facilities and programs, including foster parent programs, group homes, and special counseling services.

PROPERTY RIGHTS

Indian beliefs teach that all aspects of life are sacred. The sky is the Father and the earth is the Mother, the creators of all life. Together they form a whole, the sacred circle. All living and nonliving things come from Mother Earth. All animate and inanimate things have their own special qualities—their own inner spiritual force—which must be respected. One must establish balance and harmony with all nature and seek to understand one's relationship with all the Great Spirit's gifts.

You ask me to plow the ground! Shall I take a knife and tear my mother's bosom? You ask me to cut grass and make hay and sell it to be rich like white men! But how dare I cut my mother's hair?

Smohalla, Shahaptian, 1860s

People are a part of this whole, equal to or lesser than all other things, not above them. To traditional Indian people it made no sense to break apart the whole and sell that which was sacred, that of which one was a part. The notions of dominating or selling land were totally alien. Unlike Anglo-American society, which admired those who left their mark on the land, Indian culture taught that people should not destroy or disturb the land. Land was a sacred gift to be shared, respected, and protected for the use and enjoyment of all tribal members, present and future.

This view did not mean tribes had no concept of territorial use. Each tribe knew the boundaries of its own territory and those of other tribes. At times tribes agreed to share hunting lands. At other times they fought serious and bloody battles over hunting and fishing rights. Each Indian group also had its own system of dividing land among tribal members. Usually the headman, chief, or tribal council designated which areas families or clans were to use for farming or hunting. In sharp distinction to European tradition, all tribal members were entitled to use and enjoy the fruits of the land. The right to use the land did not depend upon one's ability to buy it. The belief that all had a right to share the land is the reason that tribes originally were willing to cede their lands to the

It may be regarded as certain, that not a foot of land will ever be taken from the Indians, without their consent. The sacredness of their rights is felt by all thinking persons in America as much as in Europe.

Thomas Jefferson, 1786

new settlers. Warfare between tribes and the new immigrants did not begin until the non-Indian demand for land jeopardized tribal hunting and, hence, tribal existence.

Feelings of reverence and responsibility for the land remain as strong among Indians today as before colonization. Without the land, tribes could not survive as spiritual, cultural, political, and economic entities. Unfortunately, however, Indian people's attachment to and reverence for the land continues to be misunderstood by much of American society.

United States' Definition of Indian Property Rights: Johnson v. McIntosh

Indian property rights were first defined by the federal courts in 1823. The Supreme Court, in *Johnson* v. *McIntosh and Graham, Lessee*, ruled that England, by virtue of discovery, possessed title to, or ownership of, Indian lands. The United States, as successor to England, inherited England's title. Tribes, the Court reasoned, did not hold title to their lands because they did not believe in individual ownership and productive use of the land. Despite this peculiar logic, Chief Justice John Marshall emphasized that Indian nations did have a right to use and occupy their lands. These lands, he wrote, could not be taken without tribal consent. When a tribe did decide to cede its land, only the United States, as the successor to England, had the right to buy it. Individuals, states, and other nations could not do so. And, as Marshall later explained in the *Worcester* case, states were also prohibited from exercising control or jurisdiction over Indian lands. Until a tribe chose to cede its land, its right to use and occupy that land was to be considered sacred and was to be protected.

Reservations

Many non-Indians do not understand the purpose of Indian reservations. Some people have the impression that reservations are like camps where Indians are confined and must live. Another mistaken impression is that reservations are like schools—that once Indians become sufficiently "civilized" and educated, they will leave the reservation and the reservation will disappear.

Both views are totally incorrect. Indian people at times feel like aliens in their own land. For them the reservation holds the key to the survival of tribal society. The reservation is the last area in the country where tribes can practice their culture and exercise their right to self-government in accordance with the values of their people.

At one time Indian nations hunted, farmed, roamed, and worshipped over the entire United States. Today Indians control only 2.3 percent of their former territory: 50.4 million acres in the continental United States (three-fourths of which is tribally owned and one-fourth individually owned)

Their rights to its exclusive enjoyment in their own way and for their own purposes were . . . respected until they abandoned them, made a cession to the government or an authorized sale to individuals. . . . It is enough to consider it as a settled principle that their right of occupancy is considered as sacred as fee-simple of the whites.

Mitchell v. *U.S.,* 1835

So long as a tribe exists and remains in possession of its lands, its title and possession are sovereign and exclusive; and there exists no authority to enter upon their lands, for any purpose whatever, without their consent.

U.S. Attorney General's Opinion, 1821

The Indians' right to "all the land within those territorial boundaries . . . is not only acknowledged, but guaranteed by the U.S."

Worcester v. *Georgia,* 1832

and 40 million acres in Alaska. This is the land known as "Indian country," governed by both Indian laws and customs and federal laws relating to Indians. Some reservations are called by other names—the pueblos of New Mexico, the colonies of Nevada, the rancherias of California, and the villages of Alaska, for instance—but all denote lands set aside for tribal use.

The size of reservations varies greatly. The Navajo reservation is the largest, occupying parts of three states and comprising approximately fourteen million acres. Only ten other reservations have more than one million acres. Most are small—too small, in fact, to adequately support their rapidly growing populations.

As settlements grew, colonies, and later the federal government, concluded treaties and agreements with tribes in which they recognized tribal boundaries. When the population of the Southeast and the Northeast expanded, the government relocated tribes to a large area between the Mississippi River and the Rocky Mountains. As white settlers filtered into this area, the government turned to a policy of establishing tribes on separate parcels of land, or reservations.

Reservations were normally established in one of three ways: by treaty, by executive order, or by congressional statute. The most common way was by treaty. Treaties, as discussed, were not grants of rights and powers *to* tribes but rather grants of land and rights *from* tribes *to* the federal government. Reservations are not lands that have been granted to tribes but lands that have been reserved by tribes for their own use. The courts refer to this principle as the reserved rights doctrine. Along with the land, tribes reserved rights to use the water, resources, and wildlife. Except in a few cases, reservation lands technically are owned by the United States but are held in trust by the federal government for the tribes' use.

Not all reservations were created by treaty. Between 1855 and 1919 the president of the United States held the authority to set aside public lands for tribal use. Reservations created in this manner are known as executive-order reservations. Treaty making ended in 1871, and presidential authority to establish executive-order reservations ended in 1919. Since then Congress alone has held the authority to take land from the public domain and set it aside for tribal use. Congress has recently established new reservations for some tribes and reestablished reservations for other tribes that had their lands taken and sold by the federal government during the termination era of the 1950s and early 1960s. Congress has also established tribal trust lands for several tribes that have recently gained federal recognition either by congressional statute or through the Federal Acknowledgment Program, a program established by the BIA in 1978 whereby tribes could obtain federal recognition.

Whereas, in the late war between Great Britain and the United States of America, a body of the Oneida and Tuscorora and the Stockbridge Indians, adhered faithfully to the United States, and assisted them with their warriors; and in consequence of this adherence and assistance, the Oneidas and Tuscororas, at an unfortunate period of the war, were driven from their homes, and their houses were burnt and their property destroyed: And as the United States in the time of their distress, acknowledged their obligations to these faithful friends, and promised to reward them: and the United State being now in a condition to fulfill the promises then made: the following articles are stipulated by the respective parties for that purpose; to be in force when ratified by the President and Senate. . . .

Article II. The Oneida and Tuscarora nations shall be secured in the possession of the lands on which they are settled.

Treaty with the Six
Nations, 1784

A few tribes do possess full title to their lands. The treaties concluded with the Five Civilized Tribes and the Senecas, for example, transferred complete ownership, or title, to these tribes. Although the Pueblos of New Mexico have no ratified treaties with the United States, they also hold complete ownership of their lands, because the Spanish and, later, the Mexican authorities recognized Pueblo land rights and confirmed them by issuing land grants. The United States agreed to honor all titles to private property valid under Mexican law, including the Pueblo land grants, when it signed the Treaty of Guadalupe Hidalgo in 1848.

As trustee of Indian lands, the United States is legally obligated to preserve and protect those lands and resources from being usurped by states or private individuals (this is discussed more fully in chapter 12). The government's trust responsibility also requires that it manage tribal lands and resources in the best interests of the tribe. The obligation to protect, however, does not prohibit Congress from changing how tribal land is held or from taking Indian lands. For example, by passing the Dawes Allotment Act of 1887, Congress radically altered land ownership on many reservations from communal to individual holdings.

International law forbids a nation from breaking a treaty, but federal law permits the United States to appropriate lands and resources secured by tribes in treaty agreements with the federal government. Even in modern times, the government has broken such treaty agreements. The Tuscarora Nation, for example, had signed treaties with the federal government in 1784 and 1789 in which possession of certain lands was guaranteed. In 1794 a grateful United States signed another treaty with the Tuscarora Nation, whose alliance had assisted the United States in its victory over England.

Then, in the late 1950s, the New York Federal Power Commission decided to use over one-fifth of the Tuscaroras' land as the site for a reservoir. The Tuscarora Nation fought the reservoir's construction with barricades and court cases. The Supreme Court ruled against the Tuscarora Nation, however, finding that, despite treaty guarantees, its land could be seized. Justice Hugo Black dissented: "Great nations, like great men, should keep their promises." Because the courts have held that a tribe's right to land and resources, if recognized and acknowledged in a treaty, *are* protected by the Fifth Amendment, the Tuscaroras were at least paid for their lands. But to many tribes, a few dollars can never compensate for the loss of ancestral lands.

TRIBAL CONTROL OF LAND

Allocating, regulating, and protecting land are primary functions, and essential elements of, a government's sovereignty. While tribal governments do exercise considerable control over their lands, the government has placed certain restrictions on that authority. Tribal governments can assign or

It may be hard for us to understand why these Indians cling so tenaciously to their lands and traditional tribal way of life. The record does not leave the impression that the lands of their reservation are the most fertile, the landscape the most beautiful or their homes the most splendid specimens of architecture. But this is their home—their ancestral home. There, they, their children, and their forebears were born. They, too, have their memories and their loves. Some things are worth more than money and the costs of a new enterprise.

There may be instances in which Congress has broken faith with the Indians, although examples of such action have not been pointed out to us. Whether it has done so before now or not, however, I am not convinced that it has done so here. I regret that this Court is to be the governmental agency that breaks faith with this dependent people. Great nations, like great men, should keep their word.

Dissenting opinion.
Federal Power Commission v.
Tuscarora Indian Nation, 1970

Signs demonstrating tribes' right to regulate their property. (Courtesy Donald L. Fixico.)

lease land to tribal members or to nonmembers. They can pass zoning laws to regulate the use of reservation land. They can evict trespassers and prevent nonmembers from entering their land. They can pass and enforce tribal conservation and environmental laws. Tribal governments also have the power to exchange or purchase land. The primary limitation on tribal authority over tribal property is that tribes cannot sell trust lands without the permission of the U.S. government.

Acquisition

Acquiring land, especially for a tribe with a small land base or one whose reservation is heavily checkerboarded, or intermixed with nontribally owned land (as a result of the allotment process), is of the utmost importance. Of the land distributed by the Dawes Commission to individuals, only 5 percent is in Indian hands today, and more than 50 percent of all reservation land in the United States is owned by non-Indians. In 1887, for example, the Sisseton Reservation of South Dakota covered about 900,000 acres. Under the Dawes Allotment Act, the government allotted approximately 300,000 acres to the two hundred tribal members and sold the remaining 600,000 acres to white settlers. Since 1887, Sisseton tribal members have sold 200,000 of their allotted acres to whites. (Many Indians were either cheated out of or forced to sell their allotments in the late 1800s and early 1900s.) Thus white ownership of the reservation now amounts to almost 90 percent.

Frequently the allotments still held by Indians cannot be used effectively because they are too small and fragmented. As original owners of allotments died, they usually divided

Over tribal lands, the tribe has the rights of a landowner as well as the rights of a local government, dominion as well as sovereignty. But over all the lands of the reservation, whether owned by tribe, by members thereof, or by outsiders, the tribe has the sovereign power of determining the conditions upon which persons shall be permitted to enter its domain, to reside therein, and to do business, provided only such determination is consistent with applicable Federal laws and does not infringe any vested rights of persons now occupying reservation lands under lawful authority.

U.S. v. Mazurie, 1975

their land equally among their heirs, with the result that, today, after several generations, some allotments are owned by more than three hundred people. Tribes refer to this as the heirship problem. Both checkerboarding and the heirship problem hamper tribal economic development and make it difficult for tribes to exercise their jurisdictional authority in Indian land. It is, for example, difficult to establish a cattle herd without an extensive area of grazing land. Similarly, it is difficult to regulate hunting rights on reservations when animals cross from Indian to non-Indian-owned lands.

The 1934 Indian Reorganization Act ended the allotment process and set aside funds to help tribes consolidate their land bases. But those funds were, and have remained, inadequate. Of the 90 million acres lost after 1890, only 3 million have been restored. In fact, tribes have lost more land since 1934 than they have acquired. Between 1934 and 1974, almost 600,000 acres were added to reservations. But more than 1.8 million acres were lost, primarily for rights of way to build reservoirs, as in the case of the Tuscarora Reservation mentioned above.

At present tribes may obtain land in one of several ways: by return of aboriginal land, federal acquisition, or tribal purchase. Tribes have wrongfully lost their aboriginal lands in several ways. Some have lost aboriginal lands illegally, without authorization by Congress. At other times the government has mistakenly omitted land from a reservation due to surveying errors. In 1972, for instance, the Yakima Nation celebrated the return of twelve thousand acres of Mount Adams, an area sacred to the tribe and lost because of a surveying error. In addition, many tribes today hold rightful claims to thousands of acres of land for which the federal government has never properly extinguished tribal title. The process of regaining lost lands, however, often involves long, costly court battles.

Federal acquisition of land for tribes can take place by acts of the secretary of the interior, who is authorized by the IRA to acquire lands for tribal use through "purchase, relinquishment, gift, exchange, or assignment," or by Congress, which also has the authority to transfer federal lands to the tribes. This is often done when a tribe can prove that the land in question was illegally taken. After a sixty-five-year struggle, the Taos Pueblo successfully obtained, in 1971, the return of 48,000 acres of sacred land. Tribal purchase of land within or outside of reservations is possible with some restrictions. The 40-acre Susanville Rancheria in California, for example, bought 120 additional acres from the Bureau of Land Management with a grant from the Department of Housing and Urban Development.

Tribal purchase of land outside reservations is subject to the restriction that it may not be held in trust by the secretary of the interior. Tribes must pay state taxes and accept state jurisdiction on such lands.

This high country is our religion. When our souls die, this is where they come. That is why this mountain is sacred to my people.

Robert Jim, former chairman, Yakima Nation

The mountain is in the palm of my hand and I want to hand it to the younger generation. We must preserve it.

Leonard Tomaskin, Yakima leader, 1982

Assignment and Leasing

Since much tribal land was lost as a result of the Dawes Allotment Act, the present trend is toward reestablishing tribal land bases. Many tribal governments actively encourage families to return their individual allotments to the tribe and hence to trust status. This prevents individual landowners from selling their allotments to outsiders. Individuals who return their allotments to the tribe are then able to apply to the tribal council for a land assignment, or lease, on a particular piece of property.

Assigning and leasing tribal lands is usually the responsibility of the tribal council, although sometimes an appointed or elected business committee carries this responsibility. A tribal member wanting to build a house, for example, would apply to the council or appropriate committee for an allotment of land. Depending on tribal law and custom, the individual might be assigned an area of land for a certain number of years or for an indefinite period. Tribal law often recognizes the rights of children to inherit their parents' assigned lands.

Tribal councils and committees also lease land to Indians or non-Indians for ranching, farming, logging, mining, and so on. A mineral lease allows a developer to extract and use or sell the minerals. The leaseholder pays the tribe royalties, based on a designated percentage of the income from the sale of the minerals. Tribal leases must be approved by the Department of the Interior and usually run for ten to twenty-five years. In 1982, Congress passed the Indian Mineral Development Act. This act confirms the right of tribes to enter into nonlease arrangements, such as joint ventures. Joint ventures allow tribes to obtain better terms and conditions—such as partial management control, environmental control, and greater revenues—than conventional leases.

Exclusion and Extradition

A sovereign's control over its territory gives it the right to decide who may enter and leave the territory. In the 1700s and early 1800s federal laws required American citizens entering Indian country to have a passport. In the 1800s the Five Civilized Tribes required passports of nonmembers entering their lands. A few Indian nations today, such as the Ojibwa Nation, located partly in Canada, issue their own passports. The traditional leaders of the Hopi Nation and the Iroquois League have traveled to international meetings using only the passports issued by their tribal governments.

Maintaining territorial control also implies the right to exclude, or evict, individuals from the government's jurisdiction. This authority is an element of a government's police power. In earlier times, being exiled from the tribe was one of the most severe punishments that a tribal government could bring against an individual guilty of violating tribal

. . . In any assignment of tribal lands which are now owned by the tribes or which hereafter may be acquired for the tribes by the United States or purchased by the tribes out of tribal funds, preference shall be given, first, to heads of families which have no allotted lands or interest in allotted lands.

Article VIII, Section 4, Constitution and Bylaws of the Shoshone-Bannock Tribes of the Fort Hall Reservation, Idaho, April 30, 1936

Lummi Ordinance L-27, May 3, 1968

The Lummi Indian Tribe has authority to exclude non-members from Tribal land, except where such members are present under the authority of Federal law.

2. Grounds for exclusion. Non-members may be excluded on one or more of the following grounds:

A. Breach of the peace, or repeated public drunkenness.

B. Entering an area of the Lummi Reservation in violation of any order or the Lummi Business Council designating such areas as closed because of fire hazard or for any other reason.

C. Failure or refusal to pay any taxes, rents or other charges justly due the Lummi

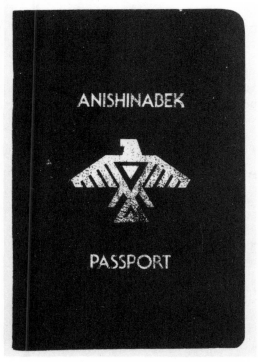
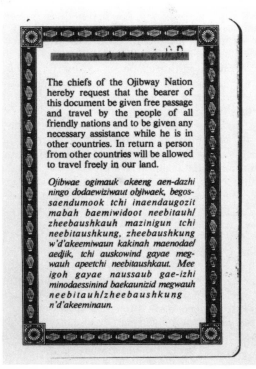

The chiefs of the Ojibway Nation hereby request that the bearer of this document be given free passage and travel by the people of all friendly nations and to be given any necessary assistance while he is in other countries. In return a person from other countries will be allowed to travel freely in our land.

Ojibwae ogimauk akeeng aen-dazhi ningo dodaewiziwaut objiwaek, begos-saendumook tchi inaendaugozit mabah baemiwidoot neebitauh/ zheebaushkauh mazinigun tchi neebitaushkung, zheebaushkung w'd'akeemiwaun kakinah maenodael aedjik, tchi auskowind gayae meg-wauh apeetchi neebitaushkaut. Mee igoh gayae naussaub gae-izhi minodaessinind baekaunizid megwauh neebitauh/zheebaushkung n'd'akeeminaun.

Passports issued by the Ojibway Nation for tribal members' use. (Courtesy Alice Brigham.)

law. (Conversely, deserting the tribe was one of the most serious crimes that could be committed.) Sometimes people were exiled for a specific period of time, and sometimes forever.

At times whole groups were, in effect, excluded or exiled from a community. When factionalism threatened a community's harmony, custom dictated that the two factions separate. Often the question of which group would leave was settled amicably. In the Southeast the decision was settled by a game of stickball, with the losers establishing a new settlement a few miles away. In 1909 the Hopis of Oraibi settled a dispute with a "push of war." A line was drawn on the ground, and it was agreed that the first leader (backed by his supporters) who was pushed across the line by the other side had to leave. By nightfall, the losing side of approximately three hundred people had packed up and left to found a new town ten miles away.

Many tribal constitutions today—the Cheyenne River Sioux constitution is typical—specifically authorize the government to exclude "non-members whose presence may be injurious to the members of the tribe morally or criminally." In 1966, after many attempts at compromise had failed, the Isleta Pueblo Tribal Council was forced to evict a Catholic

Indian Tribe after reasonable notice and opportunity to pay.

D. Unauthorized timber cutting or other activity causing physical loss or damage of any nature to Tribal property.

E. Crimes, as defined by State or Federal Law.

F. Immorality.

G. Forcing entry into any Lummi home without consent of the occupant or occupants.

H. Unauthorized property.

I. Committing frauds, confidence games or usury against Lummi people, or inducing them to enter into grossly unfavorable contracts of any nature.

J. Defrauding any Lummi of just compensation for his labor or service of any nature done at the request of the non-member.

K. Contagious disease.

priest who had shown persistent and great disrespect for the native religion and for the authority of the tribal government. In 1974 the Onondaga Nation passed a law ordering the eviction of all mixed blood families from the reservation.

A related authority possessed by tribal, federal, and state governments is the power of extradition, the surrender of an alleged criminal by one government to another. Although tribes have the inherent authority to control extradition, past court decisions indicate that the federal government will fully recognize this right only if a tribe has specifically claimed the authority in its laws. In 1976, for example, the Montana state courts refused to recognize the right of the Crow Nation to deny an extradition request from the state of Montana. The basis of the court's argument was that the Crows had not established their authority by adopting their own tribal extradition laws.

The Navajos, on the other hand, have concluded extradition agreements with the states of Arizona, New Mexico, and Utah. The Navajos have agreed that upon request by the government of any of these states, they will return any person suspected of having violated the laws of that state. The states, in return, have agreed to extradite any tribal member to the reservation to stand trial for violation of tribal law. In the mid-1970s, the state of Oklahoma requested the governor of Arizona to arrest an individual on the Navajo Reservation and return him to Oklahoma for trial. The defendant filed suit, arguing that Arizona had no authority to arrest him on the Navajo reservation. The court of appeals agreed, noting that the right of extradition properly belonged to the Navajos. Because the Navajos had signed no extradition agreement with the state of Oklahoma, the tribal government was under no obligation to return the individual to Oklahoma.

Zoning

In recent years several tribes have adopted zoning and land-use codes. Like those adopted by city and county governments elsewhere, these codes provide for the orderly development of land. The zoning code of the Oglala Sioux states that zoning is undertaken for the following reasons: to prevent overcrowding and unsanitary conditions; to establish areas where families may live in privacy; to increase public safety by reducing the possibility of fire, traffic accidents, and other dangers; to aid in planning public facilities such as schools, roads, and utilities; and to prevent the deterioration of property values that occurs when homes, stores, and factories are mixed in a haphazard fashion. The code provides that land be zoned either as residential, commercial, industrial, disposal, cemetery, or park land.

There is no question that tribes have the authority to determine zoning laws for tribally held lands or lands owned by tribal members within the reservation. The extent to which tribal governments may regulate the use of non-

**Crow Tribal Land Use Zoning Ordinance
Sec. 2. Purpose**

The controls as set forth in this ordinance are deemed necessary in order to encourage the most appropriate use of the land, to protect the social and economic stability of residential, agricultural, commercial, industrial, forest, reserved and other areas within the reservation, and to assure the orderly development of such areas; and to prevent the menace to the public safety resulting from the improper location of building and the uses thereof, and the establishment of land uses along primary highways in such a manner as to cause interference with existing and proposed traffic movement on said highways; and to otherwise promote the public health, safety, morals and general welfare in accordance with the rights reserved by the Crow Indian Nation in the Treaty.

Indian land within the reservation has not been ruled upon by the Supreme Court and remains unclear. Several lower courts have found that tribal control of land use within the reservation is a valid and important exercise of tribal self-government. The 25,000-acre reservation of the two-hundred-member Agua Caliente tribe is scattered in parcels throughout the resort town of Palm Springs, California. The tribe leases approximately 3,200 acres to hotels, condominiums, and apartment developers, the income from which makes the tribe one of the wealthiest in the United States. In 1979 the courts agreed with the tribe that it, and not the city of Palm Springs, had zoning authority over tribal lands. Since then, the two governments have established a joint zoning agreement.

CONSERVATION AND ENVIRONMENTAL PROTECTION

Conservation and environmental protection lie at the heart of Indian culture. Tribes today are restructuring their governments to include natural resource departments, and they are establishing conservation programs and enacting air- and water-quality regulations. In so doing, they are adapting modern methods to sustain traditional beliefs. Tribes of western Washington have established extensive fish-management programs to conserve and replenish fish stocks (these programs are discussed further in chapter 13). Tribes with timber resources, such as the Gila River tribe of Arizona, the Menominees of Wisconsin, and the Colvilles of Washington, have developed timber ordinances and sophisticated forest-management programs. The Colville program is discussed below.

Whereas, the lands and waters, forests, fish, game, wild rice, fruits and berries of mother earth are the most valuable and revered cultural and economic asset of Indian people; and

Whereas, these assets must be preserved for the use and benefit of ourselves, our children our children's children and their children after them; and

Whereas, it is desirable to embody conservative practices in the form of tribal ordinance which regulates the exercise of rights to hunt, fish, trap, gather rice and other usual rights of occupancy.

Preamble, Conservation Code, Lac Courte Oreilles Band of Lake Superior Chippewa Indians.

Numerous tribes throughout the country administer comprehensive fish, wildlife, and outdoor recreation programs. Shown here is the Colville Tribe, Washington. (Courtesy Gary Rankel.)

The Colville Confederated Tribe Timber Management Program

The Colville Reservation is located in north-central Washington, a land of diverse beauty and rich resources. Bordered on two sides by the Columbia River, the forested, lake-dotted mountains of the Cascades on the east slope gently to the arid plateaus on the west. The reservation stretches seventy miles from east to west and thirty-five miles from north to south. It is home to the 6,400-member Colville Confederated tribe, a confederation of eleven bands.

Known for their peacefulness, these bands never warred with the federal government during the 1850s as many of their neighbors did. In 1872, President Ulysses S. Grant established the Colville Reservation by executive order. Over the next several years bands from across eastern Washington, including the remnants of Chief Joseph's Nez Percé band, discussed in chapter 4, relocated to the reservation. Eventually the bands formed the Colville Confederated tribe.

In 1936 the Colvilles voted to reject the IRA but decided in the following year to adopt a written constitution. The constitution, which replaced the traditional system of hereditary chiefs, established an elected business council of fourteen representatives to govern the tribe. Twelve committees, each composed of from three to seven council members, were established to oversee the more than one hundred programs operated by the tribe.

Colville timber management program. (Courtesy Sheila Wilder, Confederated Band of Colville Indians.)

One of the most important committees is the Land and Forestry Committee, which is responsible for protecting the land base, preserving air and water, and conserving and managing mineral and timber resources. Approximately three-fourths of the reservation is forested with prime ponderosa pine, fir, and larch. The tribe, which has been selling its timber commercially since 1936, receives 90 percent of its tribal income from its timber resources.

Using sophisticated techniques, a forestry staff of 160 (half employed by the tribe and half by the BIA as part of its trust responsibility) works to ensure the growth and quality of the nation's timber. Logging is done on a sustained-yield basis, meaning that trees are never harvested more rapidly than they can be replaced. Only trees that have reached a certain size are tagged for cutting. Hardy, fast-growing seedlings are germinated from special seed banks and grown in carefully controlled greenhouses. Once replanted in the forests, the seedlings are monitored, thinned, and treated against disease. Two helicopters are available for fighting forest fires. The Colville foresters keep up-to-date on forest management and timbering techniques at the biannual meeting of the Tribal Timber Consortium, to which the Colvilles, as well as 128 other timber-rich tribes, belong.

Setting Standards

Courts have held that both Indian and non-Indian projects on reservations must meet the minimum environmental protection standards required by the National Environmental Policy Act of 1969 and the Surface Mining Control and Reclamation Act of 1977. Several tribes, including the Blackfeet, the Fort Apaches, the Hualapias, and the Assiniboine and Sioux tribes of the Fort Peck reservation have established their own water-quality codes. In 1986, Washington State awarded its Environmental Excellence Award to the Colville Confederated tribe for its development of a comprehensive water-quality management plan.

Some tribes have also adopted air-quality programs, and in some cases they have exercised their sovereignty by setting environmental standards that are stricter than the federal standards. The Spokane tribe of Washington and the Northern Cheyennes of Montana, for example, have designated their reservations Class I areas. This designation means that no new pollutants may contaminate the existing air quality. Because of the Northern Cheyenne's Class I designation, two power plants constructed off the reservation had to add an additional pollution-control system in 1977, because their emissions would have downgraded the reservation's air quality.

REGULATING HUNTING AND FISHING RIGHTS

Hunting and fishing hold central importance in many tribal cultures and are an economic necessity for many Indian families. The right to hunt and fish on tribal lands is included in the reserved-rights doctrine. This means that it need not be mentioned in a treaty, executive order, or statute to remain a right. Some tribes, several in Washington State, for example, also reserved in treaties and agreements their right to hunt and fish in areas outside their reservations.

The primary issue concerning Indian hunting and fishing rights is not whether tribes may hunt and fish, but whether the tribe, the state, or the federal government has the authority to control tribal hunting and fishing on and off the reservation. An even more complicated issue is the question of which government has the authority to regulate non-Indian hunting and fishing on tribal and nontribal lands within reservations.

States argue that control of all hunting and fishing within state borders is necessary for a well-regulated conservation program. Allowing tribes to hunt or fish for longer seasons and higher limits, the states insist, interferes with the more important state responsibility to preserve wildlife. Tribes argue that regulating hunting and fishing within their own territory is an important element of their culture, their sovereignty, and their right to self-government. On a practical level, the sale of tribal hunting and fishing licenses is an important source of income for many tribes and one that would be lost if state licenses were required for hunting and fishing on tribal reservation lands. The intense competition provoked between states and tribes over hunting and fishing regulation is discussed more fully in chapter 13.

Tribal Authority to Regulate On-Reservation Hunting and Fishing

The federal government's plenary power authorizes it to regulate all aspects of Indian hunting and fishing rights, on and off the reservation. However, the federal government has rarely used this authority. If there is no federal law to the contrary, tribes clearly may regulate the hunting and fishing of all individuals, tribal members or nonmembers, on tribal land. Many tribes have exercised this power by enacting comprehensive hunting, fishing, and trapping codes, which are usually directed at conservation of wildlife. They usually define the seasons, set limits, and specify manner of taking (for example, by prohibiting the use of lights at night or forbidding certain types of fishing nets). License fees are usually imposed. Tribal game wardens enforce the codes. Tribes in Washington State have established twenty-eight hatcheries on reservations—raising 30 percent of all the salmon and 23 percent of all the steelhead produced in the state.

Since the *Oliphant* decision, discussed earlier, tribes have been prohibited from pressing criminal charges against non-Indians who violate tribal game laws, but most tribes have solved this dilemma by one of two methods. Either they im-

Yakima Range and Livestock Management Code
Sec. 33.01.01: Branding Required

All livestock within the territorial boundary of the Yakima Indian Reservation must be branded pursuant to the requirements of the State of Washington Livestock Brand Law . . .

pose civil sanctions, such as fines, confiscation of equipment, or eviction from the reservation, or they ask federal agents to prosecute nonmembers under a federal trespass law that makes it a federal crime to enter Indian lands without permission for the purpose of hunting, trapping, or fishing.

Tribes in P.L. 280 states have the same authority to regulate hunting and fishing on tribal lands as those in non-P.L. 280 states. P.L. 280 specifies that the law shall not "deprive any Indian or any Indian tribe, band or community of any right, privilege or immunity afforded under Federal treaty, agreement, or statute with respect to hunting, trapping or fishing or the control, licensing or regulation thereof."

State Authority to Regulate On-Reservation Hunting and Fishing

The courts have permitted states to regulate on-reservation hunting and fishing rights in two special circumstances. If a tribe (or the federal government) has not established hunting and fishing regulations on tribal reservation lands, the state may do so, although states may not allow non-Indians to hunt and fish on tribal reservation lands from which the tribe has excluded them. State regulation is allowed in this situation mainly to conserve wildlife resources. States also have the right, upheld in the 1982 Supreme Court ruling in *Montana* v. *U.S.*, to regulate non-Indian hunting and fishing on non-Indian lands within reservations. This ruling, which held that regulation of non-Indian hunting and fishing on non-Indian reservation lands was not a necessary power of tribal self-government, was a blow to Indian sovereignty. It is consequently doubly important for tribes to exercise the authority they do possess: regulation of hunting and fishing on tribally owned lands on-reservation. Otherwise they will continue to lose portions of their sovereignty to the states.

Regulating Off-Reservation Hunting and Fishing

Several tribes—including many in Washington State, several Chippewa tribes in Michigan, and the Crows, Navajos, and Southern Cheyennes—have retained, through explicit language in their treaties, the right to hunt and fish on aboriginal lands and waters outside their reservations. These treaties often reserved for tribes the right to fish "at usual and accustomed places . . . in common with the citizens of the territory." Other treaties reserved "the privilege of hunting . . . on open and unclaimed lands" and the right "to hunt on the unoccupied lands of the United States so long as the game may be found thereon and so long as peace subsists among the whites and the Indians on the borders of the hunting districts."

Tribes that retain off-reservation hunting and fishing rights also retain the authority to regulate their members

Yakima Wildlife Management and Protection
Section 32.03.01: Reservation Closed

(1) The open range and forested area of the Yakima Indian Reservation is to remain closed to the general public with entry restricted to enrolled members of the Yakima Indian Nation, official Agency employees, persons of bona fide business or property interests and as hereinafter stated. Entry may be permitted after a permit has been secured for person(s) set forth below, limited to the purpose indicated in each section and/or in the issued permit. It shall be unlawful to take, hunt, or kill any animal or fowl or fish that are not listed on the hunting or fishing permit issued by the Yakima Indian Nation. The penalty shall be a $50 fine on each fowl and $250 for each animal.

in the exercise of these rights. States cannot require tribal members to buy state game licenses for activities on these lands, nor can a state or a private individual prevent tribal access to reserved tribal sites. The key to a tribe's exercise of this right is the operation of a comprehensive management and conservation program. Tribes must fulfill their responsibility to protect off-reservation wildlife. If they do not, or when long-range conservation interests require special action, the courts have ruled that the states can impose state regulations.

Regulating off-reservation fishing rights has become a serious issue in Washington State, because of its huge salmon industry. A federal court ruled in 1975 that United States–tribal treaties reserving to Washington tribes the right to fish "in common with the citizens of the territory" meant that tribes were entitled to 50 percent of the allowable salmon catch. A later decision, in 1979, gave the state the authority to determine the annual tonnage of salmon that could be caught safely without harming future runs. But state regulations, the court cautioned, must be reasonable and necessary for conservation and must not discriminate against tribes.

BUSINESS REGULATION

Tribes have the authority to regulate economic activity on their reservations. This includes the authority to license, tax, zone, establish businesses, and develop (or not develop) resources. Encouraging economic development that is culturally and economically suitable for their reservations is a high priority of tribal governments. Unemployment on reservations ranges from 30 to 90 percent. A 1986 study by the Interior Department found that 41 percent of Indians on reservations were living below the poverty level, compared to 12 percent of the total U.S. population. On the average, an Indian family lives on 40 percent of the income of a non-Indian family. All tribes face common obstacles in developing their reservation economies.

Obstacles to Economic Development

The greatest obstacle to tribal economic development is lack of capital. Large investments are needed to open factories, sawmills, or start most other businesses. Most tribes are poor and have no tribal funds to invest. They also have trouble getting loans because they have little collateral. Tribes do have land, but their land is held in trust and cannot be sold or used as collateral. Federal funds for development, once relatively plentiful, have been dramatically cut. Most tribes have yet to develop the managerial and technical skills needed to establish and manage business concerns. Many reservations are isolated from major economic centers by distance and poor transportation and communications facilities. An estimated 70 percent of all reservation roads are unpaved, for instance. Tribes, however, do have valuable re-

Sec. 1. Unlawful to Transact Business Without a License

It shall be unlawful for any person to engage in or carry on any business, trade, profession or calling within the boundaries of the Hopi Indian Reservation, for the transaction or carrying on of which a license is required, without first taking out or procuring license required for such business, trade, profession or calling.

Hopi Tribal Ordinance 17
December 17, 1968

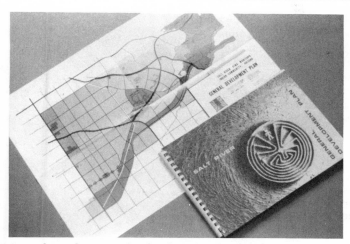

General Development Plan for the Salt River Tribe. (Courtesy National Congress of American Indians.)

sources, tax advantages, and access to flexible financing. Many tribes also enjoy abundant raw materials, and most have a large labor pool and land for business development and expansion.

Timber, Mineral, and Energy Resource Development

For two hundred years the U.S. government took the best land from Indians and pushed tribes onto land it thought of as worthless, barren, isolated, too hot, too cold, too swampy, or too arid. Ironically, much of that land is known today to contain vast mineral riches and other valuable resources. Oil wells on reservations pump more than one million barrels of oil a day. An estimated 5 percent of this country's oil and gas, one-third of its strippable low-sulphur coal, and one-half of its uranium lie on Indian lands. Tribes own thirteen million acres of forest, half of which are commercially usable. Ninety-eight reservations have dense stands of trees. The tribally owned timber company of the Fort Apache Reservation in Arizona harvests the largest stand of white ponderosa pine in the United States; the company employs more than three hundred tribal members.

In the 1920s commercial energy development on Indian reservations began in earnest with the sale of oil rights on the Osage Reservation in Oklahoma and oil and gas rights on the Navajo Reservation. Twenty years later, the Navajos, Spokanes, and Laguna Pueblo signed uranium leases. In the 1960s and early 1970s, a number of reservations signed agreements for the extraction of their coal. Many of these leases were negotiated by the BIA for flat or fixed rates instead of percentage royalties. This meant that tribes continued to receive ten to fifteen cents a ton for their coal even when the price of coal had risen from two to twenty dollars a ton.

The desire to control the development of their resources has led some tribes into joint ventures with private companies instead of simply leasing resources. In an agreement between the Blackfeet and a New York oil company, the tribe agreed to provide the land, and the company the development costs. After development costs are recovered, the profits will be shared equally. The Jicarilla Apache tribe completely owns and operates half a dozen oil wells. Future plans call for the construction of a tribally owned propane refinery.

In 1983 the Warm Springs Reservation began operating a $30-million hydroelectric plant, the only Indian-owned hydroelectric power plant in the United States. Built with tribal funds, money from a state bond issue, and a federal loan, the plant sells electricity to the Pacific Power and Light Company. The project will eventually produce $4 million in yearly sales for the tribe.

Many tribes are carefully weighing the advantages of certain types of development, especially energy development, against the possible damages to resources, the environment, and health. The development of hydroelectric power plants, for example, may endanger fish and other wildlife. Uranium mining on the Navajo Reservation has led to increases in lung disease and cancer. Many members of traditional tribes, such as the Taos, San Felipe, and Santo Domingo Pueblos and the Cheyenne and Forest County Potawatomis, believe that the scarring and destruction of land that accompanies some energy development, especially strip mining, is an act of desecration. To destroy the land is to destroy the center of the soul. Land is simply more valuable than money. If the land is destroyed, tribes are left with no choice but to assimilate. For tribes whose religious beliefs prohibit mineral exploitation, and for tribes without mineral or timber riches (only 29 percent of all Indians belong to tribes with mineral resources), improved living conditions must come through other forms of economic development.

Tribally Owned Businesses

Most tribes have no formal economy to generate capital. Their capital comes mostly from outside the reservation. Only 30 percent of tribal money originates from tribal businesses or from annuities from the sale of land or judgment awards. The remaining 70 percent of all tribal dollars are federal dollars that enter the reservation economy in the form of grants. The reservation economy is therefore highly dependent upon federal monies and especially vulnerable to cuts in the federal budget. And no matter what the source, money that does enter the reservation economy quickly leaves, spent in shops or for services off the reservation, creating demand, profits, and wages for non-Indians. The result is that off-reservation communities benefit greatly from the federal and tribal dollars flowing into or produced on reservations.

Menominee sawmill. (Courtesy Donald L. Fixico.)

Many tribes are attempting to develop economic self-sufficiency and independence by constructing their own stores and businesses on the reservations. In 1977, for example, the Shoshoni Bannocks opened a very successful shopping center on the Fort Hall Reservation in Idaho. Four years later the Navajo Nation opened a small shopping center in Chinle. The center employs one hundred people and serves thirty thousand, offering a supermarket, laundromat, general-merchandise store, and space for additional stores.

Several other tribes have opened tribally owned businesses and factories. The Blackfeet Indian Writing Company supplies thousands of pencils, pens, and markers to three hundred of *Fortune* magazine's top five hundred companies and to such institutions as Harvard University. In 1987 the tribe opened the nation's first tribally owned, federally chartered bank, in Browning, Montana. WCD Enterprises, established and operated by the Wichita, Caddo, and Delaware tribes in Anadarko, Oklahoma, manufactures straw cowboy hats for the International Hat Company, the largest hatter in the world. The Devil's Lake Sioux Manufacturing Corporation produces camouflage netting for the U.S. Army and carpeting for automobiles. The 2,500 members of the Lummi tribe in Washington own and manage a construction company, a seafood-processing plant, and a fish and oyster hatchery. These three companies have annual sales of more than $34 million. Among native Alaskan corporations, Sealaska, with 15,700 shareholders, is the most successful. In the early 1980s, it sold over $225 million worth of timber, salmon,

Inn of the Mountain Gods, a plush resort offering downhill skiing, is operated by the Mescalero Apache Tribe, New Mexico. (Courtesy Gary Rankel.)

and construction materials, placing it among the one thousand largest businesses in the United States. Several tribes, including the Warm Springs, the Mescalero Apache, and the Oneida of Wisconsin, have opened resorts.

Some tribes are beginning to establish commercial relations with foreign countries. The Japanese opened an automobile-testing facility on the Ak-Chin Indian reservation, south of Phoenix, Arizona. The Puyallup Tribe of Washington is exploring a joint venture garment factory on Puget Sound with the People's Republic of China.

Tribally regulated gaming activities exist on over one hundred reservations. The Oneidas of New York and the Ya-

The Confederated Tribes of the Warm Springs Reservation in Oregon offer an eighteen-hole golf course at their luxurious Kah-Nee-Ta Lodge and Resort. (Courtesy Gary Rankel.)

quis of Arizona are among the tribes that use bingo proceeds to fund tribal operations and services. The Oneidas have used their bingo proceeds to purchase forty-seven acres of farmland, construct a 202-room motel and a thirty-two-acre industrial park, operate a computer center and tobacco enterprises, establish fire-safety measures, research Oneida history, and set up language classes and scholarship programs. Unemployment on the reservation has decreased from 80 percent to 5 percent. In 1987 the Supreme Court ruled that the Cabazon Band of Mission Indians of California, composed of only 25 enrolled members, was allowed to operate bingo games free of state regulation.

An alternative approach to economic development is seen in the craft-oriented economy of the Zunis. The Zunis live on a barren, rugged, and generally inaccessible reservation 150 miles west of Albuquerque, New Mexico. The highly traditional Zunis have an international reputation as silversmiths for their distinctive silver jewelry inlaid with turquoise, coral, and mother-of-pearl. Although Indian jewelry is a business with yearly sales of over $.5 billion, Indian craftspeople receive only a small share of the profits, often earning only the minimum wage for their many hours of highly skilled work. Artisans often sold their products to traders who resold them at a 300 to 400 percent profit. This situation improved in 1979, when the Zuni Craftsmen Cooperative Association was established as the official marketing organization of Zuni craftspeople. The association now produces a sales catalog, enabling it to sell directly to customers, thereby eliminating the dealers and traders and allowing craftspeople to receive a greater share of the profits.

Seminole bingo hall in South Florida. (Courtesy Donald L. Fixico.)

TAXATION

The inherent authority of tribes to levy taxes has long been recognized. As early as 1857 the Muscogee Nation imposed a tax on non-Indian traders operating within the nation. The authority to tax derives from a tribe's inherent right to govern. The most important goal of taxation is to raise revenues to fund governmental services and operations, such as maintenance and operation of roads and schools and provision of care for the needy.

There are several kinds of taxes: income, business, property, severance, sales, excise, and others. The Oglala Sioux, for example, collect a tax on the income of tribal employees and plan to extend the tribal tax to state and federal employees who work on the reservation. Other tribes, such as the Quinaults and the Navajos, levy taxes on enterprises doing business on the reservation. A Navajo tribal law requires businesses grossing more than $100,000 a year to pay taxes on their profits. Some tribes charge a severance tax, which is a tax charged on resources at the time they are removed from the ground. Among the tribes that have chosen to levy severance taxes are the Blackfeet and Crow tribes of Montana, the Navajos, and the Jicarrilla Apaches of Arizona. In an effort to reduce unemployment, the Navajos, in 1988, implemented a plan to decrease taxes on businesses by an amount proportional to the number of new jobs the business provides on the reservation.

Tribal rights to impose severance taxes on nonmembers were upheld by the Supreme Court in *Merriam* v. *Jicarrilla Apache Tribe*. The Court held that the tribe could tax nonmembers by virtue of its powers to regulate economic activity on the reservation and to raise funds for governmental services as well as by virtue of its authority to exclude non-Indians from tribal lands.

Besides raising money for government services, taxes may

License Law, Amendment to

All legitimate business houses of whatsoever capacity or character engaged in the sale of all manner of dry goods, provisions, hardware, lumber, drugs, or any other article or articles known or designated as merchandise shall pay an annual tax of one percent on the first cost of all goods or merchandise offered for sale, to be ascertained by personal inspection by the Tax Collector of the original invoices of purchase. Sec. 260. All laws or parts of laws in conflict herewith are hereby repealed.

Muscogee Nation Law,
approved March 24, 1897

function as a conservation tool. If taxes are assessed on resources, companies will find it less profitable to exploit the resource quickly, thereby ensuring the tribe of a steadier income for a longer time. Taxes can also be used to encourage environmental protection. The Navajo tribe, for example, has levied a tax on two power plants that emit sulphur, a pollutant. To encourage installation of sulphur-reducing equipment, the nation instituted a sulphur emission charge based on the amount of sulphur emitted by plants within the reservation.

Another way to raise funds and to control or limit some activities and enterprises is through licensing. Licensing is both a form of taxation and an exercise of tribal police power. Requiring liquor licenses and automobile licenses, for instance, protects the health and welfare of the community. The Shoshoni and Arapaho tribes of the Wind River Reservation in Wyoming, for example, require all taverns to have a tribal liquor license. The Menominee Nation of Wisconsin, the Red Lake Chippewas of Minnesota, and the Sacs and Foxes and the Kiowas of Oklahoma raise money by issuing tribal automobile license plates to Indian and non-Indian residents.

Like other governments, tribes can levy their own excise (consumption) and sales taxes. More than fifty tribes collect excise taxes on cigarettes sold to tribal members from shops (called "smokeshops") on the reservations. A few tribes, including the Muscogees and the Zunis, place a small tribal sales tax on goods sold to tribal members on the reservation. The money raised through the Zuni sales tax has paid for lighting in certain areas of the pueblo. The Oglala Sioux also charge a tribal sales tax, which is collected by the state as part a general sales tax and then apportioned back to the tribe (this arrangement is discussed further in chapter 13).

The Supreme Court's 1980 *Colville* decision severely hampered the ability of tribes to collect revenues through excise

Taxing Ordinance

Noncompliance with any licensing and taxing ordinance of the Tribe shall constitute an offense for the punishment of which the Rosebud Sioux Court shall; in the case of a member of the Tribe, have jurisdiction. . . . Noncompliance with such order by any nonmember shall result in the loss of his license or privilege to do business on the reservation and may be removed from the reservation pursuant to Chapter 6, Section 2, of this code. . . . the Court may require as a condition to do business on the reservation, that he pay a charge or penalty in addition to any unpaid fees, taxes, or assessment in any amount not to exceed $100.00 to be determined by the council.

Rosebud Sioux Tribe,
Chap. 7, Miscellaneous
Provisions, Section 1

Sac and Fox Nation of Oklahoma license tags. (Photo by the author.)

Sac and Fox smokeshop advertisement (lower right of sign). (Photo by the author.)

taxes. Before the *Colville* decision, all individuals and businesses on the reservation were considered exempt from paying or collecting state sales and excise taxes. To raise needed revenues, many tribes ran "smokeshops," shops where they sold cigarettes and imposed their own excise tax, which was lower than the outside state tax. This allowed the tribes to sell cigarettes for lower prices than off-reservation businesses could, since the latter were required to charge a state sales tax. Then came the *Colville* decision, which did not remove tribal authority to levy taxes but did rule that tribes had to collect state excise tax on excise taxable goods sold to non-Indians. Collecting a state tax on nonmembers did not interfere with the tribe's right to self-government, said the Court.

Despite the Court's findings, the decision had unfortunate consequences for the practical exercise of tribal self-government. In effect, the decision seriously diminished the effectiveness of collecting a tribal excise tax on goods sold to non-Indians, because the addition of the state tax reduced the competitiveness of the merchandise.

RELATIONS WITH OTHER GOVERNMENTS

As discussed in chapters 2 and 3, tribes established complex and sophisticated intertribal alliances quite early in history. Between the sixteenth and eighteenth centuries various northeastern Indian nations formed a number of unions including the Huron, Mohican, Powhatan, Illinois, and Eastern Abenaki confederacies. Two confederacies, the Abenaki and the Iroquois, formed the Grand Council Fire, a "supratribal" organization, in the 1700s and 1800s. The All Indian Pueblo

Section 7—Design, procurement and issuance of registration plates.

2) The Menominee Indian Tribal Council shall determine the size, color and design of registration plates with a view toward making them visible evidence of the period for which the vehicle is registered, as well as making them a ready means of identifying the specific vehicle or owner for which the plates were issued.

Menominee Indian Motor Vehicle Code, Title 13

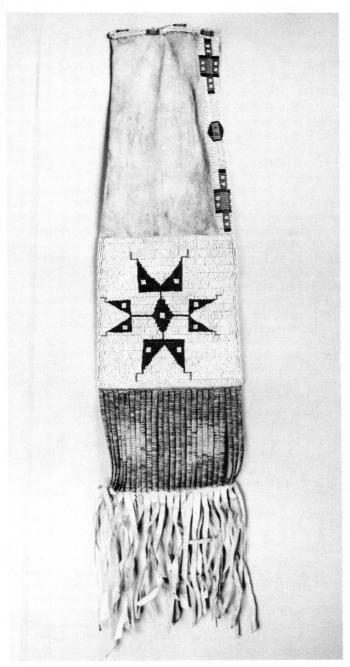

This beaded buckskin pipe bag held the peace pipe used at the Treaty of the Southern Arapahos and Utes. (Courtesy Museum of the American Indian, Heye Foundation.)

Council and the Iroquois League both have been in existence for centuries. The first recorded meeting between the Pueblo Council and Europeans occurred in 1598. Then, as now, the purpose of the council (currently composed of the governors of the nineteen pueblos) was to preserve and protect the common interests of the Pueblo Indians. Tribes continue their long tradition of cooperation today through intertribal agreements and through the formation of national, regional, and special-interest organizations.

Intertribal Agreements

As tribes seek to develop their economies and provide improved social services to their members, they have found it helpful to cooperate and join forces with other tribes. In the 1970s the Blackfeet of Montana and the Bloods of Alberta, Canada, both members of the historic Blackfeet Confederacy, signed a trade agreement in which the Blood Nation, in Canada, purchased lumber from the Blackfeet Nation, in the United States, and the Blackfeet purchased modular housing from the Bloods. The San Carlos Apaches of Arizona have established a tribal business of processing jojoba beans to produce an oil used in cosmetics and hair-care products. The San Carlos Apaches have an agreement to import their beans from the tiny Cochimi tribe in Mexico, which harvests the beans in the isolated mountains of Northern Baja, California.

In 1977 two thousand people attended a ceremony marking the end of a long-standing feud between the Southern Utes and the Comanches. The tribes had previously tried to settle their conflict in 1870, but the negotiations had ended in battle. In 1975 the elders of the Southern Utes moved to resume discussions. Two years later a ceremony involving the smoking of a peace pipe, the exchange of buffalo scrolls, and a handshake ended more than two hundred years of hostility over hunting rights. (Tribes are quite within their rights in entering into treaties with one another or with other governments. The 1871 act discussed in chapter 5 bars only the United States from signing treaties with tribes.)

National Indian Organizations:
The National Congress of American Indians

The oldest and most representative national Indian organization is the National Congress of American Indians (NCAI). Founded in 1944 and based in Washington, D.C., the NCAI represents the interests of its 160 member tribes, whose combined population totals over 400,000. The NCAI's purpose is to work closely with tribes to protect their land and natural resources, their hunting and fishing rights, and their treaty rights; to preserve their cultural values; and to increase the public's awareness of Indian and tribal affairs. The NCAI also analyzes and reports to its members information concerning legislation, judicial opinions, and government policies affecting tribal affairs.

We, the members of Indian tribes of the United States of America invoking the Divine guidance of Almighty God in order to secure to ourselves—the Indians of the United States and the Natives of Alaska—and our descendants the rights and benefits to which we are entitled under the laws of the United States, and the several states thereof; to enlighten the public toward the better understanding of the Indian people; to preserve rights under Indian treaties or agreements with the United States; to promote the common welfare of the American Indian and to foster the continued loyalty and allegiance of American Indians to the flag of the United States do establish this organization and adopt the following Constitution and By-laws.

Preamble to Constitution, National Congress of American Indians

Meeting of the United Southeastern Tribes. (Courtesy Donald L. Fixico.)

Regional and Special Interest Organizations

Since the 1960s, tribes have also formed more than a dozen regional organizations whose purpose is to improve tribal existence through collective action. Tribes of northeastern Canada and the United States (including the Micmac, Passamaquoddy, and Penobscot, for example) have, in recent years, held a series of Wabanaki Conferences (named for the powerful Wabanaki Confederacy, which flourished more than one hundred years ago) to explore mutual problems. Many of these problems arise because of the Canadian-United States border, which artificially divides more than thirty tribes and makes it difficult to develop or maintain political, economic, social, and even family relations.

Most of the other regional organizations are known as intertribal councils (ITCs). Many ITCs are involved in research, providing services, communication, and lobbying. The Intertribal Council of California (ITCC), a typical example, currently provides services to more that one hundred tribal groups throughout the state. In the past the ITCC itself offered a wide range of services to advance the economic, educational, cultural, legal, and social status of California Indians. Today, the ITCC has assumed an advisory role and has transferred program administration to local tribal groups.

In 1975, twenty-five American Indian tribes with rich energy resources formed the Council of Energy Resource Tribes (CERT). The main purpose of this organization is to assist member tribes (now numbering forty-three) in preserving and managing energy resources. In the past, tribes relied heavily on advice from outside developers. As a result, they rarely obtained adequate returns from or control over the extraction of their own resources. By monitoring important energy legislation and by providing technical assistance, CERT gives tribes an opportunity to better plan and control the development of their own resources. In 1987 representatives from eighty-two tribes established the Intertribal Agriculture Council. The council's purpose is to assist tribes in developing their agricultural potential. Forty-six million acres of the 53 million held in trust are used for agriculture. Only 40 percent of Indian farmlands, however, are used by Indians. Tribes are also increasingly entering into agreements with state and local governments in an effort to solve problems of mutual interest. Chapter 12 examines representative agreements between tribes and the federal, state, and local governments about law enforcement, resource conservation, taxation, and social services.

PROVIDING SOCIAL SERVICES

In traditional Indian society the extended family and the tribe as a whole educated the young and cared for the sick and the elderly. But the severe disruptions of tribal life during the reservation and assimilation periods left tribes unable to meet their needs in traditional ways. Responsibility for providing social services passed from the hands of tribal members to BIA agents and other outside agencies such as churches. In 1975, Congress passed the Indian Self-Determination and Education and Assistance Act in a move to return social services to tribal control. This act grants tribes the opportunity to operate many reservation programs previously administered by the bureau. This law not only supports Indian sovereignty but also encourages that social services be tailored to the special needs and unique culture of each community. Today, tribes operate more than half of the federal services provided to reservations, including assistance to the needy, law-enforcement programs, court systems, housing programs, health clinics, and schools.

Education

The education of Indian children by non-Indians began in 1568, soon after colonization, when Jesuit missionaries established a school at Havana, Cuba. The purpose of this school and the others that followed it was to "civilize" the Indians. Becoming civilized meant converting to Christianity, learning to read and write and farm, and adopting white values—individualism, materialism, competitiveness, conquest of nature, and saving for the future.

Throughout the colonial period, priests and missionaries accompanied Spanish, French, and English explorers, teach-

Purpose:
(1) "To ensure that the Indian people receive an equitable return for their resources, and are able to utilize those resources as a foundation upon which to develop stable tribal economies."
(2) "To assist the tribes in protecting their natural, social, and cultural environment from the adverse impacts of energy resource development."
(3) "To aid each tribe in acquiring the capability to manage its resources for itself."

Statement of Purpose,
Council of Energy Resource
Tribes (CERT), 1975

ing Christianity and establishing small schools in the wilderness. Later, the education of Indian youths as a solution to the hostilities on the frontier and the need for land for settlement was taken up by the new American government. The Continental Congress passed a resolution in 1775 that appropriated five hundred dollars for the education of Indian youth at Dartmouth College in New Hampshire—a school originally established to educate Indians.

Secretary of War Henry Knox and President Thomas Jefferson both argued that Indian lands could be obtained more easily and cheaply if Indians were taught to be like whites and assimilated into white culture. In its 1794 treaty with the Stockbridges, Oneidas, and Tuscaroras the United States agreed to build three grist and sawmills for the tribes and to employ persons to teach the Indians to use them. In its 1803 treaty with the Kaskaskias, the United States agreed to pay a priest one hundred dollars a year for seven years to "instruct as many of the children as possible in the rudiments of literature."

In 1819, Congress earmarked ten thousand dollars for Indian education. These funds were given to mission schools run by several denominations. These schools taught their own brand of religion—usually either Protestant or Catholic—and the English language. Stressing white values, the schools taught boys farming and blacksmithing and girls domestic skills. For the next several decades, Indian education remained the responsibility of the churches, with federal monetary support.

In 1860 the Bureau of Indian Affairs opened its first school, on the Yakima Indian Reservation in Washington State. The Yakimas negotiated for the school in 1855 as partial payment for their cession of one-third of the state of Washington. More than one hundred Indian treaties, especially those concluded between the 1850s and 1880s, included provisions for educational facilities. By the 1900s, the government was operating 138 day schools and 113 boarding schools for Indian children. Providing education had become a basic part of the government's general trust responsibility toward Indians.

It was a responsibility grossly unfulfilled, however. Indian education was poor in quality and had little or no cultural relevance. As late as the 1930s, Navajo Reservation children were literally lassoed from horseback and kidnapped by federal officials to be sent to boarding schools where they were forbidden to practice their own traditions or speak their own language, on pain of whippings or going without food.

In 1934, hoping to improve Indian education, Congress passed the Johnson-O'Malley Act. Aimed at increasing Indian children's attendance at public schools, this act gave public schools extra federal funds for all Indian children enrolled. Despite this act, statistics twenty years later showed that

We know you highly esteem the kind of Learning taught in these Colleges, and the maintenance of our young Men, while with you, would be very expensive to you. We are convinced, therefore, that you mean to do us Good by your Proposal; and we thank you heartily. But you who are so wise must know that different Nations have different Conceptions of things; and you will not therefore take it amiss, if our Ideas of this kind of Education happens not to be the same with yours. We have had some experience of it. Several of our young People were formerly brought up in the Colleges of the Northern Provinces; they were instructed in all your Sciences; but, when they came back to us, they were bad Runners, ignorant of every means of living in the Woods, unable to bear either cold or Hunger, knew neither how to build a Cabin, take a deer, or kill an enemy, spoke our language imperfectly, were therefore neither fit for Hunters, Warriors, nor Counsellors; they were totally good for nothing. We are however not the less obliged for your kind Offer, tho' we decline accepting it; and to show our grateful Sense of it, if the Gentlemen of Virginia shall send us a Dozen of their Sons, we will take care of their Education, instruct them in all we know, and make Men of them.

Conassatego, of the Iroquois League, replying to an offer by the Virginia Legislature to the Six Nations, inviting them to send six youths to be educated at the College of William and Mary, Williamsburg (1744).

Chiricahua Apache children arriving at the Carlisle Indian School, in Pennsylvania, November 4, 1886. (Courtesy Museum of the American Indian, Heye Foundation.)

Indian education remained far below national standards. In 1952 the average Indian was educated only to the fifth grade level (and on the Navajo reservation only to the first grade level). Arguing that the federal government had failed in its mission to educate Indian students, the government, as part of its termination policies shifted responsibility for Indian education to the states. Many reservation schools were closed.

In the mid and late 1960s other studies confirmed that Indian education was still ineffective and often destructive. Indian children who entered public school on a par with their white classmates or at only a slight disadvantage because of unfamiliarity with the English language, were four years behind their peers by the twelfth grade. In 1969, Senator Edward Kennedy's Special Senate Subcommittee on Indian Education published a report entitled "Indian Education: A National Tragedy—A National Challenge." The study revealed that Indian students attending public schools often encountered discrimination and racism, and that they rarely encountered a teacher who had any understanding of Indian culture or history.

To many Indian parents, the Anglo educational system represented a form of cultural genocide. It undermined Indian traditions, values, and beliefs. Indian parents acknowledged that reading and writing were useful, but they rebelled against the insistence on Anglo values—values that stressed placing one's individual needs above those of family and tribe; aggressiveness and competitiveness rather than acceptance and cooperation; achieving status through wealth and material goods rather than through wisdom and goodness.

A constant recommendation in all Indian education stud-

The same children four months later. (Courtesy Museum of the American Indian, Heye Foundation.)

ies in the 1960s and 1970s was that Indians be given greater control over the education of their children. In 1972, Congress passed the Indian Education Act, which provided funds for special bilingual/bicultural programs, for developing culturally relevant teaching materials, for training and hiring counselors, and for creating an Indian Education Bureau within the federal Office of Education. Most important, the legislation required the participation of Indians and Alaska natives in the planning of all educational projects. Three years later the Indian Self-Determination and Education Assistance Act gave tribes the opportunity to operate their own schools. Today more than fifty tribes do so. The legislation also required that all Johnson-O'Malley funds for Indian schools be administered by Indian advisory boards.

Although much remains to be accomplished, the quality and cultural relevance of Indian education has begun to improve. In 1965 less than seventeen hundred Indian students were attending college. Fifteen years later, although the Indian dropout rate from college still exceeded 35 percent, the number of Indian students in college exceeded twenty thousand. Some have been educated wholly or partly at one of twenty-three tribally affiliated colleges, such as the Navajo Community College, on the Navajo Reservation in Arizona, or Sinte Gleska (Spotted Tail) Community College, on the Rosebud Reservation in South Dakota.

Indian advisory boards on many reservations—the Hupa in California, the Paiute in Nevada, the Lummi in Washington, and the Delaware in Oklahoma, to name a few—have overseen the writing of tribal history texts and teaching materials. Tribes in the Northwest joined together in a project that encouraged elders and parents, not scholars, to produce curriculum materials on tribal history and culture.

Similarly, many schools have established bilingual programs. Some of these programs are aimed at helping children acquire English as a second language, others at helping children learn their native language. The two-thousand-member Lac Courte Oreille tribe in Wisconsin, which operates its own school, uses a computer system to teach its children Ojibwa, the native language.

The Menominee Indian School District

The Menominees (a word meaning "wild rice gatherers") were a peaceful woodland tribe that inhabited the northern Great Lakes region in the present-day state of Wisconsin. Between 1817 and 1853, the Menominee Nation signed several treaties with the United States ceding more than 255,000 acres and agreeing to remain on their forest-covered and lake-dotted 235,000 acre reservation northwest of Green Bay, Wisconsin.

In 1951, Congress terminated its relationship with the Menominees. Up to that time the Menominees had been virtually self-sufficient. They had their own sawmill, hospital, and utility company, and they enjoyed higher than average health, employment, and education. The termination process brought the tribe close to bankruptcy. Once terminated, they were required to pay property tax on their land and operate hospitals and utility companies in compliance with state codes. Their hospital closed for lack of funds, and their utility company closed as well, forcing tribal members to pay higher rates to outside companies. Tribal lands were denied trust status and placed in a corporation controlled primarily by non-Indians. Unable to pay the state taxes owed by the corporation, the tribe was forced to sell some of its lands to outsiders. No longer a reservation, the newly created Menominee County fell under state control. No longer legally Indians, many Menominees suffered a profound loss of identity, feeling neither Indian nor white. Unemployment soared. So did health problems and alcoholism.

In 1969 a group of Menominees organized against further selling of tribal lands and began lobbying Congress for redress. In 1973, Congress passed the Menominee Restoration Bill, which restored the federal-tribal relationship. The tribe began working to regain the self-sufficiency and control it had enjoyed before termination. Realizing that education was crucial to their present and future development and self-sufficiency, tribal members turned their attention toward improving their educational system.

There are now three elementary schools and one junior/senior high school on the Menominee Reservation, attended by approximately 850 Menominee students. One of the elementary schools is operated by the Catholic church; the other schools are public and accredited and are administered according to state law by a seven-member school board. All school-board members are enrolled Menominee tribal

The Mission Statement

The mission of the Menominee Indian School District is to establish an educational program, compatible with Menominee Indian heritage and with community involvement, and that provides an opportunity for all students to become proficient in the basic skills in order to be sufficiently prepared to challenge their interests and abilities and to develop confidence and respect for themselves and others so they can function in society and make responsible decisions that contribute toward their success and the betterment of their communities now and in the future.

Menominee Indian School
District Policy

Menominee Tribal High School, Keshena, Wisconsin. (Courtesy *Menominee News.*)

members elected from the reservation to three-year terms. The board levies taxes for the schools' operation, hires the schools' administrators and staff, oversees the schools' curriculum, and handles discipline problems. The Menominee school board's mission statement states its primary objective: "to provide students with a comprehensive and quality education consistent with their Menominee Indian heritage." With this goal in mind, the school board has designed a curriculum that integrates Menominee culture, language, and history into the school's program of study.

To prevent the loss of the Menominee language, the school district requires that every child from kindergarten through the sixth grade study it. High-school students may take Menominee language classes as electives. Menominee history is taught as part of the required Wisconsin history course to all fourth-grade students. Eleventh-grade students are required to take an American Indian history course in which the first semester reviews the general history of the American Indian from pre-Columbian times to the present and the second semester is devoted exclusively to Menominee tribal history and to understanding how federal policies have affected the Menominee Nation.

Students have the option of taking other courses to further their understanding of Indian cultures in general and Menominee culture in particular. Singing and drumming classes are available in which students master traditional drumming techniques and learn that the sound of the drum symbolizes the heartbeat of life. Students also learn the words and significance of a variety of different songs and chants, including powwow songs, school honor songs, and traditional songs. Traditional dances are taught, as well as the importance of differences in dress and customs among tribes.

Menominee education today is viewed as a community effort, as it was traditionally, with teachers helping teachers and community members assisting where possible. Six teachers were selected in the early 1980s to study, with the aid of a grant, tribal culture and history from pre-history to the present. Upon completion of their study they assisted other teachers in integrating aspects of Indian teachings into their classes and developing additional curriculum materials. For example, junior-high students now study Indian poetry as well as English and American literature. Students in home economics may choose projects such as weaving traditional sashes, sewing ribbon shirts, or doing beadwork. Teachers draw heavily from the reservation's own resources, especially the knowledge of the elders.

To combat the high dropout rate among Indian students, the Menominee legislature passed a law in 1980 requiring students to attend school until their eighteenth birthday, two years longer than required by state law. Parents who allow their children to become truant or to drop out of school are fined in tribal court. To help students who have special problems, the school board has developed two programs to encourage such students to stay in school. One program enables teenage mothers to care for their babies and also complete their classes. The other program allows students who have difficulty adjusting to school to carry a reduced course load.

Housing

The housing situation on Indian reservations is critical. Surveys taken in 1980 show that almost half of all Indians live in substandard housing, compared to only 12 percent of the general American population. More than 27 percent of all Indians live in overcrowded homes, compared to a national average of only 12 percent. Roughly two-thirds of Indians living in rural areas do without indoor plumbing. Overcrowding and poor sanitation cause Indians to suffer high rates of such diseases as tuberculosis and gastroenteritis. Ten out of every thousand Indian infants die before age one, a figure twice the national average.

The low income levels on many reservations are one cause of substandard housing. With the average family income on some reservations as low as nine hundred dollars a year, most Indian families simply cannot afford to build new homes or repair old ones. Second, most Indian families live in isolated areas, making it both difficult and expensive to bring in construction material and to install electricity, water, and sewage lines. Third, because most Indian families live on trust land, which, by law, cannot be sold, they cannot assume mortgages for home construction or home improvement from commercial banks and savings and loans institutions.

In 1949, Congress passed the Housing Act, enunciating a national goal that every American have a decent, safe, and sanitary home. To meet this goal, Congress began a variety of federal housing programs. Not until 1961, however, did Congress provide funds to what is now the Department of Housing and Urban Development (HUD), formerly part of

School Attendance Law:

WHEREAS, the Menominee Tribal Legislature has determined that the general welfare of the Menominee Tribe requires the regular attendance of school age children in elementary and secondary schools . . .
Section IV
1. Requirement to attend school. All persons having within their control a child between the age of 6 and 18 years when the 18th birthday shall occur during the school year be required to enroll such child in school and to maintain school attendance of such child during the school year unless the school has excused such child.

Housing for the elderly sponsored by the Muscogee Nation. (Courtesy Donald L. Fixico.)

the Department of Health, Education, and Welfare, to construct public housing on reservations. Between 1961 and
1980, HUD worked with the bureau and the Indian Health
Service (IHS) to construct 38,000 new homes on reservations. These three agencies have a cooperative agreement under which the bureau acquires and surveys the land and
builds the access roads, the IHS provides water and sanitation facilities, and HUD supplies the housing.

While tribes are supportive of federal housing assistance,
the program has suffered from poor interagency cooperation.
Housing has sometimes sat empty for lack of water and sewer
lines. HUD building requirements are insensitive to traditional (and often more efficient) housing designs. The Pueblos, for example, were at first not allowed to build their traditional and easily maintained adobe homes. The traditional
log cabins of the Plateau and Plains tribes similarly did not
meet HUD requirements for financing. Many of the Miccosukees of Florida, finding their new HUD homes oppres-
sively hot and poorly ventilated, returned to their traditional
chicksees, open-air–thatched-roof dwellings.

Another problem is that HUD regulations erode tribal
sovereignty. HUD requires that local housing authorities be
independent and answerable to HUD instead of the tribal
council. From the federal government's point of view this
arrangement has two advantages. First, tribal governments,
as sovereigns, are immune from lawsuits, while housing authorities not connected to the tribal government can be sued
for mismanaging funds. Second, by establishing an independent authority, the government hoped to eliminate tribal officials from providing housing allocations based on political
patronage or kinship. The great disadvantage to the system
for tribes is that tribal governments are faced with an important and often powerful federal presence on the reservation
over which they have no control.

The Northern Cheyenne Tribal Housing Authority

The Cheyenne Nation was originally a forest-dwelling agricultural tribe living in what is now Minnesota. Before European colonization the tribe migrated westward, where it adopted the nomadic, buffalo-hunting culture of the Plains tribes. During the early part of the nineteenth century the tribe split into two groups, one settling near the headwaters of the Northern Platte and Yellowstone rivers and the other on the banks of the Arkansas River. This separation into the Northern and Southern Cheyennes was formalized in 1851 with the Treaty of Fort Laramie. Both the Northern and Southern Cheyennes fiercely fought to protect their lands and joined the battle to defeat Custer at the Little Big Horn. Both tribes were eventually subdued, however, and forced to relocate to Indian Territory. In 1878 the Northern Cheyennes, led by two chiefs, Little Wolf and Morning Star (also known as Dull Knife), escaped and returned to Montana in the dead of winter, pursued by one thousand soldiers. Despite heavy losses from the weather and battles, the Northern Cheyennes refused to return to Indian Territory. Finally, in 1884, an executive order created a reservation of 444,157 acres for the Cheyennes in Montana, adjacent to the Crow reservation.

Today the 4,500-member tribe is governed by a 15-member council, elected for two-year terms, and a tribal chairperson, elected at large for a four-year term. Since the Northern Cheyenne Reservation is isolated from major cities and transportation routes, economic development has been difficult. Most families live on an income one-third that of non-Indian families in the state. Coal mining and livestock raising are the main sources of personal and tribal income.

The Northern Cheyenne Tribal Housing Authority was established by tribal ordinance in 1962. Since then it has helped more than five hundred families obtain safe and decent housing. The authority plans and constructs housing and also manages the housing it builds. Three types of housing arrangements are open to tribal citizens. Families who qualify may rent two-to-five bedroom houses, depending on their needs. Tenants pay an adjustable monthly rent based on their current income. Between 1962 and the late 1980s, the authority built more than sixty-five rental units, all of them maintained by authority employees.

The authority has also built more than thirty-five one- and two-bedroom apartments for the elderly and physically disabled. These apartments, constructed with wide doorways, low counter tops, and other special features, allow the elderly and the physically disabled to live independent lives in their own homes instead of in institutions. As with the low-rent housing program, individuals pay rent based on their income levels.

The third program operated by the housing authority allows families to buy their own homes. In its first decade the housing authority constructed more than 450 houses for this program. Homeowners are required to contribute one thousand dollars in either labor or material to the home's construction. Owners are charged monthly payments of not more than 25 percent and not less than 15 percent of their monthly income. Families are also responsible for repairing and maintaining their homes. If the homeowner has abided by the agreement with the authority, title is transferred to the individual at the end of a twenty-five-year period. The program has a twofold advantage. Families are able to buy homes with federal assistance and the tribe is able to subsidize additional housing with the money received from rental and homeowners' payments.

Health Care

The first explorers and settlers invariably described the Indians they met as enjoying excellent health. Traditional Indian health care, like all aspects of life, was an integral part of religion. The approach was what we today would call holistic—that is, it focused on treating the whole person, mind and body. Curing and praying ceremonies often involved the whole family and community. An array of herbal medicines was used in conjunction with the ceremonies. Angelica, for example, was used for stomachaches. Steeped elm bark quieted coughs and jimsonweed served as an anesthetic. More than five hundred drugs now listed in the *United States Pharmacopoeia* were known and used by Indians.

Traditional medicine man healing the sick. (Courtesy Library of Congress.)

By the mid-1800s, however, Indian health had declined to the point where Indian people were on the verge of extinction. Because Indians lacked the immunities that whites had to diseases such as cholera, smallpox, tuberculosis, and measles, whole tribes were virtually wiped out by these diseases, brought to North America by white explorers and colonists. A smallpox epidemic in 1837 wiped out all but one hundred of the sixteen-hundred-member Mandan tribe and killed half of the Blackfeet Nation. More than half of the Kiowa and Comanche tribes died during an epidemic of cholera.

Providing health care is an important part of the federal government's trust responsibility to Indian nations. Many treaties have specifically promised medical services in return for land. In 1954, Congress formally created the Indian Health Service (IHS) to honor its obligations. The IHS is responsible for providing health care, preventive medicine, and sanitation programs and for building and maintaining health-care facilities. In 1955, management of the IHS was transferred from the BIA to what is now the Department of Human Services.

In 1976, Congress passed the Indian Health Care Improvement Act. This act reemphasized that providing adequate health care to all Indians, reservation or urban, rich or poor, was an important part of the government's ongoing trust responsibility. Yet despite this act and the considerable progress made by the IHS in the last generation, major problems in Indian health care remain. Indians continue to die approximately eleven years earlier than non-Indians. In a 1986 study by the Office of Technology Assessment, it was reported that 37 percent of all Indian deaths between 1980 and 1982, occurred before the age of forty-five, compared to only 12 percent in the national population. Death rates from influenza and pneumonia remain twice as high for Indians as for the general population. Tuberculosis, gastroenteritis, and otis media (an ear problem) are widespread on reservations but virtually nonexistent in the dominant society. As discussed later in this chapter, hopelessness, unemployment, and a loss of identity have created a serious alcohol-abuse problem among Indians. And in the last twenty years the suicide rate among Indians has increased dramatically (by more than 130 percent), and it is twice the national average. Chronic underfunding and a lack of facilities means that an estimated one-half to three-fourths of all Indians do not receive the health care to which they are entitled by law. A federal proposal to limit federally funded health care to Indians with at least one-fourth Indian blood threatens to deprive 7,500 Indians of health care. The Navajo Nation is one of many reservations that have been working with the IHS and private agencies to improve their tribal health care. Its experiences suggest some of the problems—and the hopes for improvement—that many tribes currently face.

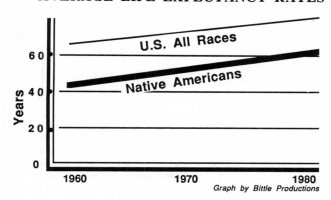

AVERAGE LIFE EXPECTANCY RATES

U.S. All Races

Native Americans

Years

60
40
20
0

1960   1970   1980

Graph by Bittle Productions

INFANT MORTALITY RATE
Deaths Per 100,000 Population

Deaths

60
40
20
0

Native Americans

U.S. All Races

1960   1970   1980

Graph by Bittle Productions

The Navajo Division of Health Improvement Services

The Navajos emigrated from Canada to the American Southwest during the fourteenth century. They refer to themselves as Dineh, meaning "the People." To the outside world they are the Navajo, a Tewa word meaning "Great Planted Fields." Unlike their Pueblo neighbors, traditional Navajos were nomadic. Typical Navajo communities were small, independent family groups, bound to other similar groups by culture, language, religion, and marriage. The Navajos quickly adapted to the horses, sheep, and goats that the Spanish introduced into the Southwest. By the 1700s, in fact, Navajo bands had come to rely on their growing sheep herds for a large part of their food and clothing.

In 1864, U.S. forces, led by Kit Carson, rounded up the Navajos and held them at Fort Sumner as prisoners of war. Four years later the Navajos were allowed to return to their homeland, between the Four Sacred Mountains in northeastern Arizona and northwestern New Mexico. Today their reservation occupies over 25,000 square miles in Arizona, New Mexico, and Utah. The largest reservation in the United States, the Navajo lands are equal in size to the state of West Virginia—an area larger than the area occupied by twenty-six of the countries in the world.

Traditionally, the Navajos had no central governing authority, being in effect a confederation of loosely knit clans. But when oil was discovered in Navajo lands in the early 1900s and the BIA needed a political entity to sign oil leases to the United States, the bureau pressured the Navajos to form a central government. Although they still operate without a written constitution, the Navajos today are governed by an extensive and sophisticated tribal government system. Their official governing body is the eighty-eight member Navajo Tribal Council. Council members are elected every four years by the 109 chapters, or local political units, into which the reservation is divided. An eighteen-member advisory committee appointed by the general council works closely with the chairperson and vice-chairperson in the overall administration of the government. The advisory committee is, in turn, assisted by thirteen specialized committees responsible for overseeing various specific areas of tribal government. Among the thirteen committees is the Health and Human Services Committee, which oversees the improvement of Navajo health care. This committee works with the IHS, the state-run Navajo Health System Agency, and several private agencies to provide health care on the reservation and to oversee tribal health-improvement programs.

While the last two decades have seen notable improvements, Navajo health care remains below the national average. Navajo life expectancy, for example, is more than ten years below the national average. Providing good services and maintaining good health is a constant struggle for several economic and social reasons. Many of the nation's 153,000 members live in isolated farming areas. Funds are scarce. Despite Navajo efforts to use craftwork (weaving, silver-smithing, and sand painting) to supplement family income, more than half of all Navajo families live below the poverty level, and many earn less than fifteen hundred dollars per year. Unemployment stands at 70 to 90 percent. Although the educational level for young Navajos is improving, the average level of education for those over twenty-five is only sixth grade. Many families still occupy the traditional one-room hogan, an earth-covered dwelling, where overcrowding and poor sanitation contribute to disease. Forty percent of the reservation housing lacks electricity, and more than half of it lacks adequate plumbing. Paved roads are scarce, making transportation to health-care facilities difficult.

The IHS must face all these difficulties in its task of providing basic health care to the Navajo people. In fulfillment of its trust responsibility, the IHS operates the Gallup Indian

The Indian men . . . are to be killed whenever, wherever you can find them: the women and children will not be harmed, but you will take them prisoners. . . . If the Indians send in a flag and desire to treat for peace, say to the bearer; [they have broken] their treaty of peace, and murdered innocent people and run off their stock: that we are going to punish them for their crimes, and that you are there to kill them wherever they can be found. We have no faith in their broken promises and we intend to kill enough of their men to teach them a lesson. I trust that this severity in the long run will be the most humane course that could be pursued toward these Indians.

Gen. James Carleton's
instructions to Kit
Carson for the roundup
of the Navajos, 1863

Medical Center, five small hospitals, three health centers, which provide twenty-four-hour care, and fifteen clinics open only at scheduled hours. The Navajo Area Health Board, made up of tribal citizens and medical personnel, oversees the IHS facilities and services. In addition, several private, nonprofit agencies (including the Navajo Nation Health Foundation, the Presbyterian Medical Services, and Project Concern) supply medical and dental care to Navajos and non-Navajos in outlying areas not served by the IHS.

In 1977 the Navajo Tribal Council created the Division of Health Improvement Services (DHIS), today one of the ten main administrative divisions of the Navajo government. The purpose of the DHIS is to provide Navajos with a comprehensive, economical, accessible, and culturally acceptable health-care service. The DHIS's programs are administered by five departments: Food and Nutrition Services; Behavioral Health; Navajo Aging Services; Preventive Health; and Health, Navajo Evaluation, and Development. The executive administration, which supervises all five departments also acts as an important link between the DHIS, the tribal chairman, and the tribal council's Health and Human Services Committee. Although federal funding cutbacks in the early 1980s brought numerous health-care programs to an end, the Navajo DHIS continues to operate several creative and innovative programs, including the New Dawn Greening Project and the Substance Abuse Program.

The New Dawn Greening Project goes straight to the roots of a primary contributing factor to Navajo health problems: poor nutrition caused by low income, lack of access to markets, and lack of refrigeration. The project was begun in 1981 to educate tribal members about nutrition, to help them grow and raise their own food, and to encourage low-cost energy conservation projects. One of the project's first undertakings was to construct a solar heated and powered greenhouse. Designed and built solely by Navajos, the greenhouse contains a classroom and a library in addition to the growing area. It has become a resource center for subjects such as building passive solar greenhouses; soil, water, and energy conservation; livestock care; planting and caring for fruit trees and houseplants; preserving and storing food; designing and growing outdoor gardens; and installing irrigation systems. Those wanting to grow their own crops can obtain free or low-cost seeds, fruit trees, and tools through the project.

One of New Dawn's long-term goals is to cooperate with each reservation community in building a self-supporting greenhouse to be used and maintained by community members. By the mid-1980s seven communities had acquired greenhouses. Another long-term program already underway is a research project on traditional Navajo practices and beliefs about food and nutrition. Historic accounts speak highly of the good health and strength previously enjoyed by the Navajo people. New Dawn hopes that educating people about their traditional foods can help improve daily nutrition. The project plans to publish cookbooks and pamphlets and to prepare slide shows for community viewing. New Dawn is also establishing seed banks and conducting experiments to attempt to resupply the once-wild plants that nearly became extinct with the arrival of white society.

The DHIS's Substance Abuse Program was created in 1982 with federal and tribal funds to educate youth and women of child-bearing age about the dangers of alcohol and drug abuse. Recognizing that the dangers of alcoholism must be taught at an early age, the tribe was particularly interested in educating its young children. Beginning in 1983, fifth and sixth graders at a number of reservation schools were given a twenty-six-unit course on alcoholism. For those youngsters most prone to alcohol abuse, the tribe initiated the Channel One Program. Channel One is a summer youth program that provides approximately sixty high-school students with a sense of responsibility and fulfillment through learning and work.

Another program is directed toward the special problems of alcohol misuse by pregnant women. Studies have shown that as few as one or two drinks a day taken by a pregnant woman can cause a birth defect known as Fetal Alcohol Syndrome (FAS). FAS is currently the second most common birth defect among the Navajos: it causes mental retardation, physical abnormalities, and stunted growth. FAS is entirely preventable. The Substance Abuse Program has trained teachers and developed teaching materials to let young women know about the dangers of alcohol to their unborn children. As does the teaching material developed for the primary grades, the Fetal Alcohol Syndrome material blends traditional Navajo beliefs with the latest information about the effects of alcohol.

Fetal Alcohol Syndrome (FAS) is a birth defect caused by women drinking alcohol during pregnancy. The purpose of this workbook is to educate and train Navajos on FAS so that "a lifetime of sadness" can be prevented. To have a son or daughter is happiness—a way of life. It is our responsibility to care for the children within us. They are our future and as Navajos they deserve lives of health and beauty—the symbol of the sash belt.

Navajo Fetal Alcohol Syndrome
Workbook

Alcoholism Programs

As mentioned above, alcoholism is one of the most serious health problems facing tribes today. American Indians, depending on their location, are six to twenty-two times more likely to die of alcohol-related diseases than are non-Indians. Alcohol is a factor in 75 to 80 percent of all Indian suicides and 90 percent of all Indian homicides. Besides threatening physical health, alcoholism often plays a central role in the breakup of families, problems with the law, and serious car accidents. Seventy-five percent of all reservation auto accidents are alcohol related. The widespread abuse of alcohol by young Indians between the ages of fifteen and twenty-four makes them four times more likely than the general population to die in automobile accidents. Statistics show that almost 20 percent of all Indian adolescents are heavy drinkers. In response to this serious problem, many tribes have established alcoholism programs. The Tsimshian Nation of the Annette Island Reserve runs one such program, discussed below.

The Annette Island Reserve Alcoholism Program

Annette Island is a rugged, fjorded, lake-filled, mountainous island off the southern coast of Alaska. It is home to the Metlakatla Indian community, composed of several clans of the Tsimshian Nation. The Tsimshians came to the island in the late 1800s under the leadership of Father William Duncan, an Anglican missionary and educator.

Father Duncan had settled in British Columbia, where he learned the native language and earned the respect of many in the native community. When interclan rivalry and violence intensified within the community—problems Duncan attributed partly to the introduction of liquor by white traders—Duncan persuaded more than eight hundred of his followers to leave British Columbia. In 1887 the group moved to Annette Island. At the community's request, three years later Congress created the Annette Island Reserve.

The thirteen-hundred-member community, whose constitution allows for anyone of Alaskan native descent to become a member upon the affirmative vote of three-fourths of the twelve-member council, is today composed of Tsimshians, Tlingits, Haidas, Eskimos, and Aleuts. The community supports itself primarily through salmon fishing and logging. The community owns a small fishing fleet, a salmon hatchery, and a salmon-processing plant. In addition it operates its own schools, health clinic, and alcoholism program, established in the 1970s.

With the aid of federal and state grants, the Metlakatla Indian Community Alcoholism Prevention Center set up a program to prevent and treat alcoholism through education and counseling. As a first step, the center produced a series of videotapes to be shown on television and throughout the reserve. In discussions at schools and businesses and with senior citizens, the center uses films to teach that alcohol is an addictive substance and that alcoholism is a disease. The center encourages individuals to seek help by stressing that the disease of alcoholism is treatable. Treatment is provided to the community's residents in the form of outpatient counseling and referrals to treatment hospitals and detoxification centers on the mainland.

The preceding chapter has shown that tribes retain a number of important rights, including the right to structure their governments; to manage their lands, resources, and economies; to administer justice; to provide social services; to levy taxes; and to deal with other governments. The manner and success with which tribes exercise these rights varies among tribes, depending upon tribal size, culture, resources, and needs.

The streamrolling effort of the "civilized society" upon the Indian people has wreaked a havoc which extends far beyond that of loss of material possessions. The American Indian and Alaskan Native are caught in a world wherein they are trying to find out who they are and where they are, and where they get in. The land which was once their "mother," giving them food and clothing, was taken. Their spiritual strengths were decried as pagan and familial ties broken. Their own form of education, i.e., that of legends, how to live, how to respect themselves and others, were torn asunder by the "White society's reading, writing and arithmetic. No culture could, or can be, expected to be thrust into a world different from its own and adapt without problems of cultural shock . . .

Reuben Snake, American Indian Policy Review Commission Report on Alcohol and Drug Abuse Task Force 11 (1976)

The exercise of tribal powers, however, is frequently constrained, changed, and even extinguished by federal and state actions. To retain their authority, tribes must exercise their rights by passing laws and establishing tribal programs. It is also important that they continually monitor the policies of the federal and state governments to ensure full protection of their inherent rights. Part 4 will discuss the past and present relationships between tribes and the federal and state governments.

TRIBAL-FEDERAL AND TRIBAL-STATE RELATIONS: AN OVERVIEW

Chapter 12 reviews the historical development, as well as the current status, of the tribal-federal relationship, focusing on the U.S. government's responsibilities to tribes and the way in which the federal government carries out these responsibilities.

Not only the federal government but state governments as well have repeatedly threatened tribal sovereignty by attempting to confiscate Indian lands, water, and other resources and by exerting jurisdiction and taxation rights over reservations. Chapter 13 examines the source of these conflicts and explores the methods used by some tribes to defuse potential conflicts and cooperate with state governments.

Finally, chapter 14 summarizes the source and powers of tribal sovereignty and the present limitations on tribal authority. In conclusion, the options that tribal governments have in directing their future development are briefly explored.

CHAPTER 12

THE TRIBAL-FEDERAL RELATIONSHIP

The United States has frequently changed the nature of its relationship with the Indian nations. It has treated tribes as international sovereigns, domestic dependent nations, wards in need of protection, and quasi-sovereign governments. These differing definitions reflect federal policies that have shifted between treating tribes as separate political entities and attempting to integrate them into mainstream America.

The federal government today describes its relationship with tribes as a trust relationship. This relationship has existed for more than two centuries. Its origins lie in tradition, international law, judicial decisions, legislation, and notions of fairness and humanity. Over the years it has undergone many changes and reinterpretations as the nation's Indian policy has changed. The tribal-federal relationship began as an equal relationship between two independent sovereigns (see table 12-1). By the late 1800s, the courts had transformed the tribes' protectorate status into that of wards under the total protection of a guardian. Today the relationship is referred to as a trust relationship that operates within a government-government setting.

From the view of many tribal people, however, the Indian nations' relationship with the federal government has never changed. Indian nations originally were, and continue to be, sovereign nations. Both parties do agree that the government-government relationship tribes maintain with the United States is based on the inherent sovereignty of each. Tribes have a right to self-determination, including the right to operate their own governments, control their own resources, and protect their own culture. The United States promised to protect remaining tribal lands and existence in exchange for cessions of vast amounts of land and an end to hostilities. The trust relationship has been acknowledged in treaties, congressional legislation, and executive proclamations.

THE PROTECTORATE RELATIONSHIP

As chapter 3 demonstrated, the early relationships between Europeans and the Indian nations centered around the important role Indian tribes played in the competition between England, France, and Spain. Vying for Indian support, the European powers signed more than five hundred treaties with various Indian nations. These treaties, which were governed by international law, or the set of laws covering interaction among nations, usually defined the relationship

Table 12-1.   Development of the Federal-Tribal Relationship

Dates	Policy	Major Laws	Relationship	Tribes' status
1770s–1820s	International sovereign to international sovereign	1783 Northwest Ordinance 1790 Trade & Intercourse Acts Treaties	Protectorate	International sovereigns
1830s–1850s	Removal	1830 Indian Removal Act Treaties	Government-government and trust relationship	Domestic dependent nations
1850s–1890s	Reservation	Reservation treaties	Guardianship	Wards in need of protection
1870s–1930s	Assimilation	1871 End of treaty making 1885 Major Crimes Act 1887 Allotment Act (Dawes Act)	Guardianship	Wards in need of protection
1930s–1950s	Indian self-government	1934 Indian Reorganization Act (Wheeler-Howard Act)	Renewal of government-government and trust relationship	Quasi-sovereigns
1950s–1960s	Termination	1953 Resolution 108 1953 Public Law 280 Urban Relocation Program	Termination of relationship	Termination of status
1960s–present	Self-determination	1968 Indian Civil Rights Act 1975 Indian Self-Determination Act 1978 Indian Child Welfare Act 1978 Indian Religious Freedom Act	Renewal of government-government and trust relationship	Domestic dependent nation/quasi-sovereigns

between the two parties as a protectorate. Under international law a protectorate is established when a weaker power accepts, without loss of sovereignty, the protection of a stronger power. In return for European protection and trade concessions, Indian nations agreed to provide friendship, military alliance, and land.

When the United States gained independence, it followed the lead of its colonial predecessors and treated the Indian nations as international sovereigns. It exerted no control over the tribes but related to them, as it did to England or to France, according to its constitutional authority to conclude treaties, wage war, and engage in commerce with other nations. Early treaties between the United States and the Indian nations generally dealt with issues of peace and war, boundaries, passports, extradition, and foreign relations. In return for Indian friendship, land, and military help the United States agreed to provide protection, trade goods, and money.

Early domestic legislation, such as the 1787 Northwest Ordinance and the trade and intercourse acts of the 1790s, supported the protectorate relationship by helping to carry out the government's agreement to protect tribal lands from unlawful settlement and fraudulent land dealing by non-Indians. The Northwest Ordinance promised that Indian "property shall never be taken without their consent; and in their property, rights and liberty, they shall never be invaded or disturbed." The 1790 Trade and Intercourse Act protected tribes against settlers' illegal land purchases by forbidding states and individuals from buying tribal lands. Only the federal government could purchase Indian lands.

In 1831 and 1832 the Supreme Court became involved in defining the status of Indian nations and their relationship to the United States. In 1830 the Cherokees sued the United States as a foreign nation, arguing that Georgia's laws did not apply to Cherokee lands and government (see chapter 4). Chief Justice John Marshall evaded the issue by ruling that the tribe was not a foreign nation but a domestic dependent nation.

The next year Marshall further explained the tribes' relationship to the United States and their rights within that relationship in *Worcester* v. *Georgia* (see chapter 4). In this ruling Marshall emphasized that the Cherokees were a nation, a distinct political community with legal rights to their land and full authority within those lands. Their treaties were as valid as the treaties the United States had made with European nations. While it was true that the tribes had placed themselves under the protection of the United States, Marshall stressed that the relationship "was that of a nation claiming and receiving the protection of one more powerful; not that of individuals abandoning their national character, and submitting as subjects to the laws of a master." This relationship, according to Marshall, was defined as a protectorate. Tribes had not lost their sovereignty; they had merely accepted another government's offer of protection in return for land cessions and friendship.

> That instrument [the Constitution] confers on Congress the powers of war and peace; of making treaties and of regulating commerce with foreign nations, and among the several states and with the Indian tribes. These powers comprehend all that is required for our intercourse with the Indians.
>
> *Worcester* v. *Georgia,* 1832

THE GUARDIANSHIP DOCTRINE

By the second half of the 1800s the country had changed its Indian policy from maintained separation to assimilation. With this change came a new interpretation of the protectorate relationship Marshall had described in the 1832 *Worcester* decision. In 1883, the Supreme Court ruled in the *Crow Dog* case (see chapter 5) that federal courts did not have jurisdiction over the murder of one Indian by another in Indian country. Angered by the Court's ruling, Congress quickly passed the Major Crimes Act of 1885 (see chapters 5 and 11). A year later, in *U.S.* v. *Kagama*, the Supreme Court reviewed the constitutionality of this act.

This time the Court held that Congress could assume criminal jurisdiction over tribes because of its role as guardian to the tribes. Tribes, the Court stated, were the nation's wards. They were also, according to the Court, weak and helpless. Hence the United States had the duty—and the right—to protect them. This decision changed the protectorate relationship into a guardianship relationship. The protectorate relationship, which emphasized tribal sovereignty, had limited federal control over tribes. The guardianship relationship functioned as a source of federal control over tribes.

A 1903 Supreme Court ruling (in *Lone Wolf* v. *Hitchcock*; see chapter 5) indicated the degree of power the federal government could assume under the guardianship doctrine. The Court ruled in this case that the federal government had the right to take Indian lands despite a treaty requiring prior Indian approval. The Court stated that Congress had plenary—or total—control over its wards. The federal government alone could determine what constituted "protection" and how to implement it.

The *Lone Wolf* decision typified guardianship-era thought that the guardianship relationship gave the federal government unlimited power over tribes. The courts repeatedly ruled that the federal government's duty to protect Indians gave it full authority to do whatever it pleased. Tribes could be protected from states and individuals, but they had no protection against the federal government. This way of thinking prevailed until the 1930s, when the courts began to limit Congress's authority over Indians and Indian lands.

A case from 1935 provides an example of such limitation. In the 1870s the U.S. government made a surveying error that gave a section of Muscogee lands to the Sac and Fox tribe. In 1891 the government sold this land, along with the rest of the Sac and Fox Reservation, to white settlers. In 1935 the Muscogees sued the government over the loss of their lands, and the Supreme Court ruled in the tribe's favor. It was true, the Court said, that the Muscogees were wards of the federal government and subject to the government's authority in managing their property. Nevertheless, the government's control over Muscogee lands was not absolute. The federal government could not take Indian lands without paying "just compensation for them . . . for that would not be an exercise of guardianship, but an act of confiscation." Indian lands guaranteed by treaty ·or by an act of Congress were protected, the Court ruled, by the Fifth Amendment to the Constitution. The Fifth Amendment guarantees that private property cannot be taken without due process of law and just compensation. The Court ruled that while Congress could take Indian lands protected by treaty, it had to pay the tribes for their loss. In this and other cases the courts began to emphasize that Congress had certain obligations to protect tribal rights. Through reinterpretation by the courts, the guardianship relationship has gradually become today's trust relationship.

CURRENT STATUS OF THE TRIBAL-FEDERAL TRUST RELATIONSHIP

The source of the trust relationship lies in international law, treaties, legislation, and judicial decisions. Since legislation is continually being passed and courts are continually deciding cases, the trust relationship is a constantly evolving one. Presently, the law states that the United States is responsible for protecting Indian lands and resources, providing social services such as health and educational benefits, and pre-

Rally on the Capitol steps, July 17, 1978, Washington, D.C., at the end of the Longest Walk protest march. (Courtesy *Akwesasne Notes*.)

serving tribal autonomy. These rights and benefits are owed to tribes as a result of promises made by the federal government in return for the cession of more than 97 percent of Indian land to non-Indians.

Protecting Tribal Property

Protecting tribal property is the most clearly defined and important aspect of the government's trust relationship. Indian tribes ceded large areas of land to the federal government in return for a promise of protection for their remaining lands and resources. This promise, the courts have concluded, extends to protecting lands; resources, such as minerals and timber; tribal funds; and water, hunting, and fishing rights. In addition, tribes are protected from state taxation of tribal lands and resources.

The federal government's obligation to protect Indian lands is stated clearly in numerous treaties, the Northwest Ordinance, the trade and intercourse acts, and many court cases. The Bureau of Indian Affairs is responsible for overseeing 53 million acres of Indian trust lands in the continental United States (10 million of which is in Indian-owned allotments) and 40 million acres in Alaska. As trustee, the federal government must prevent this land from being taken or misused by federal agencies, the states, or private individuals.

The same federal obligation protects surface and subsurface resources. It is estimated that 30 percent of all coal, 50 to 80 percent of all uranium, and 5 to 10 percent of all oil and gas reserves in the United States lie on Indian lands. One-fourth of all tribal lands are forested, with fifty-seven reservations depending substantially on income from timber sales. As trustee, the United States is obligated to assist tribes in identifying and developing these resources and preventing their misuse or mismanagement.

On many reservations, developing tribal resources and economies depends on an adequate water supply. In the semiarid west, where the scarce water supply is already overused, tribes are finding themselves in serious competition for water with states, businesses, and private individuals. Water rights are a part of the reserved-rights doctrine. When tribes ceded large amounts of their lands to the federal government and kept a smaller portion for themselves as a reservation, they also, by implication, kept for themselves enough water to make the land productive. Congress is responsible for ensuring that tribes have sufficient water for agriculture, mining, fishing, or other economic needs. Chapter 13 discusses how this responsibility, along with the responsibility to protect hunting and fishing rights, has placed the federal government as trustee and some tribes in direct conflict with many states.

Many treaties specifically guarantee to tribes hunting and fishing rights both on-reservation and off. The courts have further ruled that, unless specifically denied, all treaties contain an implicit right to hunt and fish within reservation boundaries. Tribal hunting and fishing rights have often met with intense opposition from non-Indians. Indians in the Northwest and Great Lakes regions have suffered beatings and other forms of violence for exercising their fishing rights. The federal government has sued a number of states in an effort to protect Indian hunting and fishing rights.

The federal courts have ruled that when protecting tribal property the government must meet the highest standards of loyalty, good faith, honesty, and reasonable care and skill. "Reasonable care and skill" is also required in managing tribal funds. The Bureau of Indian Affairs, with the assistance of a private investment firm, administers more than $1.8 billion belonging to Indian tribes and individuals. This money comes primarily from the sale or lease of trust resources, from tribally owned businesses, and from cash awards given by the Indian Claims Commission and other federal courts. The government, as the manager of these funds, must ensure that the monies are wisely invested.

Providing Services

In its earliest days, the U.S. government offered simple services to the Indian nations to keep them as allies against the British and Spanish. The practice of providing goods and services for Indian lands and friendship continued. In 1819, Congress appropriated money to train adult Indians in farming and to educate Indian children in reading, writing, and arithmetic. This appropriation marked the beginning of a national policy to teach Indians the ways of whites. If Indians became farmers, like non-Indians, government officials reasoned, they would no longer need hunting grounds, and the United States could, in good conscience, take away their lands.

Throughout the 1820s the government continued to offer goods and services to pacify or "civilize" tribes that were being evicted from their traditional lands. During this era entire tribes were forced onto lands unsuitable to their ways of life and inadequate for their needs. The forest-dwelling Shawnees, for example, were moved to the dry plains of Kansas; the mountain-bred Cherokees, to Oklahoma. Many hunting tribes were disarmed; others were forced to move during the winter and leave behind most of their stored food. The tribes tried to provide for themselves, but by 1865 the disruption of their ways of life had led to staggering numbers of poor, sick, and starving Indians scattered in misery across the country. At this time the idea began to take shape that the Indians were a special responsibility of the U.S. government. After the Civil War, Congress, acting out of belated concern for the people it had nearly destroyed, called upon the president to give needy tribes emergency food and clothing.

Shortly thereafter the government decided to pursue its policy of assimilation more vigorously, a move that greatly increased both federal expenditures and the role of the BIA in tribal affairs. The BIA began an education program in 1870, and in 1879 it opened its first off-reservation boarding school. After the Major Crimes Act was passed in 1885, the BIA's presence was increased by the establishment of courts of Indian offenses. By 1900 property management had become a large part of BIA operations, as a result of the Allotment Act. In 1909 the government began providing regular medical services to Indians. Although in the 1930s Congress reversed its policy of blatant assimilation with the Indian Reorganization Act and moved to strengthen tribal governments and economies, the new policy continued to increase BIA services as Congress appropriated money to tribes for economic development and technical assistance.

The bureau's expansion continued unabated until the early 1950s, when Congress, during the termination era, passed a series of laws designed to reduce the federal government's responsibility to tribes. A number of tribes were terminated and some federal services, such as education and health, were transferred from the bureau to other departments in what was then called the Department of Health, Education, and Welfare.

As discussed in chapter 5, the termination policies proved disastrous. By the 1960s, the mood of the country had changed and had embraced President Lyndon Johnson's Great Society, a series of programs designed to eradicate poverty and assist the disadvantaged.

In the 1960s tribes became eligible for a variety of programs not as beneficiaries of the government's trust responsibility but because they were government entities. Like states, counties, and cities, tribes could apply for grants designed to upgrade government services, encourage economic development, and improve health and education. The "Great Society" provided Indians with housing grants through the Department of Housing and Urban Development, economic development grants through the Department of Commerce, and training grants through the Department of Labor. By the early 1970s, tribes were receiving funds and services from a variety of agencies within the federal government.

Federal cutbacks have caused many "Great Society" programs to disappear, but the federal government's obligation to provide basic services to tribes continues. Exactly which services are required by law varies by tribe depending upon treaty provisions. The 1794 treaty with the Six Nations (Iroquois League) requires, for example, the federal government to pay each of the six tribes $4,500 per year and supply them with certain quantities of cloth. In its 1857 treaty with the Pawnees the federal government agreed to pay that tribe an annual sum of $30,000.

Educational and health-care services are explicitly required by some treaties. More generally, however, they are an obligation implied in the trust relationship. In addition,

The American Indian has purchased a prepaid program by the largest real-estate transaction in the history of the U.S. If the U.S. cannot afford the provisions of health and other benefits, then we would be happy to have our lands returned.

Everett Rhodes, M.D.,
Chairman, American Indian
Policy Review Commission,
testimony on Indian
Health Care Improvement Act

The Congress hereby declares that it is the policy of this Nation, in fulfillment of its special responsibilities and legal obligations to the American Indian people, to meet the national goal of providing the highest possible health status to Indians and to provide existing Indian health services with all resources necessary to effect that policy.

1976 Indian Health Care
Improvement Act

All enrolled Indians of at least one-quarter Indian blood are eligible for health services. Shown here is the Indian Health Service Clinic in Phoenix, Arizona. (Courtesy Donald L. Fixico.)

the 1975 Indian Self-Determination and Education Assistance Act and the 1976 Indian Health Care Improvement Act contain provisions about the government's obligation to provide these services. Section 3 of the Indian Health Care Improvement Act specifies that "it is the policy of this nation, in fulfillment of its special responsibilities and legal obligations to the American Indian people, to meet the national goal of providing the highest possible health status to Indians and to provide existing Indian health services with all resources necessary to effect that policy."

The non-Indian population generally does not understand that, while Indians are eligible for many special services (including medical and dental care, educational and employment assistance, emergency food, housing, and even funeral expenses), these services are not charity or welfare. Tribes bargained long, hard, and often unwillingly, for these benefits, and they ceded vast tracts of land in exchange for such services.

The United States is legally bound by the provisions of more than 370 treaties and agreements with Indian nations to provide various services. These treaties are the supreme law of the land. Treaty rights are, by law, property rights, and as such they are protected by the Fifth Amendment. Unfortunately, practice does not function as smoothly as theory when it comes to actually providing the services due. The

[The trust relationship] includes an obligation to provide these services, required to protect and enhance Indian lands, resources, and self-government, but also includes those economic and social programs which are necessary to raise the standard of living and social well-being of the Indian people to a level comparable to [that of] the non-Indian population.

Final Report: American Indian Policy Review Commission, 1977

BIA's budget, adjusted for inflation, decreased by more than 5 percent between 1981 and 1985. In the mid-1980s the BIA's budget accounted for less than .0115 percent of the total federal budget. Tribes sometimes are forced to pay the federal government for services rendered but not legally required by the trust relationship, even when the tribes did not request the services. For example, tribes who successfully sue the federal government for the illegal taking of their lands generally find their awards reduced by "offsets," or deductions for "services rendered."

Protecting Tribal Autonomy

As discussed in chapter 4, the Supreme Court early defined the relationship of tribes to the United States as that of a protectorate under international law, that is, the acceptance by a weaker sovereign of the protection of a stronger sovereign. This relationship, as Chief Justice Marshall emphasized, does not involve the destruction of the weaker sovereign.

As non-Indian settlement and society encroached upon and threatened tribal existence, many tribes agreed to cede their lands in the hope that by isolating themselves from threats to their culture, they could preserve their existence. They negotiated with the United States as equals, and they negotiated with one objective. They ceded land in return for a promise of protection of their remaining or new lands and their tribal existence. Toward that end, tribes carefully bargained over exactly which jurisdictional areas would be assumed by the federal government.

During the assimilation eras, the federal government reneged on its promise to protect tribal existence. The legislation of those eras—the Major Crimes Act, the Dawes Allotment Act, House Concurrent Resolution 108, and the Indian Civil Rights Act, to name a few—violated Congress's promise to respect tribal sovereignty and cultural integrity. The present era of self-determination is a return to the federal government's original promise. Two acts, the Indian Self-Determination and Education Assistance Act and the Indian Child Welfare Act, were specifically designed to protect and enhance tribal existence.

The Indian Self-Determination and Education Assistance Act of 1975 gave all tribes the right to manage the programs and services formerly provided by the BIA. This includes such services as housing, education, community development, and law enforcement. Many Indian people feared at first, and some still fear, that this act might be a form of "termination in disguise"—as soon as tribes proved they were capable of managing their own programs and services, Congress would terminate the trust relationship. To dispel this fear, the legislation states that "nothing in this act shall be construed as . . . authorizing or requiring the termination of any existing trust responsibility with respect to Indian

Wounded Knee confrontation, 1973. (Courtesy *Akwesasne Notes.*)

people." The 1978 Indian Child Welfare Act also contains a phrase guaranteeing the preservation of tribal identity: "Congress, through statutes, treaties, and the general courts of dealing with Indian tribes, has assumed the responsibility for the protection of the preservation of Indian tribes and their resources."

THE BRANCHES OF FEDERAL GOVERNMENT AND THE IMPLEMENTATION OF INDIAN POLICY

Although Indian nations' government-government relationship is maintained with Congress, the executive and judicial branches of the federal government frequently have a greater impact on Indian affairs. The following section examines the major role played by the three branches of government in establishing and implementing Indian policy. Particular attention is given to the history, function, and current status of the Bureau of Indian Affairs.

Congress

The U.S. Constitution empowers Congress to pass laws in a number of areas, including taxation, naturalization, banking, and patents. It also allows Congress to borrow money, propose constitutional changes, and conduct investigations. Article I of the Constitution authorizes Congress to regulate commerce among states, foreign nations, and Indian tribes. Article II empowers the Senate to accept or reject treaties, including Indian treaties.

The Senate Select Committee on Indian Affairs and the House Interior Committee are responsible for most of the eighty to ninety bills passed each year that affect Indian tribes directly or indirectly. Tribal officials frequently appear before these committees to express their views on proposed legislation.

In recent decades the executive branch of the government has challenged Congress's role as chief policymaker. Today the president and the president's advisers formulate the administration's policies and lobby Congress to pass the appropriate legislation. Congress, however, still retains immense power because of its control over the nation's budget. An executive decision to improve Indian health care, for example, is meaningless unless Congress appropriates enough money to build more clinics, train more medical personnel, and increase services.

The Judiciary

The federal-tribal relationship is governed by federal law. Hence the federal courts, instead of state courts, decide most cases involving Indians. Federal judges, through their power of judicial review, hold considerable power within the federal system. By ruling on the constitutionality of laws, they often act as policymakers. The Supreme Court's ruling in the *Oliphant* decision, for instance, considerably reduced Indian sovereignty by denying tribes jurisdiction over crimes committed by non-Indians on reservations.

In recent years tribal governments have turned increasingly to the federal court system to protect their rights. The federal courts have often found that federal and state governments have been violating tribal rights, sometimes for hundreds of years. In the 1970s, for example, several tribes in the eastern United States filed suit to regain lands illegally taken from them by the states. The tribes involved included the Oneidas of New York, the Narragansetts of Rhode Island, the Mashpees of Massachusetts, and the Passamaquoddies and Penobscots of Maine. Many eastern states had negotiated illegal treaties with these tribes after the passage of the 1790 Trade and Intercourse Act, which specifically forbade any state or private individual to purchase land from Indian nations. In 1975 the courts ruled that the federal government was obligated to assist tribes, whether recognized or unrecognized, in their claims under the 1790 act. The decision resulted in an out-of-court settlement in which the Maine tribes were given lands and development money in return for their illegally taken lands.

The courts cannot initiate cases or protect tribal rights until a case is brought before them. Courts do not actively search for wrongs that need to be righted. Therefore, it is important for tribal governments to have legal services available to them. The government is obligated by its trust responsibility to represent tribes in court and protect their interests. Despite this responsibility, legal aid is not always forthcoming or of adequate quality. Tribes have to convince either the attorney general's office, of the Justice Department, or the solicitor's office, of the Department of the Interior, to file a suit on their behalf. These offices have wide discretion in deciding which cases to pursue. If the Justice Department or the Interior Department refuses to initiate a case, a tribe may hire its own lawyers, but doing so is an expensive, and often unaffordable, luxury, especially for small tribes.

In addition, tribes frequently require protection from the federal government itself. At times the attorney general's or the solicitor's office must provide legal services to both sides in a conflict involving Indian tribes. In a case requesting protection of Indian fishing rights, for example, the solicitor's office may argue the case on behalf of the Bureau of Commercial Fisheries, which represents commercial fishermen, as well as on behalf of the Interior Department, which represents Indian tribes. This creates a conflict of interest, an unethical situation in all other instances of American law.

The Executive Branch

The executive branch of the government has a major impact on tribal affairs. Headed by the president, this branch is responsible for initiating, enforcing, and implementing the nation's laws and programs. Presidents may initiate policies beneficial to tribes, as President Richard Nixon did in his 1970 address outlining the policy of self-determination, or they may support harmful Indian legislation, as President Grover Cleveland did when he signed the Dawes Allotment Act. Twelve departments, including the BIA, in the Interior Department, and a variety of independent agencies aid the

President Gerald R. Ford (standing at right) meeting with tribal representatives at the White House. (Courtesy Gerald R. Ford Presidential Library, Ann Arbor, Michigan.)

president. These executive departments administer a variety
of services and programs important to tribal governments. In
the 1980s more than half of all federal funds going to Indians
came from non-BIA departments.

The Department of Labor offers employment and training
grants. These have been especially beneficial to Indian people
and tribal governments, because they have given Indians a
chance for training and jobs on their reservations, where unemployment ranges from 40 percent to 90 percent. In 1981,
Comprehensive Employment Training Act (CETA) funds,
which have since been greatly reduced, provided ten thousand jobs on reservations. These grants allowed tribal governments to offer training programs for young workers and
the elderly and also funded alcohol rehabilitation programs.

The Department of Housing and Urban Development
(HUD) provides assistance for housing and development of
rural and urban communities. HUD has cooperated with the
BIA and the IHS to set up programs for improving the deplorable living conditions on many reservations. In 1982,
HUD was financing over 90 percent of all Indian housing.
More than 140 tribes have established tribal housing authorities to oversee the construction and rehabilitation of low-cost
housing units.

The Department of Health and Human Services (HHS)
oversees the general health and welfare of all American citizens. Its programs include income assistance and health
insurance, such as Medicare and Medicaid. Other HHS agencies offer special services aimed at child care and development, the aging, and the handicapped. Indians, like all U.S.
citizens, are eligible to apply for these grants and services.
Of direct importance to Indians is the Indian Health Service (IHS), a subagency of the HHS's Public Health Service.
The IHS provides medical services, hospital care, preventive
health care, medical training, and funds for improving water
supply and wastewater treatment systems to federally recognized tribes and individual members of federally recognized
tribes living on or near a reservation.

As already mentioned, the attorney general's office, of the
Justice Department, and the solicitor's office, of the Interior
Department, represent Indian interests in court. The Justice
Department's Land and Natural Resources Division handles
most Indian resource cases. The Federal Bureau of Investigation (FBI), also located within the Justice Department, assists tribal governments in investigating crimes occurring on
Indian land. Other divisions of the Justice Department are
responsible for prosecuting crimes in Indian country, pursuing discrimination suits on behalf of Indian individuals
against non-Indians, and overseeing the compliance of tribal
governments with the Indian Civil Rights Act.

The Department of Transportation is responsible for highway development, mass transit, oil and gas pipeline construc-

tion, railroad and aviation regulations, and transportation safety. In 1975 a government report estimated that only one-quarter of all reservation roads were paved, hindering both traffic safety and economic development. In some instances the Department of Transportation, like the Department of Education, has designated tribes the "fifty-first state" and transfers their share of a program's budget to the BIA.

The Department of Education is charged with assisting citizens in establishing and maintaining efficient school systems. The Indian Education Office, located in the Department of Education, administers grants to local educational agencies for elementary and secondary school programs designed to meet the special educational needs of Indian children and adults.

The Energy and Commerce departments are directly involved in programs to help reservations achieve greater economic development. Both provide loans and other assistance to tribal governments so that they can explore for mineral deposits and develop industrial parks, tribal businesses, and recreational and tourist facilities. Department of Energy grants have funded a special interest organization, the Council of Energy Resource Tribes (CERT), which helps tribes gain greater benefits from the development of their resources.

The Department of Agriculture also funds some economic development projects and distributes commodity foods and administers supplemental food programs. Tribal governments may apply to the Farmers' Home Administration (FHA), a subagency of the department, for loans to develop farming and grazing enterprises, rural businesses and industries, and water and waste disposal systems. In addition, some tribes, the Stockbridge Munsee of Wisconsin, for example, have used a special FHA loan program to buy back lands lost through the allotment process.

The Department of the Interior is the department of the executive branch most directly concerned with tribes. Responsible primarily for the conservation and use of the nation's resources, the Interior Department administers more than 600 million acres of federal lands (including 53 million acres of continental U.S. Indian trust land and 40 million acres of Alaskan Native lands). The Interior Department also manages fish and wildlife, water, land reclamation, irrigation, development of mineral and energy resources, and the national parks.

The Bureau of Indian Affairs, within the Interior Department, is the agency directly responsible for administering Congress's relationship with federally recognized tribes. It is discussed in greater detail below.

The Bureau of Indian Affairs

The Bureau of Indian Affairs (BIA), also referred to, until 1947, as the Office of Indian Affairs and the Indian Office, is

one of the oldest agencies within the U.S. government. It
began in 1824 as a diplomatic corps to handle negotiations
between the United States and the Indian nations. Within a
century it controlled virtually every aspect of Indian existence. Today the BIA's role has come almost full circle,
evolving into an advisory agency as the tribes progress toward self-determination.

Diplomacy to Paternalism

One of the first acts of the Continental Congress was the
creation, in 1775, of three departments of Indian affairs:
northern, central, and southern. Among the first depart-
mental commissioners were Benjamin Franklin and Patrick
Henry. Their job was to negotiate treaties with tribes and
obtain tribal neutrality in the coming Revolutionary War.
Fourteen years later, the U.S. Congress established a War
Department and made Indian relations a part of its responsibilities. As the need for Indian lands and frontier hostilities
became more pressing, Secretary of War John Calhoun created the Bureau of Indian Affairs, in 1824. Eight years later
Congress officially authorized the president to appoint, with
the consent of the Senate, a commissioner of Indian affairs to
run the BIA. The commissioner supervised BIA agents, who
were essentially ambassadors with broad powers of negotiation. Their primary job was to maintain peace on the frontier, and they were authorized to sign trade agreements and
land cessions. Unlike later BIA agents, they took no part in
delivering services or regulating Indian lives.

In 1849, Congress transferred the BIA from the War Department to the newly created Department of the Interior.
With this transfer came a change in policy and responsibilities. The removal of tribes to reservations had brought about
disease and starvation, which forced the government to begin providing tribes with food and other supplies. Administering the distribution of this aid became a responsibility of
the BIA. By the 1860s, however, the agency was not discharg-
ing its duties responsibly. Unscrupulous Indian agents increased misery on reservations and generated hostility. In
1867, Congress appointed a Peace Commission to study the
problems of the BIA's administration of reservations. The
commission recommended many changes, including the appointment of honest, more effective agents and the establishment of a separate, independent agency for Indian affairs.
Some improvements were forthcoming, but the recommendation to remove the BIA from the Interior Department and
establish it as an independent agency was never followed.

During the assimilation era, in the 1880s, the BIA's presence on reservations increased dramatically. Indian agents
became responsible for operating schools, dispensing justice,
distributing supplies, administering allotments, and leasing
contracts. By 1900 the Indian agent had, in effect, become
the tribal government.

The Snyder Act

A major change occurred in 1921 with the passage of the Snyder Act. Before this act was passed, the BIA's duties were spelled out, often in confusing and contradictory terms, in scores of treaties and acts of Congress. Administration of Indian programs was further complicated because each reservation agency received its own appropriation, or allotment of money, from the federal government. The absence of a uniform policy led to chaotic administration and management in the BIA.

The Snyder Act of 1921 placed all federal Indian services under one act. It authorized the Department of the Interior to use funds for "the benefit, care and assistance of Indians throughout the United States." Expenditures were authorized for health, education, social services, law enforcement, irrigation, and for the administration of the BIA. No limit was placed on the amount of money Congress could appropriate, nor was the BIA required to ask for yearly spending authorizations from Congress—an important protection for tribes, since it meant that Congress could not simply withhold money from the BIA and thereby discontinue its operation.

Paternalism to Self-Determination

The next major change in BIA services came in response to the Meriam Report of 1928, which detailed the government's shortcomings in providing services to reservations (see chapter 5). Congress responded to the report by passing the Indian Reorganization Act (IRA), which aimed to improve tribal economies and strengthen tribal governments. BIA services were expanded to include forestry, range management, an agricultural extension service, construction, and land acquisition. BIA services continued to expand until the 1950s and 1960s, the termination era, at which time Congress dismantled some of the agency's duties. The responsibility for educating Indian children was passed to the states and Indian health care became the responsibility of the Department of Health, Education, and Welfare (now called the Department of Health and Human Services).

In the 1970s the new policy of self-determination reversed the policies of termination. Along with the new policy came greater appreciation of Indian culture and tribal governments. Congress passed a series of laws, including the Indian Self-Determination Act, the Indian Child Welfare Act, and the Health Care Improvement Act, which aimed to improve the quality of reservation life without destroying tribal government. Today the BIA is striving to change its structure and character from a management to an advisory agency. Its goals, as stated in its manual, reflect this objective: (1) To encourage Indians and train Indians and Alaska Native people to manage their own affairs under a trust re-

Raising the U.S. flag on Iwo Jima. Ira Hayes, a Pima Indian, was one of the U.S. marines who planted this flag when American forces took the island of Iwo Jima from the Japanese in World War II. Indians have served with American forces in every war with U.S. involvement since the Revolutionary War. More than 29,000 Indian men, one out of every three able-bodied men, a higher proportion than any other population group, served in World War II. The Iroquois Nation, the Muscogee Nation, the Keetoowah Cherokees, and the Lakotas formally declared war on Germany and the other Axis powers. Tribal governments bought millions of dollars' worth of war bonds, and the Crows of Montana offered their reservation's resources for the war's duration. In 1982, President Ronald Reagan proclaimed August 14 "National Code Talkers Day" to honor members of the Navajo Tribe who used their language during World War II to transmit intelligence reports. Members of the Choctaw, Chippewa, Muscogee, Lakota, and other tribes also used their languages during both world wars to the confoundment of enemies, who found the "code" unbreakable. (Photo courtesy Wide World Photos.)

lationship with the federal government; (2) To facilitate, with maximum involvement of Indian and Alaska Native people, full development of their human and natural resource potentials; (3) To mobilize all public and private aids to the advancement of Indian and Alaska Native people for use by them; and (4) To use the skill and capabilities of Indian and Alaska Native people in the direction and management of programs for their benefit.

In line with its fourth objective the BIA gives Indian applicants first consideration when hiring employees. Before the 1930s, few bureau employees were Indians. As part of the 1934 Indian Reorganization Act, Congress required that Indians be given preference in hiring. This requirement was challenged in the 1970s as unconstitutional and racially discriminatory. The Supreme Court ruled, however, that preferential hiring of Indians by the BIA did not violate the law but was proper given the government's special political relationship to tribes. Today more than 75 percent of the bureau's fourteen thousand employees are Indians.

The tribes' relationship with the bureau is often described as a "love/hate relationship." On the one hand, the bureau is the symbol of the tribes' special relationship with the federal government. On the other hand, tribes have suffered from bureau mismanagement, paternalism, and neglect. It is the hope and objective of many tribal peoples and government officials that tribes can enter into a more equal relationship with the bureau and that the bureau can truly function in an advisory capacity as opposed to dictating policy to tribes.

The federal government's relationship with tribes has wavered over the years between respect for tribal sovereignty and rights and attempts to extinquish tribal existence. The current relationship between tribes and the federal government is one of respect for tribal rights. It is an era of self-determination in which the federal government has committed itself to protecting and enhancing inherent tribal resources, rights, and the ability of tribes to manage their own governments.

CHAPTER 13

TRIBAL-STATE RELATIONS

The basis for understanding the legal relationship between tribal and state governments lies in the *Worcester* v. *Georgia* case (discussed in chapter 4). The plaintiff's argument was that the state of Georgia had no right to enforce its own laws over Cherokee lands or people. The Supreme Court agreed, ruling that states had no authority to pass laws that interfered with the federal-tribal relationship. Federal law and inherent tribal sovereignty, or the tribes' status as domestic dependent nations, ruled out any state control over tribes.

Federal law, as the *Worcester* case demonstrated, is the supreme law of the land in the areas defined as federal concerns by the Constitution and the courts. Since treaties are federal laws, a treaty between the federal government and an Indian tribe is superior to state legislation. Any state law that conflicts with a federal law or a treaty is unconstitutional and therefore illegal.

The *Worcester* case also emphasized that Indian tribes possess inherent sovereignty. States, on the other hand, are not inherent sovereigns and have no power to conclude treaties with tribes or any other nation. Tribes, because of their status as inherent sovereigns, have a higher political status than do states. States may not exercise authority over tribes unless specifically authorized by Congress (as they were by Public Law 280, discussed below) or by the tribes. States must recognize tribes as self-governing political structures.

PUBLIC LAW 280

Until 1940 no state had authority over the Indian reservations within its borders. All criminal and civil matters were handled according to either tribal or federal law. In 1940, in what was to begin the era of termination, Congress granted Kansas the power to assume criminal jurisdiction over the Kansas tribes. Six years later North Dakota was given authority to enforce its criminal laws on the Devil's Lake Reservation. In 1948, Iowa received limited criminal jurisdiction over the Sac and Fox Reservation. In 1949, California was granted authority to enforce its laws on the Agua Caliente Reservation, and the following year Congress allowed New York civil authority over New York tribes (criminal jurisdiction had been given in 1948). None of these transfers of power, however, affected tribes as did Public Law 280.

Public Law (P.L.) 280, as discussed in chapter 5, was one of a series of laws passed by Congress in the early 1950s when the national policy was to "get out of the Indian business." Passed in 1953, this law gave certain states—Cali-

They have a status higher than that of states. They are subordinate dependent nations possessed of all powers as such only to the extent that they have expressly been required to surrender them by the superior sovereign, the United States.

Native American Church v. *Navajo Tribal Council,* 1959

The Indian plays much the same role in our American society that the Jews played in Germany. Like the miner's canary, the Indian marks the shift from fresh air to poison gas in our political atmosphere; and our treatment of Indians, even more than our treatment of other minorities, reflects the rise and fall in our democratic faith.

Felix Cohen, legal scholar and special assistant to Interior Department, 1953

INDIAN NATIONS AND THE
AMERICAN POLITICAL SYSTEM

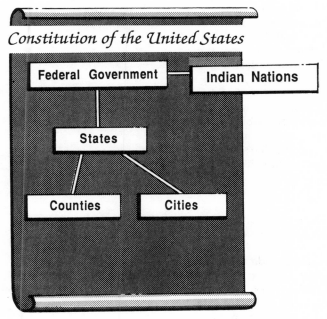

Graphic by Bittle Productions

As this chart illustrates, the relationship between Indian nations and the federal government is based on Indian nations' status as inherent sovereigns. This status means that tribes have a higher legal status than states. States, therefore, exert jurisdiction over tribes only with Congressional approval. This chart also indicates, as discussed in chapter 11, that Indian nations, whose powers spring from their own sovereignty, are only partially under the authority of the U.S. Constitution.

fornia, Minnesota, Nebraska, Oregon (excluding the Warm Springs Reservation), and Wisconsin (excluding the Red Lake Chippewa and the Menominee Reservations)—the authority to extend their criminal and civil laws onto reservations, and it offered all other states the same opportunity.

Despite a long history of arguing with the federal government about who should control Indian affairs, most states, for financial reasons, did not choose to assume criminal and civil jurisdiction over the reservations. To establish state law enforcement and court systems on the reservations would have been expensive, and states were not able to tax tribes to raise the necessary money, since reservation lands held in trust by the federal government cannot be taxed. Nor was the federal government willing to appropriate money for law enforcement.

P.L. 280 did not allow states to take total control of Indian affairs. The federal government retained the power to manage Indian trust lands. And no state was allowed to make laws changing Indian hunting and fishing rights that were protected by treaties. P.L. 280 did not technically extinguish tribal powers but allowed the state to exercise concurrent jurisdiction. In practical terms, however, state jurisdiction, when exercised, tended to supplant tribal power. From the tribes' point of view, P.L. 280 was one of the most destructive bills to tribal sovereignty ever passed by Congress.

Tribes viewed the tribal-federal relationship as one between sovereigns, a government-to-government relationship. State control of tribal matters contradicted and violated the basis of this tribal-federal relationship. Tribes were astonished that they were not consulted prior to the bill's passage and that the law did not require tribal consent before states gained jurisdiction over tribes.

Retrocession

In 1968 tribes lobbied successfully to have state jurisdiction partially retroceded, or returned to the federal government. As part of the Indian Civil Rights Act, Congress ordered that any state desiring in the future to assume jurisdiction over tribes under P.L. 280 first had to obtain tribal permission. States that had already assumed jurisdiction were allowed, with the secretary of the interior's permission, to return it to the tribes. As of the late 1980s, Nebraska, Washington, Minnesota, Nevada, and Wisconsin had returned all or part of their jurisdiction.

To determine today whether a particular tribe is operating under tribal, federal, or state law, it is necessary to know whether the state is operating under P.L. 280 and if so to what extent. That is, in P.L. 280 states one must define the particular areas in which the tribe has authorized state jurisdiction. For example, in Arizona, air and water pollution laws are the only state laws enforced on reservations. In Idaho no criminal laws are enforced on the reservation, but state laws dealing with school attendance, family relations, mental illness, traffic, welfare, and juvenile delinquency are enforced. Washington has an extremely complex system of enforcement that distinguishes between trust and nontrust lands within reservations.

P.L. 280 was theoretically attractive to states because of the long-held belief by states that their law should apply to all individuals within their borders and that no group should be exempt. Over the years states have displayed a growing interest in imposing laws on reservations concerning taxation, land use, law and order, and natural resource development. These claims of jurisdiction over tribes generally result from ignorance of tribal rights or from a desire to gain control over tribal resources. More recently, however, states and tribes have begun to realize that negotiations and mutual coopera-

The governor of Wisconsin signing a bill relating to Indians. (Courtesy *Menominee Tribal News*.)

tion are less costly than court suits, and some have worked together to solve mutual problems. The remainder of this chapter examines representative areas of conflict and misunderstanding between states and tribal governments and considers potential solutions to these problems. Some of the examples are actual cases, others are hypothetical. All are typical of the issues Indian tribes encounter every day.

LAW ENFORCEMENT

It is Friday night. A carload of non-Indian youths from off-reservation has driven into the Blackfeet Reservation in northwestern Montana to party. By midnight the youths are very drunk. They begin vandalizing homes and smashing car windows. The tribal police do not have the authority to arrest non-Indians and the county and state police have no authority to enforce law and order within the reservation.

A woman who lives a mile outside the Jicarilla Apache Reservation has called the tribal police department. She can hear someone breaking into her house. The tribal police department is close to her house; officers could be there in five minutes. But they do not have the authority to investigate crimes off the reservation. It will take the county police twenty minutes to arrive at her house.

The hypothetical examples above indicate that the problem of law enforcement is an issue of mutual concern rather than an area of competition for states and tribes. As discussed in previous chapters, however, the question of who has criminal jurisdiction on reservations can be complex. Depending on the location and the nature of the crime and whether the offender is Indian or non-Indian, any one of several different

Most tribes now have their own tribal police forces. Shown above are tribal police from the Salt River Pima Tribe (Courtesy National Congress of American Indians) and the Sac and Fox of Oklahoma (photo by the author).

law-enforcement agencies may have jurisdiction. The FBI and the BIA police (employed on some reservations) investigate all federal crimes, particularly those falling under the Major Crimes Act, whether the suspect is Indian or non-Indian. Tribal police arrest and detain tribal members accused of breaking tribal law. Tribal police may not arrest non-Indians committing crimes on reservations (this has been so since the *Oliphant* decision (discussed in chapters 5 and 11), which ruled that tribes do not possess criminal jurisdiction over non-Indians). This creates a law-enforcement problem on reservations in states that do not have jurisdiction under P.L. 280, because states may not intervene to prosecute crimes committed on reservations unless both the accused and the victim are non-Indian. In states that do have P.L. 280 jurisdiction over reservations, local (county or municipal) or state police may intervene.

    This crazy quilt of jurisdictions hampers effective law enforcement. Tribal, local, and state police frequently find it impossible to provide adequate and efficient protection to both Indians and non-Indians. Furthermore, in emergencies there is little time to work out the technicalities of which law-enforcement agency should answer the call for help. Often the appropriate agency is not the nearest one, and the nearest agency may not be able to respond because it lacks jurisdiction.

Faced with the problems caused by such complex jurisdictional issues, many tribes and local police forces, such as the Warm Springs in Oregon, the Miccosukees in Florida, the Blackfeet, Assinboines, and Lakota tribes in Montana, the Navajos in New Mexico, the Yakimas in Washington, and the Southern Utes in Colorado, have entered into cross-deputization agreements. Individual officers are made members of both the tribal and the state or local police force. Under this arrangement, if a crime requires a tribal officer, the nearest officer responds to it as a tribal officer; if it requires a state officer, the same officer can respond as a state officer.

WATER RIGHTS

The Pyramid Lake Paiute Indians have lived in northwest Nevada for hundreds of years. Pyramid Lake, which is fed by the Truckee River, is located in the middle of the Pyramid Lake Reservation. The lake also lies at the center of the tribe's spiritual and economic existence. Tribal members long depended for food on the cui-ci fish, found only in Pyramid Lake and on the Lahontan cutthroat trout, which once grew to more than 60 pounds in the lake. In the last eighty years, however, the water level in Pyramid Lake has dropped seventy feet. The cui-ci is on the endangered species list and Lahontan cutthroat trout is listed as threatened. The reason for the lake's demise is the construction of a federal dam upstream on the Truckee River.

The Tohono O'Odham, or Papago, Indians of southern Arizona are by tradition a farming people. They have used groundwater and river water to irrigate their crops from time immemorial. Water use by the city of Tucson, nearby copper mines, and non-Indian agricultural interests have now seriously depleted the water available to the Papagos for irrigation.

Water is an invaluable resource. It is crucial for farming, mining, fish and wildlife conservation, recreation, and industry, as well as for drinking and sanitation. Where there is little water, as in the arid west, determining who has the rights to the scarce supply can become an issue of life-and-death. In the eastern United States, water is considered part of the land over which it flows. Hence, eastern water rights are determined by land ownership. The titleholder of the land owns the water and may use as much as he or she needs.

But in the western states, water belongs to the state and water rights are governed by state law and the doctrine of prior appropriation. The doctrine of prior appropriation decides usage rights on a "first in time, first in right" basis.

There has been a lot said about the sacredness of our land which is our body; and the values of our culture which is our soul; but water is the blood of our tribes, and if its life-giving flow is stopped, or it is polluted, all else will die and the many thousands of years of our communal existence will come to an end.

Frank Tenorio,
former governor,
San Felipe

Whoever first began using water has the right to continue using all he or she needs, whether or not there is sufficient water for others. The user need not border the water supply but may use a pump or ditch to channel the water. The only limitation on use is that no one may use water for mining or irrigation until everyone has sufficient water for household needs. If an individual does not use the water to which he or she is entitled, the right is considered abandoned and may be taken away by the state.

Indian water rights, however, are governed by the reserved rights doctrine, not by the doctrine of prior appropriation. A 1908 Supreme Court case, *Winters* v. *U.S.*, in which the Supreme Court ruled that water bordering and running through reservations belonged to tribes and not to states, helps demonstrate how important water decisions are and also how Indian water rights are now understood. In the late nineteenth century, non-Indian farmers in Montana began irrigating their farms with water from the Milk River. About twenty years later the Gros Ventre tribe began farming on its reservation near the Milk River. The non-Indian farmers, claiming prior appropriation (that they had used the water first), built dams and reservoirs upstream to divert water from the Milk River, thereby preventing the tribe downstream from receiving any water.

The Gros Ventre tribe appealed to the federal courts, arguing that when it negotiated the 1888 agreement establishing its reservation, it understood that the Milk River belonged to it. Had this not been so, the tribe argued, it would never have accepted the agreement—land without water was useless.

The Supreme Court decided in favor of the Gros Ventres, arguing that even though the tribe had not been using the water (as the doctrine of prior appropriation would require), the water still belonged to the tribe. Indian reservations, the Court emphasized, were not lands granted to tribes by the federal government but lands reserved by tribes from the lands they had ceded to the United States. When tribes reserved these lands, the Court reasoned, they also reserved all rights to the water. The Gros Ventres' right to water dated from 1888, the date of the agreement establishing the reservation. Only individuals who began using the water before 1888 had prior water rights. Because Congress had established most reservations as a prelude to white settlement, many tribes had been using their water before white settlement and therefore had water rights by virtue of prior appropriation.

In Indian water rights cases since the *Winters* case the courts have ruled that reservations created by acts of Congress or by presidential order have the same water rights as those created by treaty. Again, the important date is the date of the reservation's establishment. In some instances, as with the Pueblos, who have irrigated their land from time immemorial, the courts have found that Indian water rights take precedence over all other claims. The courts have also reemphasized in recent cases that the amount of water a tribe is entitled to does not depend on the amount of water it used when the reservation was first established. Rather, for example, tribes have a right to use all the water that is needed to irrigate all irrigable lands on their reservations.

Despite these decisions, as the population and industries of the west grow and water becomes increasingly scarce, Indian water rights will continue to be questioned and challenged. Deciding who gets what share of the west's limited water will be a major factor in future population and development patterns both on Indian lands and elsewhere. The states need water, but so do tribes. Many tribes are only now beginning to develop farms and industry. Without water, Indian lands, Indian businesses, and Indian people will be unable to secure their futures.

> In the history of the United States Government's treatment of Indian tribes, its failure to protect Indian water rights for use on the reservations it set aside for them is one of the sorrier chapters.
>
> *Water Policies for the Future—* Final Report to the President and Congress of the United States, National Water Commission, 1973

TAXATION

Russell Bryan, a member of the Minnesota Chippewa Tribe, lives in a mobile home on trust land within the Leech Lake Reservation. In June he received a notice from the Minnesota state auditor that he owed $147.95 in personal property tax on his mobile home. He refused to pay, arguing that federal law protects him from state taxation. The state maintains that P.L. 280 gave the state authority to tax Indians.

The Oglala Sioux of the Pine Ridge Reservation own and operate a tribal grocery store. Tribal members are exempt from paying the state sales tax or the state cigarette tax imposed by South Dakota. Tribal members must, however, pay the cigarette tax imposed by the tribe. Non-Indian individuals must pay the state sales and cigarette tax. It is difficult for the grocery clerks to know which taxes to collect from which individuals.

Taxes help governments provide schools, highways, public defense, and other services. Governments at all levels have the power to tax, but not all governments tax the same items. Whether a particular government is allowed to tax a specific item or whether an individual is required to pay a certain tax are questions the courts are continually asked to decide. Whether states may tax Indians and what taxes Indians must pay are frequent issues important to Indian sovereignty and tribal self-government.

All Indians pay federal income tax, with one exception. The Dawes Allotment Act (see chapter 5), exempts from taxes income earned by Indians on their individual allotments. If the federal government so chose, however, it could tax such income, because it possesses full authority to tax tribes and Indian individuals.

State authority to tax tribal lands or the income of tribal members on the reservation is very limited. The courts have long ruled that states cannot tax either individually or tribally owned allotments. First, such lands are technically federal lands, and states may not tax any federal lands (such as national parks). Second, when tribes agreed to cede large portions of their lands and settle on reservations, the federal government promised to protect the land for the tribes' use. To allow tribal land to be taxed would penalize tribes for using their own land.

Since the late 1950s, however, many states have argued that P.L. 280 granted them power to tax Indian lands and income when it gave them civil jurisdiction over Indians. States have also argued that since tribal members are state citizens and enjoy state services, they should contribute to funding those services. But despite numerous attempts by various states to tax Indians, the courts have generally held firm. A state may not tax any land within a reservation, whether it is held in trust or non-Indian owned. Neither can a state tax the personal income of an Indian or a tribe if the income comes from reservation sources. An Indian rancher, for example, does not have to pay state taxes on profits from ranching as long as the ranch is inside the reservation. However, an Indian engineer employed by an engineering firm in Chicago would pay state income tax on the money he or she earned from the off-reservation employment. States are also barred from imposing corporate taxes on or requiring state licenses on Indian-owned businesses within reservations.

The argument for not allowing states to tax Indians on reservations is based on the following facts. First, Indian tribes are quasi-sovereigns and maintain a primary relationship with the federal government. This relationship generally rules out any form of state control, and taxation is a form of control. Second, the federal government has a legal and moral trust responsibility to protect tribal lands and tribal governments. If states are allowed to tax Indian lands, businesses, and individuals, the majority of whom are poor, they will seriously impair the ability of tribal governments to provide services and improve the lives of their people. Third, tribes, as sovereigns, have the right to maintain their own self-government, and states may not interfere with that government. Most taxation by states, the courts have ruled, interferes with tribal self-government.

The question of state and tribal taxes is complex and confusing. For instance, tribes can collect a tribal cigarette tax from Indians and non-Indians, while the state may impose state sales and cigarette taxes on non-Indians but not on Indians. To ease the difficulties of collecting and administering taxes, many tribes have negotiated tax collection agreements with their respective states. Under the agreement between the Oglala Sioux and the state of South Dakota, for example, the state collects both state and tribal sales and cigarette taxes (which are equal) on the reservation. The state returns the tribal share to the tribe, keeping a small percentage for the cost of administration.

FISHING AND HUNTING RIGHTS

A Washington State fish and game commissioner has arrested Russell Adams, a member of the Quinault tribe on a series of charges: fishing off-reservation without a state license, fishing out of season, and using illegal equipment. Adams argues at his trial that the treaties signed by his tribe in 1855 and 1856 reserved to his tribe the right to fish in this area free from state control.

A Wisconsin state fish and game warden has arrested a Winnebago Indian, Ken Funmaker, for shooting deer out of season. Funmaker argues at his trial that the hunting and subsequent feasting on deer meat are necessary to the practice of his traditional religion.

Tribal control of tribal land, water, and wildlife is crucial to tribal sovereignty, economic development, and culture. Fishing, for example, is central to the economic and spiritual survival of the tribes of the Pacific Northwest and the Great Lakes region. Hunting plays an important role within the culture of many tribes and also helps families supplement their diets. The treaties negotiated by tribes in the mid-nineteenth century reflected the importance of hunting and fishing to tribal existence. In these treaties, tribes ceded large amounts of land in return for guaranteed rights to hunt and fish on their remaining reservation lands and, in some cases, to continue hunting and fishing in off-reservation areas.

These rights, even though reserved and guaranteed in treaties, have met with stiff opposition from states. States argue that allowing tribes to control their own hunting and fishing rights is inequitable and detrimental to conservation. Tribes point out that they, unlike non-Indians, have consistently practiced conservation of natural resources.

Before the nineteenth century, salmon and other fish were abundant in the Northwest and the Great Lakes region. Tribes routinely regulated their catch, taking care that sufficient fish remained to reproduce. But by the early twentieth century, non-Indian economic development had brought devastation to the seasonal fish runs. Overfishing, pollution from logging and industries, installation of dams, and other damage to streams threatened, and still threaten, a once reliable food source.

As the salmon and other fish catches declined, non-Indian commercial and sport fishermen increasingly blamed the problem on Indian fishermen. Pressure was put on state officials to prevent tribal members from exercising their treaty rights. State game wardens blocked Indian access to traditional fishing grounds and repeatedly arrested tribal mem-

> The right of taking fish, at all usual and accustomed grounds and stations, is further secured to said Indians in common with all citizens of the Territory, and of erecting temporary houses for the purpose of curing, together with the privilege of hunting, gathering roots and berries, and pasturing their horses on open and unclaimed lands: Provided, however, that they shall not take shellfish from any beds staked or cultivated by citizens, and that they shall alter all stallions not intended for breeding-horses, and shall keep and confine the latter.
>
> Article 3, Treaty with the Nisqualli, Palallup, and other tribes, 1854

This man is gill-net fishing in the traditional Indian manner on the Klamath River, Hoopa Valley Indian Reservation, in northern California. (Courtesy Gary Rankel.)

bers for ignoring state regulations that ought not to have applied to Indians, such as fishing without a state license or using "illegal" gear (nets, for instance, instead of rod and reel). Some Indian fishermen were shot at; others had their nets slashed and their equipment destroyed. In Michigan, bumper stickers reading "Spear an Indian, save a fish" bore witness to both racial tension and non-Indians' ignorance about Indian fishing rights. Indians were fishing for a livelihood, not for recreation. As state harassment continued, Indian fishermen found it increasingly difficult to earn a living or even to feed their families.

Fishing Rights: U.S. v. Washington

In the 1960s and early 1970s, Northwestern and Great Lakes tribes began legal action in the courts to protect their fishing rights. In 1974, a federal court ruled in *U.S.* v. *Washington* that treaties signed by Washington tribes ceding more than 64 million acres to the United States guaranteed the tribes a right to fish "in common with all citizens of the territory . . . at all usual and accustomed grounds and stations." This guarantee, the court reasoned, entitled the tribes to take one-half of the state's allowable salmon catch.

The court understood that the treaties did not involve a grant to the tribes from the United States but a grant to the United States from tribes. Tribes were not given the right to fish; rather, they reserved a right they already had. The treaties, in effect, gave U.S. citizens the right to share equally with the tribes in the salmon catch. The *Washington* decision and later court cases supported the right of tribes to regulate and manage their fish resources. The courts also directed the tribes and the state to work together to protect and replenish the salmon populations.

The white man, he took over, see, after he saw there was money in fish. He just took over, you know, just steal—like stealing off the Indian. And that's how they got it. And that's why they don't want the Indian to fish, because there's big money for them. Indian is nothing to the white man. He's nothing.

Now you have to have permission to gather nuts and things from the mountains and from the desert. They didn't plant these trees here. They didn't bring the deer here. They didn't bring the fish here, and yet they say: "We give you—we give you the right to fish here—we give you." They had nothing to give in the first place. They were beggars, they were paupers. They came to this country looking for freedom of speech and to worship the way they wanted to. But when they got here they forgot when it came to the Indian. This country is built on total aggression. There was room for everyone. But now he owns everything and now he wants to take the rest of us—he wants to take away everything we have.

Nisqually Indian, 1960s

This fish hatchery, operated by the Eastern Band of Cherokee Indians in North Carolina, is used to maintain one of the most popular catchable trout fisheries in the United States. (Courtesy Gary Rankel.)

Cooperative agreements between state officials and tribes to preserve and restock wildlife have become increasingly common. In western Washington, for example, tribes established the Northwest Indian Fisheries Commission to work with state and federal game officials. Working closely with state officials, the tribes have adopted fishing regulations and instituted their own enforcement programs. They employ fishery biologists who work closely with state fishery biologists to monitor and regulate all fisheries, and they have developed thriving fish hatcheries, which account for nearly one-fourth of the salmon and steelhead trout released into area streams annually. By the late 1980s, tribes owned and operated more than sixty fish hatcheries, which produced 66 million fish a year and employed eight hundred biologists and other specialists.

Hunting Rights: The Winnebago Night Feast

The first snow has fallen, and the Winnebago tribe of Wisconsin is preparing for the Winter Feast. The Winter, or Night, Feast, one of the most important rituals in the Winnebago religion, gives thanks for a good harvest and hunt. The ceremony requires that a hunting party be formed to kill several deer for the feast.

On the night before the hunt, the hunting party retires to a sweat lodge, where ceremonies are performed to ensure a successful hunt the next day. After the hunt, the deer hide is carefully tanned and marked with the specific symbol of the spirit to whom the offering is made. The hide will later be left in the wilderness for the spirits. After preparing the hide, the tribespeople smoke the ceremonial pipe and offer the hide to the Night Spirits in thanksgiving. The feast be-

gins after this offering. Ceremonies and singing continue
until a war whoop signals the end of the ceremony and all
participants dance out of the lodge.

Just as the wine and wafer are central to many Christian religions, the deer is a dominant symbol in the Winnebago religion. The hunts and the special preparation of the deer and
hide are necessary for ceremonies such as the Winter Feast,
the Victory Dance, the Medicine Dance, and others. About
250 deer are needed each year for these ceremonies.

In the 1970s a Wisconsin state court held that state laws
prohibiting the Winnebagos from hunting deer year-round
violated their right to practice their religion. Subsequently
the state altered its hunting and fishing code to allow deer
hunting out of season by practioners of the Winnebago religion. The new rules provide for clan leaders to notify the
Department of Natural Resources the day before the hunt.
The leader must give the time and place of the hunt, the
number and names of the participants, the number of deer to
be taken, and the religious purpose for which the deer are to
be used.

ELIGIBILITY FOR STATE SERVICES

Preston Allen, a resident of the Unitah Indian Reservation
in Duchesne County, Utah, stopped by the county election
office on his way to work to cast his ballot in the county
elections. His request for a ballot was denied by the voting
precinct head. Indians, the county officials argued, did not
pay state taxes and were not state citizens. Therefore they
were ineligible to vote.

Alice Piper, a fifteen-year-old ninth grader, has been told
by county officials that because she is an Indian she may
not attend the public school in her district. Instead, she
must attend the Indian school established by the Bureau of
Indian Affairs.

These hypothetical cases illustrate the illegal denial of
state services to which Indians, as citizens, are entitled. As
discussed in chapter 5, before the 1924 Indian Citizenship
Act was passed, many Indians were denied basic political
rights, including the right to vote in federal and state elections. The citizenship act granted to Indians all the rights
granted to other state citizens, including the right to vote,
the right to an education, and the right to state welfare benefits and all other state services. Too frequently, however,
these rights have been and still are denied. Arizona Indians
were denied the right to vote in Arizona until 1948. Utah did
not allow Indians living on reservations to vote until the late
1950s, and New Mexico lifted its ban only in 1962. In 1982
legislation to prohibit reservation Indians from voting in

Have You REGISTERED To

VOTE

Don't lose out on one of

your basic FREEDOMS!

REGISTER NOW ! ! !

Make sure YOU have the chance

to express YOURSELF at the Polls

REGISTER by April 7 to vote in the May 6 Primary
REGISTER by October 6 to vote in the November 7 General Election
REMEMBER, 18-year-olds can now vote.

Distributed in the interest of
CITIZENSHIP TRAINING AND VOTER REGISTRATION
BY THE LUMBEE INDIAN CAUCUS

Voting rights poster from the 1970s distributed by the Lumbee Indians of North Carolina. (Courtesy Smithsonian Institution.)

New Mexico state and local elections was again introduced, although unsuccessfully, in the state legislature.

Federal and state attempts to educate Indian students have frequently been unsuccessful in meeting the needs of Indian students. As late as the 1950s, some states, including California, Mississippi, and Alabama, denied Indians the right to attend schools with white children. In other states, including New York and Oklahoma, officials viewed education as a process by which to integrate Indians into the dominant culture. Indian students, frequently encountering discrimination and a lack of understanding of Indian culture and history, often failed to complete high school.

THE SAN CARLOS APACHE ALTERNATIVE SCHOOL

In the 1970s the high school dropout rate among the San Carlos Apaches of Arizona was 50 percent. The reasons for this high rate were many. Through eighth grade, Apache students attended public school on the reservation, where the student body was 99 percent Indian. After grade school, they could attend either a public high school off the reservation in Globe, Arizona, or a BIA boarding school. The Globe high school, more than a thirty-minute bus ride from the reservation, is attended predominately by Anglo and Mexican-American students. The nearest BIA boarding school is 120 miles away. To attend it, students must leave their families and friends, overcome loneliness and homesickness, and adjust to students from many different tribes. Cultural differences, adjustment problems, and the pressure to work and contribute to their families' support resulted in only one-half of the Apache students completing their high-school education. In 1977, the San Carlos Apache Tribal Council, in cooperation with the school district of Globe, opened an alternative high school on the reservation. The school curriculum provides Indian students with a high-school education and helps them develop employable skills relevant to tribal enterprises. Vocational classes are taught on a cooperative basis, allowing students to earn money working for the tribe at the same time that they learn skills and earn credits toward graduation. The Globe school district provides supplies as well as a counselor and an agricultural and diversified occupations teacher. The tribe provides the school facilities, farmland, and equipment and supplies English, history, science, math, and agriculture teachers.

States have often presented tribes with the greatest threats to their sovereignty and resources. Ignorance concerning tribal rights, jealousy over tribal resources, and prejudice against Indians has resulted in state efforts to exert control over tribal peoples and territories. In recent years state governments and tribes have increasingly realized that they share common problems and that cooperation is more productive than competition. Although tribes must continuously be vigilant not to allow states to usurp their authority, tribes and states are increasingly finding it advantageous to enter into cooperative agreements for the provision of social services, the development of economies, and the protection of resources.

CHAPTER 14

THE FUTURE

American Indians were the original rulers and caretakers of the vast territory that is today the United States. Originally numbering close to five million, Indian people now number one and a half million—a minority in their own land. Although American Indian people have survived despite overwhelming odds and attempts to destroy their culture, alter their governments, and extinguish their sovereignty, tribal survival remains a question. Throughout the history of Indian-white relations, federal laws concerning tribes have too often been composed of policies designed to erase tribal rights.

Ignorance about Indian culture and competition for resources have been the two major reasons for white hostility toward Indian rights. When Europeans arrived in the Indians' world, they found societies considerably different from their own. Indian people had a holistic and spiritual approach to life. Their societies were basically communal and nonmaterialistic. Their value systems stressed cooperation, harmony, and responsibility. European culture, on the other hand, emphasized progress, materialism, individualism, competition, and property. The Europeans considered their own culture to be vastly superior to Indian society. It was incomprehensible to the English and other colonists that these "inferior" tribes did not wish to adopt the newcomers' religion, values, and practices. Europeans considered Indians "children of nature" or "savage beasts." White ignorance and misunderstanding of Indians bred contempt and racism.

The Europeans', and later the Americans', belief in their own superiority helped them to rationalize taking the Indians' lands. The tribes were viewed as intolerable obstacles to progress and Manifest Destiny. Selling Indian lands raised money for the U.S. government's operation and provided homesteads for settlers and resources for industries. To obtain Indian lands, the U.S. government broke treaties, negotiated fraudulent land deals, and passed assimilationist legislation.

Five hundred years of contact, unfortunately, have done little to reverse non-Indians' ignorance of Indian beliefs, traditions, rights, and tribal life. Many non-Indians still find it difficult to understand why many Indian people wish to retain their culture, their reservations, and their governments instead of joining mainstream American society. America is working hard to create a society of equality for blacks and

There is no "better" or "worse," only different. That difference has to be respected whether it's skin color, way of life or ideas. The Chumash have a story about this. It begins with a worm who is eaten by a bird. The bird is eaten by a cat whose self-satisfaction is disrupted by a mean looking dog. After devouring the cat, the dog is killed by a grizzly bear who congratulates himself for being the strongest of all. About that time comes a man who kills the bear and climbs a mountain to proclaim his ultimate superiority. He ran so hard up the mountain that he died at the top. Before long the worm crawled out of his body.

Kote Kotah, Chumash

other minorities and for women. The Indians' desire to be
treated differently is at odds philosophically and legalistically
with American notions of equality.

America would also benefit economically from tribal assimilation. Although tribes hold only 2.3 percent of their former lands, several tribes retain important mineral and water
rights. Today's "Indian wars" are being fought in corporate
boardrooms and law offices as tribes endeavor to protect and
control their remaining resources.

Tribal survival in the future will continue to be a struggle.
The success of that struggle will depend in part on whether
Indian people have, first, a clear understanding of their tribal
sovereignty, their rights, and their relationship with Congress, and, second, a strong tribal government responsive to
the political, economic, and cultural needs of its people

Sovereignty is power and independence. It is both the willingness to act independently and the ability or power to do
so. Tribes possess inherent sovereignty; their authority and
power to act are not delegated by the federal government
but spring from within the community and its desire to act
as one.

ELEMENTS OF TRIBAL SOVEREIGNTY

Before colonization, Indian tribes possessed complete sovereignty. Many Indian people argue that tribal sovereignty remains total today—that Indian nations have never been conquered and that all federal laws limiting tribal sovereignty
are illegal.

The federal government's argument is that Indian nations
today are quasi-sovereigns, or domestic dependent nations.
Federal law states that tribes have retained all their inherent
powers of government unless that power conflicts with a
tribe's treaty or constitution or with its status as a dependent
nation or with a congressional law. In general, these limitations mean that tribes may no longer dispose of their land
freely (the *Johnson* decisions); conduct foreign relations (the
Cherokee Nation decision); exert criminal decisions over non-
Indians (the *Oliphant* decisions); exert sole criminal jurisdiction over tribal members guilty of serious crimes (the Seven
Major Crimes Act); or sentence members convicted of lesser
crimes to longer than one year in jail or more than five thousand dollars in fines (the Indian Civil Rights Act).

In addition, the plenary doctrine (as defined in *Kagama*
and other decisions) allows the federal government to extinguish any aspect of tribal authority. In many instances,
states, as a result of P.L. 280, now have concurrent authority
with the tribal governments in criminal and civil areas.

Even accepting the federal government's interpretation of
tribal sovereignty, tribal powers remain extensive. These
powers include the authority to define their own membership; structure and operate the tribal governments; regulate

domestic relations; settle disputes; manage their property and resources; tax tribal members; regulate businesses; and conduct relations with other governments.

THE GOVERNMENT-GOVERNMENT RELATIONSHIP

All federally recognized tribes have a special relationship with the federal government. It is important to remember that each tribe's relationship with the federal government is different, depending on its treaties, its constitution, and the existence of special federal or state laws. The basic elements of the government-government relationship are that it is based on the inherent sovereignty of each party; it has been recognized in treaties, congressional statutes, and court cases; it acknowledges tribes' right to self-determination, including the right to operate tribal governments, control tribal resources, and protect tribal culture; includes federal protection of tribal resources and sovereignty in return for tribal lands and peace; it bars state interference in tribal affairs without federal and tribal approval; and it involves a weaker sovereign taking the protection of a stronger sovereign without extinguishing its own sovereignty.

For the past one hundred years the federal government has dominated the once equal government-government relationship with tribes. To regain their position as equal partners in the relationship, tribes must become more active in defining that relationship. Much federal Indian law—the *Johnson* and *Kagama* decisions, the plenary doctrine, the 1871 appropriation act ending federal treaty making, and the *Oliphant* decision—rest on questionable logic and interpretations of law. Tribal governments and individuals must not simply accept the federal government's interpretation of their rights and status. Laws, regulations, and court decisions that limit tribal sovereignty must be questioned and carefully challenged.

Tribal governments must fight to protect their rights by lobbying Congress, negotiating with other governments, and filing lawsuits when necessary. Under the plenary doctrine, the federal government has the power to extinguish tribal authority and rights. Federal law allows Indian treaties to be broken as long as tribes are compensated for their land and resources. Hence, it is vital that tribes lobby congressional representatives and testify before Congress. Tribal leaders have successfully defeated bills that would have canceled all treaties, extinguished all eastern land claims, terminated all tribes, and extinguished title to a major portion of Pueblo lands.

Plenary authority also empowers the federal government to restore extinguished tribal powers. In the future, tribes may wish to seek legislation that will, for example, increase again the sentencing limits imposed on them by the Indian Civil Rights Act, overturn the *Oliphant* decision, or restore to Congress the right to negotiate treaties with tribes.

STRONG, RESPONSIVE TRIBAL GOVERNMENT

Tribal governments are in a transition that began with independence, moved to paternalism, and is now moving to self-determination and control. As tribes reassume management of their affairs, tribal members must critically assess the structure of their governments. Many critics of tribal governments argue that such governments are not well structured to provide efficient, representative responses to the economic and social needs of the communities they represent, or to reinforce and nurture the cultural values of the community.

Criticisms

The criticisms of and proposed changes in tribal governments are as varied as the tribes themselves. Some Indian people feel that tribal governments that have retained their traditional structures offer the best protection for cultural and political survival. They argue that many tribal governments, especially those established under the Indian Reorganization Act (IRA), are based on Anglo-American political values. By incorporating majority rule, an adversarial system of justice, a one-person-one-vote concept, and the separation of church and state, these imposed governments work against the traditional Indian values of consensus, communalism, cooperation, and a holistic approach to religion and politics. Critics also charge that tribes too frequently are governed by an elite group of assimilated tribal members who do not represent the more traditional members.

Another major criticism directed at tribal governments from both traditional and assimilated factions concerns the power and structure of the tribal council. Tribal councils typically function as the executive, legislative, and judicial branches of tribal government. The council passes legislation, chooses the executive branch from among its members, and frequently appoints tribal judges and hears appeals from the tribal court. There is, then, very little separation of power, using either traditional mechanisms or Anglo-American methods. Without a system of checks and balances, the council's authority may become overly powerful and unresponsive to the needs of all tribal members.

A related criticism is that tribal councils too often involve themselves in the administrative and business operations of the tribe. In other words, council members may control hiring, firing, or budgetary decisions on the basis of their political needs (e.g., to ensure reelection) instead of on sound, objective administrative and business practices.

Solutions

Tribal leaders have offered numerous suggestions in recent years for improving the structure and operation of their governments. Some of the major suggestions include separating the executive branch from the legislative and judi-

Today tribal leaders pay little attention to the Constitution and by-laws governing them and they have no knowledge of the history of their tribe, treaties and acts of Congress. This knowledge is most important if tribal governments are to effectively improve the general welfare of their people. What is most needed are leaders who will work towards restoring their original rights as sovereign nations.

Frank Ducheneaux, former Cheyenne River Sioux Tribal Chairman

The Indian population is one of the fastest growing groups in the United States. Compared to other ethnic groups, a large percentage of the Indian population is under the age of fifteen. At council meetings and other gatherings, tribal leaders frequently speak of the obligation owed to future generations. These children from across Indian country represent the future. Shown are an Alaskan native child in costume (Courtesy Bureau of Indian Affairs), Indian children at their desks (Courtesy Bureau of Indian Affairs), and Choctaw children playing (Courtesy Mississippi Band of Choctaws.)

cial branches of government by direct election of the council chairperson and other executive officers, for instance, and by direct election of tribal judges for relatively long terms. Establishing independent appeals courts has also been suggested, as has empowering the tribal court to review the constitutionality of tribal laws, ordinances, and council decisions.

Separation of the political and administrative responsibilities of tribal government could be accomplished by employing a tribal manager to oversee the operation of tribal programs, including personnel and budgetary decisions. Political and business responsibilities could be separated by creating independently chartered business organizations. Tribal governments could increase their stability, efficiency, and capability by lengthening the terms of council members and increasing, or in some cases decreasing, the number of council members. Electing tribal officers by district would be a step toward improving tribal representation. And finally, tribal groups could increase cultural responsiveness by revising tribal codes to incorporate traditional law, by working for increased involvement of tribal elders as legislative or judicial advisers, and by establishing arbitration courts rather than, or in addition to, courts founded on an adversarial system of justice.

Many of the above changes would also increase the size and complexity of tribal governments, a change that could be either advantageous or disadvantageous. As governments increase in complexity, they become more expensive, more legalistic, and more unwieldy. As governments become more legalistic, lawyers and other non-Indian professionals might become more prominent in tribal affairs. In the end, this would offer little improvement over BIA control. The most important issue, however, is that tribal members consider and adopt for themselves the form of government that will best enable them to secure their survival.

CONCLUSION

Tribal governments are the oldest governments in existence in the Western Hemisphere. Despite common misperceptions, the U.S. Constitution was not the first government to institute democratic rule and notions of equality. Traditional tribal governments, at a time when European governments were authoritarian and hierarchical, were based on concepts of democracy, equality, freedom, and respect.

Although Benjamin Franklin incorporated aspects of the Iroquois League into the Articles of Confederation, the United States did not make the effort to learn from the tribes about their governments and their political values. Rather, Indians were viewed as obstacles to the attainment of land for settlement.

After the brief, early period of respect for tribes, born out of the need to gain their friendship and alliance in fighting European competitors, the United States turned to policies of extermination and assimilation. Tribes were first relocated to reservations, then subjected to laws designed to incorporate them into the American mainstream. Hence, throughout American history, tribes have had to deal with a federal government that has waffled between its commitment to honor its treaty obligations to respect Indian lands and sovereignty and its desire to assimilate the tribes and obtain their lands and resources.

Despite two hundred years of periodic attempts to end tribalism, tribes and their governments remain in existence. The tribal-federal relationship today is currently one sym-

Article XVI—Oath of Office

Into your care we entrust our land our people. Regardless of whether you are poor, or lack the oratory to express yourself fluently, you will, to the best of your ability, be the protector, impartially, for your people regardless of race, color, or creed, and you will give unto them the same protection and rights as you would your own. You will cherish and protect all that contains life; from the lowliest crawling creature to the human. By hasty word or deed you will refrain from hurting the feelings, both mentally and physically, of your people. In times when you, to the best of your ability and judgment, have resorted to every peaceful means of bringing reason to an individual, on a matter and that individual, through stubborness, remains contrary to the point of disrespect for the office you hold, and would, through his action, be a bad example to his fellowmen, you will question him four times if he will continue to set aside peaceful intelligent reasoning. If his answer is yes the four times, then you may strike him with the flat of your hand, and four times if necessary.

Zuni Constitution, 1934

bolized by self-determination; the recognition of tribal rights
to govern themselves and their resources according to their
own cultural values and their own assessment of their needs.

Federal law acknowledges that tribes have retained all
their rights unless they have been removed by treaty, legislation, or are inconsistent with their status as a domestic-
dependent nation. This means that tribes still possess, among
other powers, the right to structure their governments, to
define their membership, to regulate their property and resources, to levy taxes, to administer justice, and to relate to
other governments.

The federal government is obligated by the trust relationship to protect tribal resources, provide certain social services, and protect aspects of tribal autonomy. This is the
promise the United States has pledged to tribes in treaties,
legislation, and court cases. It is a promise that derives from
the tribes' agreements to cede millions of acres of their lands
and resources to the U.S. government for the settlement of
non-Indians. This special tribal-federal relationship is a political relationship, not a racial one, and it is based on the
inherent sovereignty of each party. It is a relationship that
excludes states from intervening in tribal affairs without the
consent of Congress.

A close examination of the Senecas of New York, the Muscogees of Oklahoma, the Cheyenne River Sioux of South Dakota, the Isleta Pueblo of New Mexico, and the Yakimas of
Washington, and a fleeting review of other tribes and their
programs, has shown that each tribe is different, with a different culture and a different understanding of their specific
needs. This book has also shown, however, that all tribes
seek to attain similar goals: the establishment of a responsible government, the adequate provision of social services,
and the development of tribal economy. For many tribes, it
is important to work toward these goals in a manner that
preserves and reinforces their own cultures.

What the future holds for tribal governments is unclear.
Much will depend upon the United States' willingness to uphold its historic promises and upon the vigilance of tribal
people to maintain their rights and their culture. What is
clear is that tribes have retained their governments and their
identity despite over five hundred years of attempts by non-
Indians to end tribal existence. This tenacity remains today.

IMPORTANT EVENTS IN INDIAN HISTORY

1000–1500	Iroquois League formed. The league and the All Indian Pueblo Council (date of establishment unknown) are the oldest continuing political alliances in North America.
1492	Christopher Columbus lands in present-day West Indies.
September 7, 1535	Jacques Cartier, French explorer, claims area around present-day Quebec, Canada, for France.
1539–43	Hernando De Soto leads expedition in the Southeast and establishes first contact with southeast tribes.
1540–42	Francisco Coronado's expeditions in the Southwest make European contact with the Pueblos and other tribes.
July 27, 1585	Sir Walter Raleigh and other English colonists settle at Roanoke Island, Virginia.
December 20, 1620	The *Mayflower*, carrying the Pilgrims, lands at Plymouth, Massachusetts.
March 22, 1622	Opechancanough leads Indian confederacy against white settlements in Virginia.
1638	Connecticut establishes first reservation, for remnants of the Quinnipiac tribe.
1641	The colony of New Netherlands, followed by others, offers bounties of four to eight dollars for Indian scalps.
1675–76	King Philip's War takes place in New England. This was the most destructive Indian war in colonial history.
August 10, 1680	Popé, Tewa leader of the Pueblos, and his band attack and kill more than four hundred Spanish colonists in an attempt to restore the Pueblo way of life.

March 20, 1713	South Carolina wars against the Tuscaroras, killing two hundred and capturing eight hundred at Snow Hill. The surviving Tuscaroras flee north and become members of the Iroquois League.
1754	English colonies hold the Albany Congress, at which they discuss a unified colonial-Indian policy and establish an alliance with the Iroquois League.
1760s	Several Plains tribes obtain horses from whites.
1754–63	French and Indian War.
April 27, 1763	Pontiac summons a council of four hundred Ottawa, Huron, and Potawatomi chiefs and other men to plan an attack on Fort Detroit.
May–November, 1763	Pontiac leads Indian forces that destroy every British post west of Niagara, New York, except for forts Pitt and Detroit.
October 7, 1763	England issues Royal Proclamation, which reserves for Indians the territory between the crest of the Appalachian Mountains and the Mississippi River.
1774	Lord Dunmore's War is caused by Chief Logan's revenge after frontiersmen murdered his family and by the appropriation of Shawnee and Ottawa lands in western Pennsylvania.
1775	Continental Congress names Indian commissioners for the northern, middle, and southern departments of the colonies. Their responsibilities are "to treat with the Indians . . . in order to preserve peace and friendship with the said Indians and to prevent their taking any part in the present commotion." Negotiations take place between the commissioners and the Iroquois League.
1775–83	Revolutionary War. Many Indians ally themselves with the British; some aid the United States.
1777	The new government of the United States, organized by the Articles

of Confederation, assumes authority over Indian affairs as long as the "legislative right of any State within its own limits be not infringed or violated."

September 17, 1778 First Indian treaty with the United States signed by the Delaware Nation. The United States promises military aid and admission of the Delaware Nation as a state in exchange for access of U.S. troops to Delaware lands.

1784 The Russians establish a settlement at Kodiak Island, off the southern coast of Alaska.

July 13, 1787 The Northwest Ordinance is passed by the Continental Congress, stating that "the utmost good faith shall always be observed towards the Indians; their lands and property shall never be taken from them without their consent; and in their property rights and liberty, they never shall be invaded or disturbed."

September 17, 1787 The U.S. Constitution is adopted. Article I, section 8, grants Congress the power "to regulate Commerce with foreign Nations, and among the several States, and with the Indian tribes."

1789 Congress gives the War Department authority over Indian affairs.

July 22, 1790 Trade and Intercourse Act passed.

September 19, 1790– August 3, 1795 Tecumseh leads Indian nations against the United States. Tribes included are the Mingos, Miamis, Wyandots, Delawares, Potawatamis, Shawnees, Chippewas, and Ottawas.

November 4, 1791 Little Turtle leads an Indian force of Miamis, Shawnees, and Delawares, defeating Gen. Arthur St. Clair's army of over two thousand men near Greenville, Ohio (Fort Jefferson).

August 20, 1794 Gen. Anthony Wayne defeats tribes from the Old Northwest at the Battle of Fallen Timbers, in Ohio.

1794 First Indian treaty to include provisions for education of Indians signed by the United States and the Oneidas, Tuscaroras, and Stockbridges.

June 15, 1799

GanYoDieYo, a Seneca, also known as Handsome Lake, has the first in a series of visions calling him to preach to his people and save them from corruption and degradation. His teachings are known today as the Handsome Lake religion.

1802

The U.S. Congress appropriates ten to fifteen thousand dollars annually to promote "civilization" among the Indians.

1803

United States obtains Louisiana Purchase from France, thereby acquiring vast amounts of land inhabited by Indians.

1804–1806

Lewis and Clark expedition to the Pacific Northwest makes first American contact with many northern tribes.

November 7, 1811

At the Battle of Tippecanoe, William Henry Harrison leads a force of one thousand men in destroying Tecumseh's village, Prophet's Town, in Indiana.

1812–14

During the War of 1812 with Great Britain, Tecumseh leads tribes in the Old Northwest to align with the British against the United States.

**July 27, 1813–
August 9, 1814**

Creek (Muscogee) Indian War in Alabama, Georgia, Mississippi, and Tennessee. Gen. Andrew Jackson defeats Muscogees at the battle of Horseshoe Bend, in Alabama.

1815–25

The United States signs a series of treaties with the Indian nations north of the Ohio River. These treaties signify the start of Indian removal to western lands.

**November 20, 1817–
October 31, 1818**

First U.S.–Seminole Indian War in Florida.

1819

Congress appropriates money for the "Civilization Fund," the first federal Indian education program.

1824

The secretary of war creates a Bureau of Indian Affairs within the War Department.

July 26, 1827	Cherokees adopt their first constitution at New Echota, Georgia. Chief John Ross elected president.
1828	Sequoyah's Cherokee alphabet is used to print the *Cherokee Phoenix*, the first Indian newspaper.
May 28, 1830	President Andrew Jackson's Indian Removal Bill passed.
1831	*Cherokee Nation* v. *Georgia* decision rules tribes are not foreign states but domestic dependent nations.
1832	Chief Justice John Marshall's Supreme Court decision in *Worcester* vs. *Georgia* guarantees Cherokee sovereignty. President Jackson refuses to support the decision, clearing the way for the removal of Indians westward.
1832–42	Federal government removes the Five Civilized Tribes from the southeast United States to the west.
March 29, 1835	Cherokees sign Treaty of New Echota (Georgia), agreeing to cede all their lands to the United States and prepare for their removal westward.
1835–42	Second U.S.–Seminole Indian War in Florida.
June 17, 1838	Cherokee Trail of Tears begins—a journey of over twelve hundred miles with inadequate provisions. Approximately one-fourth die along the way.
1838	Trail of Death for Indiana Potawatomis during their removal west.
December, 1847– July, 1848	Cayuse Indian War in Oregon.
1847	The Taos Pueblos join local Hispanics to overthrow their new American government.
1848	Treaty of Guadalupe Hildago signed with Mexico; many new tribes come under U.S. jurisdiction.
	Gold is discovered near Sacramento, California, leading to the extermination of thousands of California Indians.

1849	Bureau of Indian Affairs is transferred from the War Department to the newly created Department of the Interior.
1849–61	Ongoing hostilities take place with Comanche, Cheyenne, Lipan, and Kickapoo Indians in Texas.
September 17, 1851	U.S. holds Fort Laramie (Wyoming) Treaty Council with plains and mountain tribes.
1851–56	Rogue River Indian wars in Oregon.
1853	New Indian lands are acquired from Mexico in the Gadsden Purchase.
1854	Cherokee, Chickasaw, Choctaw, Muscogee, and Seminole Indian nations form a federation to deal with their mutual problems.
October 11–November 24, 1855	Yakima War, Washington Territory.
1855	Treaties signed with Indians of Oregon and Washington territories.
December 15, 1855–May 8, 1858	Third U.S.–Seminole War in Florida.
March–April, 1857	Lakota hostilities in Minnesota and Iowa.
1860–64	Military campaign against the Cheyenne Indians.
1861–65	Many tribes, especially the Five Civilized Tribes, are caught in the Civil War. Indian units fight with distinction on both sides.
1862–63	Santee Sioux Indian revolt in Minnesota and Dakota.
1863–67	Kit Carson's campaign against the Navajos.
1863–69	War against the Cheyenne, Arapaho, Kiowa, and Comanche Indians in Kansas, Nebraska, Colorado, and Indian Territory.
March 6, 1864	Navajo Long Walk begins. Eight thousand Navajos are taken to Fort Sumner, New Mexico, as prisoners of war and held under terrible conditions for three years before being allowed to leave.
November 29, 1864	One hundred and fifty peaceful Cheyennes, mostly women and

	children, massacred by Col. John Chivington's troops at Sand Creek, Colorado.
October 21, 1867	U.S. signs Treaty of Medicine Lodge with Southern Plains tribes, obtaining their agreement to move to reservations.
1867	United States acquires Alaska from Russia.
1867–68	Indian Peace Commission negotiates final treaties with Indians (the last of 370 Indian treaties is signed on August 13, 1868, with the Nez Percés).
April 29, 1868	U.S. signs Fort Laramie Treaty of 1868 with the Lakotas, agreeing, following the Lakotas' defeat by the United States, to remove forts along the Bozeman Trail.
November 27, 1868	Gen. George Custer attacks peaceful encampment of Cheyennes and Arapahos on the Washita River. Black Kettle and over a hundred other Cheyenne people are killed.
1869	Congress appoints Ely S. Parker, a Seneca Indian, to head the Bureau of Indian Affairs.
	President Ulysses S. Grant attempts to reduce the graft and corruption rampant in Indian affairs by creating the Board of Indian Commissioners (disbanded in 1933) to oversee Indian appropriations.
1870	Congress passes a law prohibiting army officers from being appointed Indian agents, prompting President Grant to turn control of Indian agencies over to various Christian denominations.
1870–86	Federal Indian policy, backed by military support, places final Indians on reservations; practice of providing food and clothing to Indians begins.
March 3, 1871	Congress passes legislation formally ending treaty making with Indian tribes.
November 22, 1872– October 3, 1873	Captain Jack leads Modoc War in Oregon and California.

1873	Military campaign against Apaches in Arizona and New Mexico.
June 2, 1876	Lt. Col. Custer's force of 267 men is annihilated by Lakotas and Cheyennes at the Little Bighorn River, in Montana.
1876–79	Hostilities with northern Cheyennes in Indian Territory, Kansas, Wyoming, Dakota, Nebraska, and Montana.
April 6, 1877	Chief Joseph and Nez Percés flee toward Canada after being attacked by the U.S. Army.
October, 1877	Chief Joseph surrenders to the U.S. Army.
1878	Congress appropriates funds to establish Indian Police forces on reservations.
September 1, 1884	Haskell Institute, an Indian training school, opens in Lawrence, Kansas.
March 3, 1885	Congress passes the Major Crimes Act.
September 4, 1886	Apache leader Geronimo and his band surrender to the U.S. Army.
February 8, 1887	Congress passes Dawes Allotment Act, providing for allotment of Indian lands in severalty.
June, 1888	Delegates from twenty-two tribes convene at Fort Gibson, Indian Territory, to discuss changing Indian Territory into an Indian state.
April 22, 1889	Oklahoma Land Run opens the Unassigned Lands, in central Indian Territory, to homesteading.
December 29, 1890	Massacre of Lakotas at Wounded Knee, South Dakota.
October, 1901	Congress passes Citizenship Act for Five Civilized Tribes.
1902–10	Bureau of Indian Affairs begins Federal Indian reclamation, forestry, and conservation programs.
1906	Congress passes the Burke Act, amending the Dawes Allotment Act, by establishing a twenty-five-year trust period.
	Most reservations and tribal governments in Indian Territory and Oklahoma Territory are liquidated

	in preparation for organizing the state of Oklahoma.
November 16, 1907	State of Oklahoma admitted to the Union.
1921	Snyder Act passed by Congress, allowing for expenditure of appropriated funds for Indians without regard to amount of Indian blood, membership in a federally recognized tribe, or residence (as long as it is in the United States).
June 2, 1924	Congress passes Indian Citizenship Act.
1928	Meriam Report, "The Problem of Indian Administration," is published.
1933	John Collier appointed commissioner of the Bureau of Indian Affairs.
June 18, 1934	Indian Reorganization Act (IRA) passed, ending allotment, providing for tribal self-government, and launching the Indian credit program. Johnson-O'Malley Act passed, offering general federal assistance to Indians.
1935	Congress passes legislation establishing Indian Arts and Crafts Board.
June 26, 1936	Congress passes Oklahoma Indian Welfare Act to provide Oklahoma tribes with provisions similar to those of the Indian Reorganization Act.
November 15, 1944	National Congress of American Indians (NCAI) founded in Denver, Colorado.
August 1, 1946	Indian Claims Commission established to end Indian land claims by making monetary compensations.
1948	Indians of Arizona and New Mexico, in separate court cases, win the right to vote in state elections.
1952	Indian relocation program established for all Indians.
June 9, 1953	U.S. Representative William Henry Harrison of Wyoming introduces House Concurrent Resolution 108, which states that Congress intends to "terminate" at the "earliest pos-

	sible time" all Indians, meaning that Congress will not recognize them as Indians and will remove all Indian rights and benefits.
August 4, 1953	Congress passes Public Law 280, giving the states of California, Nebraska, Minnesota, Oregon, and Wisconsin civil and criminal jurisdiction over reservations.
1954	First of several acts passed calling for the termination of federal trust status over Indian lands.
	Act passed transferring Indian Health Service from Bureau of Indian Affairs to the Public Health Service.
June 12, 1961	American Indian Chicago Conference held, representing 210 tribes and nations. Declaration of Indian Purpose drawn up for presentation to U.S. Congress.
Summer, 1961	National Indian Youth Council formed.
1964	Washington State tribes begin fight for fishing rights. Settled by *Boldt* decision (1974).
	Economic Opportunity Act provides means for Indians to participate in and control their own programs for economic development.
March 6, 1968	President Lyndon Johnson delivers the first special message to Congress to deal exclusively with American Indians and Alaskan Natives.
April 11, 1968	American Indian Civil Rights Act passed, guaranteeing to reservation residents many of the same civil rights and liberties in relation to tribal authorities that the U.S. Constitution guarantees to all persons in relation to federal and state authorities.
July, 1968	American Indian Movement (AIM) formed to protest the U.S. government's treatment of Indian people.
November 20, 1969– June 11, 1971	Indian activists occupy Alcatraz Island, San Francisco Bay.
April 18–23, 1970	Sit-ins held by Indians in several BIA offices.

July 8, 1970	President Richard Nixon delivers special message to Congress dealing exclusively with American Indians and Alaskan Natives and setting forth a legislative program that expresses the idea of self-determination without the threat of termination.
August 1, 1970	Puyallup Indians set up a camp on the Puyallup River in Washington State and begin fishing to reestablish their tribal fishing rights.
December 15, 1970	Taos land bill signed to return 48,000 acres of land, including Blue Lake, to the Taos Pueblo. This bill is the first legislation to restore a sizable piece of land to an Indian tribe.
December 18, 1971	Congress passes the Alaska Native Claims Settlement Act (ANCSA), which extinguishes the Alaskan Natives' title to nine-tenths of Alaska in return for 44 million acres and almost one billion dollars.
May 20, 1972	Congress restores Mount Adams, an area sacred to the Yakima Nation, to the tribe.
June 23, 1972	Congress passes the Indian Education Act of 1972, creating a BIA-level Office of Indian Education as well as a National Advisory Council on Indian Education designed to improve the quality of public education for Indian students.
November 2–8, 1972	Two hundred Indians march in Trail of Broken Treaties and occupy the Bureau of Indian Affairs Building in Washington, D.C., in protest of broken federal promises to tribes.
February 27– May 8, 1973	Two hundred Indians under AIM leadership occupy Wounded Knee, on the Pine Ridge Reservation in South Dakota.
December 22, 1973	Congress passes Public Law 93-197 restoring the terminated Menominee Indian tribe of Wisconsin to federally recognized status.
April 12, 1974	Congress passes the Indian Financing Act, making available $250 mil-

	lion in credit and grants of up to $50,000 to facilitate financing of Indian enterprises.
January 4, 1975	Congress passes the Indian Self-Determination and Education Assistance Act, expanding tribal control over reservation programs and authorizing federal funds to build needed public-school facilities on or near Indian reservations.
September 20, 1976	Congress passes the Indian Health Care Improvement Act, authorizing seven years of increased appropriations in an effort to improve Indian health care.
October 8, 1976	Congress passes a bill to terminate the Indian Claims Commission at the end of 1978. The U.S. Court of Claims is to take over cases that the commission does not complete by December 31, 1978.
February 11–July 15, 1978	Indian participants begin the Longest Walk at Alcatraz Island, California, in protest of the government's ill treatment of Indians. The walk concludes with thirty thousand marchers in Washington, D.C.
August 11, 1978	Congress passes the American Indian Religious Freedom Act (AIRFA), in which Congress recognizes its obligation to "protect and preserve for American Indians their inherent right of freedom to believe, express and exercise [their] traditional religions."
November 1, 1978	Congress passes the Education Amendment Act of 1978, giving substantial control of education programs to local Indian communities.
November 8, 1978	Congress passes the Indian Child Welfare Act, establishing U.S. policy to promote the stability and security of Indian tribes and families by giving tribal courts jurisdiction over children living on reservations.
June 13, 1979	U.S. Supreme Court awards the Lakota Nation $122.5 million for the federal government's illegal

	taking of the Black Hills, in South Dakota.
March 15, 1980	Penobscots and Passamaquoddies accept a $27 million trust fund plus $54.5 million with which to purchase 300,000 acres as a permanent land base after successfully arguing that Massachussets colony (later the state of Maine) had taken their aboriginal homeland, the northern two-thirds of Maine, in violation of the 1790 Trade and Intercourse Act.
October 27, 1986	Congress revises Indian Civil Rights Act to allow tribal courts to impose fines of five thousand dollars and one year in jail for criminal offenses.
February 3, 1988	Congress amends Alaska Native Claims Settlement Act to allow each corporation to decide whether it will sell its stock after 1991.
April 28, 1988	Legislation enacted to repeal the termination policy established by House Concurrent Resolution 108.

GLOSSARY

Aboriginal: Original; indigenous; native to a particular region.

Abrogation: The action of terminating a treaty or international agreement.

Akicitas: Fraternal societies of the Plains tribes responsible for policing camp.

Algonkian: A language family of the midwest and eastern United States, spoken by the Shawnees, Kickapoos, Delawares, Cheyennes, Potawatomis, and other tribes.

All-Indian Pueblo Council: Mutual alliance of Pueblo Indians. The first recorded meeting was in 1598, and the group was formally organized in 1965 with a constitution and bylaws.

Allotment: Surveyed reservation land distributed by the government to individual Indians under the provisions of the Dawes Allotment Act. Generally, 160 acres were allotted to heads of families; 80 acres to single persons; and 40 acres to other family members.

Alaskan Native Claims Settlement Act: 1971 act extinguishing Alaskan land claims.

American Indian Chicago Conference: A conference of Indian persons held in 1961 on the University of Chicago campus. Indian leaders in attendance issued a declaration that emphasized the goal of self-determination.

American Indian Movement (AIM): Militant Indian organization established in Minneapolis, Minnesota, in 1968. Originally founded to assist urban Indians, the organization broadened its purpose to include protesting the denial of Indian treaty rights, land rights, and social welfare.

Anasazi: Prehistoric southwestern culture that flourished in the Colorado River basin. The Anasazis excelled as basket makers, builders, and farmers.

Appeal: Complaint to a higher court or authority that a decision at a lower level was in error.

Articles of Confederation: Document adopted by the Second Continental Congress on November 15, 1777, and ratified by all states in 1781. Modeled on the structure of the Iroquois League, the articles served as the framework of the U.S. government until the Constitution was adopted in 1789.

Assimilation: The absorption of a minority culture group into the main culture body.

At-large election: Election of government officials from among members of the entire territory instead of from smaller districts.

Band: Part of a tribe.

Black drink: A purgative beverage made from the *cussena* plant and used in ceremonies by southeastern tribes as a means of cleansing and preparing worshipers.

Bureau of Indian Affairs (BIA): Agency within the U.S. Department of the Interior responsible for administering the U.S. government's relationships with Indian governments and for overseeing Congress's trust responsibility for Indian lands and existence.

Busk: Annual renewal rite celebrated by southeastern tribes; also known as the Green Corn Ceremony.

Bylaws: Set of rules adopted by an organization or assembly for governing its own meetings or affairs.

Cacique: A word of Arawakan (Caribbean Indian) origin applied by Spanish explorers and colonists to indigenous religious leaders. Among traditional Pueblos the term designated the supreme village or town priest. The Pueblo cacique is considered the primary authority in all matters religious and secular.

Calumet: Pipe used by eastern, midwestern, and plains tribes in ceremonies of religious and diplomatic importance.

Cession: The ceding or yielding of rights, property, or territory from one group or person to another.

Clan: Individuals sharing the same lineage; American Indian clans are usually represented by an animal totem.

Clan mother: Eldest female member of a clan; serves as the clan leader in a matriarchal society.

Communal: Belonging to or shared by the community.

Communal ownership: Land ownership as practiced by American Indian tribes; title was vested in the tribe rather than in individuals.

Confederacy: A league or alliance for mutual support, aid, and common action.

Consensus: An agreement or opinion held by all.

Constitution: Written or unwritten fundamental laws and principles that prescribe the nature, functions, and limits of a government and guarantee certain rights to the people.

Council: A group elected or appointed as an advisory or legislative body; council members are usually equal in power and authority.

Council of Energy Resource Tribes (CERT): Special-interest organization formed by tribes in 1975 to assist in the preservation and management of their natural resources.

Coups: Plains Indian custom of "touching" the enemy. Getting close enough to the enemy to touch but not kill was regarded as an act of bravery. Warriors recorded their coups by counting such deeds on the coup stick.

Culture: The ideas, customs, skills, arts, etc., of a given people in a given period.

Dawes Allotment Act: Also known as the General Allotment act of 1887, this act required that communally held reservation lands be allotted to individuals for ownership.

Deganwidah: Iroquois leader who created the Iroquois League approximately one thousand years ago.

Democracy: Government by the people; a government in which the supreme power is vested in the people and exercised by them either directly (pure democracy) or indirectly, through a system of representation (republicanism).

Domestic dependent nation: Term used by Chief Justice John Marshall in 1831 to characterize the legal status of the Indian nations.

Doctrine of Prior Appropriation: Test by which water rights are determined in western states; whoever first used the water is given "primary rights" to its current usage.

Dreamer religion: Established by the Shaphaptian prophet Smohalla, the Dreamer religion stressed a return to Indian traditions and the use of meditation or dreaming to find guidance and truth.

Economy: The collective material pursuits by which a community sustains itself.

Encomienda: A system by which land and its Indian inhabitants were "given" to Spanish landowners by the Spanish Crown. The Indians were forced to work for the landowners, who, in turn, were to convert the Indians to Catholicism.

Encroach: To gradually enter or force oneself upon another's property or rights.

Endogamous: A tradition dictating that members of a group marry someone from within the group.

Enumerated powers: Powers specifically listed in a constitution and granted to specific parts of a government.

Ethnocentrism: The belief that one's own ethnic group and culture are superior to all others.

Excise tax: A tax or duty on the manufacture, sale, or consumption of various commodities, such as liquor or tobacco.

Exogamous: A tradition dictating that members of a group marry partners from outside the group.

Extended family: Family membership that may include relatives other than the nuclear family.

Extradition: Surrender of an alleged criminal by one government to another that has criminal jurisdiction.

Federally recognized tribes: Tribes with whom the federal government maintains an official relationship, usually established by treaty, congressional legislation, or executive order.

Fee-simple ownership: Private ownership of land, based largely on the traditional English common-law practice of land tenure.

Five Civilized Tribes: Name given by whites to the Cherokee, Choctaw, Chickasaw, Muscogee, and Seminole tribes from the Southeast because of their adoption of certain European practices, such as a written language, written constitutions, and schools.

General Allotment Act: See Dawes Allotment Act.

General council: Supreme governing body of some tribes; traditionally composed of all adult members of the tribe.

Ghost Dance religion: Founded by Wovoka, a Paiute, in Nevada during the late nineteenth century, this religion stressed peace and special worship, including dancing, to restore tribal ways.

Government: An organization responsible for administering a group's public affairs.

Government-government relationship: relationship that exists between federally recognized tribes and the federal government. Implicit in the relationship is a recognition of tribal sovereignty and the U.S. government's obligation to protect tribal lands.

Green Corn Ceremony: See Busk.

Guardian: One who guards, protects, or takes care of another person and that person's property.

Haudenosaunee: Iroquois League; also known as the Five (and later Six) Nations.

Hotchkiss: Air-cooled, gas-operated machine gun developed in 1878.

Indian Claims Commission: Commission established in 1946 by Congress to hear suits from tribes suing for lands lost or illegally taken.

Indian country: Land on which Indian laws and customs and federal laws relating to Indians govern.

Indian Reorganization Act (IRA): Also called the Wheeler-Howard Act (1934), the IRA was formulated largely by John Collier, commissioner of Indian affairs, and was aimed at strengthening tribal governments and restoring tribal lands.

Individualism: Assumption that the individual, and not society, is paramount; that all values, rights, and duties originate in individuals and not in society; that individual initiative and action should be independent of government control.

Initiative: Laws introduced directly by the people and subject to a popular vote.

Injunction: A writ or court order either prohibiting a person from carrying out a given action or ordering a given action to be undertaken.

Inter Caetera: Papal proclamation of 1493 which drew a longitudinal (north/south) line through the Western Hemisphere. The New World to the left (west) was under Spanish control. The land to the right (east) was under Portugese control.

Iroquois League: Government and military alliance originally formed more than one thousand years ago and originally composed of five Indian nations: the Mohawks, Oneidas, Onondagas, Cayugas, and Senecas. A sixth nation, the Tuscaroras, joined in the 1700s. The league is still in existence.

Johnson O'Malley Act (JOM): Passed in 1934, this act provided supplementary funds to local school districts for improvements in Indian education.

Jurisdiction: The legal power a government has to govern its people and territory.

Kachina: A small, wooden, colorfully decorated effigy or icon figure representing a tribal deity; used by Pueblo Indians.

Kachina cult: Pueblo association, usually of all male village members above the age of early childhood but in some villages including female members as well. The cults are concerned with supernatural beings loosely connected with ancestral spirits and believed to have the power to bring rain. Kachina dances are spectacular ceremonies in which male members of the cult impersonate the Kachina by donning masks and colorful costumes.

Kiva: Pueblo ceremonial structure, circular or rectangular in shape, wholly or partly underground. These chambers are used almost exclusively by males for religious purposes and as a town forum. Leaders traditionally gathered there to discuss political, criminal, social, and military problems.

Laws of the Indies: Body of laws published by the Spanish Crown in 1681 to govern lands and natives in the New World.

Litigation: Legal contest carried out through the judicial process.

Manifest Destiny: Popular view held during the nineteeth century that the American mission was to expand its territorial limits to the Pacific Coast.

Materialism: Belief that an individual's material well-being is of great importance and that to pursue it at the expense of social and spiritual well-being is acceptable.

Matrilineal: System of social organization in which families are mother-centered and descent and property devolve through the female line.

Matrilocal: Requirement in some societies that a married couple live with the wife's mother.

Medicine: In American Indian societies, power derived from a supernatural source.

Meriam Report: A survey of Indian affairs commissioned by Congress and issued in 1928. The report detailed the deplorable conditions in which many Indians lived and called for reforms.

Micco: Highest traditional office of the Muscogee towns.

Moiety: A French word meaning *half* and referring to the division of a tribe into halves; a moiety usually comprises a cluster of clans.

Muskhogean: A language family of the Southeast, spoken by tribes including the Natchez, Choctaws, Chickasaws, Muscogees, and Seminoles.

Nacas: Traditional Lakota societies that directed the civil affairs of the tribes.

Nation: A stable, historically developed community of people who share territory, economic life, distinctive culture, and language.

National Congress of American Indians (NCAI): Organization of tribal leaders formed during the 1940s to lobby for the protection of Indian rights and culture.

National Indian Youth Conference: Organization formed by tribal youths in 1961 to provide Indian youths with a voice in policy reform.

Native American Church: Established in the early 1900s, this church's teachings combine traditional Indian beliefs and elements of Christianity with the sacramental use of peyote.

Negotiations: Discussion between two or more parties in an effort to settle a dispute.

Nomads: Groups of people who roam from place to place for particular reasons, such as to search for food.

Nonrecognized tribe: Tribe that does not maintain a government-government and trust relationship with the federal government and does not, in general, receive government services or recognition of its land base or sovereignty.

Nuclear family: Kinship group consisting of a father and mother and their children.

Patrilineal: System of social organization in which families are father-centered and descent and property devolve through the male line.

Patrilocal: Social requirement that a married couple reside with the husband's father's clan.

Peace policy: Policy formulated during the administration of President Ulysses S. Grant in the late 1860s and based on dealing with Indians peacefully in the hopes of speeding their assimilation. This policy lasted until 1877.

Plenary doctrine: Doctrine stating that the federal government has unlimited governmental control and jurisdiction over Indian tribes.

Polygamy: Plural marriages; marriage with more than one spouse.

Potlatch: Winter ceremony held by some Pacific Coast tribes. By giving gifts to their guests, individuals increased their own status.

Proclamation of 1763: Declaration by the British Government in 1763 to reserve the western portion of the previously claimed French areas for Indian use and to maintain control over the colonies.

Protectorate: Relationship between two sovereigns in which the weaker state places itself under the protection of the more powerful state.

Pueblo: Communal village built by some Southwest tribes and consisting of one or more flat-roofed structures of stone or adobe arranged in terraces and housing a number of families.

Quorum: The minimum number (usually a majority) of officers or members of a group whose presence is required for a valid decision or transaction to be made.

Rancheria: A Spanish term applied to small reservations in California.

Ratify: To confirm a treaty or amendment.

Recall: To remove an elected official from office by popular vote.

Red Power: Refers to rise of Indian militancy and Pan-Indianism in the 1960s and 1970s.

Referendum: Process of submitting an issue to popular vote.

Relocation: Federal policy formulated in 1952. Indians were relocated from rural and reservation areas to urban areas for job training and employment.

Removal Act: Act passed by Congress in 1830 authorizing the president to negotiate with eastern tribes for their removal to lands west of the Mississippi River.

Requerimiento: Royal decree issued by the Spanish government and read by conquistadors to tribes informing them of their duty to the Spanish Crown and their obligation to convert to Christianity.

Reservation: Lands reserved for tribal use.

Reserved-rights doctrine: Doctrine enunciated by the courts that tribes retain all rights to their land, water, and resources unless they have expressly granted them to the federal government.

Retrocession: Procedure by which states may return to tribes the jurisdictional powers they gained under Public Law 280.

Sachem: Iroquois chieftain.

Sales tax: Tax applied to the retail price of goods or services and collected by the retailer.

Secular: Pertaining to everyday life; nonreligious.

Sedentary: Refers to a people who establish permanent residence sites, usually to engage in agriculture, rather than living a nomadic life-style.

Self-determination: Decision-making control over one's own affairs and the policies that affect one's life.

Severance tax: Tax applied to a resource at the time of its removal from the earth.

Shaman: A priest and healer among some tribes.

Societies: Groups in which membership is determined by voluntary choice or recruitment rather than by kinship. Pueblo moieties are examples of such associations. Membership in Pueblo moieties is for life, and all members are recruited and confirmed by elaborate initiation rites.

Sovereign: Supreme in power or authority.

Sovereignty: The status, dominion, rule, or power of a sovereign.

Smokeshop: Stores on reservations, usually tribally owned, where cigarettes are sold to tribal memebers and no state sales tax is applied.

State-recognized tribes: Tribes that usually are not federally recognized but maintain a special relationship with their state government and whose lands and rights are recognized by the state.

Sun Dance: An annual renewal ceremony observed by the

Lakotas and other Plains tribes. The traditional Sun Dance included self-torture by warriors to benefit the nation's spiritual state.

Syllabary: A list or table of syllables or characters representing syllables; a language whose written characters represent syllables instead of single sounds.

Talwa: Muscogee term for a political entity having attributes of both a tribe and a town.

Taxation: Compulsory payment collected from individuals by the government and used for public purposes.

Terminated tribes: Tribes whose government-government and trust relationship with the federal government has been terminated. Most of the more than one hundred terminations occurred between 1954 and 1961.

Termination: Federal Indian policy during the 1950s that sought to end the federal government's relationship with Indian tribes as prescribed under House Concurrent Resolution 108.

Theocracy: Government by religious authorities.

Tradition: Cultural beliefs and customs handed down from ancestors.

Treaty: Formal agreement between two or more nations, relating to peace, alliance, trade, etc.

Tribe: A group of individuals bound together by ancestry, kinship, languages, culture, and political authority.

Trust: Property held by one person for the benefit of another.

Trustee: Person to whom another's property, or the management of that property, is entrusted.

Trusteeship: Term referring to the federal government's legal obligation to protect tribal land, resources, and existence.

Values: Beliefs, standards, and moral precepts.

Village: Term used to denote a community of Alaskan natives.

Wakan: Omnipotent, creative, directive force in Lakota belief.

Wampum: Small beads made of shells; used by tribes of the Notheast as money and for ornament.

Wampum belts: Red, white, purple, and black shells woven into belts and used by tribes of the Northeast as symbols of peace and war and for other international messages.

Wardship: Refers to the federal government's responsibiilty as trustee over Indians as carried out primarily by the Bureau of Indian Affairs.

Winter count: A tribal history drawn on buffalo hide and kept by the Lakota and Kiowa nations. Pictographs are drawn to represent an important event from each year.

Writ of Habeas Corpus: A written order issued by a court or a judge to bring a person before a court or judge, thereby releasing that person from illegal custody.

Zoning: The dividing of an area of land, such as a city, township, or reservation, by ordinance into sections reserved for different purposes such as housing, business, manufacturing, and recreation.

BIBLIOGRAPHY

Books

Aberle, Sophie D. *The Pueblo Indians of New Mexico: Their Land, Economy and Civil Organization.* American Anthropological Association Memoir 70. Menasha, Wis., 1948.

Abrams, George H. J. *The Seneca People.* Phoenix, Ariz.: Indian Tribal Series, 1976.

American Indian Task Force Commission. *American Indian Policy Review Commission Task Force.* 9 vols. Washington, D.C.: U.S. Government Printing Office, 1977.

Armstrong, Virginia L., ed. *I Have Spoken: American History Through the Voices of the Indians.* Chicago: Swallow Press, 1971.

Axtell, James L. *Through a Glass Darkly: Colonial Attitudes Toward the Native Americans.* Essay from Sarah Lawrence Faculty, vol. 2, no. 1. Bronxville, N.Y.: Sarah Lawrence College, 1973.

Barsh, Russel, and James Youngblood Henderson. *The Road: Indian Tribes and Political Liberty.* Berkeley: University of California Press, 1980.

Beal, Merrill. *I Will Fight No More Forever: Chief Joseph and the Nez Percé War.* Seattle: University of Washington Press, 1963. Reprint. New York: Ballantine Books, 1975.

Beck, Peggy. *The Sacred Ways of Knowledge.* Tsaile, Ariz.: Navajo Community College, 1977.

Bee, Robert L. *The Politics of American Indian Policy.* Cambridge, Mass.: Schenkman, 1982.

Berkhofer, Robert F., Jr. *The White Man's Indian: Images of the American Indian from Columbus to the Present.* New York: Alfred A. Knopf, 1978.

Billington, Ray Allen. *The Far Western Frontier, 1830–1860.* New York: Harper & Row, 1962.

Blumenthal, W. *American Indians Dispossessed: Fraud in Land Cessions Forced Upon the Tribes.* Philadelphia: G. S. MacManus, 1955.

Brookings Institution. *The Problem of Indian Administration.* 1928. Reprint. New York: Johnson Reprint, 1971.

Brooks, Harlow. "The Contributions of the Primitive American to Medicine." In *Medicine and Mankind,* edited by Iago Galdston. New York: D. Appleton-Century, 1936.

Brophy, William A., and Sophie D. Aberle, comps. *The Indian: America's Unfinished Business. Report of the Commission on the Rights, Liberties, and Responsibilities of the American Indian.* Norman: University of Oklahoma Press, 1966.

Brown, Dee. *Bury My Heart at Wounded Knee.* New York: Holt, Rinehart & Winston, 1971. Reprint. Bantam Books, 1972.

Brown, Joseph Epes, ed. *The Sacred Pipe: Black Elk's Account of the Seven Rites of the Oglala Sioux*. Norman: University of Oklahoma Press, 1953.

Burnette, Robert, and John Kaster. *The Road to Wounded Knee*. New York: Bantam Books, 1974.

Cahn, Edgar S., ed. *Our Brother's Keeper: The Indian in White America*. New York: World Publishing, 1969.

Calloway, Colin G. *New Directions in American Indian History*. D'Arcy McNickle Center Bibliographies in American Indian History. Norman: University of Oklahoma Press, 1988.

Canby, William C., Jr. *American Indian Law*. Minneapolis: West Publishing, 1981.

Capps, Ben. *The Great Chiefs*. The Old West Series. Alexandria, Va.: Time-Life Books, 1975.

Cohen, Felix S. *Handbook of Federal Indian Law, with Reference Tables and Index*. Washington, D.C.: U.S. Government Printing Office, 1942. Reprint. Albuquerque: University of New Mexico Press, 1971.

Colden, Cadwallader. *The History of the Five Indian Nations*. (Originally published in 1727.) Ithaca, N.Y.: Cornell University Press, 1958.

Collier, John. *The Indians of the Americas*. New York: W. W. Norton, 1947.

Corkran, David H. *The Creek Frontier, 1540–1783*. Norman: University of Oklahoma Press, 1967.

Costo, Rupert, ed., and Jeanette Henry. *Textbooks and the American Indian*. San Francisco: Indian Historian Press, 1970.

———. *Indian Treaties: Two Centuries of Dishonor*. San Francisco: Indian Historian Press, 1977.

Cotterill, R. S. *The Southern Indians: The Story of the Civilized Tribes Before Removal*. Norman: University of Oklahoma Press, 1954.

Crane, Leo. *Desert Drums: The Pueblo Indians of New Mexico*. Boston: Little, Brown, 1928.

Dale, Edward Everett. *The Indians of the Southwest: A Century of Development Under the United States*. Norman: University of Oklahoma Press, 1949.

Danziger, Edmund, Jr. *Indians and Bureaucrats: Administering the Reservation Policy During the Civil War*. Champaign: University of Illinois Press, 1974.

Daughtery, Richard. *The Yakima People*. Phoenix, Ariz.: Indian Tribal Series, 1973.

Debo, Angie. *The Rise and Fall of the Choctaw Republic*. Norman: University of Oklahoma Press, 1934.

———. *And Still the Waters Run: The Betrayal of the Five Civilized Tribes*. New York: Gordian Press, 1940. Reprint. Norman: University of Oklahoma Press, 1984.

———. *The Road to Disappearance: A History of the Creek Indians*. Norman: University of Oklahoma Press, 1941.

———. *A History of the Indians of the United States*. Norman: University of Oklahoma Press, 1970.

Deloria, Vine, Jr. *Custer Died for Your Sins: An Indian Manifesto*. New York: MacMillan, 1969. Reprint. Norman: University of Oklahoma Press, 1988.

————. *We Talk, You Listen: New Tribes, New Turf.* New York: MacMillan, 1970.

————. *Of Utmost Good Faith.* San Francisco: Straight Arrow Books, 1971.

————. *God Is Red.* New York: Grosset and Dunlap, 1973.

————. *Behind the Trail of Broken Treaties: An Indian Declaration of Independence.* New York: Delacorte, 1974.

DeMallie, Raymond, and Elaine Jahner, eds. *Lakota Belief and Ritual.* Lincoln: University of Nebraska Press, 1980.

DeMallie, Raymond. *Lakota Society.* Lincoln: University of Nebraska Press, 1982.

Dennis, Henry C., ed. *The American Indian, 1492–1976: A Chronology and Fact Book.* 2d ed., Dobbs Ferry, N.Y.: Oceana Publications, 1977.

DeRosier, Arthur H., Jr. *The Removal of the Choctaw Indians.* Knoxville: University of Tennessee Press, 1970. Reprint. New York: Harper & Row, Torchbooks, 1970.

Dobyns, Henry F., and Robert C. Euler. *Indians of the Southwest: A Critical Bibliography.* Bloomington: Indiana University Press, 1980.

Dockstader, Frederick J. *Great North American Indians: Profiles in Life and Leadership.* New York: Van Nostrand Reinhold, 1977.

Downey, Fairfox. *Indian Wars of the U.S. Army, 1776–1865.* Garden City, N.Y.: Doubleday, 1963.

Dozier, Edward P. "Rio Grande Pueblos." In *Perspectives in American Indian Culture Change,* edited by Edward H. Spicer, 94–186. Chicago: University of Chicago Press, 1961.

————. *The Pueblo Indians of North America.* New York: Holt, Rinehart & Winston, 1970.

————. *The Pueblo Indians of North America.* New York: Holt, Rinehart & Winston, 1970.

Drinnon, Richard. *Facing West: The Metaphysics of Indian Hating and Empire Building.* New York: New American Library, 1980.

Driver, Harold E. *Indians of North America,* 2d ed., rev. Chicago: University of Chicago Press, 1969.

Dunn, J. P., Fr. *Massacres of the Mountains: A History of Indian Wars of the Far West, 1815–75.* New York: Archer House, 1958.

Dutton, Bertha P. *Indians of the American Southwest.* Albuquerque: University of New Mexico Press, 1982.

Edmunds, R. David, ed. *American Indian Leaders: Studies in Diversity.* Lincoln: University of Nebraska Press, 1980.

Ellis, Richard N., ed. *The Western American Indian: Case Studies in Tribal History.* Lincoln: University of Nebraska Press, 1972.

Erdoes, Richard. *The Pueblo Indians.* New York: Funk & Wagnals, 1967.

————. *The Rain Dance People: The Pueblo Indians: Their Past and Present.* New York: Alfred A. Knopf, 1976.

Farb, Peter. *Man's Rise to Civilization as Shown by the Indians of North America.* New York: E. P. Dutton, 1968.

Fay, George Emory, ed. *Charters, Constitutions, and By-laws of the Indian Tribes of North America.* Museum of Anthropology, Occasional Publications in Anthropology, Ethnology Series, vols. 1–15. Greeley: University of Northern Colorado, 1967–1972.

Federal and State Indian Reservations and Indian Trust Areas. Washington, D.C.: U.S. Government Printing Office, 1974.

Fenton, William N., ed. *Parker on the Iroquois [Iroquois Uses of Maize and Other Food Plants; Code of Handsome Lake, the Seneca Prophet; Constitution of the Five Nations].* New York State Study Series. Syracuse, N.Y.: Syracuse University Press, 1968.

Fey, Harold, and D'Arcy McNickle. *Indians and Other Americans.* New York: Harper & Brothers, 1959.

Fixico, Donald L. *Termination and Relocation: Federal Indian Policy, 1945–1960.* Albuquerque: University of New Mexico Press, 1986.

Flexner, James. *Lord of the Mohawks: A Biography of Sir William Johnson.* Boston: Little, Brown, 1979.

Flexner, Stuart Berg. "Indians." In *I Hear American Talking: An Illustrated Treasury of American Words and Phrases,* 194–203. New York: Van Nostrand Reinhold, 1976.

Forbes, Jack D., ed. *The Indian in America's Past.* Englewood Cliffs, N.J.: Prentice-Hall, 1964.

Foreman, Grant. *Advancing the Frontier, 1830–1860.* Norman: University of Oklahoma Press, 1933.

———. *The Five Civilized Tribes.* Norman: University of Oklahoma Press, 1934.

———. *Indian Removal: The Emigration of the Five Civilized Tribes of Indians.* Norman: University of Oklahoma Press, 1953.

French, David. *Factionalism in Isleta Pueblo.* New York: J. J. Augustin, 1948.

Getches, David H., Daniel M. Rosenfelt, and Charles F. Wilkinson. *Federal Indian Law: Cases and Materials.* St. Paul, Minn.: West Publishing, 1978.

Gibson, Arrell Morgan. *The American Indian: Prehistory to the Present.* Lexington, Mass.: D. C. Heath & Co., 1980.

Gilbreath, Kent. *Red Capitalism: An Analysis of the Navajo Economy.* Norman: University of Oklahoma Press, 1973.

Graymont, Barbara. *The Iroquois in the American Revolution.* Syracuse, N.Y.: Syracuse University Press, 1972.

Green, Donald E. *The Creek People.* Phoenix, Ariz.: Indian Tribal Series, 1973.

Green, Michael D. *The Creeks: A Critical Bibliography.* Bloomington: Indiana University Press, 1979.

———. *The Politics of Indian Removal: Creek Government and Society in Crisis.* Lincoln: University of Nebraska Press, 1982.

Grinde, Donald A., Jr. *The Iroquois in the Founding of the American Nation.* San Francisco: Indian Historian Press, 1977.

Guie, H. Dean. *Tribal Days of the Yakima.* Yakima, Wash.: Republic Publishing, 1937.

Hagan, William T. *Indian Police and Judges: Experiments in Acculturation and Control.* New Haven, Conn.: Yale University Press, 1966.

———. *American Indians.* rev. ed. Chicago: University of Chicago Press, 1979.

Hall, Gilbert L. *The Federal-Indian Trust Relationship: Duty of*

Protection. Washington, D.C.: Institute for the Development of Indian Law, 1979.

Hamilton, Charles, ed. *Cry of the Thunderbird: The American Indian's Own Story*. Norman: University of Oklahoma Press, 1975.

Hamilton, Milton W. *Sir William Johnson and the Indians of New York*. Albany: New York State American Revolution Bicentennial Commission, 1975.

Harmon, G. D. *Sixty Years of Indian Affairs: Political, Economic and Diplomatic, 1789–1850*. Chapel Hill: University of North Carolina Press, 1941.

Hassrick, Royal B. *The Sioux: Life and Customs of a Warrior Society*. Norman: University of Oklahoma Press, 1964.

Hertzberg, Hazel W. *The Great Tree and the Longhouse: The Culture of the Iroquois*. New York: MacMillan, 1966.

———. *The Search for an American Indian Identity: Modern Pan-Indian Movements*. Syracuse, N.Y.: Syracuse University Press, 1971.

Hodge, Frederick W., ed. *Handbook of American Indians North of Mexico*. Vols. 1–2. Washington, D.C.: Smithsonian Institution, 1907–1910. Reprint. Westport, Conn.: Greenwood Press, 1970.

Hoebel, E. Adamson. *The Law of Primitive Man: A Study in Comparative Legal Dynamics*. Cambridge: Harvard University Press, 1964.

———. *The Plains Indians*. Bloomington: Indiana University Press, 1977.

Hoig, Stan. *The Sand Creek Massacre*. Norman: University of Oklahoma Press, 1961.

Holmes, Jack D. L. "Spanish Policy Toward the Southern Indians in the 1790s." In *Four Centuries of Southern Indians*, edited by Charles M. Hudson, 65–82. Athens: University of Georgia Press, 1975.

Hoover, Herbert. *The Sioux: A Critical Bibliography*. Bloomington: Indiana University Press, 1979.

Horowitz, David. *The First Frontier: The Indian Wars and America's Origins, 1601–1776*. New York: Simon & Schuster, 1978.

Hyde, George E. *Red Cloud's Folk: A History of the Oglala Sioux Indians*. Norman: University of Oklahoma Press, 1937.

———. *A Sioux Chronicle*. Norman: University of Oklahoma Press, 1956.

———. *Spotted Tail's Folk: A History of the Brule Sioux*. Norman: University of Oklahoma Press, 1961.

Indian Pueblo Cultural Center. *Our Land, Our Culture, Our Story*. Albuquerque, N. Mex.: 1977.

Indian Voices: The First Convocation of American Indian Scholars. San Francisco: Indian Historian Press, 1970.

Indian Voices: The Native American Today. San Francisco: Indian Historian Press, 1974.

Irvine, Kenneth, gen. ed. *Encyclopedia of Indians of the Americas*. St. Clair Shores, Mich.: Scholarly Press, 1974.

Irwin, Constance. *Strange Footprints in the Land: Vikings in America*. New York: Harper & Row, 1980.

Iverson, Peter. *The Navajos: A Critical Bibliography*. Bloomington: Indiana University Press, 1976.

Jackson, Curtis E., and Marcia J. Galli. *A History of the Bureau of
Indian Affairs and Its Activities Among Indians*. San Francisco:
R & E Research Associates, 1977.

Jacobs, Paul, et al. *To Serve the Devil*. Vol. 1, *Natives & Slaves*.
New York: Random House, 1971.

Jacobs, Wilbur. *Dispossessing the American Indian: Indians and
Whites on the Colonial Frontier*. New York: Charles Scribner's
Sons, 1972.

Jaenen, Cornelius J. *Friend and Foe: Aspects of French-Amer-
indian Cultural Contact in the Sixteenth and Seventeenth Centuries*. Toronto: McClelland and Stewart, 1976.

Jennings, Francis. *The Invasion of America: Indians, Colonialism,
and the Cant of Conquest*. Chapel Hill: University of North
Carolina Press, 1975.

Jones, Oakah L., Jr. *Pueblo Warriors and Spanish Conquest*.
Norman: University of Oklahoma Press, 1966.

Josephy, Alvin M., Jr., ed. *The Indian Heritage of America*. New
York: Alfred A. Knopf, 1970.

————. *Red Power: The American Indians' Fight for Freedom*.
New York: McGraw-Hill, 1971.

————. *The Patriot Chiefs: A Chronicle of American Indian Resistance*. New York: Penguin Books, 1978.

————, ed. *The American Heritage Book of Indians*. N.p.: American Heritage Publishing Co., 1982.

————. *Now That the Buffalo's Gone: A Study of Today's American
Indians*. New York: Alfred A. Knopf, 1982. Reprint. Norman:
University of Oklahoma Press, 1984.

Kappler, C. *Laws and Treaties*. Washington, D.C.: U.S. Government Printing Office, 1903.

Kickingbird, Kirke, and Karen Ducheneaux. *One Hundred Million Acres*. New York: Macmillan, 1973.

Kidwell, Clara Sue, and Charles Roberts. *The Choctaws: A Critical Bibliography*. Bloomington: Indiana University Press, 1981.

Kinney, J. P. *A Continent Lost—A Civilization Won: Indian Land
Tenure in America*. Baltimore, Md.: Johns Hopkins University
Press, 1937.

Klein, Barry T., ed. *Reference Encyclopedia of the American Indian*. 3d ed. 2 vols. Rye, N.Y.: Todd Publications, 1978.

Leach, Douglas E. *Flintlock and Tomahawk: New England in King
Philip's War*. New York: W. W. Norton, 1966.

Leacock, Eleanor Burke, and Nancy Oestreich Lurie, eds. *North
American Indians in Historical Perspective*. New York: Random
House, 1971.

Leitch, Barbara A. *Chronology of the American Indian*. St. Clair
Shores, Mich.: Scholarly Press, 1975.

————. *A Concise Dictionary of Indian Tribes of North America*.
Algonac, Mich.: Reference Publication, 1979.

Leland, Joy. *Firewater Myths: North American Indian Drinking
and Drug Addiction*. Rutgers, N.J.: Rutgers Center for Alcohol
Studies, 1976.

Levine, Stuart, and Nancy O. Lurie, eds. *The American Indian
Today*. Baltimore, Md.: Penguin Books, 1972.

Levitan, S. A., and B. Hetrick. *Big Brother's Indian Programs with Reservations*. New York: McGraw-Hill, 1971.

Liberty, Margot, ed. *American Indian Intellectuals*. St. Paul, Minn.: West Publishing, 1978.

Llewellyn, Karl N., and E. Adamson Hoebel. *The Cheyenne Way: Conflict and Case Law in Primitive Jurisprudence*. Norman: University of Oklahoma Press, 1941.

Lowie, Robert H. *Indians of the Plains*. Lincoln: University of Nebraska Press, 1982.

McKee, Jesse O., and Jon A. Schlenker. *The Choctaws: Cultural Evolution of a Native American Tribe*. Jackson: University Press of Mississippi, 1980.

McLuhan, T. C., comp. *Touch the Earth: A Self-Portrait of Indian Existence*. New York: Simon & Schuster, 1971.

McNickle, D'Arcy. *Native American Tribalism: Indian Survivals and Renewals*. New York: Oxford University Press, 1973.

————. *They Came Here First: The Epic of the American Indian*. rev. ed. New York: Harper & Row, Perennial Library, 1975.

MacWhorter, Lucuilus. *Crime Against the Yakima*. North Yakima, Wash.: Republic Print, 1913.

Maestas, John R. *Contemporary Native American Address*. Provo, Utah: Brigham Young University Press, 1976.

Mails, Thomas E. *Sundancing at Rosebud and Pine Ridge*. Sioux Falls, S. Dak.: Center for Western Studies, Augustana College, 1978.

Manypenny, George W. *Our Indian Wards*. New York: DeCapo Press, 1972.

Marhen, Jack, and Herbert Hoover. *Bibliography of the Sioux*. Metuchen, N.J.: Scarecrow Press, 1980.

Marquis, Arnold. *A Guide to America's Indians: Ceremonials, Reservations, and Museums*. Norman: University of Oklahoma Press, 1974.

Marx, Herbert L., Jr., ed. *The American Indian: A Rising Ethnic Force*. H. W. Wilson & Co., 1973.

Matthiessen, Peter. *In the Spirit of Crazy Horse*. New York: Viking Press, 1983.

Maxwell, James A., ed. *America's Fascinating Indian Heritage*. Reader's Digest Association, 1978.

Miller, Joaquin. *Unwritten History: Life Among the Modocs*. 1873. Reprint. Eugene, Oreg.: Orion Press, 1972.

Mohr, Walter H. *Federal Indian Relations, 1774–1788*. Philadelphia: University of Pennsylvania Press, 1933.

Morey, Sylvester M., ed. *Can the Red Man Help the White Man?* New York: Gilbert Church, 1970.

Morgan, Lewis Henry. *League of the Ho-De-No-Sau-Nee, or Iroquois*. Rochester, N.Y.: Sage and Brothers. Reprint. New Haven, Conn.: Human Relation Area Files, 1954.

Moquin, W., and C. Van Doren, eds. *Great Documents in American Indian History*. New York: Praeger, 1973.

Murdock, George Peter, and Timothy J. O'Leary. *Ethnographic Bibliography of North America*, 4th ed. Vol. 4, *Eastern United States*. New Haven, Conn.: Human Relations Area Files Press, 1975.

Murphy, James E., and Sharon M. Murphy. *Let My People Know:*

American Indian Journalism 1828–1978. Norman: University of Oklahoma Press, 1981.

Murray, Keith A. *The Modocs and Their War.* Norman: University of Oklahoma Press, 1959.

Nabokov, Peter., ed. *Native American Testimony: An Anthology of Indian and White Relations, First Encounter to Dispossession.* New York: Harper & Row, 1978.

Nammack, Georgiana C. *Fraud, Politics, and the Dispossession of the Indians: The Iroquois Land Frontier in the Colonial Period.* Norman: University of Oklahoma Press, 1969.

National Anthropological Archives, Smithsonian Institution. *Indian Images: Photographs of North American Indians, 1847-1928.* Washington, D.C.: U.S. Government Printing Office, 1971.

National Geographic Book Service. *The World of the American Indian.* Washington, D.C.: National Geographic Society, 1974.

National Lawyers Guild Committee on Native American Struggles, ed. and comp. *Rethinking Indian Law.* New Haven, Conn.: Advocate Press, 1981.

Neirns, Allen, and Henry Steele Commanger. *A Pocket History of the United States.* New York: Washington Square Press, 1981.

Neon, John A. *Law and Government of the Grand River Iroquois.* Johnson Reprint, 1949.

O'Kane, Walter C. *The Hopis: Portrait of a Desert People.* Norman: University of Oklahoma Press, 1953.

Olson, James C. *Red Cloud and the Sioux Problem.* Lincoln: University of Nebraska Press, 1965.

Ortiz, Alfonso, ed. *New Perspectives on the Pueblos.* School of American Research. Albuquerque: University of New Mexico Press, 1972.

Ortiz, Roxanne Dunbar. *The Great Sioux Nation: Sitting in Judgment on America.* Berkeley, Calif.: Moon Books, 1977.

———, ed. *Economic Development in American Indian Reservations.* Albuquerque: Native American Studies, University of New Mexico, 1979.

Otis, D. S. *The Dawes Act and the Allotment of Indian Land.* Norman: University of Oklahoma Press, 1973.

Paredes, J. Anthony. "Back from Disappearance: The Alabama Creek Indian Community." In *Southeastern Indians Since the Removal Era,* edited by Walter L. Williams, 123–141. Athens: University of Georgia Press, 1979.

Parker, Arthur C. *An Analytical History of the Seneca Indians.* Researches and Transactions of the New York State Archaeological Association, Lewis H. Morgan Chapter. Volume 6. Rochester, N.Y., 1926.

Parsons, E. C. *Isleta.* 47th Annual Report of Bureau of American Ethnology. Washington, D.C.: U.S. Government Printing Office, 1932.

Peckham, Howard, and Charles Gibson, eds. *Attitudes of Colonial Powers Toward the American Indian.* Salt Lake City: University of Utah Press, 1969.

Peterson, John H., Jr. "Three Efforts at Development Among the Choctaws of Mississippi." In *Southeastern Indians Since the Re-*

moval Era, edited by Walter L. Williams, 142–153. Athens: University of Georgia Press, 1979.

Pevar, Stephen. *The Rights of Indians and Tribes*. New York: Bantam Books, 1983.

Philp, Kenneth R. *John Collier's Crusade for Indian Reform, 1920–1954*. Tucson: University of Arizona Press, 1977.

Pommersheim, Frank. *Broken Ground and Flowing Waters: An Introductory Text*. Rosebud, S. Dak.: Sinte Gleska College Press, 1979.

————, and Anita Remerowski. *Reservation Street Law: A Handbook of Individual Rights and Responsibilities*. Rosebud, S. Dak.: Sinte Gleska College Press, 1979.

Powers, William. *Oglala Religion*. Lincoln: University of Nebraska Press, 1975.

Price, Monroe. *Law and the American Indian: Readings, Notes and Cases*. Contemporary Legal Education Series. New York: Bobbs-Merrill, 1973.

Prucha, Francis Paul. *American Indian Policy in the Formative Years: The Indian Trade and Intercourse Acts, 1790–1834*. Lincoln: University of Nebraska Press, 1970.

————., ed. *The Indian in American History*. New York: Holt, Rinehart & Winston, 1971.

————, ed. *Documents of United States Indian Policy*. Lincoln: University of Nebraska Press, 1975.

————. *American Indian Policy in Crisis: Christian Reformers and the Indian, 1865–1900*. Norman: University of Oklahoma Press, 1976.

————. *A Bibliographical Guide to the History of Indian-White Relations in the United States*. Chicago: University of Chicago Press, 1977.

————. *Indian-White Relations in the United States: A Bibliography of Works Published 1975–1980*. Lincoln: University of Nebraska Press, 1982.

————. *The Great Father: The United States Government and the American Indians*. 2 vols. Lincoln: University of Nebraska Press, 1984.

Reid, John Phillip. "A Perilous Rule: The Law of International Homicide." In *The Cherokee Indian Nation: A Troubled History*, edited by Duane H. King, 33–45. Knoxville: University of Tennessee Press, 1979.

Relander, Click. *Drummers and Dreamers*. Caldwell, Idaho: Caxton Printers, 1956.

Riddle, Jeff C. *The Indian History of the Modoc War and the Causes That Led to It*. San Francisco, 1914. Reprint. Medford, Oreg.: Pine Cone Publishers, 1973.

Royce, Charles C. *Land Cessions in the U.S.* 18th Annual Report of Bureau of American Ethnology, 1896–1897 (pt. 2). Washington, D.C.: U.S. Government Printing Office, 1899.

Ruby, Robert H., and John A. Brown. *Indians of the Pacific Northwest: A History*. Norman: University of Oklahoma Press, 1981.

Rydjord, John. *Indian Place-Names: Their Origin, Evolution, and Meanings*. Norman: University of Oklahoma Press, 1968.

Sabatini, J., ed. *American Indian Law: A Bibliography of Books,*

Law Review Articles, and Indian Periodicals. Albuquerque: American Indian Law Center, School of Law, University of New Mexico, 1973.

Sandner, Donald. *Navajo Symbols of Healing*. New York: Harcourt Brace Jovanovich, 1979.

Sando, Joe. *The Pueblo Indians*. San Francisco: Indian Historian Press, 1976.

Scherer, Joanna Cochan. *Indians: The Great Photographs that Reveal North American Indian Life, 1847–1929, from the Unique Collection of the Smithsonian Institution*. New York: Bonanza Books, 1982.

Schmeckebier, Laurence. *The Office of Indian Affairs: Its History, Activities and Organization*. Institute for Government Research. Service Monographs of the United States Government, No. 48. Baltimore: Johns Hopkins Press, 1927.

Schusky, Ernest. *The Right to be Indian*. San Francisco: Indian Historian Press, 1970.

————, ed. *Political Organization of Native North Americans*. Washington, D.C.: University Press of America, 1980.

Segal, Charles, and Avid Steinback, eds. *Puritans, Indians, and Manifest Destiny*. New York: G. P. Putnam's Sons, 1977.

Shames, Deborah, ed. *Freedom with Reservation: The Menominee Struggle to Save Their Land and People*. Madison, Wis.: National Committee to Save the Menominee People and Forests (Wisconsin Legal Services), 1972.

Shorris, Earl. *The Death of the Great Spirit: An Elegy for the American Indian*. New York: Mentor Books, 1971.

Smith, Edward C., and Arnold J. Zurcher. *Dictionary of American Politics*, 2d ed. New York: Barnes and Noble, 1968.

Smith, Jane F., and Robert M. Kvasnicka, eds. *Indian-White Relations: A Persistent Paradox*. Washington, D.C.: Howard University Press, 1976.

Sorkin, A. *American Indians and Federal Aid*. Washington, D.C.: Brookings Institution, 1971.

Spencer, Robert F., et al. *The Native Americans: Ethnology and Backgrounds of the North American Indians*. New York: Harper & Row, 1977.

Spicer, Edward H. *A Short History of the Indians of the United States*. New York: Van Nostrand Reinhold, 1969.

————. *Cycles of Conquest: The Impact of Spain, Mexico, and the United States on the Indians of the Southwest, 1533–1960*. Tucson: University of Arizona Press, 1972.

————. "American Indians." In *Harvard Encyclopedia of American Ethnic Groups*, edited by Stephan Thernstrom, Ann Orlov, and Oscar Handlin, 58–114. Cambridge: Harvard University Press, 1980.

Spindler, George, and Louise Spindler. *Dreamers Without Power: The Menominee Indians*. New York: Holt, Rinehart & Winston, 1971.

Splawn, Andrew Jackson. *Ka-mi-akin: The Last Hero of the Yakimas*. Portland, Oreg.: Kilham Stationery and Print Co., 1917.

Steiner, Stan. *The New Indians*. New York: Harper & Row, 1968.

Strickland, Rennard. *Fire and the Spirits: Cherokee Law from Clan to Court*. Norman: University of Oklahoma Press, 1975.

————. *The Indians in Oklahoma*. Norman: University of Oklahoma Press, 1980.

Sturtevant, William C., gen. ed. *Handbook of North American Indians*. Vol. 8, *California*. Vol. 9, *Southwest*. Vol. 15, *Northeast*. Washington, D.C.: Smithsonian Institution, 1978–1979.

Swanton, John R. *Early History of the Creek Indians and their Neighbors*. Bureau of American Ethnology Bulletin 73. Washington, D.C.: U.S. Government Printing Office, 1922.

————. *Indian Tribes of North America*. Washington, D.C.: U.S. Government Printing Office, 1952.

Symposium on Local Diversity in Iroquois Culture. Bureau of American Ethnology Bulletin 149. Washington, D.C.: U.S. Government Printing Office, 1951.

Szasz, Margaret. *Education and the American Indian: The Road to Self-Determination*. Albuquerque: University of New Mexico Press, 1974.

Taylor, Theodore W. *The States and their Indian Citizens*. Washington, D.C.: U.S. Government Printing Office, 1972.

Tebbel, John, and Keith Jennison. *The American Indian Wars*. New York: Harper & Brothers, 1960.

Terrell, John Upton. *American Indian Almanac*. New York: World Publishing, 1971.

Tooker, Elizabeth. *The Indians of the Northeast*. Bloomington: Indiana University Press, 1978.

Turner, Frederick W., 3rd, ed. *The Portable North American Indian Reader*. New York: Viking Press, 1974.

Tyler, L. *A History of Indian Policy*. Washington, D.C.: U.S. Government Printing Office, 1973.

Underhill, Ruth M. *The Navajos*. Norman: University of Oklahoma Press, 1956.

————. *Red Man's America: A History of the Indians in the United States*. rev. ed. Chicago: University of Chicago Press, 1971.

Upton, Helen. *The Everett Report in Historical Perspective: The Indians of New York*. Albany, N.Y.: New York State American Revolution Bicentennial Commission, 1980.

U.S. Department of the Interior, Bureau of Indian Affairs. *Federal Indian Policies: From the Colonial Period Through the Early 70s*. Washington, D.C.: U.S. Government Printing Office, 1973.

Utley, Robert M. *The Last Days of the Sioux Nation*. New Haven, Conn.: Yale University Press, 1963.

————. *Frontier Regulars: The United States Army and the Indian*. New York: Macmillan, 1973.

Vanderwerth, W. C., comp. *Indian Oratory: Famous Speeches by Noted Indian Chieftains*. Norman: University of Oklahoma Press, 1971.

Vaughan, Alden T. *New England Frontier: Puritans and Indians, 1620–1675*. Little, Brown, 1965.

Vecsey, Christopher, and Robert Venables, eds. *American Indian Environments: Ecological Issues in Native American History*. Syracuse, N.Y.: Syracuse University Press, 1980.

Vestal, Stanley. *Warpath and Council Fire: The Plains Indians' Struggle for Survival in War and in Diplomacy, 1851–1891*. New York: Random House, 1948.

————. *Sitting Bull, Champion of the Sioux: A Bibliography*. Norman: University of Oklahoma Press, 1957.

Vogel, Virgil J. *American Indian Medicine*. Norman: University of Oklahoma Press, 1970.

————. *This Country Was Ours: A Documentary History of the American Indian*. Harper & Row, 1972.

Waddell, Jack, and Michael Everett. *Drinking Behavior among Southwestern Indians*. Tuscon: University of Arizona Press, 1980.

Waldman, Harry, ed. *Dictionary of Indians of North America*. 3 vols. St. Clair Shores, Mich.: Scholarly Press, 1978.

Wallace, Anthony F. C. *The Death and Rebirth of the Seneca*. New York: Alfred A. Knopf, 1969.

Wardell, Morris. *A Political History of the Cherokee Nation, 1838–1907*. Norman: University of Oklahoma Press, 1938. Reprinted with new foreword, 1977.

Washburn, Wilcomb E. *The Indian and the White Man*. 1964. Reprint. Garden City, N.Y.: Doubleday, 1971.

————. *Red Man's Land/White Man's Law: A Study of the Past and Present Status of the American Indian*. New York: Charles Scribner's Sons, 1971.

————, ed. *The American Indian and the United States: A Documentary History*. New York: Random House, 1974.

————. *The Indian in America*. New York: Harper & Row, 1975.

Weems, John Edward. *Death Song: The Last of the Indian Wars*. Garden City, N.Y.: Doubleday, 1976.

Williams, Aubrey. *Navajo Political Process*. Washington, D.C.: Smithsonian Institution Press, 1970.

Williams, Walter, ed. *Southeastern Indians Since the Removal Era*. Athens: University of Georgia Press, 1979.

Wilson, Edmund. *Apologies to the Iroquois*. New York: Vintage Books, 1960.

Wise, Jennings C. *The Red Man in the New World Drama: A Politico-Legal Study with a Pageantry of American History*. Washington: W. F. Roberts, 1931. Rev. ed. with Vine Deloria, Jr. New York: Macmillan, 1971.

Wissler, Clark. *Indians of the United States: Four Centuries of Their History and Culture*. 1946. Rev. ed. edited by Lucy W. Kluckhohn, Garden City, N.Y.: Doubleday, 1966.

Worcester, Donald, ed. *Forked Tongues and Broken Treaties*. Caldwell, Idaho: Caxton Printers, 1975.

Wright, Muriel H. *Guide to the Indian Tribes of Oklahoma*. Norman: University of Oklahoma Press, 1951.

Young, Robert. *A Political History of the Navajo Tribe*. Tsaile, Ariz. Navajo Community College Press, 1978.

Zinn, Howard. *A People's History of the United States*. New York: Haper & Row, 1980.

Articles

Abler, Thomas S. "Friends, Factions, and the Seneca Nation Revolution of 1848." *Niagara Frontier* 21 (Winter 1974): 74–79.

Applen, Allen G. "An Attempted Indian State Government: The

Okmulgee Constitution in Indian Territory, 1870–1876." *Kansas Quarterly* 3 (Fall 1971):89–99.

"Arizona Project Helps Elderly Native Americans Sustain Tribal Heritage." *Aging* 263 (September 1976):7–8.

Barsh, Russel Lawrence. "Issues in Federal, State, and Tribal Taxation of Reservation Wealth: A Survey and Economic Critique." *Washington Law Review* 54 (June 1979):531–86.

———, and J. Youngblood Henderson. "Tribal Courts, the Model Code, and the Police Idea in American Indian Policy." *Law and Contemporary Problems* 40 (Winter 1976):25–60.

Beatly, Willard W. "Some Indian Contributions to Our Culture." *Childhood Education* 18 (April 1942):353–56.

Berkey, Curtis. "The Legislative History of the Indian Reorganization Act." *American Indian Journal* 2 (July 1976):15–22.

———. "Implementation of the Indian Reorganization Act." *American Indian Journal* 2 (August 1976):2–7.

Berkhofer, Robert F., Jr. "Faith and Factionalism Among the Senecas: Theory and Ethnohistory." *Ethnohistory* 12 (Spring 1965):99–112.

"Bingo is the Best Revenge." *Time* 116 (July 7, 1980):18.

Brakel, Samuel J. "American Indian Tribal Courts: Separate? 'Yes,' Equal? 'Probably Not.'" *American Bar Association Journal* 62 (August 1976):1002–1006.

Brown, Janet W. "Native American Contributions to Science, Engineering, and Medicine." *Science* 189 (July 4, 1975):38–40.

Burke, Joseph C. "The Cherokee Cases: A Study in Law, Politics, and Morality." *Stanford Law Review* 21 (February 1969):500–31.

Burnett, Donald L., Jr. "An Historical Analysis of the 1968 'Indian Civil Rights' Act." *Harvard Journal of Legislation* 9 (May 1972):557–626.

Camazine, Scott. "Traditional and Western Health Care Among the Zuni Indians of New Mexico." *Social Science and Medicine, Medical Anthropology*, 14B (February 1980):73–80.

Canby, William C., Jr. "Civil Jurisdiction and the Indian Reservation." *Utah Law Review* (1973):206–32.

Chamberlain, Alexander F. "The Contributions of the American Indian to Civilization." *Proceedings of the American Antiquarian Society* 16 (October 1903):91–126.

Chambers, Reid Peyton. "Judicial Enforcement of the Federal Trust Responsibility to Indians." *Stanford Law Review* 27 (May 1975):1213–48.

Champion, Walter, Jr. "The Road to Destruction: The Effect of the French and Indian War on the Six Nations." *Indian Historian* 10 (Summer 1977):20–33.

Clinton, Robert N. "Development of Criminal Jurisdiction over Indian Lands: The Historical Perspective." *Arizona Law Review* 17 (no. 4, 1975):951–91.

———. "Criminal Jurisdiction over Indian Lands: A Journey Through a Jurisdictional Maze." *Arizona Law Review* 18 (no. 3, 1976):503–83.

Coburn, Joe. "A Community-Based Indian Curriculum Devel-

opment Program." *Educational Leadership* 34 (January 1977):
284–87.

Cohen, Felix. "Indian Rights and the Federal Courts." *Minnesota
Law Review* 24 (January 1940):145–200.

————. "The Spanish Origin of Indian Rights in the Law of the
United States." *Georgetown Law Journal* 31 (November 1942):
1–21.

————. "How We Bought the United States." *Collier's* 117
(January 19, 1946):22–23, 62.

————. "Original Indian Title." *Minnesota Law Review* 32 (December 1947):28–59.

————. "Americanizing the White Man." *American Scholar* 21
(Spring 1952):177–91.

————. "The Erosion of Indian Rights, 1950–1953: A Case
Study in Bureaucracy." *Yale Law Journal* 62 (February 1953):
348–90.

Collins, Richard B., Ralph W. Johnson, and Kathy Imig Per-
kins. "American Indian Courts and Tribal Self-Government."
American Bar Association Journal 63 (June 1977):808–15.

Copway, George. "End of the Trail: Continual Relocation of Indians in 19th Century." *Saturday Evening Post* 248 (July
1976):25.

Dearmin, Evelyn Titus. "Project Paiute." *Journal of American Indian Education* 17 (October 1977):1–10.

Deloria, Vine, Jr. "Indian Law and the Reach of History." *Journal
of Contemporary Law* 4 (Winter 1977):1–13.

DeMallie, Raymond J. "American Indian Treaty Making: Motives
and Meanings." *American Indian Journal* 3 (January 1977):
2–10.

De Raisnes, Joseph. "Indian Civil Rights Act of 1968 and the
Pursuit of Responsible Tribal Self-Government." *South Dakota Law Review* 20 (Winter 1975):59–106.

Downs, Ernest. "How the East Was Lost." *American Indian Journal* 1 (no. 2, 1975):6–10.

Ducheneaux, Franklin."The Cheyenne River Sioux." *American
Indian* 7 (Spring 1956):20–30.

————. "The Indian Reorganization Act and the Cheyenne
River Sioux." *American Indian Journal* 2 (August 1976):8–14.

"Eastern Indian Land Claims Bill." Native American Rights
Fund *Announcements* 8 (Spring 1982):1–3.

Edwards, Everett. "American Indian Contributions to Civilization." *Minnesota History* 15 (September 1934):255–72.

Euler, Robert C., and Henry F. Dobyns. "Ethnic Group Land
Rights in the Modern State: Three Case Studies." *Human Organization* 20 (Winter 1961–62):203–207.

Fahey, Richard P. "Native American Justice: The Courts of the
Navajo Nation." *Judicature* 59 (June–July 1975):10–17.

Fairbanks, Robert A. "The Cheyenne and Their Law: A Positivist
Inquiry." *Arkansas Law Review* 32 (Fall 1978):403–45.

Fannin, Paul. "Indian Health Care: A Real Health Care Crisis."
Arizona Medicine 32 (September 1975):741–47.

Fenton, William. "Toward the Gradual Civilization of the Indian Natives: The Missionary and Linguistic Work of Asher

Wright (1803–1875) Among the Senecas of Western New York." *Proceedings of the American Philosophical Society* 100 (December 19, 1956):567–81.

Foreman, Carolyn Thomas. "Alexander McGillivray, Emperor of the Creeks." *Chronicles of Oklahoma* 7 (March 1929):106–20.

———. "The Light Horse in the Indian Territory." *Chronicles of Oklahoma* 34 (Spring 1956):17–43.

Franks, Kenny A. "The Implementation of the Confederate Treaties with the Five Civilized Tribes." *Chronicles of Oklahoma* 51 (Spring 1973):21–33.

French, Laurence. "The Death of a Nation." *American Indian Journal* 4 (June 1978):2–9.

———, and Jim Hornbuckle. "Alcoholism Among Native Americans: An Analysis." *Social Work* 25 (July 1980):275–80.

Friedman, Emily. "The Possible Dream: The Navajo Nation Health Foundation." *Hospitals* 53 (October 16, 1979):81–84.

Furman, Necah. "Technological Change and Industrialization Among the Southern Pueblo." *Ethnohistory* 22 (Winter 1975):1–14.

Garry, William C. "Jurisdictional Confusion on the Cheyenne River Indian Reservation: United States v. Dupris." *South Dakota Law Review* 25 (Spring 1980):335–71.

Giacalone, Joseph, and James L. Hudson. "A Health Status Assessment System for a Rural Navajo Population." *Medical Care* 13 (September 1975):722–35.

Gibson, Arrell Morgan. "America's Exiles." *Chronicles of Oklahoma* 54 (Spring 1976):3–15.

Gill, E. Ann. "An Analysis of the 1868 Oglala Sioux Treaty and the Wounded Knee Trial." *Columbia Journal of Transnational Law* 14 (no. 1, 1975):119–46.

Goldberg, Carole E. "Public Law 280: The Limits of State Jurisdiction over Reservation Indians." *UCLA Law Review* 22 (February 1975):535–94.

———. "A Dynamic View of Tribal Jurisdiction to Tax Non-Indians." *Law and Contemporary Problems* 40 (Winter 1976):166–89.

Graymont, Barbara. "New York State Indian Policy after the Revolution." *New York History* 57 (October 1976):438–74.

Gross, Michael P. "Indian Self-Determination and Tribal Sovereignty: An Analysis of Recent Federal Indian Policy." *Texas Law Review* 56 (August 1978):1195–244.

Haas, Theodore H. "The Legal Aspects of Indian Affairs from 1887 to 1957." *Annals of the American Academy of Political and Social Science* 311 (May 1957):12–22.

Haley, J. L. "Prelate to War: The Slaughter of the Buffalo: Red River War, 1874–1875." *American Heritage* 27 (February 1976):36–41.

Hall, Arthur H. "The Red Stick War: Creek Indian Affairs During the War of 1812." *Chronicles of Oklahoma* 12 (September 1934):264–93.

Hamilton, Milton W. "Sir William Johnson: Interpreter of the Iroquois." *Ethnohistory* 10 (Summer 1963):270–86.

Hauptman, Laurence. "Senecas and Subdividers Resistence to Allotment of Indian Lands in New York, 1875–1906." *Prologue* 9 (Summer 1977):105–16.

Havighurst, R. J. "Indian Education: Accomplishments of the Last Decade." *Phi Delta Kappan* 62 (January 1981):329–31.

Hawley, Florence. "Pueblo Social Organization as a Lead to Pueblo History." *American Anthropologist* 39 (1937):504–22.

———. "An Examination of Problems Basic to Acculturation in the Rio Grande Pueblos." *American Anthropologist* 50 (October–December 1948):612–24.

Heidenreich, C. Adrian. "Alcohol and Drug Use and Abuse Among Indian-Americans: A Review of Issues and Sources." *Journal of Drug Issues* 6 (Summer 1976): 256–72.

Herzberg, Stephen J. "The Menominee Indians: Termination to Restoration." *American Indian Law Review* 6 (no. 1, 1978): 143–204.

Hoebel, E. Adamson. "The Problem of Iroquois Law and Order." *American Indian* 2 (Spring 1945):12–20.

"The Indian Bill of Rights and the Constitutional Status of Tribal Governments." *Harvard Law Review* 82 (April 1969): 1343–73.

"Indian Givings." *Saturday Review* 5 (November 25, 1978): 28–32.

"The Indian Question, 1823–1973: 150 Years of White Attitude Toward the American Indian." *North American Review* (A Special "Heritage" Issue) 25 (Winter 1973).

"Indian Water Rights, Issue for the '80s." *Native American Rights Fund Announcements* 7 (December 1981):1–6.

Isaacs, Hope L. "American Indian Medicine and Contemporary Health Problems, Pt. 1: Toward Improved Health Care for Native Americans, Comparative Perspective on American Indian Medicine Concepts." *New York State Journal of Medicine* 78 (April 1978):824–29.

Israel, Daniel H., and Thomas L. Smithson. "Indian Taxation, Tribal Sovereignty, and Economic Development." *North Dakota Law Review* 49 (Winter 1973):267–301.

Jacobs, Wilbur. "Wampum: The Protocol of Indian Diplomacy." *William and Mary Quarterly* 3rd ser., 6 (October 1949): 596–604.

———. "The Indian Frontier of 1763." *Western Pennsylvania Historical Magazine* 34 (September 1951):185–98.

———. "Native American History: How it Illuminates Our Past." *American History Review* 80 (June 1975):595–609.

———. "Descanosora: A Note on Cadwallader Colden's Concept of the Iroquois." *Indian Historian* 8 (Summer 1975): 185–98.

Jennings, Francis. "The Constitutional Evolution of the Covenant Chain." *Proceedings of the American Philosophical Society* 115 (April 1971):88-96.

Johansen, B. "Indians for Sovereignty: The Reservation Offensive." *Nation* 226 (February 25, 1978):204–207.

Johnson, Kenneth W. "Sovereignty, Citizenship, and the Indian." *Arizona Law Review* 15 (1973):973–1003.

Kahn, Marvin, et al. "The Papago Psychology Service: A Community Mental Health Program on an American Indian Reservation." *American Journal of Community Psychology* 3 (June 1975):81–97.

Kawashima, Yasuhide. "Legal Origins of the Indian Reservation in Colonial Massachusetts." *American Journal of Legal History* 13 (January 1969):42–56.

Kellogg, Mark. "Indian Rights: Fighting Back with White Man's Weapons." *Saturday Review* (November 25, 1978):24–27.

Kennedy, Gary D. "Tribal Elections: An Appraisal after the Indian Civil Rights Act." *American Indian Law Review* 3 (no. 2, 1975):497–508.

Kickingbird, Kirke. "A Short History of Indian Education." *American Indian Journal* 1 (December 1975):2–15.

———. "'In Our Image . . . After our Likeness': The Drive for the Assimilation of Indian Court Systems." *American Criminal Law Review* 13 (Spring 1976):675–700.

Kickingbird, Lynn. "Attitudes Toward the Indian Reorganization Bill." *American Indian Journal* 2 (July 1976):8–14.

Kinnaird, Lawrence. "Spanish Treaties with Indian Tribes." *Western Historical Quarterly* 10 (January 1979):39–48.

Kleber, L. C. "Religion Among the American Indians."*History Today* 28 (February 1978):81–87.

Kniep-Hardy, Mary. "Nursing the Navajo." *American Journal of Nursing* 77 (January 1977):95–96.

Larson, J. K. "And Then There Were None: Indian Health Service's Sterilization Practices." *Christian Century* 94 (January 26, 1977):61–63.

Leland, Joy. "Alcohol, Anthropologists, and Native Americans." *Human Organization* 38 (Spring 1979):94–99.

Levenson, Dorothy. "Hopi Schooling for Two Worlds." *Teacher* 93 (November 1975):63–65.

Losada, A. "Bartolomé de las Casas: Champion of Indian Rights in 16th-Century Spanish America." *UNESCO Courier* 28 (June 1975):4–10.

Lucke, Thomas W., Jr. "Indian Law: Recognition of a Field of Values." *Indian Historian* 10 (Spring 1977):43–47.

Lujan, Philip, and L. Brooks Hill. "The Mississippi Choctaw: A Case Study of Tribal Identity Problems." *American Indian Culture and Research Journal* 4 (no. 3, 1980):37–53.

McCoy, Robert G. "The Doctrine of Tribal Sovereignty: Accommodating Tribal, State, and Federal Interests." *Harvard Civil Rights Law Review* 13 (Spring 1978):357–423.

McLaughlin, Robert. "Giving It Back to the Indians." *Atlantic* 239 (February 1977):70–85.

McNickle, D'Arcy. "Indian and European: Indian-White Relations from Discovery to 1887." *Annals of the American Academy of Political and Social Science* 311 (May 1957):1–11.

Mail, Patricia. "Hippocrates Was a Medicine Man." *Annals of the American Academy of Political and Social Science* 436 (March 1978):40–49.

Margolis, Richard J. "Red-White Relations." *New Leader* 61 (April 10, 1978):17–18.

Mater, Milton H., and Jean Mater. "American Indian Forests." *American Forests* 82 (July 1976):36–39.

Mayneg, Patrick. "Pueblo Indian Water Rights: Who Will Get the Water?, *New Mexico* v. *Aamodt*." *Natural Resources Journal* 18 (July 1978):639–58.

Medicine, Bea. "Self-Direction in Sioux Education." *Integrated Education* 13 (November–December 1975):15–17.

Meinhardt, Nick, and Diane Payne. "Reviewing U.S. Treaty Commitments to the Lakota Nation." *American Indian Journal* 4 (January 1978):2–12.

Mekeel, Scudder. "A Short History of the Teton Dakota." *North Dakota Historical Quarterly* 10 (July 1943):137–205.

Melton, M. "War Trail of the Red Sticks: Creek Indians." *American History Illustrated* 10 (February 1976):32–42.

Miles, George. "A Brief Study of Joseph Brandt's Political Career in Relation to Iroquois Political Structure." *American Indian Journal* 2 (December 1976):12–20.

Mills, C. P., Jr. "Effective Management Puts an Indian Housing Authority on the Road to Sound Practices." *Journal of Housing* 36 (June 1979):310–11.

Monguia, Anna R. "The Pequot War Reexamined." *American Indian Culture and Research Journal* 1 (no. 3, 1975):13–21.

Moore, J. H. "Racism and Fishing Rights: Michigan." *Nation* 225 (September 17, 1977):236–38.

Morton, Ohland. "The Government of the Creek Indians." Parts 1, 2. *Chronicles of Oklahoma* 8 (March 1930):42–64; (June 1930):189–225.

Mulligan, Wallace J. "The Navajo Nation Health Foundation: The Sequel to Salzburg." *Arizona Medicine* 33 (January 1976):52–54.

———. "Letter: 'Western' Health Care for Southwest Indians." *New England Journal of Medicine* 295 (August 12, 1976):454.

Nafziger, Rich. "A Violation of Trust?: Federal Management of Indian Timber Lands." *Indian Historian* 9 (Fall 1976):15–23.

Nequatewa, Edmund. *Museum Notes* 5 (no. 7, 1933):41–54.

Nolen, Curtis L. "The Okmulgee Constitution: A Step Toward Indian Self-Determination." *Chronicles of Oklahoma* 58 (Fall 1980):264–81.

Norgren, Jill, and Petra Shattuck. "Black Hills Whitewash. *Nation* 230 (May 10, 1980):577–60.

Officer, James E. "The Bureau of Indian Affairs Since 1945: An Assessment." *Annals of the American Academy of Political and Social Science* 436 (March 1978):61–72.

Olguin, John Phillip, and Mary T. Olguin. "Isleta—The Pueblo That Roared." *Indian Historian* 9 (Fall 1976):2–13.

Opler, Morris E. "The Creek Indian Towns of Oklahoma in 1937." *Papers in Anthropology* (University of Oklahoma) 13 (Spring 1972):165–80.

Ortiz, Roxanne. "Roots of Resistence: Pueblo Land Tenure and Spanish Colonization." *Journal of Ethnic Studies* 5 (Winter 1978):33–53.

———. "Wounded Knee 1890 to Wounded Knee 1973: A Study in United States Colonialism." *Journal of Ethnic Studies* 8 (Summer 1980):1–15.

Page, Jake. "Inside the Sacred Hopi Homeland." *National Geographic* 162 (no. 5, November 1982):606–29.

Page, James K., Jr. "Rebellious Pueblos Outwitted Spain Three Centuries Ago." *Smithsonian* 11 (October 1980):86–90.

Painter, Levinus K. "The Seneca Nation and the Kinzua Dam." *Niagara Frontier* 17 (Summer 1970):30–35.

Palma, Jack D., 2d. "The Winters Doctrine and the Greening of the Reservation." *Journal of Contemporary Law* 4 (Winter 1977):19–37.

Parker, Arthur. "The Senecas in the War of 1812." *Proceedings of the New York State Historical Association* 15 (1916):78–90.

Parsons, E. C. "The Laguna Migration to Isleta." *American Anthropologist* 30 (1928):602–13.

Pennington, Robert. "An Analysis of the Political Structure of the Teton-Dakota Indian Tribe of North America." *North Dakota History* 20 (July 1953):143–55.

Petete, Irving. "Science and Mythology Manage a Forest." *American Forests* 62 (September 1956):54–56.

Petros, Lynne E. "The Applicability of the Federal Pollution Acts to Indian Reservations: A Case for Tribal Self-Government." *University of Colorado Law Review* 48 (Fall 1976):63–93.

Pilling, Arnold R. "Native American Religious Rights: Constitutional Considerations." *Indian Historian* 12 (Winter 1979): 13–19.

Primeaux, Martha. "American Indian Health Care Practices: A Cross Cultural Perspective." *Nursing Clinics of North America* 12 (March 1977):55–65.

"Projects in Nevada Succeed in Helping Indians Help Themselves." *Aging* 263 (September 1976):18–20.

Reid, John Phillip. "The European Perspective and Cherokee Law." *Appalachian Journal* 2 (Summer 1975):286–93.

Rhoades, Everett. "Barriers to Health Care: The Unique Problems Facing American Indians." *Civil Rights Digest* 10 (Fall 1977):25–31.

Rice, Jon. "Health Conditions of Native Americans in the 20th Century." *Indian History* 10 (Fall 1977):14–18.

Rivers, Theodore John. "A Study of the Laws of the Ottawa Indians As Preserved in the *Ottawa First Book* (1850)." *Kansas Historical Quarterly* 42 (Autumn 1975):225–36.

Roberts, G. L. "Chief of State and the Chief: Negotiating with the Creek Indians, 1789." *American Heritage* 26 (October 1975):28–33, 86–89.

Robertson, Alice M. "The Creek Indian Council in Session." *Chronicles of Oklahoma* 11 (September 1933): 895–98.

Rogal, K. C. "Indians and Ranchers: Bad Days on the Reservation—White Ownership of Land Within Pine Ridge." *Nation* 223 (November 30, 1976):525–30.

Ryan, Joe. "Compared to Other Nations." *American Indian Journal* 3 (August 1977):2–13.

Sigleman, Lee, and Robert Carter. "American Indians in the Political Kingdom: A Note on the BIA." *Administration and Society* 8 (November 1976):343–54.

Simmons, Bradford. "Surgical Services in a Navajo Indian Hospital." *Western Journal of Medicine* 125 (November 1976): 407–10.

Spoehr, Alexander. "Creek Inter-Town Relations." *American Anthropologist* 43 (1941):132–33.

Stanley, George F. G. "The Significance of the Six Nations' Participation in the War of 1812." *Ontario History* 55 (December 1963):215–31.

Streit, Fred, and Mark J. Nicolich. "Myths Versus Data on American Indian Drug Abuse." *Journal of Drug Education* 7 (no. 2, 1977):117–22.

Sturtevant, William C. "Spanish-Indian Relations in Southeastern North America." *Ethnohistory* 9 (Winter 1962):41–94.

Swanson, Charles. "The Treatment of the American Indian in High School History Texts." *Indian Historian* 10 (Spring 1977):28–37.

"Systematic Discrimination in the Indian Claims Commission: The Burden of Proof in Redressing Historical Wrongs." *Iowa Law Review* 57 (June 1972):1300–19.

Szasz, Margaret. "The American Indian and the Classical Past." *Midwest Quarterly* 17 (October 1975):58–70.

Underhill, Lonnie E. "Hamlin Garland and the Final Council of the Creek Nation." *Journal of the West* 10 (July 1971):511–20.

"Upgrading Indian Education: A Case Study of the Seminoles." *School Review* 83 (February 1975):345–61.

Viola, Herman J. "Indians Braved Washington to See the Great Father." *Smithsonian* 12 (April 1981):72–80.

Vollmann, Tim. "A Survey of Eastern Indian Land Claims: 1970–1979." *Maine Law Review* 31 (no. 1, 1979):5–16.

Washburn, Wilcomb E. "The Historical Context of American Indian Legal Problems." *Law and Contemporary Problems* 40 (Winter 1976):12–24.

Wasser, M. "Six Nations and the State: Policy Towards Indians in New York State." *Conservationist* 30 (January 1976):36–37.

Watson, Thomas D. "Strivings for Sovereignty: Alexander McGillivray, Creek Warfare, and Diplomacy, 1783–1790." *Florida Historical Quarterly* 58 (April 1980):400–14.

Whitner, Robert. "Grant's Indian Peace Policy on the Yakima Reservation, 1870–1882." *Pacific Northwest Quarterly* 50 (October 1959):135–42.

Wilkinson, Charles F., and Eric R. Biggs. "Evolution of the Termination Policy." *American Indian Law Review* 5 (no. 1, 1977):139–84.

———, and John M. Volkman. "Judicial Review of Indian Treaty Abrogation: 'As Long As Water Flows, or Grass Grows upon the Earth'—How Long a Time is That?" *California Law Review* 63 (May 1975):601–61.

Wilkinson, Dave. "The Modoc Indian War." *American History Illustrated* 13 (August 1978):18–30.

Williams, A. M. "A Grand Council at Okmulgee." *Lippincott's Magazine* 24 (September 1879):371–75.

Wright, J. Leitch, Jr. "Creek-American Treaty of 1790: Alexander McGillivray and the Diplomacy of the Old Southwest." *Georgia Historical Quarterly* 51 (December 1967):379–400.

Wright, Muriel H. "The Great Seal of the Muscogee Nation." *Chronicles of Oklahoma* 34 (Spring 1956):2–6.

Young, Mary E. "The Creek Frauds: A Study in Conscience and Corruption." *Mississippi Valley Historical Review* 42 (December 1955):411–37.

Monographs, Reports, and Pamphlets

American Indian Lawyer Training Program. *Indian Tribes as Governments*. rev. ed. New York: John Hay Whitney Foundation, 1975.

Arizona Office of Economic Planning and Development, Indian Planning Program. *Critical Issues in Indian-State Relations*. Phoenix, Ariz., 1981.

Barsh, Russel (under the supervision of the state superintendent of public instruction, Washington State). *Understanding Indian Treaties*. 1978.

Beauchamp, William M. *A History of the New York Iroquois, Now Commonly Called the Six Nations*. New York State Museum Bulletin 76. Albany, 1905.

Civil, Religious, and Mourning Councils and Ceremonies of the Adoption of the New York Indians. New York State Museum Bulletin 113. Reprint. Albany: University of the State of New York, 1975.

Council of Energy Resource Tribes. *CERT Report*. Washington, D.C. (various issues).

Deskaheh: Iroquois Statesman and Patriot. Six Nations Indian Museum Series. Rooseveltown, N.Y.: n.d.

Drumm, Judith. *Iroquois Culture Educational Leaflet*. State Museum and Science Service, no. 5. Albany: University of the State of New York, n.d.

Indian Committee of the Philadelphia Yearly Meeting of the Religious Society of Friends. *The Story of Deganawidah: How He Planted the Tree of Great Peace and Founded the Iroquois Confederacy*. Philadelphia: n.d.

Johnson O'Malley Commission of Region IV. *The Way It Was (Anakus Iwacha)*. State of Washington, 1974.

Kickingbird, Kirke, et al. *Indian Sovereignty*. Washington, D.C.: Institute for the Development of Indian Law, 1977.

Kickingbird, Lynn, and Kirke Kickingbird. *Indians and the U.S. Government*. Washington, D.C.: Institute for the Development of Indian Law, 1977.

National Advisory Council on Indian Education. *Annual Report: 1978*. Washington, D.C.: U.S. Government Printing Office, 1978.

National Conference of State Legislatures, Commission on State-Tribal Relations. *State-Tribal Agreements: A Comprehensive Study*. N.p.: American Indian Law Center, 1981.

National Park Service. *Soldier and Brave: Historic Places Associated with Indian Affairs and Indian Wars in Trans-Mississippi West*. Washington, D.C.: U.S. Government Printing Office, 1971.

Native American Rights Fund (Boulder, Colorado). *Announcements* (various issues).

New Mexico, state of, Commerce and Industry Department. *Indians of New Mexico*. Santa Fe: N.d.

Six Nations. *The Redman's Appeal for Justice*. N.p.: March 1924.

Speck, Frank G. *The Iroquois: A Study in Cultural Evolution*. Cranbrook Institute of Science Bulletin 23. Bloomfield Hills, Mich.: 1945.

Swagerty, William R., ed. *Indian Sovereignty*. Proceedings of the Second Annual Conference on Problems and Issues Concerning American Indians Today. Chicago: Newberry Library, 1979.

Tooker, Elizabeth, ed. *Iroquois Culture, History, and Prehistory: Proceedings of the 1965 Conference on Iroquois Research*. Albany: University of the State of New York, 1970.

U.S. Bureau of Indian Affairs. *American Indians and Their Federal Relationship*. Washington, D.C.: U.S. Government Printing Office, 1972.

————. *Brief History of the Federal Responsibility to the American Indian*. Washington, D.C.: U.S. Government Printing Office, 1979.

————. *Famous Indians: A Collection of Short Biographies*. Washington, D.C.: U.S. Government Printing Office, 1977.

————. *Indian Law Enforcement History*. Washington, D.C.: U.S. Government Printing Office, 1975.

————. *Indian Water Rights*. Washington, D.C.: U.S. Government Printing Office, 1978.

————. *Indians: Wars and Local Disturbances in the United States: 1782–1898*. Washington, D.C.: U.S. Government Printing Office, 1921.

————. *Information Profiles of Indian Reservations in Arizona, Nevada, and Utah*. Washington, D.C.: U.S. Government Printing Office, 1978.

————. National American Indian Court Judges Association and Judicial Services. *Native American Tribal Court Profiles*. Washington, D.C.: U.S. Government Printing Office, 1982.

U.S. Commission on Civil Rights. *American Indian Civil Rights Handbook*. Washington, D.C.: U.S. Government Printing Office, 1980.

————. *Indian Tribes: A Continuing Quest for Survival, A Report*. Washington, D.C.: U.S. Government Printing Office, 1981.

————. *The Navajo Nation: An American Colony*. Washington, D.C.: U.S. Government Printing Office, 1975.

————. *The Southwest Indian Report*. Washington, D.C.: U.S. Government Printing Office, 1973.

U.S. Congress, Senate Select Committee on Indian Affairs. *Report on Indian Housing*. Washington, D.C.: U.S. Government Printing Office, 1979.

U.S. Department of Health, Education, and Welfare. Public Health Service. Health Services Administration. Indian Health Service. *Illness Among Indians and Alaska Natives, 1970–1978*. Washington, D.C.: U.S. Government Printing Office, 1979.

————. *Indian Health Trends and Services*. 1978 ed. Washington D.C.: U.S. Government Printing Office, 1979.

U.S. Indian Claims Commission. *Final Report: August 13, 1946—*

September 30, 1978. Washington, D.C.: U.S. Government Printing Office, 1979.

Weinman, Paul L. *Bibliography of the Iroquoian Literature: Partially Annotated.* New York State Museum and Science Service Bulletin Number 411. Albany: University of the State of New York, 1969.

Wilson, James. *The Original Americans: U.S. Indians.* Minority Rights Group Report no. 31. London: 1976.

Theses and Dissertations

Fischbacher, Theodore. "A Study of the Role of the Federal Government in the Education of the American Indian." Ph.D. diss., Arizona State University, 1967.

Fitch, James. "Economic Development in a Minority Enclave: The Case of the Yakima Indian Nation." Ph.D. diss., Stanford University, 1974.

Michael, Robert. "The Economic Problems of the Rio Grande Pueblos." Ph.D. diss., University of New Mexico, 1976.

Schuster, Helen. "Yakima Indian Traditionalism: A Study in Continuity and Change." Ph.D. diss., University of Washington, 1975.

Tribal Documents and Newspapers

All-Indian Pueblo Council. *Pueblo News.* Albuquerque, N. Mex., various issues.

————. "The Right to Remain Indian: The Failure of the Federal Government to Protect Indian Lands and Water Rights." Report submitted to the U.S. Commission on Civil Rights. Albuquerque, N. Mex.: November 8, 1972.

Cheyenne River Sioux Tribe. *Constitution and Bylaws of the Cheyenne River Sioux Tribe.* Amended, 1980. Eagle Butte, S. Dak.

Indian Pueblo Cultural Center. *Our Land, Our Culture, Our Story.* Albuquerque, N. Mex.: 1977.

Iroquois League of Six Nations. *The Great Law of Peace of the Longhouse People.* Mohawk Nation, Rooseveltown, N.Y.: *Akwesasne Notes,* 1977.

Kickapoo Tribe of Oklahoma. *Children's Code, Title 4* (Draft). N.p., n.d.

Mississippi Band of Choctaw Indians. *Revised Constitution and Bylaws of the Mississippi Band of Choctaw Indians.* Amended, 1974. Philadelphia, Miss.

————. *Choctaw Industrial Park.* Philadelphia, Miss.: 1982.

Mississippi Band of Choctaw Indians, Tribal Council. *Chahta Hapia Hoke—We are Choctaw.* Philadelphia, Miss.: 1981.

Muscogee Nation. *Constitution and Laws of the Muscogee Nation.* Published by authority of the Muscogee National Council. St. Louis: Levison and Blythe Stationery Co., 1880.

————. *Acts and Resolutions of the National Council of the Muskogee Nation of 1893 and 1899,* inclusive. Muskogee, Indian Territory: Phoenix Printing, 1900.

————. *Constitution of the Muscogee Nation.* August, 1979. Okmulgee, Okla.

———. *Muscogee Nation News.* Okmulgee, Okla.: various issues.

———. *Muskogee National Council.* Pamphlet. N.p., n.d.

Pace, Robert E., comp. *The Land of the Yakimas.* Yakima Indian Nation Tribal Council, 1977. Toppenish, Wash.

Pueblo of Isleta. *Constitution for the Pueblo of Isleta, New Mexico.* February 23, 1970. Isleta Pueblo, N. Mex.

———. *Pueblo of Isleta Legal Code.* Vol. 1, *Civil and Criminal Ordinances.* July 2, 1976. Isleta Pueblo, N.M.

Pueblo of Isleta Tribal Council. *Isleta: Goals and Objectives.* Pamphlet. August 1976. Isleta Pueblo, New Mexico.

Seneca Nation of Indians. *Constitution of the Seneca Nation of Indians, 1898* (as amended September 12, 1978). Salamanca, New York.

———. *Program Fact Sheets for 1980.* Irving, N.Y.: 1980.

———. *Seneca Country.* Pamphlet, n.d. Salamanca, New York.

Yakima Indian Nation. *Yakima Nation Review.* Toppenish, Wash.: various issues.

Yakima Treaty Council. *Treaty Centennial: The Yakimas, 1855–1955.* June 1955. n.p.

INDEX

DATE DUE

SEP 2 2 1997			